PENGUIN BOOKS

THE UNCOLLECTED SHERLOCK HOLMES

Sir Arthur Conan Doyle was born in Edinburgh in 1859 and died in 1930. Within those years was crowded a variety of activity and creative work that made him an international figure and inspired the French to give him the epithet of 'the good giant'. He was the nephew of 'Dickie' Doyle the artist, was educated at Stonyhurst, and later studied medicine at Edinburgh University where the methods of diagnosis of one of the professors provided the idea for the methods of deduction used by Sherlock Holmes.

He first set up as a doctor in Southsea and it was while waiting for patients that he began to write. His growing success as an author enabled him to give up his practice and to turn his attention to other subjects. He was a champion of those whom he believed had been wrongly convicted, as witness his attempt to prove the innocence of Oscar Slater; a sportsman; an amateur detective himself, for whose help there were occasional demands; a volunteer physician in the Boer War; an historian; and late in life a convert to spiritualism.

His greatest achievement was, of course, his creation of Sherlock Holmes, who soon attained international status and constantly decoyed him from his other work; at one time Conan Doyle killed him but was obliged by public protest to restore him to life. And in his creation of Dr Watson, Holmes's companion in adventure, and chronicler, Conan Doyle produced not only a perfect foil for Holmes but also one of the most famous characters in fiction. Penguin publish all the books about the great detective, *A Study in Scarlet, The Sign of Four, The Adventures of Sherlock Holmes, The Memoirs of Sherlock Holmes, The Hound of the Baskervilles, The Return of Sherlock Holmes, The Valley of Fear, His Last Bow, The Case-Book of Sherlock Holmes* and *The Penguin Complete Sherlock Holmes*.

Richard Lancelyn Green is the author of the Soho Series *Bibliography of Conan Doyle*, compiled in collaboration with John Michael Gibson with whom he has edited a series of Conan Doyle's works, including the *Uncollected Stories* and *Essays on Photography*; his previous writings about Sherlock Holmes include an edition of the 1901 burlesque *Sheerluck Jones*.

Sir Arthur Conan Doyle

THE UNCOLLECTED SHERLOCK HOLMES

COMPILED BY
RICHARD LANCELYN GREEN

Penguin Books

Penguin Books Ltd, Harmondsworth, Middlesex, England
Penguin Books, 40 West 23rd Street, New York, New York 10010, U.S.A.
Penguin Books Australia Ltd, Ringwood, Victoria, Australia
Penguin Books Canada Ltd, 2801 John Street, Markham, Ontario, Canada L3R 1N4
Penguin Books (N.Z.) Ltd, 182–190 Wairau Road, Auckland 10, New Zealand

First published 1983

Made and printed in Great Britain by
Cox & Wyman Ltd, Reading
Set in Linotron Goudy by
Rowland Phototypesetting Ltd,
Bury St Edmunds, Suffolk

Contents

Preface

This volume, an addendum to the four long stories and fifty-six short stories which comprise the main collected works, includes all Conan Doyle's other writings about Sherlock Holmes, his parodies, plays, prefaces, and reminiscences; there are also a number of interviews and articles, including two by J. M. Barrie. Each piece is preceded by an introductory note giving an account of its origin and composition.

The main introduction traces the background to the stories, making use wherever possible of direct quotations from letters, interviews, and similar sources to illustrate Conan Doyle's own opinions and those of his friends and contemporaries. The longest sections are devoted to Joseph Bell, the model for Sherlock Holmes, and to William Gillette, who portrayed the detective on the stage; but consideration is also given to the influence of Edgar Allan Poe, to the *Strand Magazine* and its editor, to the reactions of the reading public at home and abroad, and to other similar or related topics, such as Doyle's own interest in crime.

I trust that no apology will be necessary for the number of quotations and that the piling up of data will not tire the patience of the reader. I have not tried to give my own views, but rather to present the opinions of those best, or better, qualified to speak on the subject. I hope that this book will serve as a tribute to Arthur Conan Doyle, to his fine sense of humour, his modesty, and above all to his integrity as the creator of one of the greatest figures of popular fiction, and that it will enable readers to see Sherlock Holmes, not only through the eyes of Dr Watson, but also through those of his creator.

My special thanks go to Mr Beverley Nichols for permission to include his interview with Conan Doyle, to Mr Charles Farrell for his interesting reminiscences and for allowing me to quote from his letter in the *Stage*, and to Brigadier J. N. Stisted, a descendant of Dr Joseph Bell and the present owner of the letters to him from Conan Doyle. I would also like to express my gratitude to the friends who have helped me. In England these include Owen Dudley Edwards, John Michael Gibson, Stanley Mackenzie, and Nicholas Utechin; while in America, my warmest thanks go to Marvin P. Epstein, also to J. Bliss Austin, Peter E. Blau, Redmond A. Burke, Cameron Hollyer, Andrew Malec, and John Bennett Shaw.

Acknowledgements and thanks are also due to the curators, librarians, and staff at the British Library, the Metropolitan Toronto Central Library, the Humanities Research Center at the University of Texas, the Berg Collection in the New York Public Library, the Philip S. Hench Collection at the University of Minnesota, and to the Arthur Conan Doyle Foundation in Switzerland.

To all the other people whose work has been drawn upon – those from whose publications quotations are taken, whether they be the humblest journalist condemned to anonymity or the best known writers, and those who may feel that I have made use of their research – I wish to extend my deepest appreciation.

Finally I would like to thank all the members of Sir Arthur Conan Doyle's family for their many kindnesses, and to express the hope that my own admiration and respect have enabled me to do justice not only to Sherlock Holmes but also to the memory of his creator.

London, 1983   *Richard Lancelyn Green*

Introduction

Arthur Conan Doyle, the creator of Sherlock Holmes, was born in Edinburgh in 1859 and died in Sussex in 1930. Although he had a full and active life he never succeeded in freeing himself from the 'notorious character' on whose fame his own reputation rested, nor could he avoid the natural curiosity of the public or, in the end, deny them the additional stories for which they clamoured. If on occasion he did regret ever having written a word about Sherlock Holmes, experience showed that once created he could not be destroyed, so the murderous threats became less serious and were at all times accompanied by a smile or a laugh. In his autobiography he was to say of Holmes that he 'has been a good friend to me in many ways. If I have sometimes been inclined to weary of him, it is because his character admits of no light or shade.'[1] And he confessed a few years later that the Sherlock Holmes stories had never interfered with his other work: 'I have not in actual practice found that these lighter sketches have prevented me from exploring and finding my limitations in such varied branches of literature as history, poetry, historical novels, psychic research, and the drama. Had Holmes never existed I could not have done more, though he may perhaps have stood a little in the way of the recognition of my more serious literary work.'[2]

As the creator, he alone could shock those who swore by Sherlock Holmes, by swearing at him, and he rather enjoyed the reaction of horror which this provoked. After one such occasion, when he had vented his irritation at some unsuccessful golf strokes by wishing Holmes out of existence, Herbert Asquith wrote: 'I thought that a world without Sherlock Holmes would have a serious gap in it, a void which sooner or later would somehow have to be filled; but it was a relief to feel that though it was possible for the author to kill him with one stroke of the pen and revive him with another, he could never with all the pens in the world expunge him from memory, or make him vanish from the earth as though he had never been.'[3] The truth was that Doyle could have destroyed Holmes's standing by writing inferior stories; instead he took the greatest care to preserve the honour and integrity of the character and was always on his guard lest standards should slip, and on the defensive when it was implied that they had.

Any discussion of Sherlock Holmes must begin with the three basic components which lay behind his creation. These are Doyle's own character – his medical training, background, and the influence of other people with whom he was associated; then the example and methods of an Edinburgh professor, Dr Joseph Bell; and thirdly the writings of Edgar Allan Poe. The first provided the necessary details of people and of their eccentricities, the second showed how best to recognize and observe habits and occupations by outward signs, and the third revealed that such observation might be employed in a form of fiction now firmly established as the detective story, but then very much in its infancy.

Dr Waller, Dr Budd, and Dr Doyle

Details of Doyle's life will be found in the section entitled 'The Background to Sherlock Holmes', which is based on his autobiography. However, Doyle does not refer there to one person who had a profound influence on his life, and gives another a fictional name; he also perhaps did not realize that his own practice as a G.P. in Southsea had provided characters and a setting which he utilized in his stories. These points will therefore be touched upon here.

Dr Bryan Charles Waller is a character whose very existence was for a long time shrouded in obscurity, even though he shared and paid for one of the houses in which Doyle's family lived. He was only a few years older, but he took an active interest in Doyle's early education and coached him for his examinations. He was also an assistant of Dr Joseph Bell and a witness to the decline of Conan Doyle's father. In spite, or perhaps because, of his proximity to the family, Doyle ignored him and came to despise him. The dislike may have been caused by Waller having jilted one of his sisters, or because he regretted that his family, and his mother in particular, who spent many years of her life in a cottage on Waller's estate, should have become indebted to him. Characteristics of 'the doctor' can, however, be traced in his work – most obviously in the letter from B. C. Haller which appears in the early story, 'Uncle Jeremy's Household'. As Waller had a consulting-room in the Edinburgh house, he could by a stretch of the imagination be described as an Ur-Holmes to Doyle's Watson, and by extension, Doyle's mother could be a prototype for Holmes's housekeeper. 'Though she retained the bearing of a duchess,' Doyle said of her in a passage later deleted from his autobiography, 'she had the worn hands of a charwoman.'[4]

George Turnavine Budd, another early influence, was a fellow student at Edinburgh with whom Doyle shared a house and practice in Plymouth during the summer of 1882. He was the inspiration for Crabbe in a short story, first published in 1884, called 'Crabbe's Practice' and, under the name 'Cullingworth', appears as the protagonist in *The Stark Munro Letters* written ten years later. The novel was based to a certain extent on events which had occurred in the Durnford Street consulting-room and at Budd's home on the Hoe at 6 Elliot Terrace. Although Doyle mentioned George Budd (and his younger brother, Arthur) by name when writing his autobiography, the name 'Cullingworth' was substituted in the published versions so as to protect the feelings of the family who, after Budd's death in 1889, had received some financial assistance from Doyle. Budd's name was not mentioned publicly in connection with Conan Doyle until 1931, when W. H. Hosking started doing research for a biography. Thereafter, as the novel purported to cover some of the most formative years of Doyle's life and to show his mental and spiritual development, there was an attempt to present Budd as a forerunner of Holmes. They do share certain habits and qualities, but Budd's fiery temperament, his unpredictable nature, and his marriage to a slip of a girl have more in common with Professor Challenger.

The partnership with Budd was shortlived, and Doyle decided to set up in practice on his own. He first visited Tavistock on the fringes of Dartmoor. The journey provided ideas which he subsequently used in a short story, in one of his photographic essays, and even perhaps in *The Hound of the Baskervilles*, but the town proved to be well endowed with medical practitioners. He therefore returned to Plymouth and took the Irish steamer to Southsea, an offshoot of Portsmouth, where early in July 1882 he established himself in Elm Grove at Bush Villa (or 1, Bush Villas). When he first set eyes on the house in which he was to create Sherlock Holmes, he had little besides a brass plate – and that he quickly replaced: 'I took the most central house I could find,' he told a friend in Edinburgh, 'determined to make a spoon or spoil a horn, and got three pounds worth of furniture for the Consulting room, a bed, a tin of corned beef and two enormous brass plates with my name on it.'[5] A red lamp was also procured, but neither that nor the plates attracted patients in quite the numbers which Doyle had hoped. A dental surgeon over the road, William Henry Kirton, came to his assistance by passing cases on to him, and these were soon swarming in 'at a rate of about two a week'.[6]

Doyle was then joined by his brother, Innes, who had been born in 1873. 'Duffy', as he was affectionately known, made himself at home, and a place was found for him as a day pupil at a private school which prepared boys for the Navy. He may well have been the inspiration for the Boots at Baker Street who was later given the name 'Billy' as he did, on occasion, fulfil a similar role; but he was also a companion who was easily impressed and who never ceased to be amazed at the observations and deductions of his elder brother. Doyle relished the effect which his superior wisdom had on such a young mind, and on one whose unintentional humour was always a source of merriment. Innes shared the house until 1885, when he went to a public school in Yorkshire, and thereafter to a military academy. He died in 1919, having risen to the rank of Brigadier-General. If he was not the original of Dr Watson, he was at least a warm-hearted and good-natured companion, and, it seems, the only person who ever shared lodgings with Conan Doyle.

Southsea also provides a suitable candidate for the original of Mrs Hudson of 221b Baker Street in the person of Doyle's own housekeeper. After Innes had joined him, he followed the advice of a friend and, in exchange for the basement flat, got a decent woman (in fact he got two, as the first was accompanied by a lady who claimed to be a sister). She may have had the qualities attributed to Mrs Hudson or, if not, at least those of Mrs Turner, who on one or two occasions stood in for Mrs Hudson. The lady who replaced her certainly had the right qualities. She was described by the Rev. E. Elliot, a friend of Doyle and one of Innes's teachers, as 'a kindly old Scotchwoman who had been a servant to the family and was a mother both to him and his little brother and must have been the greatest help and comfort to the young doctor in his struggles'.[7]

If such speculation is correct and Innes and the housekeeper were the prototypes of Billy, Watson, and Mrs Hudson, then it is clear that Doyle himself must have been in some ways the original of Sherlock Holmes. He was, or considered himself to be, a 'Bohemian'. He may not have used a seven-per-cent solution, but he had as a student studied drugs. His copy of *The Essentials of Materia Medica and Therapeutica* has some impressive marginalia and doggerel verse summarizing the points made in the text; and what is thought to be his earliest published letter, in the

British Medical Journal of 20 September 1879, describes the effect upon himself of increased doses of the drug gelseminum.

In the summer of 1878, four years after his first visit, Doyle was in London, where he stayed with his relations at Clifton Gardens in Maida Vale. He 'roamed about' the city but, though his relations were kind, he feared that he was 'too Bohemian for them and they too conventional for me'.[8] Matters might have been different if he had married Elmo Welden, which he seriously contemplated, before sailing for the West Coast of Africa in October 1881; but he was dissuaded, and a few days before the ship sailed telegraphed to the agent (who was called Watson) to say that he would be coming aboard unmarried. When he got to Southsea, though he had visits from his sisters and girlfriends, he was soon admitting that he had become 'a most awful Bohemian from knowing so few ladies'.[9] In his room on the first floor he would have had a table of chemicals for his medical work and possibly for photographic experiments; certainly he had scrapbooks and commonplace books, and much of the paraphernalia which he later described at Baker Street. He was also filling his mind with unusual details gleaned from papers read at the local clubs and societies of which he was a member. The most important of these was the Portsmouth Literary and Scientific Society, and the titles of the lectures he attended are by themselves sufficient to show their probable influence – such as 'The Army Doctor and his Work in Wartime' on 20 November 1883, or a paper by James Charlton, 'Incidents of a Journey from Chicago to Vancouver and British Columbia', on 2 April 1885 which included a full description of Salt Lake City and its Mormon inhabitants.

Doyle was married on 6 August 1885. Although this caused a domestic upheaval, his day-to-day routine continued as before. There were visits to patients, to coroners' inquests, and to the South Hants Eye and Ear Hospital, where he was a part-time voluntary worker, but more and more of his time was being devoted to writing and, if Dr George Sanderson is to be believed, he was doing little else. Sanderson was one of a group of doctors, the others being Doyle, Dr Royson Pike, Dr Trimmer, and Dr Keith Welsh, who met each morning. They were all great friends and, according to Sanderson, 'would spend about half an hour together (not longer) daily, and then go about our business. Dr Doyle would go to his house and get on with his writing.'[10] Doyle's consulting-room did resemble a study, and he acquired the ability to break off in mid-sentence and resume without hesitation after dealing with a patient or visitor.

Doyle's literary powers had developed early; he wrote his first story at the age of six, and by the time he was at school he was putting his ability as a story-teller to good use as a means of acquiring jam tarts. He was from an early age an omnivorous reader, and the period he spent at Stonyhurst and afterwards at Feldkirch in Austria was formative not only because of what he was taught, but also because of what he saw and heard. Memories of the school, of the buildings, pupils, and teachers may well have surfaced in his later work. One of his contemporaries, the Marqués de Villavieja, even claimed that he already had the qualities of Sherlock Holmes: 'I believe his detective instinct must have been well developed even then, for he was very observant and very thorough.'[11] This has led to the suggestion that Doyle's closest friend, James Ryan, may have been one of the many prototypes of Dr Watson. But it is safer to assume that his powers of observation owed their development to Dr Joseph Bell.

The Original of Sherlock Holmes: Dr Joseph Bell

With 'The Mystery of Sasassa Valley', published anonymously in *Chambers's Journal* on 6 September 1879 and the first story by Conan Doyle to appear in print, the author enclosed a second story called 'The Recollections of Captain Wilkie'. This was mislaid and did not resurface until 1895, by which time its full significance could be appreciated. It contains a direct tribute to Dr Joseph Bell, under whom Doyle served as a dresser or outpatient clerk at the Edinburgh Royal Infirmary. The narrator says:

> 'I used to rather pride myself on being able to spot a man's trade or profession by a good look at his exterior. I had the advantage of studying under a Professor at Edinburgh who was a master of the art, and used to electrify both his patients and his clinical classes by long shots, sometimes at the most unlikely of pursuits, and never very far from the mark. "Well, my man," I have heard him say, "I can see by your fingers that you play some musical instrument for your livelihood, but it is a rather curious one – something quite out of my line." The man afterwards informed us that he earned a few coppers by blowing *Rule Britannia* on a coffee-pot, the spout of which was pierced to form a rough flute. Though a novice in the art compared to the shrewd Professor, I was still able to astonish my ward companions on occasion, and I never lost an opportunity of practising myself.'[12]

Doyle became a student of Edinburgh University in October 1876, and the following year paid four guineas to attend the classes on surgery which were given by Joseph Bell. He paid as much again a year later for a sixteen-month course of clinical surgery. 'Bell's staff was so well organized,' one fellow-student later said of the Friday clinics at the Royal Infirmary, 'that there was no loss of time; the patients, all prepared in the side-room, were run into the theatre at great speed, diagnosed and run out again. It was here that Conan Doyle, then an ordinary student like ourselves, observed, studied, and took notes, which he utilized thereafter in his stories.'[13] Doyle made good use of his time and learnt a great deal about the cases and diseases which he handled and the methods by which they might be traced. His practical and theoretical work was supplemented by 'outdoor practice' in the employ of local doctors. He spent a few weeks in Sheffield with a Dr Richardson, four months in Shropshire with Dr Henry Francis Elliot (a former resident physician at the Royal Infirmary), and a number of longer periods in Birmingham as a paid assistant to Dr Reginald Ratcliffe Hoare who, with his wife, Amy, and other members of his family, was numbered among Doyle's closest friends. Doyle could have said, as did the pupil of the Edinburgh Professor in 'Captain Wilkie': 'I am a medical man, and observation is everything in my profession.' And how prophetic was the reply which this elicited from Captain Wilkie: 'I thought you were a detective, at first, but I couldn't recall your face at the time I knew the force.'[14]

Few people recalled Dr Joseph Bell when the Sherlock Holmes stories began appearing in the *Strand Magazine* in 1891, but this was soon remedied. In May 1892, the public were made aware of the Edinburgh Professor, as he was described in 'A Talk with Dr Conan Doyle' by Raymond Blathwayt which appeared in the *Bookman*. When asked how he had 'evolved, apparently out of his own inner consciousness, such an extraordinary person as his detective Sherlock Holmes', Doyle replied:

> 'Oh! But, if you please, he is not evolved out of any one's inner consciousness. Sherlock Holmes is the literary embodiment, if I may so express it, of my memory of a professor of medicine at Edinburgh University, who would sit in the patients' waiting-room with a face like a Red Indian and diagnose the people as they came in, before even they had opened their mouths. He would tell them their symptoms, he would give them details of their lives, and he would hardly ever make a mistake. "Gentlemen," he would say to us students standing around, "I am not quite sure whether this man is a cork-cutter or a slater. I

observe a slight *callus*, or hardening, on one side of his forefinger, and a little thickening on the outside of his thumb, and that is a sure sign he is either one or the other." His great faculty of deduction was at times highly dramatic. "Ah!" he would say to another man, "you are a soldier, a non-commissioned officer, and you have served in Bermuda. Now how did I know that, gentlemen? He came into the room without taking his hat off, as he would go into an orderly room. He was a soldier. A slight authoritative air, combined with his age, shows he was an N.C.O. A slight rash on the forehead tells me he was in Bermuda, and subject to a certain rash known only there."

'So I got the idea for Sherlock Holmes. Sherlock is utterly inhuman, no heart, but with a beautifully logical intellect.'[15]

Doyle had sent Bell a copy of The White Company and, at the time of the Blathwayt interview, was corresponding with him. Each went out of his way to compliment the other. Bell was delighted that Doyle had demonstrated the importance of observation, but, when giving some suggestions of his own, insisted that Holmes owed less to his example than Doyle claimed. In a letter dated 4 May 1892, which also touched on the critical reception given to The White Company, Doyle wrote:

Many thanks for your most kind and genial letter which was a very great pleasure to me. It is most certainly to you that I owe Sherlock Holmes, and though in the stories I have the advantage of being able to place him in all sorts of dramatic positions I do not think that his analytical work is in the least an exaggeration of some of the effects which I have seen you produce in the out-patient ward. Round the centre of deduction and inference and observation which I have heard you inculcate I have tried to build up a man who pushed the thing as far as it would go –

further occasionally – and I am so glad that the result has satisfied you, who are the critic with the most right to be severe.

I think that a fine thing might be done about a bacteriological criminal, but the only fear is lest you get beyond the average man, whose interest must be held from the first and who won't be interested unless he thoroughly understands. Still, even so, I should think that something might be done on these lines. I should be glad, if you should find yourself with ten minutes to spare, if you would give me an idea of the case which you speak of, and indeed I should be very grateful for any 'spotting of trade' tips, or anything else of a Sherlock Holmes nature.

The book will come out about September, and I should much like to inscribe your name upon the fly-leaf, if the dedication will not be an intrusion. I am sure that no other name has as good a right to the place.[16]

The letter produced an immediate response from Bell and, three days later, Doyle wrote again to acknowledge the information which he had been sent and to reassure Bell that it would be of value:

Your letters are really of great value to me and I am exceedingly obliged to you for the details which you so kindly furnished. The deserter-cobbler is admirable, and I wish I had a dozen more such cases. I am going to do 12 more Sherlock Holmes sketches next year so that I am insatiable for material. All you tell me is most useful. I have a lot more things which I have devised myself, and altogether I think that he will not fall away at all.

Your sketch too of the crime is capital. It wants a sort of second plot to run parallel with the first, and to drag some other red herring across the scent besides the ex-soldier. But there is the nucleus – and indeed much more than the nucleus, of something very good. I shall certainly – with your kind permission – avail myself of the idea.[17]

A month later, Doyle was approached for another interview, this time by Harry How, a staff reporter who was
making his name with a series of 'Illustrated Interviews' in
the *Strand Magazine*. He spent 'A Day with Dr Conan Doyle'
in June 1892 and his account was published in the August
1892 issue of the magazine. Doyle now mentioned Bell by
name and explained that he had been a clerk in Bell's ward:

> A clerk's duties are to note down all the patients to be
> seen, and muster them together. Often I would have
> seventy or eighty. When everything was ready, I would
> show them in to Mr Bell, who would have the students
> gathered round him. His intuitive powers were simply
> marvellous. Case No. 1 would step up.
>
> 'I see,' said Mr Bell, 'you're suffering from drink. You
> even carry a flask in the inside breast pocket of your coat.'
> Another case would come forward.
>
> 'Cobbler, I see.' Then he would turn to the students,
> and point out to them that the inside of the knee of the
> man's trousers was worn. That was where the man had
> rested the lapstone – a peculiarity found only in cobblers.
>
> All this impressed me very much. He was continually
> before me – his sharp, piercing grey eyes, eagle nose, and
> striking features. There he would sit in his chair with
> fingers together – he was very dexterous with his hands –
> and just look at the man or woman before him. He was
> most kind and painstaking with the students – a real good
> friend – and when I took my degree and went to Africa the
> remarkable individuality and discriminating tact of my old
> master made a deep and lasting impression on me, though
> I had not the faintest idea that it would one day lead me to
> forsake medicine for story writing.[18]

The day after How's visit, Doyle began to worry in case
Bell should take offence, and therefore wrote to warn him
that How would endeavour to contact him:

> I am afraid that my little sketches have had the effect of

setting a newspaper man on your trail with as great persistence as ever Holmes showed to any of his criminals. Mr Harry How (who did Professor Blackie lately) was out here yesterday, and on my mentioning in the course of the interview about the influence which your teaching had in making us observe, deduce, &c., he departed with full intentions of writing to you and getting all he could from you to embellish his article with. I thought that I should write to you independently to say that I have nothing to do with the matter, and that I hope you won't consider me in the least in deciding whether to give him what he wants or not. I should be sorry if you were bothered in any way in consequence of my having made use of your teachings.[19]

Bell, however, was happy to comply with Harry How's wishes and the following letter was printed at the end of the article:

> 2 Melville Crescent
> Edinburgh
>
> 16 June 1892

Dear Sir,
   You ask me about the kind of teaching to which Dr Conan Doyle has so kindly referred, when speaking of his ideal character, 'Sherlock Holmes'. Dr Conan Doyle has, by his imaginative genius, made a great deal out of very little, and his warm remembrance of one of his old teachers has coloured the picture. In teaching the treatment of disease and accident, all careful teachers have first to show the student how to recognize accurately the case. The recognition depends in great measure on the accurate and rapid appreciation of *small* points in which the diseased differs from the healthy state. In fact, the student must be taught to observe. To interest him in this kind of work we teachers find it useful to show the student how

much a trained use of the observation can discover in ordinary matters such as the previous history, nationality, and occupation of a patient.

The patient, too, is likely to be impressed by your ability to cure him in the future if he sees you, at a glance, know much of his past. And the whole trick is much easier than it appears at first.

For instance, physiognomy helps you to nationality, accent to district, and, to an educated ear, almost to a county. Nearly every handicraft writes its sign manual on the hands. The scars of the miner differ from those of the mason. The shoemaker and the tailor are quite different.

The soldier and the sailor differ in gait, though last month I had to tell a man who said he was a soldier that he had been a sailor in his boyhood. The subject is endless: the tattoo marks on hand or arm will tell their own tale as to voyages; the ornaments on the watch chain of the successful settler will tell you where he made his money. A New Zealand squatter will not wear a gold mohur, nor an engineer on an Indian railway a Maori stone. Carry the same idea of using one's senses accurately and constantly, and you will see that many a surgical case will bring his past history, national, social, and medical, into the consulting-room as he walks in. Dr Conan Doyle's genius and intense imagination has on this slender basis made his detective stories a distinctly new departure, but he owes much less than he thinks to

yours truly, Joseph Bell. [20]

As well as the letter, How was able to reproduce a photograph of Joseph Bell taken by A. Swan Watson of Edinburgh. It was, it seems, the one which Bell had sent Conan Doyle, to which reference was made in How's article, and for which acknowledgement was given in a letter dated 16 June 1892:

12 Tennison Road
South Norwood

My dear Mr Bell,

Thank you very heartily for the photograph which I shall much value. Your permission will rejoice the cockles of Mr Harry How's heart. It is an exceedingly character-istic and excellent likeness.

We had a good laugh over Miss Dorothy. Holmes is as inhuman as a Babbage's Calculating Machine, and just about as likely to fall in love. The *Strand* insists on having a dozen more of his adventures for next year, and I am in great dread of letting him tail off. I have done the first one however of the new series and he is still going strong. I expect the book to come out about September. The Elections have demoralized the publishers.

With kindest regards,

Yours very truly, A. Conan Doyle[21]

The Adventures of Sherlock Holmes, to which he was referring, was published on 14 October 1892. It was dedi-cated: 'To My Old Teacher, Joseph Bell, M. D., &c., of 2, Melville Crescent, Edinburgh.' This led Robert Louis Stevenson, when complimenting Doyle on Holmes, to say in a letter of 5 April 1893: 'Only the one thing troubles me; can this be my old friend Joe Bell?'[22] In Samoa there might still have been some doubt, but not in England. Bell repaid the compliment by reviewing the book for the December 1892 issue of the *Bookman*. His article, which bore the title of the book, was later used as a preface for the Warwick House Library edition of *A Study in Scarlet* and for most of the subsequent editions. It did not worry the publishers that he had not read the first story. His 'Note', which was retitled 'Mr Sherlock Holmes', proved ideal for their purpose, as only the final paragraph had mentioned the individual stories, and this, of course, they omitted.

Doyle had warned Bell, in a letter dated 7 July 1892, that

'one effect of your identity being revealed to the readers of
the *Strand* will be that you will have ample opportunity for
studying lunatic letters, and that part at least of the stream
which pours upon me will be diverted to you.' He gave as
examples a mystic youth from Glasgow who would put the
time of composition – such as 7.14 p.m. – on his letters, one
from the south of Portugal, an American lady with a curved
spine, a Liverpool merchant 'who burns to know who Jack
the Ripper is', and the many folks who 'believe that their
neighbours are starving maiden aunts to death in hermetic-
ally sealed attics'.[23] Doyle's prediction was fulfilled to a certain
extent. The Press and the public were eager for examples of
Bell's powers of observation. The initial interest subsided for
a while, but it was renewed at the time of Holmes's death in
December 1893. During that month Bell and Dr Henry
Littlejohn were appearing on behalf of the Crown at the
Ardlamont trial in Edinburgh. It was a very appropriate
moment for Bell to be interviewed, and Lincoln Springfield,
who was a representative of the *Pall Mall Gazette* at the trial,
managed to get an invitation to spend an evening with him
at his house in Melville Crescent. Springfield recalled in his
autobiography:

> He was a dear old boy – white-haired, keen-eyed,
> ruddy-faced and clean-shaven, in a black velvet dinner-
> jacket; and at first, amused and chuckling over my iden-
> tification of him with the great detective of fiction, he
> warded me off with assurances that it was nothing to do
> with him – that Doyle was the clever man, and not he. But
> I got him talking a bit.[24]

Springfield's interview, 'The Original of Sherlock Holmes',
was first published in the *Pall Mall Gazette* on 28 December
1893. It was reprinted in the *Pall Mall Budget* the following
week, and extracts were given in various American magazines and newspapers, such as the *Book Buyer* and *Harper's
Weekly*. Unlike Dr Gunn, who later said that Doyle 'held an

average position as a student, and was not specially brilliant',[25] Bell, without knowing of his literary inclinations, regarded him as one of the best students he had taught: 'He was exceedingly interested always upon anything connected with diagnosis, and was never tired of trying to discover all those little details which one looks for.' Bell recalled that he had on one occasion deduced that a patient was Irish and that he had walked across the links:

> Conan Doyle could not see how I knew that, absurdly simple as it was. On a showery day, such as that had been, the reddish clay at bare parts of the links adheres to the boot, and a tiny part is bound to remain. There is no such clay anywhere else round the town for miles. Well, that and one or two similar instances excited Doyle's keenest interest, and set him experimenting himself in the same direction – which, of course, was just what I wanted, with him and all my other scholars.[26]

Many stories, true and apocryphal, and many versions of the same story were to be told of Bell's powers of observation. Every student who had been a contemporary of Doyle – and many who had not – were at one time or another to give an account of their experiences. The apocryphal stories were legion. 'Holmes's Early Mistake', which appeared in the *Evening Standard* after Doyle's death, could stand for them all:

> Doyle and Bell were awaiting a train in Edinburgh when Doyle pointed out a tall man whose hand was continually stealing to his side. Doyle deduced that he was a soldier in mufti, unconsciously groping for his sword to make sure that it was in the correct position. The professor, doubtful, suggested a polite inquiry. Doyle therefore approached the stranger. He was a butcher. His hand had been reaching for his steel![27]

Whatever Bell thought of his own powers of observation –

and according to one student who had been an outpatient clerk at the same time as Doyle he would never accept that he was wrong and so might say 'This man won't admit that he is a Shetlander, but he is one all the same'[28] – he always insisted that the credit for Sherlock Holmes should go to Conan Doyle. 'The only credit I can take to myself,' he said in the 1893 interview, 'is that appertaining to the circumstances that I always impressed over and over again upon all my scholars – Conan Doyle among them – the vast importance of little distinctions, the endless significance of the trifles.'[29]

During the remainder of his life Bell's name was inextricably linked with that of Sherlock Holmes and since his death has often only been remembered because of it. At the time of the *Pall Mall Gazette* interview Bell told his future biographer Jessie M. E. Saxby: 'The fiends of your profession won't let me alone, and I am haunted by my double whom you so hate, namely Sherlock Holmes.'[30] She used this in her biography to suggest that he shared her own dislike, but he was probably more flattered than annoyed. In an article called 'The Real Sherlock Holmes', published in *Good Words* in March 1902, an occasion was described – before the question of Holmes's original had been settled – when Bell overheard some ladies discussing the stories and treating the hero as if he were a real person. He at first only admitted that he knew the man, but on returning to the room announced: 'I am Sherlock Holmes.'[31] He soon became accustomed to hearing his name coupled with that of Sherlock Holmes and even treated as synonymous with it.

Although Doyle did later admit that some of the suggestions which Bell had given him were impractical, he never missed an opportunity of acknowledging his debt. One of the few occasions on which they met was on 1 October 1900, when Bell agreed to share the platform at the Literary Institute in Edinburgh and to lend his support to Doyle as the prospective Unionist candidate for the Central Division of the city. Their presence together provoked some frivolous questions. At the close of the meeting Bell told the audience that he had probably known Doyle before anyone else in the room and that if he was 'half as good a member of Parliament as he was a dresser in the Edinburgh Royal Infirmary, he would be one of the best members of Parliament'.[32] Despite this support, Doyle failed to win the seat.

Joseph Bell died on 4 October 1911. A tribute by Conan Doyle appeared the following day in the *Daily Express*:

> Personally, I can say very little of Dr Joseph Bell, for I have never met him in his own house, and really only knew him as my professor. As such I shall always see him very clearly; his stiff, bristling, iron-grey hair, his clear, half-humorous, half-critical grey eyes, his eager face and swarthy skin.
>
> He had a very spare figure, as I remember him, and walked with a jerky energetic gait, his head carried high and his arms swinging. He had a dry humour and remarkable command of the vernacular, into which he easily fell when addressing his patients.[33]

He was to be more forthcoming in his autobiography written just over a decade later.

Sir Henry Littlejohn, an expert on forensic medicine, was also one of Doyle's professors. He was noted for the extremely dramatic and convincing way in which he demonstrated his subjects. Doyle coupled his name with that of Bell in a speech to Graduates of Edinburgh University at the Hotel Avenue, Nairobi, on 4 March 1929. He explained how he had read a number of detective stories and been horrified by the way the solutions were reached. 'He reflected that neither Joe Bell nor Littlejohn would have gone about things in that way. And, reflecting on their methods first induced him to write a detective story from the point of view of the scientific man.'[34] Dr Harold Emery Jones, another of Doyle's contemporaries at Edinburgh, was one of the few people to have mentioned Henry Littlejohn in this connection. He did so in an article about Joseph Bell called 'The Original of Sherlock Holmes' which appeared in *Collier's Weekly* on 9 January 1904. It was then used as the introduction to a three volume edition of *Conan Doyle's Best Books*, which consisted entirely of pre-copyright works and so had wide and cheap distribution. It was very influential, but few were convinced by his claim that if Bell were indeed the inspiration, then 'the absurd fiction that Conan Doyle drew upon Poe for his ideas' would be 'silenced for ever'.[35] Not even the editor of *Collier's* could allow that to stand without some qualification. Sherlock Holmes had been endowed with greater humanity than Poe's Dupin, but there were many points in common which neither the greater ingenuity nor the more real personality could disguise.

The Father of the Detective Story: Edgar Allan Poe

When Doyle visited America for the first time in 1894, he was asked if he had been influenced by Edgar Allan Poe when he wrote the Sherlock Holmes stories:

> 'Oh, immensely! His detective is the best detective in fiction.'
> 'Except Sherlock Holmes,' said somebody.
> 'I make no exception,' said Dr Doyle, very earnestly. 'Dupin is unrivalled. It was Poe who taught the possibility of making a detective story a work of literature.'[36]

This at least was his answer as reported by the *New York Times*. Doyle did admit that he had also known a 'schoolmaster' who 'deduced irrefutable facts from reasoning', but the implication was that Edgar Allan Poe had been the major influence.

In the early notes for A Study in Scarlet, Sherrinford Holmes says to Ormond Sacker: 'Lecoq was a bungler – Dupin was better. Dupin was decidedly smart – his trick of following a train of thought was more sensational than clever but still he had analytical genius.'[37] In the book itself, Watson is so impressed by the way Holmes had inferred that he had been in Afghanistan that he compares him to Dupin. Holmes replies: 'No doubt you think that you are complimenting me in comparing me to Dupin, now in my opinion, Dupin was a very inferior fellow. That trick of his of breaking in on his friend's thoughts after a quarter of an hour's silence is really very showy but superficial. He had some analytical genius, no doubt; but he was by no means such a phenomenon as Poe appeared to imagine.'[38]

There is no reason to believe that Poe did consider Dupin a phenomenon. When he began 'The Murders in the Rue Trianon Bas' in which C. Auguste Dupin made his début, he can have had no idea that he was giving birth to the modern detective story, nor when it was published as 'The Murders in the Rue Morgue' in April 1841 did it arouse any particular interest among readers. It is, however, the earliest story in which the detective is the central character and in which the art of precise analysis is of greater interest than the mystery itself. Poe wrote a number of stories which involve detection, but there were only two others in which Dupin was the central character, 'The Mystery of Marie Rogêt' and 'The Purloined Letter'. When the second of these was published in Great Britain in Chambers's Edinburgh Journal on 30 November 1844, taken directly from The Gift, it received the highest praise for its acute observation of mental phenomena and for the apt illustration of the play of two minds, and this was the quality which appealed to Conan Doyle.

The beginning of 'The Purloined Letter', in which Dupin and his unnamed companion are enjoying the 'twofold luxury of meditation and a meerschaum',[39] was to be the model for many of the Sherlock Holmes stories. But Holmes's most obvious debt, despite what he said, was to the mind-reading episode in 'The Murders in the Rue Morgue'. This served as the inspiration for the sequence in 'The Adventure of the Cardboard Box' when Holmes breaks into Watson's thoughts: 'You may remember,' Holmes says, 'that some little time ago when I read you the passage in one of Poe's sketches in which a close reasoner follows the unspoken thoughts of his companion, you were inclined to treat the matter as a mere *tour-de-force* of the author.'[40] And this had induced him to do the same and show that it was possible.

Poe's *Tales of Mystery and the Imagination* was a book which Doyle had with him at Feldkirch in 1876 and which he may have known before then. He judged it second only to Macaulay's *Essays* as a major influence on his life: 'I read it young when my mind was plastic. It stimulated my imagination and set before me a supreme example of dignity and force in the methods of telling a story.'[41] Poe is mentioned by name in a number of his early stories, and one in particular is of interest for the association between Dupin and Sherlock Holmes. This is 'The Fate of the Evangeline', which was published in the 1885 Christmas number of the *Boy's Own Paper*, having been rejected a year earlier by *Blackwood's Magazine*. The narrator begins the story by reproducing various newspaper reports about the missing yacht, the *Evangeline*; one is a leader from the *Scotsman* which discusses the mystery and considers the theories which have been put forward to account for it:

> 'It would be well,' the *Scotsman* concluded, 'if those who express opinions upon such subjects would bear in mind those simple rules as to the analysis of evidence laid down by Auguste Dupin. "Exclude the impossible," he remarks in one of Poe's immortal stories, "and what is left, however improbable, *must* be the truth."'

Dupin had formulated these rules in 'The Murders in the

Rue Morgue' where he ascertained that no one could have
used the doors, then turned his attention to the windows.
Those in the front room were in full view and could not have
been used; therefore the murderer or murderers must have
passed through the windows of the back room. The police
had discounted this as an impossibility, but Dupin told his
companion: 'It is not our part, as reasoners, to reject it on
account of apparent impossibilities. It is only left for us to
prove that these apparent "impossibilities" are, in reality,
not such.'[43] Doyle's own version was considerably better.
In *The Sign of Four*, written in 1889, Holmes is confron-
ted by a similar problem, and asks Watson: 'How often
have I said to you that when you have eliminated the impossible, whatever remains, *however improbable*, must be the
truth?'[44]

The remark was to become closely associated with Sherlock Holmes. He used it again in 'The Adventure of the
Beryl Coronet' (1892) and in 'The Adventure of the Bruce-
Partington Plans' (1908). It also appears in 'The Lost Special', one of the Round-the-Fire stories written in 1898,
where there is an extract from a letter to *The Times* by a
'recognized authority': '"It is one of the elementary prin-
ciples of practical reasoning," he remarked, "that when the
impossible has been eliminated the residuum, however improbable, must contain the truth."'[45] This has been used as
evidence to suggest that the 'authority' was Sherlock Holmes
and that 'The Lost Special' and a companion story, 'The
Man with the Watches', are 'apocryphal' Sherlock Holmes
stories; but, as the 'recognized authority' is wrong and as his
reasoning is shown to be at fault, it would be doing Holmes as
great a disservice to associate him with the inferior fellow as
it would to suggest that he had written the leader in the
Scotsman!

Doyle frequently acknowledged that he owed a great deal
to Poe. In 'To an Undiscerning Critic', the light-hearted
verses written in 1912 as a reply to a poem by Arthur

Guiterman which had accused him of 'shameless ingratitude', he wrote:

> As the creator I've praised to satiety
> Poe's Monsieur Dupin, his skill and variety,
> And have admitted that in my detective work,
> I owe to my model a deal of selective work.[46]

Doyle also acknowledged his debt in the introduction which
he wrote for the Sherlock Holmes stories in the Author's
Edition, and in *Through the Magic Door* (1907), where he
calls him the 'master of all':

> To him must be ascribed the monstrous progeny of
> writers on the detection of crime – *'quorum pars parva fui!'*
> Each may find some little development of his own, but his
> main art must trace back to those admirable stories of
> Monsieur Dupin, so wonderful in their masterful force,
> their reticence, their quick dramatic point. After all,
> mental acuteness is the one quality which can be ascrib-
> ed to the ideal detective, and when that has once
> been admirably done, succeeding writers must neces-
> sarily be content for all time to follow in the same main
> track.

'The Gold Bug' and 'The Murders in the Rue Morgue' were
the stories which Doyle considered the best: 'These two have
a proportion and a perspective which are lacking in the
others, the horror or weirdness of the idea intensified by the
coolness of the narrator and of the principal actor, Dupin in
the one case and Le Grand in the other.'[47]
    As the main speaker at the Poe Centenary Dinner, given
under the auspices of the Authors' Club at the Hôtel
Métropole on 1 March 1909, Doyle described the tragic
circumstances of Poe's life, praised his poetry, and said of the
stories that they were 'one of the great landmarks and
starting points in the literature of the past century': 'For
those tales have been so pregnant with suggestion, so stimu-

lating to the minds of others, that it may be said of many of
them that each is a root from which a whole literature has
developed.' As an example, he mentioned the 'exploits of
M. Dupin', and asked: 'Where was the detective story until
Poe breathed the breath of life into it?'[48]

Describing his visit on 4 June 1922 to the cottage at
Fordham, near New York, where Poe had spent the last years
of his life, Doyle wrote:

> His face looks at you from every wall, austere, coldly
> intellectual, cruel in its precise accuracy. He had every
> quality save humour, and of that there was not a trace. But
> he was surely the greatest originator of various story-types
> that ever lived. He was so sure of himself that he never
> troubled to work out a reef, but he just picked a nugget or
> two, and then turned away to prospect elsewhere. He was
> the real father of the detective story, of the buried-treasure
> story, of the Jules Verne semi-scientific story, of the purely
> morbid story, and of nearly every other sort that we now
> use. If every man who owed his inspiration to Poe was to
> contribute a tithe of his profits therefrom he would surely
> have a monument greater than the pyramids, and I for one
> would be among the builders.[49]

In his 'Talk' with Raymond Blathwayt in 1892, Doyle said
that the theoretical side of detective works had always had a
great charm for him, and that in his opinion Dupin was the
best detective in fiction, followed by Lecoq, Gaboriau's
hero. Lecoq may have been 'a miserable bungler' in the eyes
of Sherlock Holmes, but during the eighteen eighties Gaboriau's sensational novels were all the rage, and Conan Doyle
was one of those who enjoyed them. 'I have read Gaboriau's
Lecoq the Detective, *The Gilded Clique*, and a story concerning
the murder of an old woman, the name of which I forget,' he
wrote shortly before he began his own detective story. The
missing title, *The Lerouge Case*, was then added, and he
continued: 'All very good. Wilkie Collins, but more so.'[50] If

he could not feel the same about other detective stories, they at least revealed the main weakness. 'The great defect of the detective of fiction,' he said in the 1892 interview, 'is that he obtains his results without any obvious reason. This is not fair, it is not art.'[51] Detective stories were not his only reading matter, Dickens, Wilkie Collins, and others, were familiar to him, and in the second part of A Study in Scarlet it was Bret Harte and Robert Louis Stevenson (or his wife) whose influence was most apparent.

Stevenson's story, 'The Pavilion on the Links', which is itself in the nature of a detective story, had made a deep impression on Conan Doyle at the time of its appearance in the Cornhill Magazine. He always preferred that version to the one which appeared in the New Arabian Nights, but he knew both and was, perhaps, also influenced by the other stories in the book – though it is unlikely, as some have suggested, that the President of the Suicide Club was the inspiration for Professor Moriarty, or that Prince Florizel and Colonel Geraldine lay behind Holmes and Watson. No one, however, can doubt the influence of another book by Stevenson, The Dynamiter, which contains the Mormon story of the 'Destroying Angel'. Doyle was to describe this in an article on Stevenson as among the most vivid and lucid in fiction: 'How are we to forget the lonely fire in the valley, the white figure which dances and screams among the snow, or the horrid ravine in which the caravan is starved.'[52]

Patronymics and Prototypes

By the end of 1885 Doyle was ready to attempt his first detective story. All that remained was to find a title and to choose the names for his characters. In one of his common-place books he made a short entry under the heading 'A Tangled Skein' which was then crossed out and replaced by 'A Study in Scarlet'. This is the only evidence to suggest that he contemplated using another title. Underneath he had written:

> The terrified woman rushing up to the cabman. The two going in search of a policeman. John Reeves had been 7 years in the force, John Reeves went back with them.[53]

There was nothing remarkable about the title, but the choice of the name Sherlock Holmes was inspired, and after it had gained world-wide currency, it was natural that Doyle should be asked about its origin. He always claimed that he did not remember how he had chanced upon it: 'I don't know how I got that name,' he told Bram Stoker in an interview before his second marriage – then added: 'I was looking the other day at a bit of paper on which I had scribbled "Sherringford Holmes" and "Sheridan Hope" and all sorts of other combinations.'[54] Alternative names are also mentioned in his autobiography where he says that he still possessed 'the leaf of a notebook with various alternative names'.[55] This may have been the single sheet of notes headed 'A Study in Scarlet' which gives the name of the future Dr Watson as 'Ormond Sacker' and that of the 'sleepy eyed young man', the consulting detective, as 'Sherrinford Holmes'; but it has no other combinations.

'Holmes' was chosen, according to Doyle, because it was common, and therefore preferable to the 'Sharps' and 'Ferrets' of contemporary detective fiction, and it almost certainly came from Oliver Wendell Holmes, who spent three months in England in 1886, from 9 May to 21 August, when he was given an honorary degree by Edinburgh University. Doyle had already used the name in an essay called 'After Cormorants with a Camera' which was published in 1881. Holmes was there considered an unsuitable companion as he 'neither smoked nor drank'.[56] All the photographic essays showed the influence of the *Breakfast Table* series, and Doyle always had the highest regard for their author. He was to describe Oliver Wendell Holmes in *Our American Adventure* as his 'favourite essayist', as one of his 'spiritual and literary fathers': 'The gentle laughing philosopher whether as autocrat, poet, or professor, made a very deep mark upon my young mind. Glorious fellow, so tolerant, so witty, so worldly-wise.'[57] And in *Through the Magic Door* he said of him: 'Never have I so known and loved a man whom I had never seen.'[58] There were, of course, other people with the same name whom Doyle could have known. Both David and James Holmes received medical degrees at Edinburgh University in 1877, one an M.B., the other an M.D.; Timothy Holmes would also have been known to him as the author of standard works on surgery which were quoted by Joseph Bell in his published writings and in his lectures. But only the 'Sage of Boston' deserves or is worthy of such a nominal association. That there was some confusion in people's minds is shown by a story which was current shortly after the death of Oliver Wendell Holmes in 1894. It concerned a lady in high society who, in the words of Arthur Mee, 'on hearing somebody discussing Dr Doyle's hero, broke in with the remark that she was "almost heart-broken when he died", adding that "his *Autocrat of the Breakfast Table* has long been a favourite of mine"'.[59]

The name 'Sherlock' could have been derived from Patrick Sherlock, who was Doyle's contemporary at Stonyhurst; or Doyle may have come across the name of William Sherlock in Macaulay's *History of England*. But he never referred to either of these as his source; instead he gave the credit to a cricketer whom he first mentioned in a speech at the 1921 Stoll Convention Dinner, and again, for example, in an interview to mark his 69th birthday. Many of the syndicated obituary articles, such as those in the *Portsmouth Evening News*, the *Yorkshire Telegraph*, and the *Belfast Telegraph*, mentioned that Doyle had been 'an enthusiastic and useful cricketer in his younger days', and added: 'In those days there was a famous bowler named Sherlock. "I cannot really be certain," he said a little while ago, "but it is possible that the name of the bowler Sherlock stuck in my mind, and Holmes also may owe its origin to cricket." '[60] This was given wider currency by Vincent Starrett, who mentioned it in an article in the *Atlantic Monthly* for July 1932 which was included a year later in his influential book, *The Private Life of Sherlock Holmes*. Having stated (though, as he admitted later, without authority) that Doyle's love for the works of Oliver Wendell Holmes had 'dictated' the choice of the surname, he mentioned in a footnote that Doyle was once quoted in a newspaper as saying: 'Years ago I made thirty runs against a bowler by the name of Sherlock, and I always had a kindly feeling for that name.'[61] What Doyle had originally said on 28 September 1921 was:

> I remember playing in a match and my old friend, Colonel English, who is present, played in it too, between the United Services and the MCC. The MCC brought down against us two fine bowlers in Attewell and Sherlock. I had the good fortune to scrape up twenty or thirty runs against them, and I think the name Sherlock impressed itself on my mind.[62]

Though still popular today, this explanation is open to doubt, as Doyle probably realized. In the first place, Robert English, who had just retired from the Army and taken up film acting, was an ardent cricketer, but would have been only twelve years old when the first Sherlock Holmes story was written; moreover, he did not play for the United Services against the MCC until June 1898. As for the cricketer called Sherlock, although there was one with this name who played club cricket for Devonshire and who could conceivably have been known to Doyle when he was in Plymouth in 1882, it is quite clear that he was actually referring to Frank Shacklock and to a match which took place after the name had been chosen. Even so, Shacklock could have been known to Doyle before then, as he had played for various Scottish teams when Doyle was in Edinburgh; after that he joined Derbyshire, and in 1886 became a member of the Nottinghamshire team. If Doyle did try various combinations, then Frank Shacklock and another member of the Notts team, Mordecai Sherwin, could between them have supplied the name (the 'Mordecai' perhaps suggested 'Mordecai Smith' in *The Sign of Four*); but the match in which Doyle played for the United Services, and Frank Shacklock for the MCC, took place in Portsmouth on 25 and 26 April 1890. Doyle scored twenty runs, and caught Shacklock.

Whatever Shacklock's claim, the names of other cricketers certainly influenced Conan Doyle. He mentioned two in his 1921 speech: Mycroft and Rylott. The first, given to Holmes's elder brother, derived from Thomas and William Mycroft, who were famous Derbyshire players. William had played for the MCC against the United Services in 1889 when Doyle was a member of the other team. The second was certainly in Doyle's mind when he came to dramatize *The Speckled Band*, in which the central character is called Dr Grimesby Rylott, and may also have inspired the name 'Roylott' which was used in the story itself. It was taken from Arnold Rylott, a famous Leicestershire bowler.

It is easy to understand why Doyle became confused, for with hindsight a match such as that between Derbyshire and Lancashire on 22 May 1884 can be disconcerting when one finds Shacklock, Mycroft, and a player called Watson appearing together. Cricket enthusiasts were quick to correct Doyle's initial mistake, but the idea that the name of the great detective was based on a cricketer was given added authority in the obituary for Conan Doyle which appeared in the 1931 edition of *Wisden's*: 'It is said that Shacklock, the former Nottinghamshire player, inspired him with the Christian name of his famous character, Sherlock Holmes, and that of the latter's brother Mycroft was suggested by the Derbyshire cricketers.'[63]

Both Patrick Sherlock and Frank Shacklock could have

been in Doyle's mind in March 1886 when he decided upon
the name. In August 1885, during his honeymoon, Doyle
had visited Dublin as a member of the Stonyhurst Wander-
ers' cricket team, having first played one match at the school
in Lancashire, so it is quite possible that he would have heard
reports of, or even have met, the first. Shacklock was in the
news at the beginning of 1886 because of his decision to
move from Derbyshire to Nottinghamshire. There are also,
of course, a number of other less serious contenders, such as
The Sherlocks, a novel by John Saunders, or Sheridan Le
Fanu's *A Lost Name*, in which Carmel Sherlock has many of
the attributes of Doyle's Sherlock Holmes. Among those
whose first name it was is Lieutenant-General Shurlock
Henning, listed in the index of the 1885 *Army List* as
'Sherlock Henning'. Born in 1829, he entered the army in
1849 and retired in 1885 – having served in the Crimea,
India, and in the Abyssinian Campaign of 1868 – and on 26
December of that year was given the rank of Lieutenant-
General. As he lived until 1898, he would have seen his
previously obscure Christian name made familiar, but
whether he ever assumed that he was responsible for it is not
known. Later, in the United States, there was a Sherlock
Witherington Holmes (born 1907), a Sherlock Gordon
Holmes (born 1920), and a Sherlock Holmes of Memphis,
Tennessee. A Sherlock Holmes died in Chicago in November 1948 at the age of 61, and another, according to the
house magazine of the Post Office, was working two years
later in the Dartford sorting office.

Many people have been suggested as the source for Dr
John H. Watson, of whom some are worth mentioning. One
is Herbert Thurston, the Jesuit historian. Three years older
than Doyle when he arrived at Stonyhurst in 1871, he was
placed in the class above him, but they became friends, and
for their own amusement collaborated on a comic guide to
the school. Thurston's connection with Watson is a devious
one. In May 1885 Doyle wrote a story called 'Uncle Jeremy's

Household' which is in some ways a prototype of the later Sherlock Holmes stories. The Holmes character, who has few similarities to his distinguished successor, is called Hugh Lawrence, but he lives in Baker Street and he has a companion with the name John H. Thurston. A more plausible candidate, and one who had medical qualifications of a considerably higher standard than those of his fictional counterpart, is Dr Patrick Heron Watson, Joseph Bell's assistant at the Edinburgh Royal Infirmary and one of the finest surgeons of the day. The name, however, which fits most closely is that of Dr James Watson of Southsea. He became an active member of the Portsmouth Literary and Scientific Society, and eventually its President. The first meeting he attended, at which Doyle was also present, was on 11 November 1884; he was elected a member two weeks later, and there were many subsequent occasions when he and Doyle were both present, such as 22 December 1885 and 16 March 1886. Watson was in the chair at the farewell dinner given to Conan Doyle at the Grosvenor Hotel, Southsea, on 12 December 1890. His claim to be the source of the name is enhanced by a slip which occurs in 'The Man with a Twisted Lip' where Watson is called 'James' by his wife.

Another person put forward as the original of Dr Watson is Alfred Herbert Wood, who replaced Charles Terry as Doyle's private secretary shortly after the end of the Boer War. Born in Portsmouth in 1866, he was educated at Portsmouth Grammar School, winning an open scholarship to Brasenose College, Oxford. After taking his M.A., he returned to Portsmouth and taught at his old school. Cricket and football first brought him into contact with Conan Doyle as both, for example, played with the United Services against the MCC. Although Doyle said of Wood in 1921 that he had been 'mixed up in my life ever since as young men we played both cricket and football in the same team',[64] it is unlikely that Wood made any great impact that early.

He served in the 5th Royal Sussex Regiment in France during the Great War and reached the rank of major. Thereafter he became closer to the popular conception of Dr Watson.

Finally there is Dr David George Thomson. He first met Conan Doyle in Edinburgh, and they remained close friends for the remainder of their lives. Thomson, who was three years older, took his M.B. and C.M. in 1878 (as did Watson), and was then employed as a house surgeon in the Edinburgh Royal Infirmary under Dr Joseph Bell. He and Doyle shared an interest in photography, and both contributed articles to the *British Journal of Photography*. Thomson became an M.D. in 1881. He then served as an assistant physician at the Derby County Asylum, held the same position at the Camberwell House Asylum, and in 1886 became the superintendent of the County Mental Hospital in Norwich, where he remained until his death in 1923. Doyle was a frequent visitor, and he and Thomson were stalwarts of the hospital cricket club. On one occasion, according to Dr J. Spence Law, who did locum work, Doyle asked Thomson:

> 'What do you think of Dr Watson?'
> 'I think he's a bit of an ass,' said Thomson.
> 'I'm sorry you think that,' said Conan Doyle. 'I rather modelled him on you.'[65]

The First Book About Sherlock Holmes

Doyle started *A Study in Scarlet* in March 1886 and had completed it by the end of the following month. He and his wife were confident that it would do better than its predecessor, then still known as 'Girdlestone & Co.': 'We rather fancy,' Doyle's wife told her sister-in-law, 'that *A Study in Scarlet* may find its way into print before its elder brother.'[66]

It was sent first to James Payn, the editor of the *Cornhill Magazine*. He returned it on 7 May with a covering letter which was almost illegible and open to various interpretations, some complimentary and some less so. 'Payn's Opinion', as Doyle described it in his scrapbook, appears to have been as follows:

> My Dear Sir,
>   I have kept your story an unconscionably long time but it so interested me that I wanted to finish it. It's capital. The best of the 'shilling dreadfuls' – except Stevenson's. I may say we don't publish books at that price. It's too long – & too short – for the 'CM'.
>
> Truly, J. Payn[67]

'Shilling dreadful' were the words which stood out, but those which followed were indecipherable. Maybe, as others have supposed, Payn wrote: 'The size of the "shilling dreadful" – except Heavens, I wish they wouldn't publish books at that price. It's too long – & too short – for the "CM".' If this had been intended as a compliment, and Stevenson's *Dr Jekyll and Mr Hyde* had appeared shortly before as a 'shilling dreadful', then it failed to hit the mark; even so, it was more encouraging than what followed.

Arrowsmith's of Bristol, who had made their fortune with Hugh Conway's *Called Back* and whose Christmas annuals were ideally suited for a novel like *A Study in Scarlet*, missed their opportunity of another and potentially greater fortune by allowing the manuscript to remain unread from May until July when it was returned. 'I missed Conan Doyle,' Arrowsmith admitted later. 'He came to me with *A Study in Scarlet*. I was a stupid young beggar, and I let it go. He should have told me the kind of book it was going to be.'[68] Frederick Warne, the next recipient, was quick to reject the manuscript when it was offered at the end of August. Doyle felt close to despair. He told his mother that his 'poor *Study*' had never even been read by anyone except Payn, and added:

'Verily literature is a difficult oyster to open.'[69] But he was confident that all would come well in the end.

In September the dog-eared manuscript was on its way to Ward, Lock and Company. They replied on 30 October:

> Dear Sir,
>   We have read your story A Study in Scarlet, and are pleased with it. We could not publish it this year, as the market is flooded at present with cheap fiction, but if you do not object to its being held over till next year we will give you £25/–/– (Twenty-five Pounds) for the copyright.
>   We are Dear Sir, Yours faithfully, Ward, Lock & Co.

This was far from ideal, less than Doyle had received three years earlier for the serial rights of 'J. Habakuk Jephson's Statement', but he intimated that he would accept the offer if he were allowed a small royalty. The publishers were adamant. On 2 November they answered:

> Dear Sir,
>   In reply to your letter of yesterday's date. We regret to say that we shall be unable to allow you to retain a percentage on the sale of your work as it might give rise to some confusion. The tale may have to be inserted together with some other, in one of our annuals, therefore we must adhere to our original offer of 25£ for the complete copyright.
>   We are Dear Sir, Yours truly,
>   For Ward, Lock & Co. &c.[70]

With some reluctance Doyle accepted. The contract was drawn up on 20 November and his meagre cheque was dispatched the same day. Twelve months then elapsed before A Study in Scarlet was published as the main story in the 1887 edition of Beeton's Christmas Annual, with Food for Powder, 'A Vaudeville for the Drawing Room', by R. André, and The Four-Leaved Shamrock, 'A Drawing-room Comedietta in Three Acts', by C. J. Hamilton.

One of the few inside accounts of the negotiation between the author and the publisher, and one that is slightly suspect and fanciful, was given by Coulson Kernahan in 1934, in an article called 'Personal Memories of Sherlock Holmes'; he claimed that it was his wife who had 'discovered' Sherlock Holmes. In 1886 she had been shown the manuscript by her husband, Professor George T. Bettany, who worked for Ward, Lock and Company as an adviser and as the editor of various popular series; he asked her whether he should read it, and she told him: 'This is, I feel sure, by a doctor – there is internal evidence to that effect. But in any case, the writer is a born novelist. I am enthusiastic about the book, and believe it will be a great success.'[71] If she did say that, then it was in marked contrast to her later feelings. In the *Young Man* of February 1900, for example, when discussing 'The Younger Writers of To-Day', she complained that 'Dr Conan Doyle is the saddest case of decadence';[72] he had proved himself a competent historical novelist with *Micah Clarke* and *The White Company*, 'yet has steadily declined since the evil hour which saw him invent one Sherlock Holmes'. Even if she had not 'discovered' Sherlock Holmes, she should have known that the 'evil hour' preceded the historical novels.

In 1889 Kernahan became a junior editor at Ward, Lock and Company and shortly afterwards an assistant editor of the English edition of *Lippincott's Magazine*. He claimed in his 1934 article that he had come across the file copy of *Beeton's Christmas Annual* for 1887. He asked if anything might be done with *A Study in Scarlet* and was told: 'It served its purpose, and did respectably as the Annual, but the sales were not great, and few reviewers had anything to say of it.'[73] He, however, with great foresight encouraged the firm to re-issue it. The Annual had in fact been favourably reviewed and had sold out within a fortnight of its publication. Doyle knew early in 1888 that there would be a separate edition and he probably suggested that it should be illustrated by his father.

The first separate edition was published in July 1888 with

six rather infirm drawings by Charles Altamont Doyle, perhaps based on members of the artist's family. They bore no similarity to the later conceptions of Sherlock Holmes, and were far less successful than the heavy designs by D. H. Friston which had appeared in the Annual. The book, with its red printed paper covers, its cheap string binding and pages of advertisements, was prefaced by the publisher, who paid Doyle the compliment of comparing his book with Archibald Clavering Gunter's contemporary best-seller, *Mr Barnes of New York*, and with *Shadowed by Three*, the sensational adventures of the detective Francis Ferrars which had been published in 1884 and written by Emma M. Murdoch under the pseudonym 'Lawrence L. Lynch, Ex-Detective'. The preface was as follows:

This book contains a story of thrilling interest, in which the expectation of the reader, and his faculties for conjecture and deduction are kept in employment from first to last. The *Study in Scarlet*, and the unravelling of the apparently unfathomable mystery by the cool shrewdness of Mr Sherlock Holmes, yield nothing in point of sustained interest and gratified expectation to the best stories of the school that has produced *Mr Barnes of New York*, *Shadowed by Three*, &c., &c.; and the description of the deadly Mormon association of tyranny and vengeance, is as true in its features as it is enthralling in interest.

The work has a valuable advantage in the shape of illustrations by the author's father, Mr Charles Doyle, a younger brother of the late Mr Richard Doyle, the eminent colleague of John Leech, in the pages of *Punch*, and son of the eminent caricaturist whose political sketches, signed 'H.B.', were a feature in London half-a-century ago.

The original issue of this remarkable story having been exhausted, it is now presented to the public in a new form, with these additional attractions, in the full expectation that it will win a new and wide circle of readers.[74]

The expectation was fully justified. Andrew Lang was one of those to be struck by the story; in his 'At the Sign of the Ship' column in the January 1889 issue of *Longman's Magazine* he praised the book as 'an extremely clever narrative, rich in surprises', and admitted that he 'never was more surprised by any story than when it came to the cabman';[75] Doyle had, he believed, come 'nearer to the true Hugh Conway than any writer since the regretted death of the author of *Called Back*'.

The preface stated that Doyle's description of the Mormons was true in its features, and Doyle may have based it on the entry in the *Encylopaedia Britannica*, or on the lecture he had heard at the Portsmouth Literary and Scientific Society, or on any number of books and articles which were then current. But Bishop Charles W. Nibley of the Church of the Latter Day Saints was to criticize it in 1923 when Doyle was on his second American 'adventure'. Nibley was angry that the author of such a book should be welcomed in Salt Lake City and that he should have taken money from its inhabitants. He called for an apology. Doyle stood by what he had said, but he was very favourably impressed by what he saw in Utah and pleased when the Mormons put their assembly hall at his disposal:

> It was the more magnanimous because in my early days I had written in *A Study in Scarlet* a rather sensational and overcoloured picture of the Danite episodes which formed a passing stain in the early history of Utah. This could have been easily brought up to prejudice opinion against me, but as a matter of fact no allusion was made to it save by one Gentile doctor, who wrote and urged me to make some public apology. This of course I could not do, as the facts were true enough, though there were many reasons which might extenuate them. I thought it better to leave the matter alone and confine my attention and remarks to the present.[76]

Mr Barnes of New York, which was mentioned in the early

preface, had been a theatrical as well as a literary success and this may have encouraged Doyle to dramatize his own story. The Portsmouth *Crescent* mentioned on 28 September 1888, in an article about Conan Doyle, that *A Study in Scarlet*, having gained a 'world wide reputation', was to be dramatized. As there is an unpublished play by Doyle which deals with the same subject and uses many of the same characters, it has always been presumed that the dramatization was made and that this 'Drama in Three Acts', first known as 'A Study in Scarlet' and then renamed 'Angels of Darkness', was the result. The characters include John Ferrier; his daughter, Lucy; his Chinese laundryman, Ling-Tchu; and an Irish help, Biddy McGee. There is, too, a traveller in notions called Elias Fortescue Smee, and an unorthodox Mormon, Hiram Cooper. The villains of the piece who threaten Ferrier when he refuses to give up his daughter in marriage are the Elder Johnstone, the leaders of the Avenging Angels, John Drebber and Lovejoy Stangerson, and two of their followers. Then there are the two heroes, Jefferson Hope and John Watson, M.D., a San Franciso practitioner, as well as the aristocratic English globe-trotter Sir Montague Brown. The first two acts take place in Utah and the third, which exists in a completed and an uncompleted version, is set in San Francisco at the boarding-house of Mrs Carpenter and her daughter, Rose. The John Watson of the play appears to have no connection with the companion of Sherlock Holmes, but some of the other characters and the plot have points in common with *A Study in Scarlet*. Holmes himself is conspicuously absent.

The Sign of the Four: or, The Problem of the Sholtos

At the end of August 1889 Doyle was in London at the request of Joseph Marshall Stoddart, the managing editor of *Lippincott's Magazine*, as was Oscar Wilde. The ensuing literary meeting – one of the most remarkable and unlikely ever to take place – was responsible for two famous works of fiction. Unlike Wilde, who does not appear to have mentioned the occasion, Doyle was fond of recalling it, not least because he learnt that Wilde had actually read one of his books and, what was more, had enjoyed it. Even after Wilde's fall from grace, Doyle retained a kindly feeling for him, as he believed that he should have been in a consulting-room rather than a prison. In a speech about his literary contemporaries given in Australia in 1920, Doyle said of their meeting:

> On one occasion an American who was visiting London in order to secure cheap stories from the new writers, invited us to dinner with the intention of doing business afterwards. Wilde was one of the younger authors there, and I was also one of the company. The result of the dinner was that I wrote *The Sign of Four*, and Wilde wrote *The Picture of Dorian Gray*. [77]

The meeting took place at the Langham Hotel, and there was one other guest, Thomas Patrick Gill, M.P., the editor of the *Catholic World* and former editor of the *North American Review*, who had been a member of the Mission of the Irish Parliamentary Party which had just visited America. Stoddart had been in England for some weeks making arrangements with Ward, Lock and Company for the publication of the English edition of *Lippincott's Magazine*; Ward, Lock might have mentioned Doyle's name to him, but, as he had also called on the editors of other magazines and as James Payn told Doyle that he had recommended him to Lippincott, it seems that Payn was the person ultimately responsible for the invitation.

The contract was drawn up on 30 August, the same day, it seems, as the dinner itself, with Doyle to receive one hundred pounds for a story of not less than 40,000 words. The author, writing to Stoddart on 3 September, stated that this was 'entirely satisfactory' and he was especially pleased as it only covered the serial publication. His letter continued:

> As far as I can see my way at present my story will either be called 'The Sign of the Six' or 'The Problem of the Sholtos'. You said you wanted a spicy title. I shall give Sherlock Holmes of A *Study in Scarlet* something else to unravel. I notice that everyone who has read the book wants to know more of that young man. Of course the new story will be entirely independent of A *Study in Scarlet* but as Sherlock Holmes & Dr Watson are introduced in each, I think that the sale of one might influence the other. I wish therefore that your firm would reprint A *Study* in America and give me some dollars for it.[78]

This suggests that the subject of the book had not been agreed on at the Langham Hotel, even though Doyle was to say later that it was the success of the first Sherlock Holmes book in America which had led Lippincott's to ask for a sequel. Lippincott's did reprint A *Study in Scarlet* as a result of his suggestion; published in March 1890, it is the earliest American edition known.

The new story was completed at the end of September 1889. It was some thousand words over the agreed figure and filled 160 pages of manuscript. Doyle had not, however, decided upon the title, so on 1 October he again wrote to Stoddart:

> You promised to collaborate with me in this book, so I want you to name it, which will surely make you a bona fide collaborator. 'The Sign of the Four' strikes me as likely to be popular, but a trifle catchpenny. 'The Problem of the Sholtos' is more choice, though less dramatic. On you be the burden of choosing. I wish also that your reader would look over the proofs. It would save sending twice across the Atlantic.

> I have finished it & sent it to your London agents. I

think it is pretty fair, though I am not usually satisfied with my own things. It has the advantage over *The Study in Scarlet* not only as being much more intricate, but also as forming a connected narrative without any harking back as in the second part of *The Study*. Holmes, I am glad to say, is in capital form all through. You will see that *The Study* is alluded to in it, and I believe that you have a demand for it if you would get it out at the same time.[79]

The Sign of the Four; or, The Problem of the Sholtos was published both in America and England in the February 1890 issue of *Lippincott's Magazine*, and Doyle was well pleased with it and with the frontispiece by Herbert Denman. He wrote to Stoddart in March asking him to thank the artist. His letter continued:

By the way there is one very obvious mistake which must be corrected in book form – in the second chapter the letter is headed July 7th, and on almost the same page I talk of its being a September evening. Again in the first chapter the same post office is called Wigmore Street & Seymour Street. The first is correct.

By the way it must amuse you to see the vast and accurate knowledge of London which I display. I worked it all out from a post-office map.[80]

The reviews on both sides of the Atlantic were also encouraging, as was the reaction from the readers. Doyle told Stoddart on 17 March 1890:

I was so glad that 'The Sign of the Tom' as the *N.Y. Herald* called it made some friends. It seemed to be fairly fortunate over here also. I did not see a single review out of 30 or 40, which my Press Agency sent me, which was not very kind, from the 'This is the best story I ever read in my life', of one priceless critic, down to more discriminating & less flattering reviews. It's a triumph ever to get a rise out of you shrewd people on the other side, but a Philadelphia tobacconist actually wrote to me under cover to you, to ask me where he could get a copy of the monograph in which Sherlock Holmes describes the difference in the ashes of 140 different kinds of tobacco. Rather funny, isn't it?[81]

The tobacconist in Philadelphia may have been the first to confuse fact and fiction but he was by no means the last. When the Scribner Book Store in New York issued a catalogue of material from Vincent Starrett's collection in 1943, it contained 'a few extraordinary and unique items' dreamed up by Starrett. One of these was *An Inquiry into the Nature of the Ashes of Various Tobaccos* by Sherlock Holmes, a rare second edition published in Tibet in 1893! Dave Randall, who was responsible for the catalogue, recalled:

> No sooner was the catalogue distributed when who should present himself at Scribner's but the late great George Arents, with his librarian, panting to buy it for his collection at the New York Public Library. Arents was a humourless man, though an important customer, and didn't think the hoax was at all funny when I explained the non-existence of the book. Starrett, however, was absolutely entranced with the success of his efforts when I related the incident.[82]

The Sign of Four was published in book form in October 1890 in the attractive Standard Library of Spencer Blackett. 'Dr Doyle's admirers will read the little volume through eagerly enough,' the *Athenaeum* commented in its review which had failed to mention the name of Sherlock Holmes, 'but they will hardly care to take it up again.'[83]

The Strand Magazine and its Editor

A pirate edition of *The Sign of Four* was published in New York in March 1891 by P. F. Collier in the 'Once a Week

Library' with an anonymous story at the end called 'The Siege of Sunda Gunge'. Some people thought it must be by Doyle, but it was actually written by Herbert Greenhough Smith who, at the end of the previous year, had joined George Newnes as the future editor of the *Strand Magazine*. Smith was born in 1855 and educated at St John's College, Cambridge; he had been a private tutor, then a journalist with various newspapers and magazines, and an associate editor of *Temple Bar*. The first number of the *Strand Magazine* was dated January 1891, and during that month A. P. Watt, Doyle's literary agent, sent in a story called 'The Voice of Science'. This marked the beginning of an association between the author and the magazine which lasted until Doyle's death. The magazine was to publish all the subsequent Sherlock Holmes stories as well as many of Conan Doyle's other major works; the first story appeared in March 1891 and the last in December 1930.

After his return from Vienna Doyle set up in practice as an eye specialist in Devonshire Place (or 2, Upper Wimpole Street), and it was here during April 1891 that he wrote the first of the adventures of Sherlock Holmes. Greenhough Smith recalled the delight with which these stories were received in a 'Thumbnail Sketch' of Conan Doyle in *John O'London's Weekly* on 19 April 1919:

> Well I remember how, many years ago, when the *Strand Magazine* was making its start in a tiny room at the top of a building in a street off the Strand – a sanctum approached through a room crammed with typewriters, with machines incessantly clicking – there came to me an envelope containing the first two stories of a series which were destined to become famous over all the world as the 'Adventures of Sherlock Holmes'. What a God-send to an editor jaded with wading through reams of impossible stuff! The ingenuity of plot, the limpid clearness of style, the perfect art of telling a story! The very handwriting, full of character, and clear as print.[84]

Smith used the article again as the basis for Conan Doyle's obituary in the *Strand Magazine* in 1930, which was the same year that he relinquished his position as editor. In December 1930 he was interviewed by the *World's Press News* and again mentioned Doyle's association with the *Strand Magazine* and the excitement caused by the arrival of the first Sherlock Holmes stories. Doyle, he explained, had divided his time between medicine and literature and had written various novels without creating 'any great sensation in the literary world':

> Then he tried short stories, and A. P. Watt, his agent, sent me the first two of Sherlock's *Adventures*. I realized at once that here was the greatest short story-writer since Edgar Allan Poe. I can still remember rushing into Mr Newnes' room and thrusting the stories before his eyes. He read them with an appreciation equal to my own, and forthwith secured Conan Doyle to write the famous series of *Adventures*, which eventually ran to over fifty stories.[85]

Without the encouragement and pressure exerted by Greenhough Smith Doyle might not have written as many stories about Sherlock Holmes as he did. He was always grateful for the editor's suggestions, some of which were based on material which had been sent for publication, and some the result of Smith's own interest in criminal cases. The plot for 'The Problem of Thor Bridge', which was based on a real suicide case described in Hans Gross's *System der Kriminalistik*, as well as a number of other possible plots, some practical and some impractical, originated with the editor. The magazine itself, especially the 'Curiosities' page, provided further ideas. A letter from a convict put together out of words cut from a Bible, and a snake puzzlebox made by Boer prisoners-of-war on St Helena that would prick the hand which opened it, may well have been the source for the letter in *The Hound of the Baskervilles* and for the box sent to Sherlock Holmes in 'The Adventure of the Dying Detective'. There is certainly little doubt that the two false horseshoes, illustrated in the May 1903 issue, were the inspiration for those used in 'The Adventure of the Priory School'. The real ones were discovered in the moat of Birtsmorton Court, near Tewkesbury, and were designed to leave in one case the print of a cow's hoof and in another that of a child's foot.

In a deleted passage of his autobiography, Doyle described Greenhough Smith as a man 'whose rather melancholy exterior which has earned him the name of "Calamity Smith" conceals a very real humanity and a broad literary instinct'.[86] He had a great respect for Smith's judgement, and much of his writing was tailored to suit the tastes of the editor. Doyle once said that if he were the father of Sherlock Holmes, Smith was the 'Accoucheur',[87] and he wrote on the cover of the manuscript of 'The Adventure of the Golden Pince-Nez' which he gave him in February 1916: 'A Souvenir of 20 years of collaboration.'[88] Their letters covered every detail from the initial idea to the final presentation in the magazine, and, after Smith's death in 1935, it was his friendship with Conan Doyle which received most attention in his obituaries. Doyle was the author most closely associated with the success of the Strand Magazine and the only one (with the possible exception of Winston Churchill) whose name on the cover was sufficient by itself to raise the circulation. It is a measure of Greenhough Smith's ability as an editor that Doyle should have remained so faithful and that he resisted the offers from the editors of other magazines who would have paid almost any price for the rights to an original Sherlock Holmes story.

Sidney Paget

'A Scandal in Bohemia' appeared in the Strand Magazine in July 1891. It was illustrated by Sidney Paget, whose work met with the approval of the author. 'Should you see the Artist who did my "Sherlock Holmes",' Doyle told the editor on 9 July, 'I wish you would tell him how very much I appreciate his rendering. I hope the blocks may be preserved so that my future publisher may have the refusal of them.'[89] Paget's drawings were to establish the popular conception of Sherlock Holmes, at least among English readers, though Doyle later admitted that it was somewhat unlike his original idea. In the manuscript of his autobiography, parts of which were published in America in *Collier's Weekly* on 29 December 1923, he was to say:

I saw him as very tall – 'over six feet, but so excessively lean that he seemed considerably taller,' said *A Study in Scarlet*. He had, as I imagined him, a thin razorlike face, with a great hawk's-bill of a nose, and two small eyes, set close together on either side of it. Such was my conception. It chanced, however, that poor Arthur Paget, who, before his premature death, drew all the original pictures, had a younger brother whose name, I think, was Harold, who served him as a model. The handsome Harold took the place of the more powerful but uglier Sherlock, and, perhaps from the point of view of my lady readers it was as well.[90]

When the copy reached the *Strand Magazine*, 'Arthur' was corrected to 'Sidney' though 'Harold' was allowed to stand. The editor could hardly complain as he, or somebody close to him, had confused the names at the start. It seems that the drawings which Walter Paget had done for the *Illustrated London News* of the Gordon Relief Expedition had caught the editor's attention and he was chosen for the Sherlock Holmes stories, but as no one could recall the first name, the offer went instead to Sidney Paget. Walter did, however, become famous as the model for Sherlock Holmes. He was so like his brother's drawings that he was several times mistaken for the great detective; on one occasion for instance, according to his niece, when he was attending a musical recital at the Bechstein Hall a woman was heard to say as he walked past: 'Look, there's Sherlock Holmes.'[91] Many of the characters in the drawings were based on friends and members of the Paget family. One was Sidney Paget's brother-in-law, Stephen Martin; and it is believed that Dr Watson was based on a contemporary of Paget's at the Royal Academy School, a certain Alfred Morris Butler. Furniture and clothing from the Paget household also appeared, and it was the artist's own deerstalker which was responsible for the now quintessential piece of headgear. The *Bristol Observer* had shown Holmes wearing a deerstalker in its issues of 7 and 14 June 1890 when it reprinted *The Sign of Four*, but it is undoubtedly Sidney Paget's drawings for 'The Boscombe Valley Mystery' and for 'Silver Blaze' which are the most perfect of their type and the main inspiration of all subsequent interpretations. His delineations of Sherlock Holmes, as the *Strand* rightly claimed in December 1895, 'had their share in the popularity of that wonderful detective'.[92] Sherlock Holmes himself had acknowledged the part played by the artist. In Sidney Paget's diary at the time of his marriage there is the following entry:

> June 1st, 1893. Our Wedding Day . . . Was most delighted at breakfast time to find a beautiful silver cigarette case from 'Sherlock Holmes' had come as a present.[93]

It was from Conan Doyle. 'I think that was the nicest idea possible,' Paget's mother-in-law confided to her daughter, 'that case from "Sherlock Holmes".'[94] The artist was kept busy during his honeymoon doing the illustrations for the Holmes stories. 'Wrote letters and read Sherlock Holmes,' he noted in his diary a few days after his wedding; and on the 12th: 'After breakfast began drawing (S.H.) worked till 1 o'clock.' Until his death on 29 January 1908, he was the illustrator most favoured by Conan Doyle, and was responsible for all the drawings for the Sherlock Holmes stories in the *Strand Magazine*. The later artists, including Walter

Paget, who did the illustrations for 'The Adventure of the Dying Detective', were less successful.

The Adventures of Sherlock Holmes

Doyle only intended to do six adventures of Sherlock Holmes, but they proved so popular that he was asked to write more. 'The *Strand* are simply imploring me to continue Sherlock Holmes,' he told his mother on 14 October 1891. 'The stories brought me on an average £35 each, so I have written by this post to say that if they offer me £50 each, irrespective of length, I may be induced to reconsider my refusal.'[95] The proprietors readily complied, and by 11 November he had written a further five; he listed their titles in another letter to his mother, and added: 'I think of slaying Holmes in the sixth and winding him up for good and all. He takes my mind from better things.'[96] But he was restrained by her protestations and used an idea which she had suggested instead. 'During the holidays,' he told her at the beginning of the new year, 'I finished my last Sherlock Holmes tale "The Adventure of the Copper Beeches" in which I used your lock of hair, so now a long farewell to Sherlock. He still lives, however, thanks to your entreaties.'[97] There was understandable relief in the new offices of the *Strand Magazine*, and in the December issue Doyle was included among the 'Portraits of Celebrities at Different Times of their Lives'; the accompanying note assured the reader: 'There are few better writers of short stories than Mr Conan Doyle, and it gives us great pleasure to announce that the extraordinary adventures of Sherlock Holmes, which have proved so popular with our readers during the past six months, will be continued in the new year.'[98]

In February 1892 Doyle was persuaded to undertake a further series. 'Under pressure,' he explained, 'I offered to do a dozen for a thousand pounds, but I sincerely hope that they won't accept it now.'[99] It was a forlorn hope as the magazine was under very different pressures and was therefore quick to accept his conditions. Doyle had a number of other literary and social commitments to deal with first, but by the end of June he had written three of the new series and was confident that he had enough material for the remainder. It was during that month that Harry How paid his visit. He learnt a number of interesting facts about Sherlock Holmes which he made known to the readers of the *Strand Magazine*:

> Dr Doyle invariably conceives the end of his story first, and writes up to it. He gets the climax, and his art lies in the ingenious way in which he conceals it from his readers. A story – similar to those which have appeared in these pages – occupies about a week in writing, and the ideas have come at all manner of times – when out walking, cricketing, tricycling, or playing tennis. He works between the hours of breakfast and lunch, and again in the evening from five to eight, writing some three thousand words a day. He receives many suggestions from the public. On the morning of my visit the particulars of a poisoning case had been sent to him from New Zealand, and the previous day a great packet of documents relating to a disputed will had been received from Bristol. But the suggestions are seldom practicable. Other letters come from people who have been reading the latest of his stories, saying whether they guessed the mystery or not. His reason for refraining from writing any more stories for a while is a candid one. He is fearful of spoiling a character of which he is particularly fond, but he declares that already he has enough material to carry him through another series, and merrily assures me that he thought the opening story of the next series of 'Sherlock Holmes', to be published in this magazine, was of such an unsolvable character, that he had positively bet his wife a shilling that she would not guess the true solution of it until she got to the end of the chapter.[100]

Another member of the household, Doyle's youngest sister, who herself became an author under the pseudonym 'H. Ripley Cromarsh', was also given the opportunity to test her wits against those of Sherlock Holmes. 'A London Woman's Diary' in the *News Chronicle* of 9 July 1930 recalled:

> While he was still a young writer Sir Arthur used to offer a prize (a guinea, I think it was) to his youngest sister, a very beautiful and brilliant girl, long since dead, if she could guess the end of the particular 'Sherlock Holmes' he was busy on. He gave her half the story and left her to work out the end. Once or twice she succeeded too.[101]

If both accounts are true, it would seem that his wife was at something of a disadvantage. On the art of the detective story, Doyle was to say years later that the main thing 'is to make your detective as sharp as possible, and to get some ingenuity into the plots. The stories should be clear-cut, but always with certain reservations, so as to maintain the interest of the readers to the conclusion.'[102] In this he was as successful with his new stories as with the earlier ones, but he had decided that Holmes would have to be destroyed.

The Death of Sherlock Holmes

J. M. Barrie was one of the first, outside the immediate family, to know that Holmes's death was being planned. He recalled in *The Greenwood Hat* how he had asked Doyle to help him complete a comic opera, *Jane Annie*, and adds in parentheses: 'I sat with him on the seashore at Aldeburgh when he decided to kill Sherlock Holmes.'[103] (Whether this was in September 1892 or later is not clear.) Another person who learnt of Doyle's intention was Frederic Villiers, the war artist/correspondent who on 14 December 1892 gave his popular lecture 'Here, there, and everywhere' to the Upper

Norwood Literary and Scientific Society. Villiers visited Doyle, who had proposed the vote of thanks, in order to borrow a drawing by Dickie Doyle. He was received in the usual hearty and breezy manner, but he could see that there was something on Doyle's mind: 'I discovered that he had finally come to the conclusion that his old and valuable friend Sherlock Holmes must die.' It was painful news, but Doyle explained that he was tired of the detective and, although perplexed as to the method, longed to be free to write on other subjects:

> But first of all he must settle what manner of death Sherlock Holmes should die.
>
> 'A man like that musn't die of a pin-prick or influenza. His end must be violent and intensely dramatic.'
>
> I could see that my dear friend of many happy monthly parts was doomed. The author of his being was inexorable on this point, and I left the house with a touch of sadness in my heart. [104]

Some uncertainty surrounds the composition and publishing history of the story in which Holmes was presumed to have met his death. Doyle's biographers, quoting a letter to his mother dated 6 April 1893 in which he said 'I am in the middle of the last Holmes story, after which the gentleman vanishes, never more to reappear. I am weary of his name', [105] have assumed that 'The Final Problem' was referred to, and have therefore concluded that Doyle visited Switzerland in the spring. This, however, does not appear to be the case. Doyle had, at the end of 1892, accepted an invitation from Frederick Atkins and William J. Dawson, the editors of the Young Man, to be a guest lecturer in the following year at the special summer gathering in Lucerne. It was held at the beginning of August, and that was the occasion on which Doyle visited the Reichenbach Falls.

Back in England at the end of the month, he wrote to his publisher about his latest book:

The second Holmes book, which I suppose you will bring out before Xmas, I think of naming *The Memoirs of Sherlock Holmes*. This is to give a distinctive title so that buyers may not muddle it up with the *Adventures*.

Then I want the second story, 'The Cardboard Box', to be omitted, and the one about Holmes's death to come in at the end so as to complete the dozen. The story omitted is rather more sensational than I care for.[106]

The letter, dated 28 August, was followed by another insisting that 'The Final Problem' should be included, which would imply that the last story was an afterthought. There is plenty of other evidence to support this theory. The American serial rights for the second collection, for example, were taken by *Harper's Weekly*, and yet they did not have the rights to 'The Final Problem'. As late as 5 November 1893, Doyle was writing to his agent, A. P. Watt: 'I hope we will find an American opening for Sherlock Holmes' death . . . But if not it doesn't matter. Or should we compromise for £50. Nothing less.'[107] The rights actually went to McClure, who first syndicated the story in various newspapers and then included it in his own magazine. As far as the publication in book form is concerned, there are the pencilled notes on the letter written at the end of August:

Omit the story referred to – & circle for revised proofs of the collection. Better write him that own edition is about ready to print & unless the changes referred to are radical, we wd. prefer to make them in 2d. Edition – We do not think the copyright would be endangered unless the changes are radical.

Doyle was concerned lest differences between the two editions should affect the copyright, and the last point was a reference to this. In fact the first American edition did differ from the first English edition: although it was called *The Memoirs of Sherlock Holmes* and included 'The Final Problem', the running title at the head of each page was still 'The Adventures of Sherlock Holmes', and the second story was not omitted. All this was changed in the second edition. Further evidence that the story was independent of the series is to be found in Doyle's account book for 1893. On 20 October there is a separate entry for 'Sherlock Holmes last story', showing that he was paid £180 for it. The curious point about the letter quoted above is that Doyle speaks of a dozen stories, whereas without 'The Cardboard Box' and with 'The Final Problem' there are only eleven.

Doyle and his wife reached Lucerne at the beginning of August 1893 and stayed at the Hôtel de l'Europe. He gave a number of lectures, but it was his preoccupation with the matter of Holmes's death which made the greatest impact on the other people present. According to Dr Lunn, who was in the chair, after giving his talk on George Meredith at the Old Catholic Church on 9 August, Doyle turned to Dawson and said: 'I am tired of Sherlock Holmes, and am going to find a suitable place in which to kill him.'[108] Lunn also referred to this occasion during an interview for *Tit-bits* in 1896. The conversation had turned to the local guides at Grindelwald, when the interviewer interrupted to say that some were becoming over-imaginative: 'They are beginning to point out the spot where Sherlock Holmes was killed.' Lunn then replied:

It's curious you should mention that, for it was when Conan Doyle was lecturing for us at Lucerne that he turned to me and said: 'I have made up my mind to kill Sherlock Holmes; he is becoming such a burden to me that it makes my life unendurable.' It was the Rev. W. J. Dawson who suggested the spot, the Reichenbach Falls, near Meiringen, where Conan Doyle finished the great detective, so I was an accessory before the fact.[109]

There is more than a grain of truth in this statement. After his lectures and some enjoyable days in the company of the

Rev. Silas K. Hocking, Benjamin Waugh, and the editors of
the Young Man, Doyle and his wife set out for the Rhône
Valley by way of the Gemmi Pass, and W. J. Dawson
accompanied them part of the way. From Meiringen they
ascended the Reichenbach Falls to the Baths of Rosenlaui
and then made their way to the ridge of the Great Scheidegg.
Dawson described the route from the other direction and the
Falls themselves in an article which appeared in the Young
Man in April 1894:

> I took this route the reverse way last year with Dr
> Conan Doyle, and thus became an unintentional accom-
> plice to the murder of the lamented Sherlock Holmes,
> whose last struggle occurs in this place of horrible beauty.
> The decree had gone forth that Sherlock Holmes must
> die, and it is a tribute to Dr Doyle's sense of artistic fitness
> that he finally selected this spot for the tragedy. The water
> pours over a curving precipice into a huge cauldron, from
> whose black depth rises a cloud of vapour, through which
> the morning sun flashes innumerable rainbows. The eye
> vainly searches the abyss for any bottom; the depth seems
> infinite, and the thunder that rises from the boiling
> cauldron is terrific. A narrow path winds along the edge of
> the abyss, from which the scene may be viewed in all its
> grandeur.[110]

Once in the Rhône Valley the Doyles made their way to
Vispach, where they again encountered Silas Hocking who,
like them, was intending to take the train up to Zermatt and
then climb to the Riffelalp Hotel. The hotel, which com-
manded superb views of the Matterhorn and its surrounding
valleys, was owned by the Seiler family and was especially
popular with English tourists. The Archbishop of Canter-
bury and his wife were among the guests, and one morning
their son, E. F. Benson, joined Doyle and Hocking on an
excursion to the Findelen Glacier. As they walked through
the pine woods the conversation turned to Sherlock

Holmes. Doyle agreed that his detective stories had made him famous, but he felt that he could do better work, and did not wish to be known only as the creator of Sherlock Holmes. They reached the top of the glacier, and as they crossed the great frozen river, the conversation was resumed. Hocking described what followed in an article which appeared in the *New Age* on 24 January 1895:

> 'Whether you like Sherlock Holmes or not,' I said, 'he's been a gold mine to you.'
>
> 'Anyhow,' he said, 'I shall kill him off at the end of the year.'
>
> 'Nonsense!'
>
> 'If I don't,' he said with a laugh, 'he'll kill me.'
>
> We paused on the edge of a gaping crevasse, which gashed the glacier almost from side to side.
>
> 'How are you going to finish him?' I asked.
>
> 'I don't know; I haven't decided yet,' he said thoughtfully.
>
> I stooped over and looked down into the blue treacherous abyss at my feet.
>
> 'Why not bring him out here,' I questioned, 'and drop him down a crevasse? That would finish him off effectually, and save all the trouble and expense of a funeral.'
>
> He laughed heartily. 'Not a bad idea,' he said.

Doyle did not make use of this idea; he chose the Reichenbach Falls instead which, as Hocking remarked, 'disposed of him quite as effectually, and with a somewhat better chance of bringing him to life again if he should be that way inclined'.[111]

Further accounts of this visit were given in the 1920s. The first was G. B. Burgin's in his *Memoirs of a Clubman*, published in July 1921. He gave Silas K. Hocking's account of how he had suggested a means of killing Sherlock Holmes. E. F. Benson was mentioned by name, unlike the earlier article, and was given credit for having brought up the subject. When Doyle announced his intention, Hocking interposed:

> 'He must have been a good friend to you.'
>
> 'Oh, I don't deny that,' he laughed, 'but the fact is he's become a sort of nightmare – an old man of the sea about my neck. If I don't kill him soon he'll kill me.'

By then they had reached the yawning crevasse, and as they stood looking down into the greeny-blue depths Hocking suggested that Holmes might be dropped down such a crevasse. 'Not a bad idea,' Doyle laughed. 'I'll have to think about it.'[112]

Hocking included the story in his own autobiography, *My Book of Memory*, which was published in 1923. As in the earlier accounts, Doyle stated that he wished to do away with Sherlock Holmes: 'The fact is,' he said, 'he's got to be an "old man of the sea" about my neck, and I intend to make an end of him.' 'Rather rough on an old friend,' Hocking suggested, 'who has brought you fame and fortune.'[113] The talk then went on with Benson making out a strong case for the continuance of Holmes. They reached the crevasse and Hocking made his famous suggestion.

A footnote to this story was given on 7 March 1941. On 4 March (two months too soon though it was) *The Times* carried a leader in memory of Sherlock Holmes who had disappeared at the Reichenbach Falls 'fifty years ago today'. The world at large was rapidly disappearing – Bush Villa, the house in Southsea where Doyle had written the first two Sherlock Holmes stories, had been destroyed two months earlier during the Blitz – but Sherlock Holmes proved himself 'the one fixed point in a changing age'.[114] J. H. Marlow, writing to the editor of *The Times* from the vicarage at Bozeat, recalled that Hocking, whom he had met in Switzerland in 1904, had told him how ten years earlier Doyle had said: 'I have got to get rid of Sherlock Holmes somehow and I do not quite know how to do it.' A few weeks later Doyle had sent Hocking a postcard from Meiringen saying: 'Have dropped Sherlock Holmes down the Reichenbach Falls.'[115]

Doyle was using black-edged notepaper during October and November 1893, but this was for his father who had died on 10 October. That and the serious chest symptoms which his wife developed shortly afterwards allowed him to keep Holmes's death in perspective, but there was a sense of elation and some satisfaction when he was able to write in his diary: 'Killed Holmes.'[116] Though if ever a murderer was to be haunted by the man he had killed and to be forced to atone for his act, it was the creator, turned destroyer, of Sherlock Holmes.

Some Posthumous Adventures

The news became public in November 1893 when *Tit-bits* announced that 'The Death of Sherlock Holmes' would be appearing in the Christmas number of the *Strand Magazine*. This, as expected, caused considerable indignation among the readers. 'The news of the death of Sherlock Holmes has been received with most widespread regret,'[117] *Tit-bits* commented shortly afterwards. Mourning bands were to be seen in the city, foreign newspapers reported the event as the main news of the day, and there was considerable disquiet at the next shareholders' meeting of the magazine when George Newnes mentioned the 'dreadful event'.[118] 'We pleaded for his life in the most urgent, earnest and constant manner,' *Tit-bits* assured its readers when announcing the Sherlock Holmes Memorial Prize: 'Like hundreds of correspondents, we feel as if we had lost an old friend whom we could ill spare.'[119] Other leading journals and newspapers noted Holmes's death with similar concern and many carried obituary notices and memorial verses. '"Tragic Death of Mr Sherlock Holmes",' said the *Sketch* on 20 December, 'is a piece of literary intelligence which will come as a bereave-

ment to the thousands who have month after month followed with breathless interest the exploits of Mr Conan
Doyle's hero. The fatal accident takes place in the *Strand*.'[120]
Punch, however, not without prescience stated: 'There is
no proof positive given by any eye-witness whose veracity is
unimpeachable of the death of the great amateur detective as
it has been reported in the *Strand Magazine*', and asked,
'Where is the merry Swiss boy who delivered the note and
disappeared?'[121]

The sense of loss was felt throughout America. Edward
Sandford Martin, writing in *Harper's Weekly*, feared that
there was every reason to believe that Sherlock Holmes had
lost his life:

> At any rate, he has disappeared, and though his re-
> mains have not yet been found, the proof is almost
> absolute that he died a violent death. His many admirers
> will cling to the last to the hope that he may be found
> alive; but that seems so remote a possibility that the more
> reasonable solace, such as it is, appears in the chance that
> his brother, whose perceptions are well known to be
> marvellously acute, may be roused by this bereavement
> from the indifference which has so long impeded him, and
> be restored to a useful and active life.[122]

Mycroft remained firmly ensconced in the Diogenes Club,
but Sherlock Holmes had already assumed an independent
character, so that Anthony Hope seemed to be stating the
obvious when he remarked a few years later that nobody ever
asked who Holmes was or in which book he figured; and few
would have denied Holmes's 'world-wide notoriety', as it was
described by W. J. Dawson in a character sketch of Conan
Doyle published in July 1894:

> Colonial judges quote him in their addresses to the jury,
> and London magistrates tell stammering and stupid
> police-officers to go to Sherlock Holmes if they would be

clever and wise. He is spoken of with familiarity in newspaper articles, and his shade is invoked with every fresh episode of undiscovered crime. He is even treated as a real and living person, and victims of the burglar have been known who were quite ready to retain his services, if his whereabouts could be discovered.[123]

Doyle had indeed been receiving letters addressed directly to Sherlock Holmes; some were sent to Scotland Yard to be forwarded, others were delivered at various addresses in Baker Street, but most, if not all, eventually reached him. He told Raymond Blathwayt in 1892:

I get many letters from all over the country about Sherlock Holmes. Sometimes from schoolboys, sometimes from commercial travellers who are great readers, sometimes from lawyers pointing out mistakes in my law. One letter actually contained a request for portraits of Sherlock at different periods of his life.[124]

Although spared the more bizarre requests, such as those seeking a lock of Holmes's hair, Joseph Bell was also a recipient of letters. In *Cassell's Saturday Journal* of 15 February 1893, Conan Doyle was reported as saying:

Both Dr Bell and myself are constantly receiving letters from persons in distress, inviting us to unravel some mystery or other in connection with the family, to use our best endeavours to trace some missing relative, or to bring to justice some delinquent whom the police have failed to capture. These letters are very amusing at times, and often contain particulars and details so elaborate as to be astonishing.[125]

Doyle would later take such letters seriously, but at this period they gave rise to amusement rather than concern. He often referred to them in his talks about Sherlock Holmes, such as those he gave in America in 1894, and he was to mention them in his speech at the Authors' Club Banquet which was held in his honour in June 1896:

> One curious outcome of the stories was that the public would insist upon identifying me with my character, and that from all quarters of the world, varying as widely as from San Francisco to Moscow, I had private communications detailing family mysteries which I was at once to come and unravel. I had no idea before that there were so many mysteries in existence. I refused to take any of them in hand, and I don't suppose that their solution was seriously delayed upon that account.[126]

He may have been accustomed to such letters, but the uproar which followed Sherlock Holmes's death came as a surprise. One correspondent began her letter: 'You beast!'[127] (or, as the story varied in the telling, 'You Brute!').[128] Doyle found that he had become the scapegoat and that the crime was held against him. In his 1896 speech he admitted:

> I have been much blamed for doing that gentleman to death, but I hold that it was not murder, but justifiable homicide in self defence, since, if I had not killed him, he would certainly have killed me. For a man who has no particular astuteness to spend his days in inventing problems and building up chains of inductive reasoning is a trying occupation. Besides it is better not to rely too much upon the patience of the public, and when one has written twenty-six stories about one man one feels that it is time to put it out of one's power to transgress any further.[129]

The public refused to believe that Doyle's decision to kill Holmes could be justified by the claim that they had, or would have, shown hostility towards the great detective; on the contrary they were more than anxious to see him restored to life. Some sought consolation in an assurance given by *Tit-bits* that the author had promised he would 'at some future date, if opportunity may occur, give us the offer of some posthumous histories of the great detective';[130] and others noted that although it was assumed that Holmes was dead, there was no death certificate to prove it. There was a good chance that Doyle might relent. The cartoon in *To-Day* on 30 December 1893 had made this point. It showed George Newnes standing in a state of shock by the open coffin of Sherlock Holmes and asking: 'Great Scott! Doyle, is he dead?' To which the corpse replied: 'It's all right, Guv'nor; the doctor knows what to do when you want me.'[131] In private Doyle admitted that though he had no intention of doing so, he could either revive Sherlock Holmes or record more of the cases which had preceded his death. When asked by David Christie Murray in 1896 if there would be further stories, he replied: 'Poor Holmes is dead and damned. I couldn't revive him if I would (at least not for years), for I have had such an overdose of him that I feel towards him as I do towards *pâté de foie gras*, of which I once ate too much, so that the name of it gives me a sickly feeling to this day.'[132]

During 1894 Doyle worked on the first of the Brigadier Gerard stories, but he knew that when he reached America in October Sherlock Holmes would be at the front of people's minds. Even in his own study Holmes was very much in evidence: there were original drawings by Sidney Paget, and a large portrait bust of the detective by F. L. Wilkins. Robert Barr, an editor of the *Idler* and the author of one of the earliest Sherlock Holmes parodies, was among the first to see the bust which, though no one knew at the time, was to provide the inspiration for the opening story in *The Return of Sherlock Holmes*. The interview with Robert Barr was published in a shortened form in the *Idler*, but it was really intended for *McClure's Magazine*, where it appeared in its entirety as a 'Real Conversation'. In the course of it, Barr referred to the bust:

'Who is the statesman?' I asked.

'Oh, that is Sherlock Holmes,' said Doyle. 'A young sculptor named Wilkins, from Birmingham, sent it to me. Isn't it good?'

'Excellent. By the way, is Sherlock Holmes really dead?'

'Yes; I shall never write another Holmes story.'[133]

By the time this article appeared in *McClure's Magazine* in November 1894 Doyle was in America, where he was subjected to many similar questions. A day after his arrival, the *New York Daily Tribune* informed its readers that Doyle 'thought Sherlock Holmes was probably dead. He admitted that he might escape, and be revived, but did not think it at all likely that he would.'[134] The audiences soon forgave the author for his rash act, and by the end of his tour he had made many friends. His stories were already highly popular, and for many Americans Holmes was quite as real as the author himself. Parodies and jokes flourished on both sides of the Atlantic, and Holmes's name was invoked as readily in America as it was in England.

One story syndicated in various newspapers during that November had the curiously prophetic subtitle 'How a Boston Detective Out-Sherlocked Holmes', for on 6 December 1894, at the end of his tour, Doyle, as guest of honour at the Aldine Club in New York, amused the audience by relating an anecdote about Sherlock Holmes which was to prove one of the most resilient of all and one which he later referred to as typical of the apocryphal tales which 'go round and round the press and turn up at fixed intervals with the regularity of a comet'.[135] It was an account of his arrival in Boston. There were a dozen or so cabmen and he instinctively called to the one who had a book projecting from his pocket. He asked to be driven to one of two hotels in Boston where he thought his manager, Major J. B. Pond, would be waiting for him. The observant cabman told him that he would find Major Pond at Parker's Hotel, and when they reached the hotel he asked Doyle for a ticket to his lecture in place of the fare. Doyle felt he 'had to be gruff or laugh outright', and so said:

> 'Come, come, I am not accustomed to be beaten at my own tricks. Tell me how you ascertained who I am, and you shall have tickets for your whole family, and such cigars as you smoke here in America, besides.'

> 'Of course we all knew that you were coming on this train – that is, all of the members of the Cabmen's Literary Guild,' was the half apologetic reply. 'As it happens, I am the only member on duty at this station this morning, and I had that advantage. If you will excuse other personal remarks, your coat lapels are badly twisted downward, where they have been grasped by the pertinacious New York reporters. Your hair has the Quakerish cut of a Philadelphia barber, and your hat, battered at the brim in front, shows where you have tightly grasped it, in the struggle to stand your ground at a Chicago literary luncheon. Your right overshoe has a large block of Buffalo mud just under the instep, the odour of a Utica cigar hangs about your clothing, and the overcoat itself shows the slovenly brushing of the porters of the through sleepers from Albany. The crumbs of a doughnut on the top of your bag – pardon me, your luggage – could only have come there in Springfield, and stencilled upon the very end of the "Wellington", in fairly plain lettering, is the name, "Conan Doyle".'

Now I know where Sherlock Holmes went when he died. That leaves me free to write any more adventures of his that I wish as long as I locate them in Boston.[136]

The following day there were full reports of the speech in the newspapers, and six years later, in his book *Eccentricities of Genius*, Major Pond gave Doyle's full version. The other people who had been present, such as William Ellsworth and Frederic Villiers, were also to recall the story on many subsequent occasions, but it was the version given by Pond which appeared most often; the American *Bookman* was particularly fond of it and never missed an opportunity of repeating it, and it was soon equally well known in England. It then assumed a life of its own and resurfaced under various different guises. The version which Doyle gave in his autobiography concerned a cabman in Paris who had correctly named the various European cities which Doyle had visited by looking at the labels on his trunk. A typical example of the other versions appeared in the *Sunday Express* the day before Doyle's death. It purported to be a 'true tale' told by a 'Taxicabman for 20 Years':

> Another interesting fare was Sir Arthur Conan Doyle. The only time I drove him I managed to puzzle the creator of Sherlock Holmes.
>
> 'Thank you, Mr Conan Doyle,' I said when he tipped me. He looked surprised, and asked how I knew him. I replied that, although I had never set eyes on him before, to use his own language, 'I had established his identity by a process of deduction.'
>
> This interested him, and he asked me how I had managed it. When I replied that his name was written all over his luggage I think he was disappointed.[137]

So might he have been by the limp retelling of such a good story!

'After a glorious career, happily and decently dead'[138] was what H. G. Wells said of Sherlock Holmes in his bicycling idyll, *The Wheels of Chance*, published in 1896. But, in fact, Holmes refused to die. On 15 July 1896, the *Cape Times* announced in all seriousness that Sherlock Holmes and Dr Watson had arrived in South Africa. How they obtained their information is not clear, but it had nothing to do with Conan Doyle, who was by then back in England after spending the previous winter at the Mena House Hotel near the Pyramids, and acting during the spring as a special correspondent for the *Westminster Gazette*. 'Sherlock Holmes in the Desert' was the caption to a drawing by H. C. Seppings-Wright in the *Illustrated London News* of 16 May 1896 which showed Conan Doyle on a somewhat recalcitrant camel that had gone down on its front legs; but it was left to Hugh S. Maclauchlan to establish the best Egyptian story about Sherlock Holmes, and this he did in 'An Appreciation of Dr Doyle's Work' which appeared in the *Windsor Magazine* for October 1896. Maclauchlan, a former editor of the *Portsmouth Evening News* and of the *Hampshire Telegraph*, was a close personal friend of Conan Doyle in Southsea and one of the earliest admirers of his literary work. In his article he wrote:

> Dr Doyle was at the Pyramids a few months ago, and a strange story has been whispered in this country of an announcement that was made to him by his hotel keeper. He was informed – so the story goes – that Sherlock Holmes had been translated into Arabic and issued to the local police as a text-book. The Nile valley has its humorists, unconscious or otherwise.[139]

The story was consolidated by the *Bookman* in April 1902 when J. E. Hodder Williams in 'The Reader' article about Doyle said:

> Even beneath the shadow of the Pyramids his reputation of detective story writer had grown to vaster proportions than he himself had ever contemplated. In Egypt he first was made aware that 'Sherlock Holmes' had been translated into Arabic, and issued to the local police in the form of a reliable and handy text-book![140]

None of the correspondents on the Dongola expedition appears to have known of this rumour, nor, it seems, did Conan Doyle himself, or he would surely have referred to it in his speech at the Authors' Club dinner in June 1896. There was also no mention of it in '"Sherlock Holmes" in

Egypt', which appeared in the *Strand Magazine* in August 1913. This article described the methods of the Bedouin trackers, which were similar to those of Sherlock Holmes as far as footprints were concerned – though if these were a true reflection of those used by the Egyptian police, then, rather than Sherlock Holmes, they should have handed out copies of 'The Three Princes of Serendip', *Zadig*, or the works of Fenimore Cooper; and they would also have found use for another article in the *Strand Magazine*, that in the November 1914 issue on 'Black "Sherlocks"', as its author believed that the native trackers of Australia surpassed the Bedouins. However, true or not, Doyle in time came to believe that the Egyptian system, like those used in France and China, was based on that of Holmes.

Holmes may not have been in South Africa in 1896, but rumours that he was in Edinburgh did have a firm foundation. Late in the summer Conan Doyle received a request from his old university for a contribution to a special number of the *Student* in aid of the Field Bazaar which was to raise money to provide and equip a sports pavilion for a new playing field. To the surprise and delight of many, a short Sherlock Holmes parody was the result (see pp. 147 ff.). Although it disappointed those who had hoped that the detective would be restored to life, and irritated the purists who complained that Watson could not have been an M.B. of Edinburgh University in 1896 as he had gained his M.D. at London University in 1878, it did suggest that Doyle might be on the point of relenting. His resolve was certainly beginning to weaken.

Two years later he was working on a series of short stories, and for a time the editor of the *Strand Magazine* hoped that Sherlock Holmes might figure in them. But Doyle told him:

> 'Detective Stories' would not fairly characterize them, and I want to give myself a very free hand so that in case any tap runs dry I can turn on another. I should therefore not say anything about Detectives or Holmes in the

announcement. To say however that they deal in mystery and adventure would be true, also that they are concerned with the weird and the terrible.[141]

Two of the 'Round the Fire' series contained references to an unnamed authority on crime whose letters to the Press sounded as though they might be the work of Sherlock Holmes. The first, 'The Story of the Man with the Watches', which appeared in July 1898, mentioned a letter in the *Daily Gazette* 'over the signature of a well-known criminal investigator';[142] and a month later, 'The Story of the Lost Special' included an extract from a letter to *The Times* 'over the signature of an amateur reasoner of some celebrity'.[143] Both stories had plots which would have been ideal material for Sherlock Holmes – as did others in the same series – and it seems that Doyle was only restrained by his vow never to revive him.

In 1897 Sherlock Holmes made a posthumous reappearance in America through the mediumship of John Kendrick Bangs. After the success of *A House-Boat on the Styx*, he wrote *The Pursuit of the House-Boat*, a further account of 'the Divers Doings of the Associated Shades', though this time 'under the leadership of Sherlock Holmes, Esq.'; the book was dedicated 'To A. Conan Doyle, Esq. With the author's sincerest regards and thanks for the untimely demise of his great detective which made these things possible.'[144] If there were any fears that Doyle would take offence, they were soon dispelled. On receiving a copy, he wrote to Bangs: 'How very good of you to inscribe your most amusing and original book to me! I begin to have hopes of immortality now that I have got onto your fly-leaf.'[145] Later, in 1905, when it was known that Holmes was alive, Bangs wrote the adventures of Raffles Holmes, a son of the great detective who combined the qualities of his father with those of his grandfather, the gentleman burglar A. J. Raffles.

Holmes and Raffles

Raffles made his first appearance in *The Amateur Cracksman*, published in March 1899. The author, E. W. Hornung, was Conan Doyle's brother-in-law, and the book was dedicated 'To A.C.D. This form of flattery.'[146] Not only had the name been taken from Doyle's novel, *The Doings of Raffles Haw*, but the hero and his companion, Bunny, owed a great deal to Sherlock Holmes and Dr Watson. Doyle said of Hornung:

> I think I may claim that his famous character Raffles was a kind of inversion of Sherlock Holmes, Bunny playing Watson. He admits as much in his kindly dedication. I think there are few finer examples of short-story writing in our language than these, though I confess I think they are rather dangerous in their suggestion. I told him so before he put pen to paper, and the result has, I fear, borne me out. You must not make the criminal a hero.[147]

Just as he thought Sherlock Holmes had damaged his own literary reputation, so he felt the Raffles stories 'harmed Hornung, for they got between the public and his better work'.[148] It was the price of popularity and was more costly for Hornung, for he was often accused of having provided criminals with their inspiration.

As a result of their family ties, many attempts were made to encourage Doyle and Hornung to collaborate on a book or play in which Holmes and Raffles would appear together. Doyle was totally against the idea. He told Greenhough Smith on 14 April 1911 that, though he was constantly being asked, he could not do it as his inspiration would fail. His feelings were echoed by the American *Bookman* in January 1903 when a New York publisher first put the idea forward. Such a book, it said, would rapidly develop into a farce: 'Yet so long as one keeps it from going beyond the theoretical stage the idea is deliciously suggestive.'[149]

Trumbull White was the most persistent in his attempts to

interest Doyle and Hornung. He first toyed with the possibility in February 1903 when he was put in charge of the Chicago *Red Book*. His representative in London, Seth Westcott Moyle, received a firm refusal when he asked Doyle, but this did not deter White, who continued during the years that followed to try and persuade Doyle, as well as Hornung, William Gillette, and Kyrle Bellew (who had dramatized *Raffles*). By twice visiting Doyle at his house, he eventually received permission. Doyle was still adamant that he would have nothing to do with it himself, but, according to the account which White published in the American *Bookman* in 1922, he did say: 'I will give you Sherlock Holmes and Hornung will give you Raffles. If you want to write it, it may be done by you, with our permission and our good will.'[150] This was in 1913. Because of the war and later the death of Hornung, nothing ever came of it.

Another person interested in the idea was the impresario and 'natural born gambler' George C. Tyler, who later persuaded William Gillette to make a farewell tour as Sherlock Holmes. Although he confused their relationship, he said of Doyle and Hornung:

> My idea was to get the two cousins to collaborate on a play that sicked Sherlock Holmes on Raffles and let nature take its course. I knew that I could get Bellew to do Raffles again at the drop of a hat and Frohman was willing enough to contribute William Gillette, the creator of Sherlock Holmes on the stage, as his share of a joint production. But it turned out to be a case of the proverbial irresistible force tangling up with the immovable object. Neither author could be persuaded to let his pet character get the worst of it in a battle of wits, and, after all, something had to happen or there wouldn't be any play.[151]

As neither Doyle nor Hornung had control over the cinema rights, Holmes and Raffles were shown together on film. The earliest appears to be *Sherlock Holmes II*, made in

1908 by the Danish company, Nordisk, and released in Great Britain in November of that year as *Raffles Escapes from Prison*, and in the United States the following February as *The Detective in Danger of His Life. Raffles' Escape from Prison*.

Hornung is also remembered for what Doyle called his 'criticism upon Sherlock Holmes': 'Though he might be more humble, there is no police like Holmes.'[152] And this, according to a later editor of the *Strand Magazine*, was the only relic of Sherlock Holmes which survived in its files after the Second World War.

The inversion of Sherlock Holmes by Hornung was to set the pattern for a whole generation of detective-story writers who knew that they could not compete on the same ground and so were forced to find characters as dissimilar as possible. Baroness Orczy faced the predicament a year or two later when in need of a detective who 'must in no way be reminiscent of Sherlock Holmes';[153] she chose the Old Man in the Corner. A. E. W. Mason settled on a French detective 'as physically unlike Mr Sherlock Holmes as he could possibly be'.[154] E. C. Bentley in *Trent's Last Case* wanted a human being rather than a 'heavy' sleuth, and to make the 'hard-won and evidently correct solution of the mystery turn out to be completely wrong'.[155] Agatha Christie, well steeped though she was in 'the Sherlock Holmes tradition', knew one thing about her detective: he would be 'Not like Sherlock Holmes.'[156]

Sherlock Holmes on the Stage: William Gillette

Although Doyle was reluctant to revive Sherlock Holmes in the pages of the *Strand Magazine*, he did at the end of 1897 contemplate and work on a play. The 'Green Room Gossip' column of the *Daily Mail* said on 15 December:

To set at rest all kinds of unauthorized rumours, it may

be as well to state that Dr Conan Doyle is at work upon a drama which has for its raison d'être and central character the infallible Mr Sherlock Holmes, and, further, that Mr Tree has expressed a lively interest in the projected play. At present this, I am officially informed, is all. [157]

Herbert Beerbohm Tree soon afterwards went down to Hindhead to hear the play and, according to his biographer, suggested a number of rather absurd changes. He wanted to play both Moriarty and Sherlock Holmes until Doyle pointed out that they both appeared together; he then intimated that he might play Holmes in a beard. Doyle was naturally surprised and asked what the public would make of it. Tree said that they would know that he was disguised for a purpose and that it was up to the author to say for what purpose. Doyle could not do this and began to have doubts about the whole idea. In a letter to his mother which appears to have been written at the beginning of 1898 he said:

I have grave doubts about Holmes on the stage at all – it's drawing attention to my weaker work which has unduly obscured my better – but rather than re-write it on the lines which would make a different Holmes from my Holmes, I would without the slightest pang put it back in the drawer from which it emerged. I dare say that will be the end of it – and probably the best one. [158]

The *Candid Friend* of 9 November 1901 described what followed:

For a while, Dr Doyle's version was put aside. Then, in the author's words, Mr Addison Bright suggested Mr Gillette as the man for the part. Again the play was despatched; again, after an interval, it was returned. But, this time with a difference: Mr Gillette found it impracticable as it stood, but, foreseeing enormous stage possibilities in the character, made an alternative proposal. Given *carte blanche* in the matter of selection of incidents,

compression or expansion, as circumstances might demand, he would write a play on the subject. To this course
Dr Doyle assented on advice, finally discarding his own
five-act version.[159]

Gillette steeped himself in the stories, but emerged to say
that he found it impossible to transfer Holmes to the stage.
Charles Frohman, his manager, insisted, and after four
weeks the play was written. Another and better known
version of how the play came about was that when Gillette
was in London playing in Secret Service, Frohman showed
him a cutting from a newspaper published in the western part
of the United States which contained a manufactured interview with Conan Doyle in which he was made to say that if
anybody ever dramatized or played Sherlock Holmes, it
would be William Gillette. According to an article in the
Strand Magazine, he had said nothing of the kind, and at that
time had not even met Gillette or had any correspondence
with him. The suggestion had in fact been made in the
'Green Room Gossip' column of the Daily Mail, which ties in
with the third version, that given by Frohman's biographers.
Frohman and Gillette, they said, were both in London
during July 1898 when they were struck by the popularity of
Sherlock Holmes; Frohman suggested that they should make
a bid for the rights and Gillette agreed. Doyle was contacted
and gave his consent on condition that there was no 'love
business' in the play.

At the end of October, or the beginning of November,
Frohman wired to Gillette asking him to press ahead with
the proposed play as all the necessary arrangements had been
made. Gillette then wrote to Conan Doyle asking what
liberties he might take. He was delighted with the answer, as
Doyle told him, in the words of the Strand Magazine, that he
'might marry the detective, or murder him, or do anything
he pleased with him, preferring to leave a stage detective in
the hands of a master actor'.[160]

During the early hours of 23 November 1898, disaster

struck. The Baldwin Hotel in San Francisco and its adjoining theatre at which Gillette's company was playing *Secret Service* was destroyed by fire; Frohman thereby lost a considerable amount of property, including, as the *New York Times* noted, 'the original manuscript of the dramatization of Conan Doyle's novel, *Sherlock Holmes*, which Mr Gillette has been working upon for the last three weeks. This Mr Frohman regards as the most serious loss of the entire property, as it was the only copy of the dramatization in existence, and it will undoubtedly entail considerable time and expense to secure another copy.'[161] However, the play was soon rewritten, now in four rather than five acts. Gillette based his work primarily on the first of the short stories and on the last. He it was who gave the page at Baker Street the name of 'Billy' (which Doyle himself later used), and some would say, though it does not appear in any of the published versions, that he was responsible for coining the phrase: 'Elementary, my dear Watson!' Certainly, many of the early versions did contain the line: 'Elementary, my dear fellow.'[162]

He brought the script over to England in the spring of 1899 and in May took it to Hindhead for Doyle to see. The reaction was highly favourable. Doyle, according to Frohman's biographers, 'liked the play immensely and made no objection whatever to the sentimental interest. In fact, his only comment when Gillette finished reading the manuscript was: "It's good to see the old chap again."'[163] Doyle retained the script so as to make a few minor alterations, and on 12 June it was given a copyright performance at the Duke of York's Theatre in London. It opened in America at the Star Theatre, Buffalo, on 23 October 1899, and on 6 November reached New York, where it ran until the following June. In August 1901, after an American tour, Gillette sailed for England. A few performances were given in Liverpool before it opened at the Lyceum Theatre on 9 September. Doyle's name always appeared alongside that of

William Gillette in the credits, and when he attended the first night in London he was presumed to be a joint author. He gave his own impressions in the interview with the *Candid Friend* which were summarized as follows:

> Of the merits of this play, as contrasted with his own, Dr Doyle permits himself to speak with equal frankness and in the warmest terms. Although much of his own work has gone into the making – the first and last stories of the series being ingeniously dove-tailed, and the dialogue, in parts, a literal transcript – he looks at it quite impersonally. The new Holmes, he recognizes, is weaker than the original, for the latter was never thawed by love. But:
>
> 'In reading the play,' he said, 'I recognized at once that it was the work of a highly-skilled workman. The MS. literally bristled with points, and I realized what an art it is to write for the stage.'[164]

'You seem to have carried London once more by storm,' Doyle told Gillette shortly before Christmas: 'Everyone I meet tells me the same thing.'[165] He was inviting the American members of the cast to spend Christmas with him so as to see a little of English country life. From Gillette he received an illustrated Christmas card containing photographs and drawings which bore the legend: 'Mr Sherlock Holmes at the Lyceum Theatre, London, presents his Compliments and the Best Wishes of the Season.' On it Gillette had written: 'Did you ever imagine that Sherlock Holmes would be sending his compliments to his maker? Good wishes, dear Doyle.'[166]

Gillette did become the living embodiment of Sherlock Holmes, certainly as far as the Americans were concerned, though there was also a story to the effect that on his arrival in Liverpool there was a messenger from the London and North Western Railway with a letter for him. Uncertain how he would recognize the actor, he asked one of the passengers and was told: 'Do you know Sherlock Holmes?'

The messenger replied that he had read the stories in the *Strand Magazine*. 'That's all you need to know,' said the passenger. 'Just look around till you see a man who fits your idea of what Sherlock Holmes ought to be, and that's he.'[167] This was precisely what Frederic Dorr Steele was to do when he needed a model for his illustrations. W. H. Hyde and Sidney Paget, who had illustrated the first stories, made very little impact in America compared with Steele, who, using the drawings and photographs from the souvenir programme of the play, had his first great success with the magnificent series of drawings for *The Return of Sherlock Holmes* in *Collier's Weekly*; he also illustrated all the subsequent stories. By the time of Gillette's last tour in 1929–30, Steele was able to say in the souvenir programme: 'A glance at Hyde's pictures', or, he added later, Sidney Paget's, 'shows a marked unlikeness to our present conception of the character. That conception was entirely created by Mr Gillette.' He also answered the question: 'Which came first, Gillette's play or Steele's pictures?' It was, of course, the play: 'I made my models look like him, and even in two or three instances used photographs of him in my drawings. But while the actor was seen by thousands, the magazines and books were seen by millions.'[168] Although he used photographs, Steele did not actually see Gillette until 1929. For *The Return* he used an Englishman called Robert King, and for the later stories a certain Frank B. Wilson and his sons. He met Doyle only once, at the luncheon given for him by Mark Sullivan of *Collier's*. Rather than commending either Paget or Steele himself, Doyle reserved his praise for Cyrus Cuneo. 'I had not needed to be self-effacing,' Steele remarked afterwards: 'Sir Arthur effaced me.'[169]

Gillette and Conan Doyle remained firm friends. The actor was always a welcome guest at Conan Doyle's house and called upon him whenever he was in England. One critic spotted him among the audience on the first night of Doyle's *The Speckled Band*. He was in London in 1914, when he tried with Doyle's help to join the Allies as an engineer; he was offered, though rejected, the title role in *The Return of Sherlock Holmes* (the 1923 play); and his last visit during Doyle's lifetime was in March 1928. On that occasion Doyle invited him to the Grotrian Hall where, on Sunday 25 March, he was lecturing on spiritualism, and then on the following Tuesday to his flat in London where he was entertaining an American medium called Arthur Ford. Describing this occasion in his weekly column for the *Sunday Express*, Doyle said:

> Among others who were witnesses of Ford's perform-ance was Mr William Gillette, the American actor, whose impersonation of Sherlock Holmes is vividly remembered in this country. He expressed himself as deeply interested and surprised.
>
> He was amused by my assurance that if Sherlock Holmes had ever shown signs of mental discernment it was on the day when he saw that this subject, defaced by fraud and scorned by high-brow man, was in very truth the greatest advance forward which man had ever made into the unknown.[170]

He was not being serious, although spiritualism was a subject in which he passionately believed. He had said much the same to Hayden Church when the American journalist interviewed him at the Grosvenor Hotel on 11 November 1918. Church asked what Sherlock Holmes would say about spiritualism, and Doyle replied: 'I suppose I am Sherlock Holmes, if anybody is, and I say that the case for Spiritualism is absolutely proved.'[171]

Gillette, who eventually played Sherlock Holmes over 1,300 times on the stage, on radio, and in a film, was asked at the beginning of 1928 to consider a revival. He had his doubts, but by June of the following year had agreed to do a farewell tour. His manager, Clayton Hamilton, sought and got a vast collection of letters addressed to Gillette from

distinguished people in all walks of life expressing their
delight at Gillette's decision. As well as appearing on a
poster and in a special booklet, extracts were given in the
souvenir programme. Conan Doyle, writing on 25 October
1929 from the Hotel Angleterre in Copenhagen, said:

> My dear Gillette
>
> May I add my word to those which are addressed to you
> upon the occasion of your return to the stage. That this
> return should be in *Sherlock Holmes* is of course a source of
> personal gratification, my only complaint being that you
> make the poor hero of the anaemic printed page a very
> limp object as compared with the glamour of your own
> personality which you infuse into his stage presentment.
> But in any case you are bringing back to the world
> something very precious in your own great powers, and I
> rejoice to know it.
>
> Yours always, Arthur Conan Doyle[172]

Although Gillette was averse to the idea of a printed
edition of the play, he allowed himself to be overruled. An
acting version was published by Samuel French in 1922. As
this claimed to be 'adapted by Arthur Conan Doyle and
William Gillette from the story by Arthur Conan Doyle
entitled "The Strange Case of Miss Faulkner"', its title page
had to be cancelled – there being no such story. On the
typescript, it was described as 'an original play written by
William Gillette under an arrangement with Sir Arthur
Conan Doyle for the exclusive right to make use of the title
and the character of "Holmes" for dramatic and film presentation'. But this was highly debatable, and neither Doyle
nor his lawyers would accept that any such arrangement had
been made. The royalties from the play were divided equally
between Gillette, Doyle, and Charles Frohman, and, as a
result, Doyle found within a few years that he had benefited
to the tune of $45,000. A revised edition of the play was
published in America in 1935 under Gillette's name and

included some of the revisions made for the final tour, by which time Gillette was so old that the final scene in which Holmes becomes engaged to Alice Faulkner looked, or would have looked, slightly ridiculous. The title page of the American edition was also altered at a late stage. 'A play' was put into upper case italics at the insistence of Doyle's widow and of his eldest son. 'This is essential,' Denis Conan Doyle explained on 4 October 1934, 'as otherwise the publication would be confused with the Sherlock Holmes books.'[173]

The run of *Sherlock Holmes* at the Lyceum ended in April 1902 and was followed by an eight week tour of the provinces. By then there were also two other touring companies on the road, a North and a South company. H. A. Saintsbury was in charge of the northern company. His tour opened with a production of his own play, *Jim, the Romance of a Cockney*, soon followed by the far more successful *Sherlock Holmes*. The young boy in the first and Billy in the second were played by Charles Chaplin. It was his first major role and he was always grateful for the opportunity which Saintsbury had given him; he considered that Saintsbury was the ideal actor for the role of Sherlock Holmes, 'a living replica of the illustrations in the *Strand Magazine*',[174] and better than Gillette himself.

Chaplin took part in the three tours on the main northern circuit, and was preparing to visit the smaller theatres when he was called to London to play Billy in Gillette's short curtain-raiser, *The Painful Predicament of Sherlock Holmes*. This had been given its first performance on 23 March 1905 at a benefit performance for Joseph Jefferson Holland at the Metropolitan Opera House, New York, when it replaced another play which could not be ready in time. It was hastily written and quickly learnt, and, as a 'fantasy in about one tenth of an act', it was originally called *The Frightful Predicament of Sherlock Holmes*. A further performance under the title *The Harrowing Predicament of Sherlock Holmes* was given on 14 April 1905 at a benefit in aid of the Actors' Society of

America. But its longest run was in London at the Duke of York's Theatre, where it was given for two weeks, beginning on 3 October 1905, in an attempt to improve the ailing fortunes of Gillette's new play, *Clarice*. The joke of the play was that Holmes never said a word. Chaplin recalled:

> I had the opening lines, bursting into Holmes's apartment and holding on to the doors while the madwoman beats them outside, and then, while I excitedly try to explain to Holmes the situation, the madwoman bursts in! For twenty minutes she never stops raving incoherently about some case that she wants him to solve. Surreptitiously Holmes writes a note, rings a bell and slips it to me. Later two stalwart men lead the lady off, leaving Holmes and me alone, with me saying: 'You were right, sir; it was the right asylum.'[175]

Even with the curtain-raiser *Clarice* was doomed, and both came off on 14 October. In their place Gillette mounted a revival of *Sherlock Holmes* with Chaplin playing Billy. This enabled him to recover some of his losses, and by Christmas he was back in America. He never again appeared as Sherlock Holmes in England, but his picture often did, as, for example, on 27 February 1907 when *Vanity Fair* published a cartoon by 'Spy'. It was something of an honour to sit for Leslie Ward and to become Spy's 'Sherlock Holmes', as it might otherwise have been Doyle himself.

The only time that Doyle mentioned Chaplin was at the annual dinner of the Savage Club in 1925 when he admitted that he had made one great theatrical blunder:

> I made the mistake of my life over the drama. At one theatre in London there was a boy playing the page in *Sherlock Holmes*. If I had said to him that 'Although I have a fairly good income and you have £2 a week, I will go halves with you for life', I should have done exceedingly well, for that little boy's name was Charlie Chaplin.[176]

It seems unlikely that Doyle actually met Chaplin at the time, but he did meet another little boy on 25 May 1923 during his American tour; this was Jackie Coogan, who, though he was only eight, had already earned several million dollars. 'They asked me to be photographed with him,' Doyle recalled: 'so I employed the time telling him a gruesome Sherlock Holmes tale, and the look of interest and awe upon his intent little face is an excellent example of those powers which are so natural yet so subtle.'[177]

Sherlock Holmes Redivivus: The Hound of the Baskervilles

When Gillette's play opened in America, Doyle's mind was full of the South African war, and he found it difficult to concentrate on literary work. During the second week of December 1899 the situation became so serious that he decided to volunteer. He was not accepted because he had had no previous experience, but when he heard that John Langman was fitting out a field hospital he offered his services as a doctor and thereby got the chance to go out to South Africa. He was at Bloemfontein at the beginning of April 1900, and though most of his time was occupied in dealing with the serious outbreak of enteric fever, he did manage to do some work on his history of the war. He also sat for a drawing by Mortimer Menpes whose daughter, Dorothy, the 'Painter's Youngest Daughter', prepared his notes for publication. The article, 'Conan Doyle at the Front', appeared in M.A.P. (Mainly About People) on 14 July 1900:

> When the Painter talked of his Sherlock Holmes series, Conan Doyle smiled and said that that work was not good. Sherlock Holmes being merely a mechanical creature, easy to create because he was soulless. 'Why,' he said, 'one story by Edgar Allan Poe would be worth any number of stories on the plane of Sherlock Holmes.' The Painter

asked him which story of the series he liked best, and he
said: 'Perhaps the one about the serpent, but I can't for the
life of me remember the name of it!' 'But, doctor,'
exclaimed the Painter, 'you are not a fair judge of your
own work.' 'Oh, yes,' he said, 'I am though. It's a curious
thing,' he added, 'in real life I have no capacity for
detecting anything. I never had that power; I never could
discover anything.' He was simply amazed at the Painter's
acuteness in discovering that there was a missing dot on an
Orange Free State stamp surcharged V.R.I.![178]

A few days before this article appeared, Doyle had boarded
the *Briton* at Cape Town on his way home. It was to prove a
memorable journey and one which led indirectly to the most
famous of the Sherlock Holmes stories. Among the many
distinguished people on board were two war correspondents,
H. W. Nevinson, who was recovering from a severe bout of
fever, and Bertram Fletcher Robinson, the nephew of Sir
John Robinson of the *Daily News*, who had been acting for
the new *Daily Express* of which he later became the editor.

The journey cemented the friendship between Doyle and
Robinson, and when Doyle lost his temper with Major Roger
Raoud Duval, who had suggested that the British used
Dum-Dum bullets, it was Robinson who made peace between them. The initial apologies were not accepted, but a
letter which Robinson procured from Duval successfully
averted what might otherwise have been a 'serious
incident'.[179]

Doyle was back in London by August 1900 and almost
immediately left for Edinburgh, where he stood as a candidate in the 'khaki' elections. His failure and the backwash of
enteric fever lowered his spirits to such an extent that he
would have welcomed the opportunity which came in March
1901 of a short holiday in Norfolk with Robinson. They
stayed at the Royal Links Hotel in Cromer, and it was from
there that Doyle scribbled a short note to his mother
mentioning the title of a new novel:

Fletcher Robinson came here with me and we are going to do a small book together *The Hound of the Baskervilles* – a real creeper.

Cromer, Norfolk   Your own, A.[180]

J. E. Hodder Williams, in the *Bookman* of April 1902, gave more details of how Doyle's story came about:

With his friend Mr Fletcher Robinson he found himself at Cromer, where a long Sunday was spent together in friendly chat. Robinson is a Devonshire man, and he mentioned in conversation some old county legend which set Doyle's imagination on fire. The two men began building up a chain of events, and in a very few hours the plot of a sensational story was conceived, and it was agreed that Doyle should write it. When he came to working out the details, he found, however, that some masterful central figure was needed, some strong man who would influence the whole course of events, and his natural reflection was: 'Why should I invent such a character when I have him already in the form of Holmes?'[181]

Doyle had to return to London, but from there he went down to Devon. His host, Bertram Fletcher Robinson, the son of Joseph Fletcher Robinson, had spent his childhood at Park Hill, Ipplepen, and, before going up to Jesus College, Cambridge, had attended Newton College in Newton Abbot, so he was familiar with many of the local Devonshire legends, a great number of which concerned dogs and hounds. It is not known for certain exactly what Robinson told Doyle. His close friend Max Pemberton, who as editor of *Cassell's Magazine* had published the articles about Robinson's extensive tour through Europe, believed that the initial inspiration was not a Devonshire hound but the 'ghost-hound' of the Norfolk marshes. Pemberton thought that he might have had a part in the preliminary stages of the book as Robinson was a frequent visitor to his house in Hampstead and had there heard the legend of the phantom dog; Pember-ton had been told of 'Old Shuck', or 'Black Shuck', by a marshman, Jimmy Farman, whose dog had been terrified by it. This, he said, had reminded Robinson of the people on Dartmoor who were also convinced of the existence of a phantom hound and had given him the idea for the book.

On 2 April 1901 Doyle wrote to his mother on the headed notepaper of Rowe's Duchy Hotel, Princetown:

> Dearest of Mams,
>   Here I am in the highest town in England. Robinson and I are exploring the moor over our Sherlock Holmes book. I think it will work out splendidly – indeed I have already done nearly half of it. Holmes is at his very best, and it is a highly dramatic idea – which I owe to Robinson.
>   We did 14 miles over the moor today and we are now pleasantly weary. It is a great place, very sad & wild, dotted with the dwellings of prehistoric man, strange monoliths and huts and graves.[182]

No doubt in the course of their peregrinations they visited the prehistoric enclosure at Grimspound, learnt of the ancient tenement of Merripit, saw the Hound Tor, and heard tales of escaped convicts. Robinson was an invaluable guide. 'The story owes its inception to my friend, Mr Fletcher Robinson,' said a footnote to the first part of *The Hound of the Baskervilles* in the *Strand Magazine*, 'who has helped me both in the general plot and in the local details.'[183] And in the book itself Doyle added a letter addressed to Robinson: 'It was to your account of a West Country legend that this tale owes its inception. For this and for your help in the details all thanks.'[184] Or, in the first American edition: 'It was your account of a west country legend which first suggested the idea of this little tale to my mind. For this, and for the help which you gave me in its evolution, all thanks.'[185]

The acknowledgement to Robinson quickly became – and

has remained – a subject for debate. The editors of the American *Bookman*, after seeing the first part of the serial, said that while it primarily concerned the authors and their publishers, 'We have very little hesitation in expressing our conviction that the story is almost entirely Mr Robinson's, and that Dr Doyle's only important contribution to the partnership is the permission to use the character of Sherlock Holmes.'[186] This assumption may appear ridiculous, but there is some truth in it, certainly if one of Robinson's closest friends, the novelist Archibald Marshall, is to be believed. He described Robinson as a great inventor of stories:

> He gave Conan Doyle the idea and plot for *The Hound of the Baskervilles*, and wrote most of its first instalment for the *Strand Magazine*. Conan Doyle wanted it to appear under their joint names, but his name alone was wanted, because it was worth so much more.[187]

There can be no doubt that the very least which Robinson did was to provide the legend, though nowhere is it actually mentioned by name. Sabine Baring-Gould in his *A Book of the West*, published in 1899, gives one version of a legend which is the most likely source:

> There existed formerly a belief on Dartmoor that it was hunted over at night in storm by a black sportsman, with black fire-breathing hounds, called the 'Wish Hounds'. They could be heard in full cry, and occasionally the blast of a hunter's horn on stormy nights.[188]

Another version is associated with Sir Richard Cabell (or Capel) of Brooke Manor, Buckfastleigh. James Branch Cabell, in a letter to his distant relative which appeared in his book, *Ladies and Gentlemen*, in 1934, described how in October 1677 Sir Richard's pact with the devil expired and fire-breathing hounds gathered at midnight around the manor. In obedience to their summons, he mounted his black mare and rode away across the moor. When his body was discovered it was badly mangled and scorched, while his throat had been torn open. Branch Cabell, who had come across the suggestion in *Devon and Cornwall Notes and Queries*, was in no doubt that this had inspired the famous novel. 'Well, Sir,' he added, 'and afterward – a long while afterward, in the year of grace 1902 – one Dr A. Conan Doyle took over your story, renaming you Hugo Baskerville. He reduced the company of your familiars to a single beast; and he lugged into your story a superfluous "yeoman's daughter" . . . Doyle wrote, in brief, with you as his point of departure, *The Hound of the Baskervilles*; and he made out of your legend a striking book.'[189]

Buckfastleigh is close to Ipplepen, and the legend was well known. Doyle was to say in the preface to the 1929 omnibus volume that the story arose from a remark by Fletcher Robinson 'that there was a spectral dog near his home on Dartmoor'.[190] Doyle almost certainly stayed at the Robinson family home and there met the man who believed that he had supplied the name used in the title; this was Henry, or Harry, Baskerville, the coachman at Park Hill. He recalled years later:

> Mr Doyle stayed for eight days and nights. I had to drive him and Bertie about the moors. And I used to watch them in the billiards room in the old house, sometimes they stayed long into the night, writing and talking together.[191]

Harry Baskerville believed that Fletcher Robinson had intended to write the story even before the outbreak of the Boer War; he had also been asked for permission to use his name, as proof of which he could produce a copy of *The Hound of the Baskervilles* which was inscribed: 'To Harry Baskerville, with apologies for using the name. Fletcher Robinson.'

Harry Baskerville was descended from the ancient Norman family which had originated at Basqueville in Nor-

mandy. The main branch settled at Eardisley Castle in Herefordshire, and its descendants were until recently at Clyro
Court, just inside the Welsh border. These Baskervilles were
neighbours of, and intermarried with, the Vaughans of
Hergest Court who had a legend of a Black Hound. It has
been said that Conan Doyle stayed at Kington, near Hergest
Court, when he was writing the story and that the historic
house at Dunfield with its double avenue served as the
inspiration for Baskerville Hall. There is also a tradition that
Doyle visited the Welsh borders in 1897 or 1898, that he saw
the famous old inn sign at Clyro, and that he asked the
Baskervilles at Clyro Court for permission to use the name.
The sole surviving member of the Baskerville family has been
quoted as saying of the Baskerville seat:

> Everybody knows that Conan Doyle heard the tale of a
> phantom hound that haunted the Vaughans at Hergest
> Court, ten miles from here. He asked my grandmother if
> he could use the family name because Baskerville was
> more romantic than Vaughan. She agreed, provided he
> spirited the hound far away from here into the West
> Country. [192]

The grandmother in question, Dorothy Nesta Baskerville,
who succeeded her brother after he was killed in action in
1918, would have been very young at the time, and many
have doubted the tradition which only really became popular after Dr Maurice Campbell's paper, 'The Hound of the
Baskervilles – Dartmoor or Herefordshire?', which was written in 1953; but there is supporting evidence given by
Greenhough Smith, the editor of the Strand Magazine. He
said in 1930 that Robinson's share in the transaction was 'to
draw the attention of Conan Doyle to the tradition of the
fiery hound in a Welsh guide-book'. [193]

Greenhough Smith had been one of the first to know that
the story was being written. Doyle told him:

I have the idea of a real creeper for the *Strand*. It is full of surprises, breaking naturally into good lengths for serial purposes. There is one stipulation. I must do it with my friend Fletcher Robinson, and his name must appear with mine. I can answer for the yarn being all my own in my own style without dilution, since your readers like that. But he gave me the central idea and the local colour, and so I feel his name must appear. I shall want my usual £50 per thousand words for all rights if you do business.[194]

When he had decided to use Sherlock Holmes, the price was doubled:

The price I quoted has for years been my serial price not only with you but with other journals. Now it is evident that this is a very special occasion since as far as I can judge the revival of Holmes would attract a great deal of attention. If put up to open competition I could get very particular terms for this story. Suppose I gave the directors the alternative that it should be without Holmes at my old figure or with Holmes at £100 per thou. which would they choose?

And he added: 'Holmes is at a premium in America just now.'[195] The directors had no difficulty in making up their minds; they took both the English and American rights.

The figure of £100 per thousand words supports what Archibald Marshall later said about the arrangement made between Doyle and Fletcher Robinson (or 'Bobbles', as he was known to his friends):

They were paid £100 a thousand words, in the proportion of three to one. As I put it to Bobbles at the time, 'Then if you write "How do you do?" Doyle gets six shillings and you get two.' He said he had never been good at vulgar fractions, but it sounded right, and anyhow what he wrote was worth it.[196]

The first part of *The Hound of the Baskervilles* appeared in the *Strand Magazine* in August 1901. Its success was immediate and the interest evoked by the name of Sherlock Holmes was as great as ever. The public, said Hodder Williams in 1902, 'has shown that during an absence of six years they have not entirely lost interest in him'.[197] There were long queues at the offices of the *Strand Magazine* and at local bookstalls and, it was said, bribes were being offered so that readers might have their copies early.

Harper's Weekly, in America, celebrated Sherlock Holmes's return on 31 August 1901 in its 'Notes of a Bookman' by publishing a series of documents from foreign newspapers, the agony columns of *The Times*, from the letters and telegrams which had passed between Holmes and Watson, and from a number of other sources. The great detective had, the magazine revealed, been working as a waiter in Switzerland and was now anxious to return home. It was excellent and highly amusing chaff. But the American *Bookman* went a stage further. Impatient to know the end of the story, correspondents started sending in solutions of their own. Edgar Allan Poe had done this very successfully after reading the first instalment of *Barnaby Rudge*, but *The Hound of the Baskervilles* produced some extraordinary ideas. The main theory, the ingenuity of which, according to Arthur Bartlett Maurice, was commended by Conan Doyle, was produced after four issues. The Baskervilles suffered from a hideous deformity: they had the feet of a hound! The later theorists, who took this for granted, suggested that the girl chased by the wicked Sir Hugo had given birth to a child, and that the escaped convict, Selden, was Rodger Baskerville. Doyle himself, according to Edmund Pearson in the American *Bookman* of August 1932, provided the best epitaph for these theories: 'They were all far astray. Mr Arthur Bartlett Maurice told me that they were read by Dr Doyle, who intimated that they were worthy of Gregson and Lestrade.'[198] The last letters about the theory were published when the truth was known, and the *Bookman* commented that the story 'was in a minor way a really great serial. In fact, in that form it has proved the most successful book since *Trilby* came out in parts in *Harper's Magazine*.' The number of letters which they had received about the hound foot theory, 'contradicting or affirming it',[199] showed how widespread was the interest.

If the scenes in England were unprecedented, those in America were no less surprising. *The Hound of the Baskervilles* was reprinted in the newspapers and there were so many orders for the first edition that the publisher kept setting back the publication date so as to have sufficient to meet the demand. Pages of the manuscript were dispatched across America to publicize the book, while the demand for the earlier stories increased to such an extent that limited editions of only fifty thousand copies were not uncommon. Between two and five thousand copies of a first edition were sufficient to make a best-seller in England, but for *The Hound of the Baskervilles*, twenty-five thousand was only the beginning. On both sides of the Atlantic the interest in Sherlock Holmes seemed to be increasing and it was clear that readers would not be averse to a new series.

The Return of Sherlock Holmes

During the spring of 1903 an offer was received from Collier's in America. Would the author consider reviving Sherlock Holmes if he were offered twenty-five thousand dollars for six stories, or thirty thousand for eight, or forty-five thousand for thirteen? Doyle gave his answer on a postcard: 'Very well, A.C.D.'[200] No conditions were attached, but it was hoped that Sherlock Holmes might find himself on the other side of the Atlantic.

Doyle's mother was worried that the great detective might not live up to past expectations; but once a start had been made, Doyle was confident that all would be well:

Dearest Mammie,

I don't think you need have any fears about Sherlock. I am not conscious of any failing powers, and my work is not less conscientious than of old. I don't suppose any man has ever sacrificed so much money to preserve his ideal of art as I have done, witness my suppression of *Girdlestone*, my refusal to serialize *A Duet* and my refusal to republish in a book the Round the Fire series of stories. I have done no short Sherlock Holmes stories for seven or eight years and I don't see why I should not have another go at them. I might add that I have finished the first one, 'The Adventure of the Empty House'. The plot, by the way, was given to me by Jean; and it is a rare good one. You will find that Holmes was never dead, and that he is now very much alive.[201]

The lady to whom he referred, Jean Leckie, had become a close friend and, after his wife's death, became the second Lady Conan Doyle.

Although the editor was pleased with the first story, he expressed some reservations about the 'Solitary Cyclist' and the 'Norwood Builder' which followed it. Doyle, who was staying at the Hill House Hotel at Happisburg, replied on 14 May 1903. He felt that he had a fairly sane view of his own work, and told the editor:

This is what I think about these two stories.

The second 'The Norwood Builder' I would put in the very first rank of the whole series for subtlety and depth. Any feeling of disappointment at the end is due to the fact that no crime has been done & so the reader feels bluffed, but it is well for other reasons to have some of the stories crimeless.

Take the series of points, Holmes's deductions from the will written in the train, the point of the bloody thumb mark, Holmes's device for frightening the man out of his hiding place, &c. I know no Holmes story which has such a succession of bright points.

As to the Cyclist story I did not like it so well nor was I satisfied with it & yet I could make no more of it. It has points but as a whole is not up to the mark.

He then spoke of his intense disinclination to continue the stories and hoped that Greenhough Smith would now appreciate why he had for so long resisted the temptation to do so:

It is *impossible* to prevent a certain sameness & want of freshness. The most one can do is to try to produce such stories that if they had come first and the others second, they would then have seemed fresh and good.[202]

A few days later he was more confident: 'I have a strong bloody story for the fourth, "The Adventure of the Dancing Men".'[203] This he suggested might be put as the third story and so separate the two crimeless ones. He also went over the 'Solitary Cyclist':

It strikes me as a dramatic & interesting & original story. The weakness lies in Holmes not having more to do. But Watson now prefaces his account by meeting this criticism. I have gone over it carefully & can do no more to strengthen it. I consider that these four stories will beat any four *consecutive* Holmes stories that I have done.[204]

In a letter to his mother he spoke of 'three bull's-eyes and an outer'.[205] His problem was not writing the stories – that was the easiest part – but finding suitable plots. He was anxious to talk these over with somebody, and probably did so, not only with his friend, Jean Leckie (who actually wrote out part of the final story in the series), but also with Hornung, as many of the later stories, such as 'Charles Augustus Milverton' and 'The Priory School', did borrow their plots from the Raffles stories. He also wondered how the public would receive the new stories. Here he need not have worried. Holmes's popularity was as great as ever, though that could not prevent a few people finding fault with the stories, or at least with aspects of them.

The cryptogram used in 'The Adventure of the Dancing Men' was inspired by the stick figures drawn by a child (the child, according to a neat theory subsequently denied by the person in question, being G. J. Cubitt, who was staying at the Hill House Hotel and whose surname was clearly an influence). But a similar puzzle had also appeared in *St Nicholas* in May 1874 where the figures were known as the 'restless imps'. A doctor in America drew Doyle's attention to this fact and, for his pains, received the following reply:

> Dear Sir,
>   Pure coincidence.
>   Yours truly, A. Conan Doyle.[206]

This would have been the end of it had not Lyndon Orr decided to chronicle the 'Case of Coincidence' for the American *Bookman* of April 1910. His sense of injured pride rather biased his judgement. The point which seemed so important to him was a mere trifle as far as Doyle was concerned.

It was more serious when the logic or reasoning was called into question, as occurred in 'The Adventure of the Priory School'. Was it, as Holmes had said, possible to tell which way a bicycle was travelling by examining the tracks? When a carriage was involved, Doyle had had no doubts, nor had there been any evidence of dissatisfaction on the part of the readers. Holmes had said, for example, in 'The Adventure of the Greek Interpreter', 'you may have observed the same wheel-tracks going the other way. But the outward-bound ones were very much deeper – so much so that we can say for a certainty that there was a very considerable weight on the carriage';[207] but with the Priory School bicycle, which used an idea (and almost the same words when it came to the

Dunlop and Palmer tyres) from the Raffles story 'The Wrong House', it was a different matter. The editor passed on a number of letters, and Doyle then replied:

> I don't suppose you take much notice about what cranks write, but with regard to the two letters from Dublin you sent me – both from the same person by the way – you may be interested to know that I have just been out, tried it on my bike, and got the impressions as in the story, the hind wheel cutting across the line of the front one. I then took a photo of the tracks but don't know if it will come out. If it does I'll send it for publication.[208]

Although Doyle does not appear to have sent the photograph, he did forward one by H. Grose which had reached him from Australia. This was published with the 'Curiosities' in the August 1904 issue of the *Strand Magazine* and showed eight miners posing as 'dancing men' to spell out the name of their mine.

Bicycles and motor cycles were very much on Doyle's mind because he was investing in a company which manufactured them, but he had been an advocate for many years: 'I have myself ridden a bicycle most during my practice as a physician and during my work in letters,' he said in 1896. 'In the morning or the afternoon, before or after work, as the mood o'ertakes me, I mount the wheel and am off for a spin of a few miles up or down the road from my country place.'[209] There was nothing incongruous about Sherlock Holmes on a bicycle, but the idea of his using a motor cycle was less appealing. The representatives of the magazine *Motor Cycle* did ask about the possibility when they visited Doyle at Undershaw. Their article appeared in the magazine on 27 February 1905 when Holmes was safely out of the way:

> We could not leave 'Undershaw' without referring to our old friend Sherlock Holmes. 'Shall we hear of the famous detective hunting down his quarry, accompanied

by his faithful Watson, both mounted on "Mysterious Motors"?' we asked.

'No,' said Sir Arthur. 'In Holmes' early days motor bicycles were unthought of, even by *his* fertile brain, and now he has retired into private life.'[210]

Watson was to be found at the wheel of a car a few years later, so perhaps the question was not as absurd as it seemed.

Although Doyle at one point threatened to limit the number of stories to eight, he eventually found sufficient material for thirteen. The hardest to do were those in the middle of the series and, as a way out of the impasse, there was a suggestion that he might visit America. The *Evening News* announced on 8 June 1903:

> A letter from Sir Conan Doyle says that he is going to spend the summer at Montauk (New York), in order to revive Sherlock Holmes in a series of stories and mysteries of American origin. With a view of obtaining local colour, he has leased a hotel which is usually vacant in the summer, but in winter is a sporting centre.[211]

Nothing seems to have come of this plan, which may have been only a rumour, but the acting secretary of the President of the United States did write to Doyle's publishers asking for information. The letter of 27 July said: 'The President has heard that Sir Conan Doyle will soon be in this country, and wishes me to ask if you know when he will be here and where he can be reached after his arrival.'[212]

Sherlock Holmes in Retirement

'The Adventure of the Second Stain' was the final story, and this once again brought Holmes's career to its conclusion by sending him down to Sussex to keep bees. The author was fully determined that the detective should enjoy complete seclusion. Holmes had grown older as the stories progressed, but it was still a somewhat premature retirement. The world first learnt of his imminent departure when it was announced in the October *Bookman*, and that was quickly followed by the excellent interview, 'The Last of Sherlock Holmes', which appeared in the *Daily Mail* on 8 October 1904. The interview was so convincing, especially when extracts were published in other newspapers, that at least two people wrote offering their services.

From the Isle of Wight there was a letter from M. Gunton, who gave the address of the Hon. Pauline Emily Cranstoun, the daughter of the tenth Baron Cranstoun:

> To Sir Conan Doyle, Bart.
>
> Will 'Mr Sherlock Holmes' require a housekeeper for his country cottage at Xmas? I know someone who loves a quiet country life, and 'Bees' especially – an old fashioned quiet woman.
>
> Yours faithfully, M. Gunton
>
> c/o The Hon. P. Cranstoun, Hurst Hill House, Totland Bay, I. of Wight
>
> 10 Oct. 1904[213]

Doyle believed that the letter was serious, though the inverted commas might suggest otherwise. A second letter, addressed to Sherlock Holmes, came from W. Herrod, F.E.S., lecturer and apiarian specialist, lecturer on poultry, a gold, silver, and bronze medallist, and an expert on every aspect of bee-keeping:

> W.B.C. APIARY
> OLD BEDFORD ROAD
> LUTON, BEDS
> 10.10.1904
>
> Dear Sir,
>
> I see by some of the morning papers that you are about to retire and take up beekeeping. I know not if this be

correct or otherwise, but if correct I shall be pleased
to render you service by giving any advice you may require.

I make this offer in return for the pleasure your writings
gave me as a youngster, they enabled me to spend many &
many a happy hour. Therefore I trust you will read this
letter in the same spirit that it is written.

Yours faithfully, W. Herrod[214]

Both these letters, though without the names or addresses,
were given by A. St John Adcock in an article about Conan
Doyle for the November 1912 *Bookman*. He considered the
second to be 'curiously charming': 'its sincere, spontaneous
gratitude is an infinitely better thing than the most laudatory
criticism written by those who sit in the judgement seats.'
And he added: 'I forgot to ask Sir Arthur whether in replying
to this and others he made it clear that Sherlock Holmes
could not oblige them because, in the words of Mrs Gamp,
"there ain't no sich person"; but I hope he did not.'[215]

Doyle admitted on so many occasions that he knew
nothing whatever about bees or about bee-keeping that his
hosts in Australia decided to end his state of blissful ignorance. On 14 January 1921 he and his family were taken to
the largest bee-farm in Australia, the Redbank Plains Apiary
at Brisbane run by H. L. Jones. Describing the occasion in
The Wanderings of a Spiritualist, he said:

> Ever since I consigned Mr Sherlock Holmes to a bee
> farm for his old age, I have been supposed to know
> something of the subject, but really I am so ignorant that
> when a woman wrote to me and said she would be a
> suitable housekeeper to the retired detective because she
> could 'segregate the queen', I did not know what she
> meant. On this occasion I saw the operation and many
> other wonderful things which made me appreciate
> Maeterlinck's prose-poem upon the subject.[216]

Other letters to Sherlock Holmes were more mundane; his

autograph was much in demand, as shown by this letter from
Worthing, dated 18 November 1904:

> Dear Sir,
>
>   I trust I am not trespassing too much on your time and
> kindness by asking for the favour of your autograph to add
> to my collection. I have derived much pleasure from
> reading your Memoirs, and should very highly value the
> possession of your famous signature. Trusting you will see
> your way to thus honour me, and venturing to thank you
> very much in anticipation, I am, Sir,
>
>   Your obedient servant, Charles Wright
>
> P.S. Not being aware of your present address, I am taking
> the liberty of sending this letter to Sir A. Conan Doyle,
> asking him to be good enough to forward it to you.[217]

A further letter, dated 10 June 1910, from an admirer in New
York may also be given here:

> I have read with great interest the reminiscences of your
> detective achievements, as recorded by your friend, John
> H. Watson, M.D. I would like you to know how greatly I
> admire your skill in every way; but especially in that great
> case which goes by the name of *The Hound of the Baskervil-
> les*. Might I ask you, as a special favour to myself, to send
> me your autograph? You cannot think how delighted I
> would be to add it to my collection.[218]

These letters were less remarkable than those which came
from other foreign countries where the reputation of Sherlock Holmes was scaling new heights and where the reaction
was often bizarre.

Sherlockitis

The Sherlock Holmes stories were popular throughout
Europe, but France was the country most enamoured of the

detective. It was there in 1906 that Maurice Leblanc gave
birth to *Arsène Lupin, Gentleman-Cambrioleur*, which was
first published in *Je Sais Tout*. In the third story Leblanc
mentioned a great English detective, Herlock Sholmès, who
was far more intelligent than any of the French detectives
with whom Lupin had to deal. The last story in the book,
'Herlock Sholmès arrive trop tard', prepared for what was to
follow and probably also provided the inspiration for the
message to Sherlock Holmes from Arsène Lupin which was
concealed in a piece of chalk and handed to Conan Doyle at
a billiard match (see p. 291). Sholmès arrives too late to
prevent Lupin from ransacking a castle, but they do meet on
the road, and at the end of the story a parcel is discovered
addressed to 'Herlock Sholmès, Esq, from Arsène Lupin'
which contains Sholmès's watch. The English detective
thereupon prophesies that he and Arsène Lupin will meet
again. This they did on various occasions, the most famous
being the next collection, *Arsène Lupin contre Herlock
Sholmès*, where Sholmès is given more character and where
he is accompanied by his faithful Wilson. No praise was high
enough for the English detective. In the chapter entitled
'Herlock Sholmès ouvre les hostilités', Leblanc wrote:

> Et puis, c'est Herlock Sholmès, c'est-à-dire une sorte de
> phénomène d'intuition, d'observation, de clairvoyance et
> d'ingéniosité. On croirait que la nature s'est amusée à
> prendre les deux types de policier les plus extraordinaires
> que l'imagination ait produits, le Dupin d'Edgar Poë, et le
> Lecoq de Gaboriau, pour en construire un à sa maniere,
> plus extraordinaire encore et plus irréel. Et l'on se deman-
> de vraiment, quand on entend le récit de ces exploits qui
> l'ont rendu célèbre dans l'univers entier, on se demande si
> lui-même, ce Herlock Sholmès, n'est pas un personnage
> légendaire, un héros sorti, vivant du cerveau d'un grand
> romancier, d'un Conan Doyle, par exemple.[219]

The Arsène Lupin stories, and a play derived from them,

were equally popular in England, though the name of the detective was changed in some translations to Holmlock Shears. As he was frequently outwitted, it was probably just as well that Doyle had in the first place refused the author permission to use the real name.

Commenting on his use of Sherlock Holmes, in an interview with Charles Henry Meltzer in 1913 Leblanc said:

I have been accused of pilfering Conan Doyle. That is hardly fair. I have read Conan Doyle, and I admire his works. I have not pilfered him. It was a friend of mine who suggested my introducing Sherlock Holmes into my stories, and the idea seemed natural. But I admit that I have not been wholly fair in my descriptions of that character. Whenever Lupin meets him, Lupin conquers. And though, of course, Conan Doyle owed much to Gaboriau, I confess that I regret some things I have written of his hero. Not only because I may have been unjust. But – well, because I may have offended English sentiment.[220]

A French adaptation of Gillette's *Sherlock Holmes* by Pierre Decourcelle, which opened at the Théâtre Antoine on 20 December 1907, also enjoyed a prodigious success. Firmin Gemier played Holmes, and Doyle was to say at the 1925 Savage Club dinner, at which Gemier was also a guest, that his performance was the 'greatest theatrical representation of Holmes ever made'.[221] Shortly after the French play had opened, Arthur Bartlett Maurice gave the following description of the French 'Sherlockitis':

M. Decourcelle's play, with M. Gemier in the title rôle, has now reached almost three hundred performances at the Théâtre Antoine, a very remarkable run for Paris. The result of this successs has been exceedingly annoying to the French police officials. One Parisian out of five nowadays considers himself a Sherlock Holmes, and consequently everybody is asking why M. Hamard should fail where the English detective would have succeeded in no time. In connection with two recent sensational murders two Paris papers have been setting forth their versions of how these mysterious crimes are committed, in the form of interviews with Sherlock Holmes. The other day a foot-man stole a casket containing ten thousand francs' worth of jewels and concealed it in a hole in the ground in the Bois de Boulogne. When finally forced to confess, he declared that he had been so much impressed by the cunning of Holmes and the skill of Moriarty as a criminal that he wished to imitate them and commit theft in a scientific and artistic manner.[222]

The methods of Sherlock Holmes were to influence the police in France, aided no doubt by the 'étude médico-légale' of Dr J. Bercher who in 1906 produced a volume (one of a number of similar studies) entitled *L'Œuvre de Conan-Doyle et la police scientifique au vingtième siècle*, with a preface by Dr R. A. Reiss, Professeur de Police Scientifique à l'Université de Lausanne.

Sherlockismus and Sherlockholmitos

Whatever the French could do, the Germans considered they could do better. Like the English, who for a time used the verb 'to sherlock', the Germans created a new word 'sherlockieren' meaning to track down or deduce. In 1908, Alfred Lichtenstein's *Der Kriminalroman. Eine literarische und forensisch-medizinische Studie mit Anhang: Sherlock Holmes zum Fall Hau* was published in Munich. Six years later, under the Heidelberg imprint of Carl Winter, appeared Friedrich Depken's *Sherlock Holmes, Raffles und ihre Vorbilder. Ein Beitrag zur Entwicklungsgesichte und Technik der Kriminalerzählung* which quoted the complaint of the *Kölnischen Zeitung* of 1908: 'Der Sherlockismus ist eine literarische Krankheit, ähnlich der Werthermanie und dem romantischen Byronismus.'[223] And this was no less than the truth.

The Kaiser himself was partial to the Sherlock Holmes stories, which were among the books he had specially bound to suit the colour scheme of the bedroom on his royal yacht. In his capital, Berlin, the Verlagshaus für Volksliteratur und Kunst had in 1907 produced the first ten volumes of *Detektiv Sherlock Holmes und seine weltberühmten Abenteuer*, of which by 1910 there were to be a further 146. These were not translations, but what *The Times* called 'the free creations of a mythological fancy, rather like the Eastern legends of Alexander the Great, preserving little association with the original beyond the name'.[224]

Four of the German plagiarisms were translated into Spanish in 1908, and three years later the entire series was taken over by a firm in Barcelona. Although these *Memorias íntimas de Sherlock Holmes* represented, in the words of the American *Bookman*, 'the imaginative work of hack writers',[225] they soon became the favourite reading matter of Spanish-speaking people not only in Spain but also in Mexico, Cuba, and Latin America. The interest in Señor Sherlock Holmes of the South Americans, who, in turn, coined the word 'Sherlockholmitos', was shared by those of Portuguese origin: Brazil, for example, produced at least one serious study, Elysio de Carvalho's *Sherlock Holmes no Brasil*, published in Rio de Janeiro in 1921.

The Reverend Gerald Herring was to tell the readers of one newspaper that on a visit to Russia in 1908 he had found the whole country 'crazy about Sherlock Holmes. Even the peasants (those who could read) had got hold of copies, cheaply printed, and, no doubt, pirated.'[226] These were, in fact, some of the thousand or more sensational novels published in Russia during that year which were classed as 'Nat Pinkerton and Sherlock Holmes Literature'. One Russian critic considered that the craze 'foreshadows a complete change in the Russian reader, the decay of the literature of passivity, and the rise of a new literature of action and physical revolt'.[227] If the pastiches were indeed undermining the state, the Tsar and his family in St Petersburg were unconscious of it, and were themselves fervent admirers of the original stories – an interest shared by their successors, who, having first banned the books on account of their author's spiritualist beliefs, later recommended them for the Red Army as 'a model of magnificent strength and great culture'.[228] Carmen Sylva, the Queen of Romania, like other royalty, emperors, and princes, was also a firm devotee, as were various Presidents of the United States and such diverse figures as Marshal Tito and President Syngman Ree of Korea. The most remarkable, however, was the Sultan of Turkey.

An article on Abdul Hamid II had followed 'The Final Problem' in the pages of the *Strand Magazine* in December 1893, and this may explain the Sultan's interest. When Doyle was in Constantinople on his honeymoon at the end of 1907, he and his wife were invited to attend the weekly 'selamlik' where they saw the Sultan with his 'dyed beard' accompanied by the ladies of the harem as they passed down to their devotions.[229] The Sultan sent word that he had read Doyle's books and would gladly have seen him had it not been the month of Ramadan. Then, in an interview through the Chamberlain, he presented him with the Order of the Medjedie, and his wife with the Order of the Chevekat. Within less than two years, the 'Red Sultan' was deposed. In *Golden Horn*, Francis Yeats-Brown gave a dramatic account of how this came about, and of how the Sultan spent one of his last evenings in power, that of 23 April 1909. Having first dictated a message to the rebellious army units:

He sent for his Chamberlain to read aloud to him: a new Conan Doyle story had appeared in the *Strand Magazine*, and as usual it had been immediately translated by the Press Bureau in Yildiz Kiosk. So Abdul Hamid passed the long hours, with a shawl over his knees, lying on a divan, smoking, listening to the adventures of Sherlock Holmes, while the Army of Liberation closed in round the Palace.[230]

The story was 'The Adventure of the Bruce-Partington Plans'. Just as the Sultan had shared in the death of Sherlock Holmes, so Holmes shared his final hours in power.

More evidence of Holmes's influence in Turkey was given by Frederick Hamer in a letter to *The Times* shortly after Doyle's death:

> In 1920 it was decided to complete the occupation of Constantinople in a military sense. Acting on sure information, certain 'nationalist' elements, which might have organized resistance, were rounded up in the early hours of the morning, and later in the day the occupation of the Turkish War Office and Admiralty were effected without incident. The Turkish populace, however, insisted that the great English detective Sherlock Holmes must have been behind the scenes, informing the High Command with his keen intellect and directing the measures which led to the removal of the recalcitrants and the consequent peaceful completion of the military occupation.[231]

Further afield, the reactions provoked by Sherlock Holmes were no less surprising. One of the earliest was in Samoa where, as Doyle recalled in his autobiography, Robert Louis Stevenson had read the stories to his servants:

> He had been retailing some of my Sherlock Holmes yarns to his native servants – I should not have thought that he needed to draw upon anyone else – and he complained to me in a comical letter of the difficulty of telling a story when you had to halt every moment to explain what a railway was, what an engineer was, and so forth. He got the story across in spite of all difficulties, and, said he, 'If you could have seen the bright feverish eyes of Simelè you would have tasted glory.' But he

explained that the natives took everything literally, and that there was no such thing as an imaginary story for them. [232]

Many years later, the *Sunday Express* was able to report the following 'odd thing' that had happened:

> At a cinema at Wad Medani, Sudan, a Sherlock Holmes serial so excited the natives that they demanded to see the remaining instalments there and then. The manager could not oblige. Rioters wrecked the cinema. [233]

It was out of regard not for their cinemas but for their morals that the ever-cautious Swiss reacted against Sherlock Holmes, or at least against the pernicious influence of the detective story. The Geneva correspondent of *The Times* stated on 14 February 1910 that the Federal Railways Company had issued an order prohibiting the sale of detective stories and thereby banning Sherlock Holmes, and that this had forced his creator to come to his defence:

> Sir Arthur, in a letter to the chief of the Federal Railway Company, points out that there is nothing in his detective stories to shock anybody, and that he is in no way responsible for the bad literature and worse morals of the stories which have inundated the Continent. [234]

The Swiss newspapers were sympathetic towards his point of view, but they still felt that drastic measures were necessary, and a number of authorities in other towns followed the example set by the railway company.

The Crimes Club and Jack the Ripper

'Dr Conan Doyle, the creator of Sherlock Holmes, has admitted that he would never make a good detective,' said the *Pictorial Magazine* in July 1905:

But on one occasion he successfully carried out a little piece of detective work. He was at a tailor's, when he noticed a very unprepossessing man who was selecting some material for a pair of trousers, and the man seemed to have a great aversion to any material with a stripe in it, from which Conan Doyle deduced that he must be an ex-convict. To satisfy his curiosity on this point he visited a number of prisons, and at length came upon the man's portrait hung in the rogues' gallery.[235]

This would appear to be an apocryphal story, but it was true that Doyle often insisted that his own powers of detection were limited, though that did not stop people from writing to him – indeed he had been receiving requests for help ever since the earliest Sherlock Holmes stories had appeared. According to the 1908 article in *Collier's*, the experience was repeated when he was in South Africa at the time of the Boer War: 'There he was the recipient of envelopes, pieces of writing, and other things with the request that he would examine them and deduce all sorts of facts.'[236] When he was back in England, however, he began to take a closer interest, and when interviewed by the *Candid Friend* towards the end of 1901, he spoke readily about the problems that were submitted to him. 'Such a one,' said the paper, 'is now engaging his attention, but its development is more likely to be treated at Scotland Yard than in the pages of the *Strand Magazine*.'[237] This referred to a registered envelope, postmarked 23 May 1901, which contained three half sheets of blank paper and which had been sent from Western Canada to Mr Rome, a former employee of Whitaker's, the publisher of the famous Almanack. Doyle was asked for his opinion by Cuthbert W. Whitaker and during September sent the leaves to Scotland Yard to be tested for secret writing. Nothing, however, was discovered. Nor was an explanation found for the words 'Conf[l] films (or 'Tonf[e] . . . films') and 'Report Sy' which appeared on the outside of the envelope.

In 1901 Doyle wrote a series of 'Strange Studies from Life'; they were based on real crimes but were constrained by the limitations of the subject and weakened by the introduction of fictitious elements. Doyle realized from the start that they were unsatisfactory, and when he received letters of complaint from the relatives of those involved was glad that he had done no more than the first three.

Doyle's real initiation into the wonders of criminology came three years later, at the time when the Adolph Beck case was on everybody's mind. Beck had been imprisoned in 1896, released in 1901, and then rearrested in 1904 even though he was entirely innocent. He was on the point of being returned to prison when the real culprit was discovered. The case and the demand for compensation were given wide publicity in the *Daily Mail* by G. R. Sims, who was a friend of Beck. Doyle, who, according to his obituary in the *Daily Telegraph*, had also taken part in the agitation which led to Beck's release, used the articles and letters by Sims as his model for the investigation into the Edalji case.

On 17 July 1904 Doyle paid his first visit to the Crimes Club (or 'Our Society'), at the invitation of its founder and Honorary Secretary, Arthur Lambton. The club, of which Doyle was made a life member, had been founded the previous year and many of the early members were already known to him, while others were to become close friends as a result. As well as Lambton, the early members included J. B. Atlay, J. Churton Collins, Dr Herbert Crosse, H. B. Irving, A. E. W. Mason, S. Ingleby Oddie, C. A. Pearson, Max Pemberton, and Bertram Fletcher Robinson. All, it seems, were present at a dinner held in the Great Central Hotel in 1904. Many famous cases were discussed and the actual objects used by criminals were handed round; reformed criminals were also occasionally invited as guests.

One case which interested the members was that of Jack the Ripper. In 1894 Conan Doyle had been asked by an

American journalist how Sherlock Holmes would have tracked 'the notorious Whitechapel miscreant'. His answer, as reported in the *Portsmouth Evening News* of 4 July 1894, was as follows:

> I am not in the least degree either a sharp or an observant man myself. I try to get inside the skin of a sharp man and see how things would strike him. I remember going to the Scotland Yard Museum and looking at the letter which was received by the police, and which purported to come from the Ripper. Of course, it may have been a hoax, but there were reasons to think it genuine, and in any case it was well to find out who wrote it. It was written in red ink in a clerkly hand. I tried to think how Sherlock Holmes might have deduced the writer of that letter. The most obvious point was that the letter was written by someone who had been in America. It began 'Dear Boss', and contained the phrase, 'fix it up', and several others which are not usual with the Britishers. Then we have the quality of the paper and the handwriting, which indicate that the letters were not written by a toiler. It was good paper, and a round, easy, clerkly hand. He was, therefore, a man accustomed to the use of a pen.
>
> Having determined that much, we can not avoid the inference that there must be somewhere letters which this man had written over his own name, or documents or accounts that could be readily traced to him. Oddly enough, the police did not, as far as I know, think of that, and so they failed to accomplish anything. Holmes's plan would have been to reproduce the letters in facsimile and on each plate indicate briefly the peculiarities of the handwriting. Then publish these facsimiles in the leading newspapers of Great Britain and America, and in connection with them offer a reward to anyone who could show a letter or any specimen of the same handwriting. Such a course would have enlisted millions of people as detectives in the case.[238]

A chance to visit Whitechapel came in 1905 as a result of his membership of the Crimes Club. S. Ingleby Oddie, with the aid of Dr Gordon Brown, a friend who was the City of London Police Surgeon, arranged for a visit which took place on 19 April 1905. Oddie, Doyle, Churton Collins, H. B. Irving, and Herbert Crosse met outside the Police Hospital in Bishopsgate and, in the company of three City detectives who were well versed in the murders, visited the nine sites in Whitechapel where the victims had been found, as well as seeing the place where the trunk was discovered. They also visited Petticoat Lane, the Jews' fowl-slaughtering houses, a dosshouse, and the like places. Collins recalled in his diary: 'Conan Doyle seemed very much interested, particularly in the Petticoat Lane part of the expedition, and laughed when I said "Caliban would have turned up his nose at this."'[239]

It would have been in poor taste for Sherlock Holmes to have attempted to solve the Ripper murders, but his original, Dr Joseph Bell, did turn his mind to the subject. He and a friend made independent investigations and put their conclusions into envelopes which they exchanged; as one name appeared in both, this was communicated to the police. 'It was about this time,' *Tit-bits* said in their obituary article about Bell, 'that the series of murders came to an end.'[240]

Arthur Lambton always regarded the case of Adolph Beck as the first great triumph of the Crimes Club, as G. R. Sims was also a member; the club could then take credit for Churton Collins's investigation of the Merstham Tunnel Mystery (a case which may have given Doyle the idea for 'The Adventure of the Bruce-Partington Plans'), for H. B. Irving's criminological studies, for Arthur Diosy's work on the Ripper case, and not least for Conan Doyle's examination of the Edalji case, which was his first major attempt at detective work.

George Edalji: A Special Investigation

George Edalji, whose father was a Parsee, had been found guilty in 1903 of cattle maiming, and had also been charged with writing a series of anonymous letters. After his conviction, the case was taken up by the Hon. Roger Dawson Yelverton, who had also been closely involved in the Beck case. Yelverton had been the Chancellor and Chief Justice of the Bahamas in the early 1890s and became the Chairman of the League of Criminal Appeal, having, since 1888, advocated the establishment of a Criminal Court of Appeal. He prepared a memorial about George Edalji, which was signed by some 10,000 people and then sent to the Home Secretary. This was not immediately effective, but a series of articles in *Truth*, which demonstrated the impossibility of Edalji's guilt, led to his release on 19 October 1906 with a four year ticket of leave. Edalji then began 'protesting his innocence' in a series of articles which were published in the Manchester *Umpire* between 11 November and 16 December 1906. It was these articles which led Doyle to become involved.

After a visit to Hindhead on 28 December 1906, Churton Collins noted in his diary: 'Had a delightful time with Conan Doyle who is on fire with the Edalji case: going to deal exhaustively with it in the *Daily Telegraph*.'[241] Shortly afterwards Doyle sent him a copy of his statement asking him to cast an acute eye over it: 'You are probably conversant with the facts and have views thereon. To me, coming fresh to it, it seems a case which calls aloud to Heaven.'[242] His summary of the evidence or 'Special Investigation' appeared in the *Daily Telegraph* on 11 and 12 January 1907. It was based on the documents supplied by Yelverton, though Doyle had also spent a day at the scene of the crime, Great Wyrley, Staffordshire, and had had a meeting with Edalji at the Grand Hotel, Charing Cross. He noted that Edalji was of good character; there was evidence of a conspiracy against his family which stretched back at least fifteen years; his movements on the evening of the maiming were all accounted for; the handwriting expert who claimed the anonymous letters were by Edalji had been at fault in the Beck case; the letters named Edalji, which was most unlikely if he were their author; and, above all, his eyesight was so bad that he would have been unable to reach the scene of the crime in the stated time.

As a result of the publicity, the Home Office agreed to make a fresh examination, and an advisory committee was established. It acknowledged that Edalji was innocent of the charge of cattle maiming, but maintained that he had written some of the anonymous letters and so did not recommend any compensation. Doyle therefore felt that he must prove that the letters were not by Edalji. At the end of May, he wrote three articles about the handwriting based on the expert opinion of Dr George Lindsay Johnson who, in the Dreyfus case, had traced the incriminating 'Bordereau' document to Major Esterhazy. Doyle also, as he thought, had conclusive evidence as to the identity of the true culprits, and therefore prepared a full statement of the 'case against Royden Sharp of Cannock' and against his brother Wallie whom he believed to be an accomplice. Before submitting it to the Home Office, he showed it to the other members of the Edalji Committee, which included Churton Collins (who in March 1907 published an account of the case in the *National Review*), Jerome K. Jerome, and Sir George Lewis. Lewis advised him that there was insufficient evidence on which to bring a conviction, and this was the answer given to F. E. Smith when a question was raised in Parliament.

Doyle was warned by the Staffordshire police that he would be libelling an innocent man if he published his findings, even if he used different names, so his statement never became widely known. He did, however, hint at his discoveries using the name 'Peter Hudson' or 'X'. Some of his arguments were convincing, others less so; Sharp, for example, was not known to Edalji so his reasons for implicating him could only have been racial. But Doyle did receive a great deal of help from local people, such as Wilfred Greatorex, who had been Sharp's trustee and had himself received anonymous letters. The rejection by the Home Office was a source of great irritation, as it discredited his findings (which he had insisted were no more than the basis for an investigation) and made it appear that he had failed where Sherlock Holmes would so easily have succeeded.

Doyle's major contribution to the Edalji case was as a publicist. He did not consider his opinions infallible. In the introduction to a later pamphlet about the cattle maiming, he said:

> As for the very incomplete investigation which I, living at a distance and only knowing the place by a single visit, have been able to make, I have never contended that it was in any way exhaustive, or more than an excellent foundation upon which those who had the power and the opportunity might have built. [243]

The whole business had been most unsatisfactory, as no one had been prepared to admit the initial blunder: 'Instead of recognizing that I had no possible object save the end of justice, and that it was their function in this country to see that justice was done,' he said of the Home Office at the time, 'they took an obvious side in favour of impeached officialdom, and made me feel at every point that there was a hostile atmosphere around me.' [244] He repeatedly brought Edalji's case to the notice of each new Home Secretary, but always in vain. 'After many years,' he wrote in his autobiography, 'I can hardly think with patience of the handling of this case.' [245] Edalji had, at least, received a free pardon, though, as he admitted in Pearson's Weekly on 6 June 1907, this had been thrown at him without a word of apology and with the insinuation that he had written the letters. He could only regard it as 'the grossest insult'.[246]

Whatever the truth may have been, the details of the Edalji case soon became confused with the legends. Max Pemberton, for example, a fellow member of the Crimes Club, was to describe it as a 'brilliant vindication' of Edalji, who was 'absolutely exculpated by Conan Doyle's brilliant analysis';[247] and Dr Lindsay Johnson, in a reminiscence of Conan Doyle, suggested that the case had been something of a triumph. Having mentioned his connection with the Dreyfus case, he said:

> I was so successful in my investigations that Sir Conan Doyle got me to undertake a considerable amount of detective work for him, as he was always trying to defend the innocent, and many people at the present time owe their liberty to his exertions on their behalf. I may add that I was the means of liberating the Indian Edalji, and of running to earth the real criminal, and of getting the police to arrest him on a certain day a month later in a specified spot near Liverpool to the astonishment of the Attorney-General, and all the officers of Scotland Yard, after they had given up the case as hopeless.[248]

The Case of Oscar Slater

Doyle soon found that he was being given credit for having engineered the release of Edalji from prison. The defence lawyers in the Slater case were, apparently, under this impression and hoped that Doyle might do the same for Oscar Slater, who had been arrested in New York at the beginning of January 1909 and charged with the murder in Glasgow on 21 December 1908 of Miss Marion Gilchrist. Slater was tried in May, found guilty, and sentenced to death by hanging, though this was commuted to penal servitude for life after a memorial by Ewing Speirs and a petition signed by 20,000 people had been lodged with the Scottish Secretary.

When he was approached in the summer of 1912, Doyle was reluctant to involve himself in the case, as Slater was a far less pleasant character than Edalji; but it was impossible for him to read the facts without 'feeling deeply dissatisfied with the proceedings, and morally certain that justice was not done'.[249] He therefore agreed to write a booklet, as he had done three years earlier with the Congo, to draw the public's attention to the possibility and probability of a miscarriage of justice. He believed that the case was vitiated from first to last, that it was based on a false clue, and supported by untrustworthy evidence. His booklet was little more than a summary of the arguments in Slater's favour, but there was what seemed to be an original suggestion, that the murderer or murderers had been seeking a document rather than jewellery, and that the theft of a brooch, if indeed it was stolen, was merely a blind. This idea had a psychic origin. William Strang, who had been present at a séance shortly after Slater was arrested, sent Marshall Hall an acount of what Miss Gilchrist and her murderer had said. 'I have come for that paper,' said the stranger. She replied that it was not there. What paper did he want? one of them asked. 'My will,' she answered.

The Case of Oscar Slater was published on 21 August 1912. 'If the British public agree with my views,' Doyle told the readers of the *Daily Mail*, 'it is for them to see that the case is reopened.'[250] Some support was forthcoming, and Sir Herbert Stephens sent an important letter to *The Times*, but it could not offset the wave of hostile criticism directed against the book. Nearly two years passed. 'Just as I had begun to despair, however, that justice would be done,' Doyle wrote in April 1914 in a new introduction to his booklet, 'a few public spirited men in Glasgow began to move independently in the matter and I am informed that an inquiry will be held.'[251] This was established by the Secretary for Scotland

and presided over by James G. Millar, K. C., who called in James Hart, the Procurator Fiscal for Lanarkshire, and the Chief Constable. The commission sat between 23 and 25 April 1914, but on 17 June the Scottish Secretary announced that no case had been made to justify a re-trial. Doyle was unable to hide his contempt for this 'farce'. It was a fiasco because Sir John Lamb had directed that it should not relate to the 'conduct of the trial' or to the actions of the police, that it should be held in camera and that the witnesses should not be under oath, and that Slater himself should not be present. The two people who had been called in to help were both closely involved with the original trial and were therefore considered tainted.

Slater continued to serve his life sentence, while Doyle made occasional efforts to get a new trial. In 1925 a message smuggled out of Peterhead Prison by a fellow inmate, William Gordon, reached Doyle, who asked that Slater might now be released on humanitarian grounds; this did not occur until 1927. In July of that year Doyle published William Park's *The Truth about Oscar Slater*, to which he had contributed an introduction; on 23 October, the *Empire News* published an admission by Helen Lambie, one of the main witnesses against Slater, that she had 'blundered'; finally, in November, the *Daily News* had a retraction from the other major witness, Mary Barrowman. As a result, the Secretary for Scotland let it be known that the prisoner would be released, and on 15 November 1927 Slater was once again a free man.

The case was remitted to the Scottish Court of Appeal in June 1928, with a full hearing in July. Doyle attended and, while Craigie Aitchison argued the case, was able for the first time to see Slater in the flesh. On 20 July the conviction was quashed, and a few days later Doyle gave his 'last words on the case' in the *Sunday Times*. He asked: Why had the new evidence never been heeded? Both Helen Lambie and Mary Barrowman had shown themselves unreliable from the start and had since retracted their statements; what of Mrs Hamilton, a witness who had seen the murderer and been prepared to swear on oath that it was not Slater? Why had her evidence been disallowed at the original trial? What of Inspector Trench, who had taken evidence from a relative of Miss Gilchrist, a Miss Birrell, who said that Lambie had told her that Miss Gilchrist expected to be murdered, and had also informed her that the murderer was not Slater? What of the brooch which had been used as evidence against Slater, but which was proved to be different from the one thought to be missing from the Gilchrist flat? Doyle hoped that those who were responsible for Slater's ordeal might answer for their actions, and that those people whose lives had been ruined in the attempt to prove his innocence might yet receive compensation: 'And so I retire from a task which has cost me some expense, much time, considerable worry, and no satisfaction, save that the good name of Scottish jurisprudence has been restored.'[252]

There was one final twist. Although Slater was given an *ex gratia* payment of £6,000 by the Government, he was left to pay his own costs, and Doyle, who had made himself responsible for these up to £1,000, expected to be reimbursed. Slater refused. Doyle threatened to take the matter to a court of law but was persuaded to settle the matter amicably: 'It was a painful and sordid aftermath to such a story,' he admitted in the revised edition of his autobiography, 'but I have reflected since that one could hardly go through eighteen years of unjust imprisonment and yet emerge unscathed.'[253] Doyle had, at least, lived long enough to see Slater freed, and he felt that the case had served a useful purpose in that it led to the establishment of the Appeal Court in Scotland. 'Many a poor devil in the future,' he said, 'will see his last chance of safety in the tribunal which had its origin in Oscar Slater's misfortunes.'[254]

Another case which interested Doyle and of which he had the inside story from the American detective, William J.

Burns, was that of Leo Frank, a Jew who had been held for the murder of a child in Atlanta, Georgia. He said of it in 1915:

> In the case of Frank, as of Slater, a case was made up of shreds and patches, a little suspicion here, a racial prejudice there, absolutely false statements as to fact, vague allegations of previous evil conduct, witnesses whose opinions were moulded by suggestion – all the familiar array by which Justice is baffled. The man was condemned to death. And here America showed that it had what England lacks. In England it is only by the long-drawn, inconclusive agitation of a few amateurs that a reversal can be hoped for. In America the friends of the ill-used man can turn to Burns.[255]

In private, Doyle wondered if Slater had not been used as a scapegoat to protect somebody else whose identity was known to the police, and he also wondered if there was any truth in the rumour that Slater was known to have committed a murder and the Gilchrist case was merely used as a means of cornering him. But whatever the truth and whatever his own achievement may have been, his involvement, as the creator of Sherlock Holmes, gave the case a great deal of publicity.

Famous Crimes and Other Mysteries

Doyle's advice was sought in connection with various murder cases and mysteries, and in some he did take an active interest. His name has been mentioned in connection with the disappearance of Camille Cecille Holland. She was a wealthy spinster of fifty-five who in 1898 met and fell under the spell of Samuel Herbert Dougal. The following year they moved to the Moat Farm near Saffron Walden. Although they were not married, Miss Holland let it be known that she would not tolerate Dougal's flirtation with a maid, and shortly afterwards she disappeared. Her whereabouts remained a mystery, though suspicion naturally fell on Dougal, and he was arrested on 19 March 1903 when it was discovered that he had been forging Miss Holland's signature in order to transfer money into his bank account. A search at the farm led to the discovery of the remains of the corpse in an old drainage ditch. Dougal was tried in June 1903 and, having been found guilty, was hanged on 14 July. Before the mystery had been solved, Doyle was one of those who suggested that the corpse might be found at the Moat Farm and he thought the moat might be an obvious place to look.

Doyle's advice was also sought by Sir Arthur Vicars, a distant relative who, as the Ulster King of Arms, had previously helped Doyle's mother to trace her descent. Being also the Knight Attendant on the Order of St Patrick, he was seriously implicated in the theft of the regalia, or Irish Crown Jewels, from Dublin Castle which was made known on 6 July 1907. He refused to attend a Vice-Regal Commission appointed the following January to discover whether he was guilty of negligence, and was thereupon declared guilty and dismissed from his post. Vicars, his half-brother Pierce O'Mahony, and Francis Shackleton, the brother of Ernest Shackleton, were the prime suspects. Although many letters passed between Doyle and Vicars, it was not a case with which he wished his name to be associated as he feared that it would hamper his efforts in the Edalji case by making him appear, in his own words, as a 'universal busybody'. When a rumour of his involvement appeared in the Press he was at pains to deny it.

The 'Brides in the Bath' case is another famous crime which interested Doyle. He is said to have arranged an experiment to see if it were possible for a woman to drown in a bath and, having found that it was not, to have correctly deduced that the various deaths were the work of one man. The enormity of the crime came to light in January 1915 when the father of Alice Burnham read in the *News of the World* of the drowning of Margaret Lofty in her bath; it was so similar to his own daughter's death that he informed the police, and they came across a third victim, Beatrice Mundy, who had died in her bath in July 1912. George Joseph Smith was arrested by Inspector Neil in March 1915 and charged with the three murders.

A famous case which occurred almost on Doyle's doorstep was the murder of Elsie Cameron in December 1924 at Blackness near Crowborough. Bernard Spilsbury was called in and found evidence on which to convict Norman Thorne, or, to give him his full name, John Norman Holmes Thorne. The trial took place in March 1925 and Thorne was sentenced to death. The case went before the Court of Criminal Appeal, where the verdict was upheld. Doyle, like the *Law Journal* and a number of other people, was dissatisfied. He had been over the scene of the crime and his opinion was given in the *Morning Post* on 21 April 1925, the day before Thorne was executed:

> 'I think that there is just one chance in a hundred,' said Sir Arthur to a representative of the *Morning Post* yesterday, 'that Thorne was not guilty of murder, and as long as there is one, I do not think he ought to be hanged. The evidence is strong, but it is circumstantial. Personally, I am against capital punishment except in very extreme cases, and to justify it I think the evidence should be stronger than it was in this case.'[256]

Some cases of people who had disappeared were sent to Doyle as a last resort when the police had been unable to help. A few of these are mentioned in 'Some Personalia about Mr Sherlock Holmes' (below, pp. 277 ff.), and there are sketchy details about others. There was one case where a man had disappeared though was known to have gone to Sweden. When his relatives approached Doyle, they were told that he would be found in a certain part of London, and to their amazement his theory proved correct. There were also local mysteries, such as burglaries, though here, as Doyle admitted, his methods proved less effective.

One of the most curious cases in which Doyle was involved was heard at the Mark Cross Petty Sessions on 22 April 1913 when he spoke in defence of his collie dog, Roy, who was accused by a local farmer of having killed a sheep. Doyle argued that a dog of five or six years old was unlikely to have done so; he pointed out that there were sheep in a field which was closer to his house than the one in which the alleged incident had taken place and that they had never been molested; but his strongest point was that Roy had a disease which prevented him from eating anything hard – even bread had to be soaked. A vet gave evidence of the faulty conformation of the dog's jaw, the bailiff of a local farm was on hand to say that Roy had never interfered with his sheep, and Doyle's chauffeur was prepared to give evidence that the dog had never molested sheep on the road. But, before all the witnesses could be called, the Bench stopped the case, dismissed the summons against Doyle, and vindicated the dog's character. It is probably no coincidence that the devoted wolfhound of Professor Presbury in 'The Adventure of the Creeping Man' should have been given the name Roy. He, it will be recalled, slipped his collar and tried to kill his master or, as Holmes said, the monkey which was masquerading as his master.

Although Doyle built up a large library of books on crime, many of which came from the sale of W. S. Gilbert's collection in 1911, he was never greatly interested in the psychology of the criminal. If he believed a man to be innocent, he felt it his duty to see that justice prevailed; but if he thought him guilty, he had little sympathy. He visited a number of prisons in America and was more often than not appalled at the inhumanity he saw, but his attitude towards 'hardened offenders' was that they should be imprisoned for life. Crime was in his opinion equivalent to a contagious disease, and it was in the interests of society that its carrier should be locked away.

The Case of the Man Who was Wanted

At the beginning of 1911, Doyle received through the post a typed copy of 'The Case of the Man who was Wanted', a rather poor Sherlock Holmes story by a young architect in Barnsley called Arthur Whitaker. Its author, with some effrontery, suggested that Doyle might like to collaborate with him. Doyle replied on 7 March, encouraging Whitaker to change the names and to try and get it published on his own. Collaboration, he said, was out of the question as it would reduce by 75 per cent the price that publishers would be prepared to pay. 'Sometimes,' he continued, 'I am open to purchase ideas which I lay aside and use at my own time in my own way.'[257] He had done so once before and had given ten guineas for an idea; this he would be prepared to do again, though he made it clear that he could not guarantee to use it and that Whitaker could not expect to get any personal credit from it. Whitaker accepted Doyle's offer of ten guineas, which was duly paid on 14 March 1911. He also retained a carbon copy of his story and, fortunately, the letter from Conan Doyle. The story, with its ungainly title and its many inconsistencies, though obviously not by Doyle, was nevertheless published under his name after his death. The mistake was quickly corrected, however, to the relief of those who had read it.

Doyle made no use of the Whitaker story, nor of another similar piece known simply as the 'Plot for Sherlock Holmes story'. Although the second is included in this volume because it has been attributed to Conan Doyle, there can be very little doubt that it was sent to him; it may be that the real author was the recipient of the other ten guineas.

Studies in the Literature of Sherlock Holmes

The honour of being the first true Sherlockian critic is generally given to Frank Sidgwick, whose 'Open Letter to Dr Watson', criticizing the dates in *The Hound of the Baskervilles*, was published in the *Cambridge Review* on 23 January 1902. Andrew Lang, however, in the *Quarterly Review* of July 1904 and in his monthly column for *Longman's Magazine*, proved himself a more worthy critic of Dr Watson. But the first to pay scholarly attention to the entire opus was Ronald Knox. As boys, he and his brothers wrote a critique of *The Sign of Four* which, with five orange pips, they sent to Conan Doyle. As an undergraduate, Knox expanded the original article which, under the title 'Studies in the Literature of Sherlock Holmes', became widely known when he included it in 1928 in his *Essays in Satire*. Using the works of such distinguished commentators as M. Papier Maché and Herr Sauwosch, Knox discussed the textual and chronological problems found in Dr Watson's narratives, and was able to infer, among other things, that Watson, like his brother, had suffered from drink and had in *The Return of Sherlock Holmes* been reduced to patching together clumsy travesties of his earlier experiences. The studies, first read to the Gryphon Society, were published in the Oxford *Blue Book* in July 1912. Knox sent a copy to Conan Doyle, whose reply was delightfully modest and unassuming:

> I cannot help writing to you to tell you of the amusement – and also the amazement – with which I read your article on Sherlock Holmes. That anyone should spend such pains on such material was what surprised me. Certainly you know a great deal more about it than I do, for the stories have been written in a disconnected (and careless) way, without referring back to what had gone before. I am only pleased that you have not found more discrepancies, especially as to dates. Of course, as you seem to have observed, Holmes changed entirely as the

stories went on. In the first one, *The Study in Scarlet*, he was a mere calculating machine, but I had to make him more of an educated human being as I went on with him. He never shows heart – save in the play – which one of your learned commentators condemned truly as a false note.

One point which has not been remarked by the learned Sauwosch . . . is that in a considerable proportion of the stories – I daresay a quarter – no legal crime has been committed at all. Another point – one of the few in which I feel satisfaction but which I have never seen mentioned – is that Watson never for one instant as chorus and chronicler transcends his own limitations. Never once does a flash of wit or wisdom come from him. All is remorselessly eliminated so that he may be Watson.[258]

Doyle then explained – as Holmes had been 'too indolent' to do so himself – about the Priory School bicycle, and he ended, with 'many thanks and renewed amazement', by suggesting that he had said more than enough on the subject. Knox was also later to believe that such critical exegeses were becoming tiresome, but the enthusiasm of other commentators has continued unabated.

221b Baker Street

One of the recurrent problems in Sherlockian scholarship is the actual location of 221b Baker Street. The arguments based upon its proximity to post offices or to Oxford Street need not be mentioned here, but a few theories are, perhaps, relevant. Although Doyle said in his autobiography, 'Many have asked me which house it is, but that is a point which for excellent reasons I will not decide',[259] he did on one occasion, according to Sebastian Lamb, a writer on legal subjects, reveal its whereabouts. They were both walking in

Baker Street when Doyle pointed to No. 61 and said that that was where Holmes lived. This rather contradicted the assertion made in 'The Adventure of the Empty House' that the famous rooms were opposite – or, in the original manuscript, 'exactly opposite' – Camden House. An American, Dr Gray Chandler Briggs, who mapped Baker Street, found Camden House as No. 118, with No. 111 opposite to it. In a letter to Frederic Dorr Steele, on 30 October 1921, he explained that he had revealed his discovery to Conan Doyle, who was 'amazed' to learn that Camden House really existed: 'He told me in such seriousness that I could not doubt him that he did not believe he had ever been on Baker St in his life and if he had it had been many years ago – so long that he had forgotten!'[260] Doyle was probably pulling Briggs's leg as far as the last point was concerned, but the identification of Camden House seemed conclusive.

The son of Doyle's friend Malcolm Morris was later to insist in his book *Back View* that the original house was actually No. 21, as this had once belonged to the Morris family – but the evidence produced by Harold Morris to support his theory is far from conclusive. Those who correspond with Sherlock Holmes today will find that their letters are delivered to a building society who has a legal right to the address. In 1949, one of Doyle's sons sought an injunction against the *London Mystery Magazine* to prevent it from using the address. Justice Wynn-Parry refused to grant it, stating that there was no such address as 221b Baker Street, but that the number was contained in an office block owned by the building society.

Supplementary Sherlock Holmes Stories

In the years before the First World War, Doyle, having already had some success with a one-act play, *Waterloo*, emerged as a dramatist. There was *Brigadier Gerard*, then *The*

Fires of Fate (based on *The Tragedy of the Korosko*), and in 1910 he took the gamble of producing a boxing play, *The House of Temperley*; its failure led to the new Sherlock Holmes play, *The Speckled Band*, or, as it was first known, *The Stonor Case*. As well as the Edalji and Slater cases, he was active in his condemnation of the Belgian misrule of the Congo and was a fundraiser for the British team in the doomed 1916 Berlin Olympics. He also found time to write a few supplementary Sherlock Holmes stories, the first of which, 'Wisteria Lodge', reached the editor of the *Strand Magazine* shortly after Easter in 1908. Doyle confessed that he had found it a difficult story to write, but, he said, 'I have done my best.'[261] He also solved the problem which had been worrying Greenhough Smith since Sidney Paget's death at the beginning of the year by choosing Arthur Twidle as the illustrator. Doyle had been delighted with the artwork Twidle had done for *Sir Nigel*; he was also responsible for the illustrations in the Author's Edition and so had already done drawings for the Sherlock Holmes stories.

Doyle's interest in real crime provided useful ideas for the new stories. As well as the Merstham Tunnel Mystery, for example, the theft of the Irish Crown Jewels could well lie behind 'The Adventure of the Bruce-Partington Plans'. Smith was even to suggest that Doyle might use his experiences in the Edalji and Slater cases as the basis for some story, though Doyle felt that, in the case of Slater at least, the subject was too delicate and too near to self-advertisement.

After an operation at the beginning of 1909, Doyle went to Cornwall. This enabled him to gather data, as well as learning a little Cornish, with the result that he wrote a Holmes story concerning a 'Cornish Horror'. The special publicity which it received was unprecedented, as, on 7 December 1910, the first and, it seems, the only issue of the *Daily Strand* was primarily devoted to it. The illustrated 'tabloid' newspaper, marked 'Priceless', carried the head-

line: 'Mysterious Horror in Cornwall'; below it there were six
'Striking photographs from the scene of the crime'. One
showed 'The Rev. Mr Roundhay (nearest the camera)
telling of the discovery of the crime', and another was of
'The man in charge of the investigations' – he needed no
introduction. Inside there were further details, but the full
story was only to be found in the *Strand Magazine*, which
contained an eye-witness account by Dr Watson which he
had entitled 'The Adventure of the Devil's Foot'. There
were two further cases the following year and one a year
later. Then in 1913 came 'The Adventure of the Dying
Detective'. Its title at first caused some alarm, as it was feared
that Holmes's death might be imminent, but it was soon
learnt that he was neither dead nor dying. 'The day when
Holmes will really die,' Doyle told Greenhough Smith on
one occasion, 'will be the day when I think that I am letting
him down.'[262]

The Valley of Fear

If Greenhough Smith had any worries, they were dispelled at
the beginning of 1914 when Doyle let him know that he was
working on a new Sherlock Holmes novel. Smith asked for
information, and on 6 February Doyle replied:

> The *Strand* are paying so high a price for this story that I
> should be churlish indeed if I refused any possible informa-
> tion.
> The name, I think, will be *The Valley of Fear*. Speaking
> from what seem the present probabilities it should run to
> not less than 50,000 words. I have done nearly 25,000, I
> reckon roughly. With luck I should finish before the end
> of March.
> As in the *Study in Scarlet* the plot goes to America for *at
> least* half the book while it recounts the events which led
> up to the crime in England which has engaged Holmes's

services. You will remember that in *S in S* it was a Mormon drama. In this case it is the Molly McQuire Outrages in the Coalfields of Pennsylvania tho' I change all names so as not to get into possible Irish politics. This part of the story will contain one surprise which I hope will be a real staggerer to the most confirmed reader. But of course in this long stretch we abandon Holmes. That is necessary.

Across the top of the letter, he put: 'I fancy this is my swan-song in Fiction.'[263] As this was not what Greenhough Smith wished to hear, he asked for an explanation. 'As to the "swan-song" or goose cackle what I mean,' said Doyle, 'is that if I had a good competence I would devote myself to serious literary or historical work.'[264] He then explained that his procedure had been to write two opening Sherlock chapters and then to branch off into the American section; this made it difficult for him to send anything which would not give a false impression. But he promised to concentrate on the first part. By 23 March he had reached the 50,000-word mark, and the book was finished at the beginning of April. A number of changes were made in the month which followed for reasons of greater accuracy, and further changes were deemed necessary in England when war was declared. Those of German origin, for example, changed their nationality and became Swedish.

The Valley of Fear is based on the exploits of James McParlan in the coal region of Pennsylvania as recorded by Allan Pinkerton in *The Mollie Maguires and the Detectives*, and also, perhaps, in F. P. Dewees' *The Molly Maguires. The Origin, Growth, and Character of the Organization*, both published in 1877. But Doyle was very anxious to conceal the source so that he did not become involved in Irish politics. He insisted that the publicity should give no reference to the organization:

One word about the Molly McQuires would in my

opinion be most dangerous. It was an Irish organization and the Irish are exceedingly touchy upon the point. I make it vague & international with nothing to offend anyone. It would be a *most serious error* to be definite in the matter. Any advance matter must be *very* cautiously done & should pass my censorship.[265]

His attempt to conceal the origin had very little effect in America. The New York *Bookman*, for example, in April 1915 suggested that Doyle might have made some use of his conversations with the private detective William J. Burns, but believed there were 'reasons for thinking that the proto-types of the Scowrers were the Molly Maguires of former days'.[266] Doyle may have discussed the case with Burns in 1913, and it is highly likely that Burns suggested one or two alterations when the two men met in New York the following year – but it would also appear that Doyle had received a first-hand account from William Pinkerton, whom he met on a Transatlantic crossing. The 'Sherlock Holmes of America' was extremely annoyed when he saw the book and found that there was no mention of Pinkerton and no acknowl-edgement. His general manager, Ralph Dudley, recalled:

> W.A.P. raised the roof when he saw the book. At first he talked of bringing a suit against Doyle but then dropped that after he had cooled off. What made him angry was the fact that even if Doyle was fictionizing the story, he didn't have the courtesy to ask his permission to use a confiden-tial discussion for his work. They had been good friends before but from that day on their relationship was strained. Mr Doyle sent several notes trying to soothe things over and while W.A.P. sent him courteous replies he never regarded Mr Doyle with the same warmth.[267]

Due acknowledgement was given in the preface to the 1929 omnibus volume, where Doyle stated that the book had 'had its origin through my reading a graphic account of the Molly

McQuire outrages in the coalfields of Pennsylvania, when a young detective drawn from Pinkerton's Agency acted exactly as the hero is represented as doing'.[268]

The first part of the new serial appeared in September 1914, and the *Strand Magazine* commissioned a special coloured frontispiece for it from Frank Wiles. This was sent to Doyle, who wrote on the back: 'This comes nearest to my conception of what Holmes really looks like.'[269] Whether he meant that it was the best drawing he had ever seen or merely the best of a batch which had been sent is not known.

The War Service of Sherlock Holmes

With the outbreak of hostilities in August 1914, the country was gripped by war fever, and spies and suspected spies were being rounded up in droves. Among them was William Gillette, who found himself stranded in London. Having moved from the Savoy to the Palais Royal in Kensington, he returned one day to find two detectives awaiting him who had already been through his papers and discovered a plan of the British Embassy in Paris (which Gillette had acquired for use in the play, *Diplomacy*). Gillette urged the detectives to ring Conan Doyle, and this they eventually did, saving Gillette the indignity of being hauled off to Scotland Yard. A German Secret Service man was less fortunate. He had established an office at Stanley House, Sherwood Street, Piccadilly, where he operated as a moneylender using, on a brass plate outside, the inconspicuous name 'Sherlock Holmes'. Others before him had masqueraded as the great detective, the strangest being a certain Stephen Sharp who, it is said, became convinced that he actually was Sherlock Holmes and therefore made many urgent efforts to see Conan Doyle. Eventually the police had to be brought in to dissuade him, but even then he sent a number of threatening letters. But when the war came there was no doubt on which side Mr Holmes would be fighting. 'We feel sure that he has long since answered the call to the colours and is serving in that high capacity for which he is so admirably fitted,'[270] said the American *Bookman* in December 1914.

Conan Doyle was content to leave Sherlock Holmes to work behind the scenes while he busied himself with rifle clubs, propaganda, and research for a history of the British campaign in France and Flanders. In June 1916 he was invited to visit the Italian front, and this encouraged him to seek and obtain permission to go behind the French and British lines as well. In France he had an opportunity of seeing his son and also his secretary. The menu for a banquet held there in his honour, specially designed by an orderly called Muiremont, was later described by Robert Donald, the editor of the *Daily Chronicle*, who had arranged Doyle's visit:

> The medallion at the top represents the Sherlock Holmes coat-of-arms – a revolver, a pipe, and a violin. The lion and the unicorn are seen in the top corners, and the thistle and the shamrock at the bottom, while in the centre are the German and Austrian eagles, represented as being hanged.[271]

Among the guests was General Humbert, of whom Doyle said:

> He fires his remarks like pistol shots at this man or that. Once to my horror he fixed me with his hard little eyes and demanded, 'Sherlock Holmes, est ce qu'il est un soldat dans l'armée Anglaise?' The whole table waited in an awful hush. 'Mais, mon général,' I stammered, 'il est trop vieux pour service.' There was general laughter, and I felt that I had scrambled out of an awkward place.[272]

Sherlock Holmes had already infiltrated the German lines, as Doyle had sent news to prisoners of war by pricking out words on the pages of *The Valley of Fear*. But it was left to others to suggest what Holmes might be doing. The *Sketch*, for example, on 28 July 1915 reproduced illustrations of a 'Musical Farce in Seven Paroxysms Aboard Ship' which had been attended by Admiral Jellicoe and some eight hundred officers and which showed Sherlock Holmes and Dr Watson in pursuit of a German submarine. Finally Conan Doyle decided to reveal the true story of how Holmes had come to the aid of his country, and on 7 March 1917 completed 'His Last Bow', which he subtitled 'An Epilogue of Sherlock Holmes'. He felt that it was one of his most important stories and therefore one over which it was worth spending a considerable amount of time. His anxiety lest the artist give away the identity of 'Altamont' and other problems delayed its publication until September 1917. In the magazine, at Doyle's own suggestion, it was given the subtitle 'The War Service of Sherlock Holmes', while the cover proclaimed 'Sherlock Holmes outwits a German spy'.

'His Last Bow' gave its name to the fourth collection of short stories, published on 22 October 1917. It included 'The Adventure of the Cardboard Box', which had appeared in the *Strand Magazine* in January 1893. Doyle had excluded it from *The Memoirs of Sherlock Holmes* – at least from all but the first American edition – and had transferred the opening sequence to 'The Adventure of the Resident Patient'. This mind-reading episode now reappeared in its original place. The omission of the story had intrigued a number of people, such as Arthur Bartlett Maurice, who gave it the status of a 'suppressed'[273] story, but when they read it, they remained uncertain as to why Doyle had originally excluded it.

After reading *His Last Bow*, Vincent Starrett wrote an article 'In Praise of Sherlock Holmes' which he subsequently sent to Conan Doyle. As he was to become one of the most distinguished Sherlockians and the author most responsible for the revival of interest in Sherlock Holmes after Doyle's death, the letter which he received in reply is of some interest:

> Dear Mr Vincent Starrett
>
> It was really very kind of you to write so heartily about Holmes. My own feelings towards him are rather mixed as I feel that he has obscured a good deal of my more serious work, but that no doubt will right itself in time – or if not, it does not really matter. I am so busy with my history of the war, and see so clearly how many changes, additions &c will be needed, that I feel I have mortgaged the rest of my life, but really I could not have done so to a better cause. To drop a leaf of laurel on our dead boys would be the best top up to my life's work I could imagine.
>
> Yours sincerely, A. Conan Doyle[274]

The Disappearance of Agatha Christie

By 1920 Doyle had completed his history of the war and had turned his attention to the subject of spiritualism, but Sherlock Holmes refused to stay in retirement. First there was the new series of films with Eille Norwood, then Doyle's own play, *The Crown Diamond*, which inspired or was inspired by 'The Adventure of the Mazarin Stone'; then there was a speech to be given at the 1921 Stoll Convention Dinner; and, as before, there were various ideas which he felt must be used for new Sherlock Holmes stories. He was also asked to write a 'book' for the Queen's Dolls' House. But, although Holmes was never forgotten, most of Doyle's time was occupied in travelling, lecturing, and studying with the aim of spreading and popularizing the psychic revelation.

The tracing of crime was one area where spiritualism could offer help. In 1920 Doyle wrote an article entitled 'A New Light on Old Crimes' which described how mysteries had been solved by mediums, and when he was in Australia shortly afterwards he met a successful psychometrist who had been able to trace a missing man merely by using a boot which had belonged to him. When Oscar Gray, a seventeen-year-old schoolboy, disappeared from Liverpool Street Station on 15 September 1921, Doyle's advice was sought by the parents. He contacted two trained clairvoyantes and presented them with a coat which had belonged to the boy. 'The results were by no means perfect,' he admitted in a letter to the *Daily Express*, 'but I am sure that Mr and Mrs Gray found consolation in them, and in some ways they were very accurate.'[275] The boy was discovered on 16 October having enlisted as a private in the Royal Engineers under an assumed name. The clairvoyantes had been able to state that he was alive and that he would be found, but they could not say where. As he was discovered at Crowborough, almost within sight of Doyle's house, it was a rather unimpressive example of the power of psychometry.

A far more famous disappearance was that of Agatha Christie who, having had an argument with her husband, left her house on 6 December 1926; her car was found abandoned in a quarry on the Surrey Downs. Doyle obtained a glove which belonged to her and showed it to Horace Leaf, who informed him that the lady was not dead and that she would be heard of within a few days. She was then discovered to be at a hotel in Harrogate. Doyle announced his findings after the mystery had been solved, when they were of very little interest, but he was convinced that they were genuine and that psychometry had a great potential: 'Now supposing that instead of being the glove of an innocent lady, it had been the weapon of an assassin, or the coat of his victim, is there any reason why the result should not have been equally accurate?'[276] The psychometrist would, he believed, be part of every well-equipped police station in the future. The police, however, were not greatly impressed. 'The whole thing is absolute bunkum,' said the Chief Constable of Salford when shown Doyle's letter in the *Morning Post* about

the Christie case; and a 'high police official' in London
exclaimed: 'We do not keep hopeless lunatics in the police
forces of this country.'[277]

The Last Sherlock Holmes Stories

Conan Doyle was the main guest at the Savage Club Dinner
on 5 December 1925. The illustrated menu drawn in his
honour shows Sherlock Holmes ascending the guillotine
platform, saying to Sidney Carton: 'They've got the wrong
man.' Carton answers: 'I know; but it is the only way.' In
fact, as far as Conan Doyle was concerned, the only way of
ending Sherlock Holmes was by writing a sufficient number
of stories to produce a final volume. Six had been written by
the beginning of 1925, then at the end of the following year
he agreed to do a final series of six. These began publication
in October 1926 with 'The Adventure of the Three Gables',
followed by two which had Sherlock Holmes as the narrator.
They were not the most successful, but they were not, the
author hoped, as bad as some people were making out. One
of those who complained was John Gore, and Doyle replied
to the criticism by saying:

> I read with interest, and without offence, your remarks
> about the Holmes stories. I could not be offended for I
> have never taken them seriously myself. But still even in
> the humblest things there are degrees, and I wonder
> whether the smaller impression which they produce upon
> you may not be due to the fact that we become blasé and
> stale ourselves as we grow older. My own youthful
> favourites no longer appeal.
>
> I test the Holmes stories by their effect on fresh young
> minds and I find that they stand that test well. I believe in
> my own critical capacity, for it is very detached, and if I
> were to choose the six best Holmes stories I should
> certainly include 'The Illustrious Client' which is one of

the last series, and also 'The Lion's Mane' which is the next to appear. 'The Noble Bachelor' which you quote would be about bottom of the list.

I have always said that I would utterly abolish him the moment he got below his level, but up to now, save for your note (which may perhaps prove symptomatic) I have seen no sign that he has lost his grip.[278]

'After Thirty-five Years', the leader in *The Times* of 10 December 1926, was far more appreciative, saying of Sherlock Holmes: 'To whom else has it been given to share life so long with so persistent, though fictitious, a contemporary? For though Watson is no more, Holmes, as can be gathered from the magazine to which he has been steadily faithful – the *Strand* – is still bee-farming in Sussex, and in his green old age, for he must be over seventy, has broken the habit of a lifetime by becoming his own biographer. His creator ought indeed to be proud of him.'[279] When this appeared Doyle had just finished the last story. He had told Greenhough Smith that the main difficulty was finding suitable plots, and Smith had sent some ideas of his own. Thanking him for these and commenting on the new stories Doyle said:

These ideas are admirable – especially the paper house. But I don't see that I could use them. I am engaged on what I hope will work out as the sixth of the S.H. series, 'The Adventure of the Black Spaniel'. I honestly think that these six will compare in plot and treatment with any consecutive six I have done. At the same time I cannot hide from myself that the public has lost the sense of novelty with Holmes and his methods. This has been helped by the repeated Parodies. Therefore even if I could keep him on the same level I can't expect, do what I will, to produce the same effect.[280]

The story to which he referred was eventually to be known as 'The Adventure of Shoscombe Old Place', though on the manuscript he put 'The Adventure of Shoscombe Abbey'. It was published in the *Strand Magazine* in April 1927, the last to appear there, though Doyle had devised a competition, announced the previous month, to discover which stories were considered the best and to see if he really was as impartial a judge as he liked to believe. The results and his list with the reasons for his choice appeared in June 1927, and that was his last contribution about Sherlock Holmes, but of this he was unaware when in December 1926 he had written to announce that the very last story had been completed:

> My dear Smith,
>   I hear that *The Times* has been handing it out *in a leader* to me, Holmes, and the *Strand*. It will do no harm. I have done the sixth Sherlock, 'The Adventure of Shoscombe Abbey'. It's not of the first flight, and Sherlock, like his Author, grows a little stiff in the joints, but it is the best I can do. Now farewell to him for ever!
>   Yours always, A. Conan Doyle[281]

In July 1930 the world learnt that Conan Doyle, the creator of Sherlock Holmes, was dead. Two months earlier he had made a recording in the Small Queen's Hall in Regent Street for His Master's Voice, and when this was released after his death it served as an epitaph, for one side contained an explanation of how he had come to write the Sherlock Holmes stories. He said:

> With regard to Sherlock Holmes I was, when I wrote it, a young doctor, and had been educated in a very severe and critical medical school of thought, especially coming under the influence of Dr Bell, of Edinburgh, who had most remarkable powers of observation. He prided himself that when he looked at a patient, he could tell not only their disease but very often their occupation and place of residence. Reading some detective stories I was struck by

the fact that their results were obtained in nearly every case by chance – I except, of course, Edgar Allan Poe's splendid stories, which, though only three in number, are a model for all time. I thought I would try my hand at writing a story where the hero would treat crime as Dr Bell treated disease, and where science would take the place of chance. The result was Sherlock Holmes, and I confess that result has surprised me very much, for I learn that many schools of detection working in France, in Egypt, in China and elsewhere have admittedly founded their system upon that of Holmes. To many he seems to be a real person; and I have had numerous letters from time to time addressed to him from all parts of the world, and the most quaint requests, including what was virtually an offer of marriage. His autograph also is much in demand. [282]

These were his last words about Sherlock Holmes; they echoed what he had said previously in a talking film produced during the summer of 1927 by Jack Connolly for Movietone News. Against the background of his New Forest house, Conan Doyle recalled how the Holmes stories had come about and how the example of Joseph Bell had suggested to him that scientific reasoning might be applied to the study of crime. He had first thought out the hundred little dodges and touches by which his detective might reach his conclusions, and had then written the stories:

At first, I think, they attracted a little, very little, attention. But after a time, when I began the short *Adventures*, one after the other, coming out month after month in the *Strand Magazine*, people began to recognize that it was different to the old detective, that there was something there that was new. They began to buy the magazine, and it prospered, and so, I may say, did I. We both came along together, and from that time Sherlock Holmes fairly took root. I've written a good deal more about him than I ever intended to do, but my hand has been rather forced by kind friends who continually wanted to know more. And so it is that this monstrous growth has come out, out of what was really a comparatively small seed.[283]

What Doyle had written about Sherlock Holmes, other than the stories themselves, is what follows. Few people will consider that he said too much, and many will be grateful to his friends for having forced his hand by continually wanting to know more.

THE FIELD BAZAAR

The Field Bazaar, modelled on an earlier Union Bazaar, was held in the Music Hall of Edinburgh University on 19, 20, and 21 November 1896 to raise money to build and equip a sports pavilion for a new playing field near the Craiglockhart Station. The stalls contained a wide variety of goods from all over the world, and there were military bands, a demonstration of Röntgen rays, concerts and a *café chantant*, as well as a special Theatre of Varieties. The fair was opened on the first day by the Chancellor of the University, A. J. Balfour, and on the second by the Lord Provost. Over £3,000 was raised by the five hundred or so students who attended (a third of the total number) and by members of the general public.

Instead of a souvenir album, there was a special Bazaar Number of the *Student* with contributions by Robert Barr, J. M. Barrie, Walter Besant, Professor Blackie, S. R. Crockett, Sir William Muir, Professor Saintsbury, Jessie M. E. Saxby, Israel Zangwill, and Conan Doyle – a list which few other magazines could have rivalled. It was published on 14 November (though dated 20 November) and cost a shilling. It was so successful that a second printing was needed to meet the demand.

It had been rumoured that Conan Doyle would actually revive Sherlock Holmes, but though he did not do so, his gentle and affectionate parody was very relevant to the occasion. Holmes should, however, have spoken of equipping a new athletics ground rather than of extending a cricket field, as it was, at the time of the bazaar, laid out as two Rugby pitches and one Association Football pitch.

'The Field Bazaar' was Doyle's first contribution to the *Student*. His only other piece was a letter written in 1915 in honour of the students and graduates who were sacrificing their lives for their country; but, as a graduate of the University and, after 7 April 1905, also an honorary graduate, his name did appear in the magazine. 'The careful reader could tell from nearly every one of his novels,' said the *Student* on 10 February 1892, 'that the writer was educated in every department of medical knowledge'; and recalled: 'During his student days Mr Doyle took a great interest in athletics, and has played both cricket and football in the University teams.'[284]

On 20 November 1896 Doyle was at the Omar Khayyam Club and so could not attend the bazaar in person.

The first separate edition of 'The Field Bazaar', in an edition of 100 copies, was privately printed in England by the Athenaeum Press for A. G. Macdonnell, who took copies to America for distribution at the first state dinner of the Baker Street Irregulars in 1934. A hardback edition, limited to 250 numbered (and 25 unnumbered) copies, was published on 1 July 1947 by Edgar Smith's Pamphlet House, the exclusive distribution rights being held by Ben Abrahamson's Argus Bookshop in Chicago.

'I should certainly do it,' said Sherlock Holmes.

I started at the interruption, for my companion had been eating his breakfast with his attention entirely centred upon the paper which was propped up by the coffee pot. Now I looked across at him to find his eyes fastened upon me with the half-amused, half-questioning expression which he usually assumed when he felt that he had made an intellectual point.

'Do what?' I asked.

He smiled as he took his slipper from the mantelpiece and drew from it enough shag tobacco to fill the old clay pipe with which he invariably rounded off his breakfast.

'A most characteristic question of yours, Watson,' said he. 'You will not, I am sure, be offended if I say that any reputation for sharpness which I may possess has been entirely gained by the admirable foil which you have made for me. Have I not heard of débutantes who have insisted upon plainness in their chaperones? There is a certain analogy.'

Our long companionship in the Baker Street rooms had left us on those easy terms of intimacy when much may be said without offence. And yet I acknowledge that I was nettled at his remark.

'I may be very obtuse,' said I, 'but I confess that I am unable to see how you have managed to know that I was . . . I was . . .'

'Asked to help in the Edinburgh University Bazaar.'

'Precisely. The letter has only just come to hand, and I have not spoken to you since.'

'In spite of that,' said Holmes, leaning back in his chair and putting his finger tips together, 'I would even venture to suggest that the object of the bazaar is to enlarge the University cricket field.'

I looked at him in such bewilderment that he vibrated with silent laughter.

'The fact is, my dear Watson, that you are an excellent subject,' said he. 'You are never *blasé*. You respond instantly to any external stimulus. Your mental processes may be slow but they are never obscure, and I found during breakfast that you were easier reading than the leader in *The Times* in front of me.'

'I should be glad to know how you arrived at your conclusions,' said I.

'I fear that my good nature in giving explanations has seriously compromised my reputation,' said Holmes. 'But in this case the train of reasoning is based upon such obvious facts that no credit can be claimed for it. You entered the room with a thoughtful expression, the expression of a man who is debating some point in his mind. In your hand you held a solitary letter. Now last night you retired in the best of spirits, so it was clear that it was this letter in your hand which had caused the change in you.'

'This is obvious.'

'It is all obvious when it is explained to you. I naturally asked myself what the letter could contain which might have this effect upon you. As you walked you held the flap side of the envelope towards me, and I saw upon it the same shield-shaped device which I have observed upon your old college cricket cap. It was clear, then, that the request came from Edinburgh University – or from some club connected with the University. When you reached the table you laid down the letter beside your plate with the address upper-most, and you walked over to look at the framed photograph upon the left of the mantelpiece.'

It amazed me to see the accuracy with which he had observed my movements. 'What next?' I asked.

'I began by glancing at the address, and I could tell, even at the distance of six feet, that it was an unofficial communication. This I gathered from the use of the word 'Doctor' upon the address, to which, as a Bachelor of Medicine, you have no legal claim. I knew that University officials are pedantic in their correct use of titles, and I was thus enabled to say with certainty that your letter was unofficial. When on your return to the table you turned over your letter and allowed me to perceive that the enclosure was a printed one, the idea of a bazaar first occurred to me. I had already weighed the possibility of its being a political communication, but this seemed improbable in the present stagnant condition of politics.

'When you returned to the table your face still retained its expression, and it was evident that your examination of the photograph had not changed the current of your thoughts. In that case it must itself bear upon the subject in question. I turned my attention to the photograph therefore, and saw at once that it consisted of yourself as a member of the Edinburgh University Eleven, with the pavilion and cricket-field in the background. My small experience of cricket clubs has taught me that next to churches and cavalry ensigns they are the most debt-laden things upon earth. When upon your return to the table I saw you take out your pencil and draw lines upon the envelope, I was convinced that you were endeavouring to realize some projected improvement which was to be brought about by a bazaar. Your face still showed some indecision, so that I was able to break in upon you with my advice that you should assist in so good an object.'

I could not help smiling at the extreme simplicity of his explanation.

'Of course, it was as easy as possible,' said I.

My remark appeared to nettle him.

'I may add,' said he, 'that the particular help which you have been asked to give was that you should write in their album, and that you have already made up your mind that the present incident will be the subject of your article.'

'But how —!' I cried.

'It is as easy as possible,' said he, 'and I leave its solution to your own ingenuity. In the meantime,' he added, raising his paper, 'you will excuse me if I return to this very interesting article upon the trees of Cremona, and the exact reasons for their pre-eminence in the manufacture of violins. It is one of those small outlying problems to which I am sometimes tempted to direct my attention.'

HOW WATSON LEARNED
THE TRICK

The decision to build a Dolls' House for the Queen was taken in 1920. Designed by Sir Edwin Lutyens, the architect of New Delhi, who produced the first plans in the spring of the following year, it was completed in 1924. As a gift to Queen Mary from the people of Great Britain, it was on display at the British Empire Exhibition at Wembley, and was afterwards moved to Windsor Castle.

The library is on the ground floor and is entered through a door to the right of the main hall, though it can be seen to its best advantage when the outer walls are raised. It is panelled in walnut and divided by columns at either end; the bookshelves are on each side of the fireplace and against the side walls. There is a painted ceiling by William Walcot, and the pictures are by Frank Reynolds, Arthur Cope, and William Nicholson. The room is richly furnished with cabinets of drawings, globes, and other objects suitable for a Royal library, while the books include printed editions of the classics and original manuscript works by the leading authors of the day.

The honorary librarian was Princess Marie Louise, and she was responsible for the acquisition of the manuscripts. She wrote to each of the authors, who were to include Barrie, Conrad, Hardy, Kipling, and Somerset Maugham, asking them to contribute. The letter to

Conan Doyle, from the Ambassadors' Court at St James's Palace, was dated 29 August 1922:

> Dear Sir Arthur
>
> You have doubtless heard that a number of artists, authors, craftsmen and others have conspired to present to the Queen a Dolls' House or model residence in miniature, in which everything that one would find in a King's Palace today is reproduced with minute accuracy so that it will have a great historical value in the future.
>
> For the Library little books in the autograph of their writers are being prepared and will be specially bound.
>
> May I ask if you will be so good as to contribute one of these; either something already published which I would ask you to be so kind as to copy out, or preferably something original? I enclose a small blank book for the purpose.
>
> Believe me
Yours sincerely
Marie Louise[285]

Conan Doyle used his blank book for a parody of Sherlock Holmes. The manuscript covers thirty-four pages, and there are three blank pages at the beginning and end. Although the scale of the Dolls' House was one inch to a foot, some leeway was allowed so that the authors would have sufficient room to use their own hand-writing, but even so the book is only an inch and a half high, an inch and a quarter wide, and half an inch thick. The 'Unpublished Novelette', as Doyle called it in a covering letter, was bound by Sangorski and Sutcliffe. It is in red leather with gilt borders on the upper and lower covers; the upper one is embossed with the Queen's cipher and crown, and both covers have three dots set into each corner. The spine is divided by ribbing into five panels, each edged in gilt, with the title in the one second

from the top: HOW WATSON / LEARNED / THE TRICK;
and the author's name in the one below: CONAN /
DOYLE.

The parody was included in *The Book of the Queen's
Dolls' House Library* which was edited by E. V. Lucas and
published in June 1924 as a companion volume to *The
Book of the Queen's Dolls' House*; the two volumes came in
a cardboard slipcase and were limited to 1,500 copies.
Permission to include the piece had been given by Major
A. H. Wood, Doyle's private secretary, in a letter dated
28 May 1923. Doyle himself was in America, but his
secretary felt sure that he would 'be glad for you to act as
you wish with reference to the publication of his
booklet'.[286]

The American publication rights were held by
Frederick A. Stokes Company, and, with their permission, 'How Watson Learned the Trick' was reprinted in
the *New York Times* on 24 August 1924. It was first issued
separately, with the imprint of 'Camden House', Chicago, in September 1947 in an edition of 60 copies
privately printed for Robert J. Bayer and Vincent
Starrett.

Watson had been watching his companion intently ever
since he had sat down to the breakfast table. Holmes
happened to look up and catch his eye.

'Well, Watson, what are you thinking about?' he asked.

'About you.'

'Me?'

'Yes, Holmes, I was thinking how superficial are those
tricks of yours, and how wonderful it is that the public should
continue to show interest in them.'

'I quite agree,' said Holmes. 'In fact, I have a recollection
that I have myself made a similar remark.'

'Your methods,' said Watson severely, 'are really easily
acquired.'

'No doubt,' Holmes answered with a smile. 'Perhaps you will yourself give an example of this method of reasoning.'

'With pleasure,' said Watson. 'I am able to say that you were greatly preoccupied when you got up this morning.'

'Excellent!' said Holmes. 'How could you possibly know that?'

'Because you are usually a very tidy man and yet you have forgotten to shave.'

'Dear me! How very clever!' said Holmes. 'I had no idea, Watson, that you were so apt a pupil. Has your eagle eye detected anything more?'

'Yes, Holmes. You have a client named Barlow, and you have not been successful in his case.'

'Dear me, how could you know that?'

'I saw the name outside his envelope. When you opened it you gave a groan and thrust it into your pocket with a frown on your face.'

'Admirable! You are indeed observant. Any other point?'

'I fear, Holmes, that you have taken to financial speculation.'

'Hou *could* you tell that, Watson?'

'You opened the paper, turned to the financial page, and gave a loud exclamation of interest.'

'Well, that is very clever of you, Watson. Any more?'

'Yes, Holmes, you have put on your black coat, instead of your dressing gown, which proves that you are expecting some important visitor at once.'

'Anything more?'

'I have no doubt that I could find other points, Holmes, but I only give you these few, in order to show you that there are other people in the world who can be as clever as you.'

'And some not so clever,' said Holmes. 'I admit that they are few, but I am afraid, my dear Watson, that I must count you among them.'

'What do you mean, Holmes?'

'Well, my dear fellow, I fear your deductions have not been so happy as I should have wished.'

'You mean that I was mistaken.'

'Just a little that way, I fear. Let us take the points in their order: I did not shave because I have sent my razor to be sharpened. I put on my coat because I have, worse luck, an early meeting with my dentist. His name is Barlow, and the letter was to confirm the appointment. The cricket page is beside the financial one, and I turned to it to find if Surrey was holding its own against Kent. But go on, Watson, go on! It's a very superficial trick, and no doubt you will soon acquire it.'

TO AN UNDISCERNING CRITIC

'To an Undiscerning Critic' was written as a reply to one of Arthur Guiterman's 'Letters to the Literati' addressed 'To Sir Arthur Conan Doyle' which was first published in *Life*, New York, on 5 December 1912, then in *London Opinion* on 14 December 1912, and which was collected in 1915 in Guiterman's volume *The Laughing Muse*.

Two small changes were made to Guiterman's poem by Lincoln Springfield, the editor of *London Opinion*, and as this text was the one which Conan Doyle saw, these have been retained. In line 20, where Guiterman referred to Doyle's pamphlet, *The War in South Africa*, as a vindication of the South African war and as proof that it was not 'an atrocity', the poet originally put in parentheses 'as most of us think'; this became 'as some of us think'; and in line 36, Springfield changed 'More than a trifle to Poe and Gaboriau' to 'Clearly a trifle to Poe and Gaboriau'.

Lincoln Springfield had been interested in Sherlock Holmes since 1893 when he interviewed Joseph Bell for the *Pall Mall Gazette*. He might have brought the poem to Doyle's attention, or it may be that Doyle came across it independently. The reply was published in *London Opinion* on 28 December 1912, and was prefaced by a short note: 'In "LO" the week before last appeared one of our "Letters to the Literati", mixing admiration and gentle criticism in a rhymed address to Sir Arthur Conan Doyle. Sir Arthur sends me the following spirited reply.'

Although Doyle did have a copy of the poem in his scrapbook and mentioned it in his speech at the 1921 Stoll Convention Dinner, it was Springfield who kept it before the public by reprinting it in his autobiography, *Some Piquant People*, which was published in 1924.

The allusions in the poem to Poe and Gaboriau are based on the comments made by Sherlock Holmes in *A Study in Scarlet*. Guiterman's comparison between Doyle and Maurice Hewlett is explained by the fact that Hewlett had been an earlier recipient of one of his 'Letters'.

Letters to the Literati

To Sir Arthur Conan Doyle

Gentle Sir Conan, I'll venture that few have been
Half as prodigiously lucky as you have been.
Fortune, the flirt! has been wondrously kind to you,
Ever beneficent, sweet and refined to you.

Doomed though you seemed – one might swear without
    perjury –
Doomed to the practice of physic and surgery,
Yet, growing weary of pills and physicianing,
Off to the Arctic you packed expeditioning.

Roving and dreaming, Ambition, that heady sin,
Gave you a spirit too restless for medicine;
That, I presume, as Romance is the quest of us,
Made you an Author – the same as the rest of us.

Ah, but the rest of us clamour distressfully,
'How do you manage the game so successfully?
Tell us, disclose to us how under Heaven you
Squeeze from the inkpot so splendid a revenue!'

Then, when you'd published your volume that vindicates
England's South African raid (or the Syndicate's),
Pleading that Britain's extreme bellicosity
Wasn't (as some of us think) an atrocity –

Straightway they gave you a cross with a chain to it –
(Oh, what an honour! I could not attain to it,
Not if I lived to the age of Methusalem!)
Made you a Knight of St John of Jerusalem!

Faith! as a teller of tales you've the trick with you!
Still there's a bone I've been longing to pick with you:

Holmes is your hero of drama and serial;
All of us know where you dug your material
Whence he was moulded – 'tis almost a platitude;
Yet your detective, in shameless ingratitude –

Sherlock your sleuthhound, with motives ulterior,
Sneers at Poe's 'Dupin' as 'very inferior'!
Labels Gaboriau's clever 'Lecoq', indeed,
Merely 'a bungler', a creature to mock, indeed!

This, when your plots and your methods in story owe
Clearly a trifle to Poe and Gaboriau,
Sets all the Muses of Helicon sorrowing.
Borrow, Sir Knight, but be candid in borrowing!

Still let us own that your bent is a cheery one,
Little you've written to bore or to weary one,
Plenty that's slovenly, nothing with harm in it,
Much with abundance of vigour and charm in it.

Give me detectives with brains analytical
Rather than weaklings with morals mephitical –
Stories of battles and man's intrepidity
Rather than wails of neurotic morbidity!

Give me adventures and fierce dinotheriums
Rather than Hewlett's ecstatic deliriums!
Frankly, Sir Conan, some hours I've eased with you
And, on the whole, I am pretty well pleased with you.

Arthur Guiterman

To An Undiscerning Critic

Sure, there are times when one cries with acidity,
'Where are the limits of human stupidity?'
Here is a critic who says as a platitude,
That I am guilty because 'in ingratitude,
Sherlock, the sleuth hound, with motives ulterior,
Sneers at Poe's Dupin as very "inferior".'

Have you not learned, my esteemed commentator,
That the created is not the creator?
As the creator I've praised to satiety
Poe's Monsieur Dupin, his skill and variety,
And have admitted that in my detective work,
I owe to my model a deal of selective work.

But is it not on the verge of inanity
To put down to me my creation's crude vanity?
He, the created, the puppet of fiction,
Would not brook rivals nor stand contradiction.
He, the created, would scoff and would sneer,
Where I, the Creator, would bow and revere.

So please grip this fact with your cerebral tentacle,
The doll and its maker are never identical.

Dec. 14/12   Arthur Conan Doyle

THE STONOR CASE

Conan Doyle took a six-month lease on the Adelphi Theatre in London at the beginning of February 1910 after he had failed to find a manager prepared to produce his boxing play, *The House of Temperley*, which required a large cast, lacked a major starring role, and involved a prize fight. Doyle's production opened on 11 February, but the costs were high, the initial outlay being about £2,000 and the rent and salaries working out at about £600 a week. Although it opened with a full house, the play had a limited appeal: 'The furore for boxing had not yet set in. Ladies were afraid to come, and imagined it would be a brutal spectacle,'[287] were the reasons given by Doyle in his autobiography. The various attempts to improve the play's fortunes, such as a one-act play by Mrs Caleb Porter, *The Marauder*, which was added in March, or *A Pot of Caviare*, a one-act play specially written by Doyle himself which replaced it on 19 April, failed and the losses continued to mount.

The play's fate was sealed by the King's death on 6 May. It had a devastating effect on all the theatres, the more so as nobody had realized that the King was seriously ill until the day before he died. In common with other theatres, the Adelphi closed on 9 May and, although performances were announced for 14 and 16 May, the theatre was dark for the lying-in-state and for the funeral. It then remained closed, except for a few special performances, until the beginning of June. Doyle could have sublet the theatre, but he preferred to try and recover his losses by turning to Sherlock Holmes, much as Gillette had done in 1905 when *Clarice* had failed. 'I had signed a contract to take over the Adelphi until the end of the season,' Doyle said in an interview with the *Referee*, 'so as the position was serious and as I had nothing with which to replace *Temperley*, I was compelled to make an effort and I wrote *The Speckled Band*. We had that drama actually in rehearsal three weeks after I commenced it.'[288]

It is possible that Doyle first thought of writing an entirely new play and it may be that *The Crown Diamond* (pp. 247 ff.) dates from this period, but if so it was soon put aside in favour of a dramatization of one of the best known and most popular Sherlock Holmes stories, 'The Speckled Band'. The new play was called *The Stonor Case*, but as others wished to stay on familiar ground the title reverted to *The Speckled Band* before it opened. Doyle did not, however, stick rigidly to the story, and there were a number of changes, even in the names of the characters: Dr Grimesby Roylott appears in the play as Dr Grimesby Rylott; his stepdaughters, Helen and Julia Stoner, become Violet and Enid Stoner; and Percy Armitage, who had been the fiancé of Helen Stoner, gives his name to the village grocer who befriends Enid Stoner. A number of characters from other stories also enter the play. Mary Morstan, who had become engaged to Dr Watson in *The Sign of Four*, is mentioned as his fiancée, and Milverton, who had been shot in the story bearing his name, appears as one of Holmes's clients.

The Speckled Band does have some weaknesses, as Doyle himself admitted: 'The real fault of this play was that in trying to give Holmes a worthy antagonist I overdid it and produced a more interesting personality in the villain. The terrible ending was also against it.'[289] Holmes enters the drama too late and his clients are irrelevant to the action; the play is more concerned with Rylott than with Holmes; and the end, when it comes, comes too quickly. Holmes does not appear to do as much as he should and his mental agility looks less impressive when not seen through the eyes of Dr Watson. *The Stonor Case*, the original version, is in some ways better than the revised version published in 1912 by Samuel French. The stage directions which are Doyle's own are kept to a minimum, and there are many small variations including a few of some importance: Billy does not prevent Holmes taking his cocaine – a sequence which was added later as it was deemed unsuitable to show Holmes indulging himself in this way – but he does lock Dr Rylott into the waiting-room. Perhaps the most notable change is that in *The Stonor Case* Holmes straightens the poker bent by Dr Rylott. This is one of the most memorable incidents in the story and appears to have been discarded only because no suitable prop could be found. This version also includes the sequence with Mrs Soames, a client of Sherlock Holmes who had been led to believe that her husband had been killed in Chicago whereas he had in fact remarried. 'I took Mrs Soames out,' Doyle explained to Lyn Harding when congratulating him on the success which he and the play were having in Chicago in February 1914, 'because I felt as if the Audience were held too long from the plot.'[290]

Some members of the *Temperley* cast were given rôles in the new play, but the principal characters were brought in from outside. H. A. Saintsbury was chosen to play Sherlock Holmes, having already made the part his own in a touring production of William Gillette's play. He had given his five hundredth performance as early as 21 December 1903 and his thousandth performance as Holmes occurred during the run of *The Speckled Band* on 30 July 1910, so he had no difficulty in stepping into the rôle. Dr Grimesby Rylott was played by Lyn Harding, who had been a member of Beerbohm Tree's company at His Majesty's Theatre and had made his name in various Shakespearean rôles and as Bill Sikes in *Oliver Twist*. During the rehearsals of *The Speckled Band* which he directed, Harding had some disagreements with Conan Doyle over the way the character should be presented. Doyle had envisaged a melodramatic stage villain, but Harding favoured a more complex interpretation based on a man whom he had met in Scotland twenty years before. J. M. Barrie was eventually called in to adjudicate and persuaded Doyle to allow Harding a free hand. The decision was warmly applauded by the critics, one of whom gave a vivid description of the impression which Harding conveyed: 'A weird face, pallid, with sunken eyes, set in a ragged fringe of iron-grey hair, nervous fingers that could not be still, and contorted themselves in strange, fantastic gestures, sudden jerky movements, and sharp changes of manner and voice, and glances aside as at something haunting, and through all looming a vast conceit of himself.'[291]

The Speckled Band opened on 4 June 1910. 'We produced *The Speckled Band* last night,' Doyle told his mother the following day. 'It went wonderfully well. I don't think I have ever seen a play go so well.'[292] The audience were delighted and made their feelings known to the author when he took his curtain call; the critics were also full of admiration. Even E. F. Spence, who had been unduly harsh about the earlier play by Gillette which he parodied with Malcolm Watson in *Sheerluck Jones*, only found fault with Holmes's lack of legal knowledge, as the document put in front of Enid Stonor would have been invalid whether signed or not, but, like the other critics, he was impressed by Harding's performance and by the excellence of Saintsbury's disguises, which actually deceived the audience – a deception which may have been helped by the appearance in the programme of 'Mr C. Later' as the actor playing Peters, the butler. This was, of course, Sherlock Holmes in disguise, but at least one critic, having either not waited until the end or with his tongue firmly in his cheek, found room in his review to praise Mr Later's performance. Whenever Saintsbury subsequently played Holmes, C. Later played Peters, and both rightly claimed to be in their 'original parts'.

On 8 August 1910, at the end of Doyle's season at the Adelphi, the play transferred to the Globe Theatre. Two touring productions were already on the road and plans were in hand for an American production. *The Speckled Band* was revived at the *Strand Theatre* in February 1911, and there was a new production at the St James's Theatre in 1921. Doyle was in the audience on the opening night, 22 September 1921, and later, when he learnt that the play was only breaking even, agreed to forgo his royalties because he had been so grateful to the actors, Harding and Saintsbury, for turning theatrical defeat into a dramatic victory.

The use of a real snake in the first production and its lifeless performance was the subject of one of Conan Doyle's favourite anecdotes. It will be found elsewhere in this volume (p. 311) and also in *The Wanderings of a Spiritualist* which describes his visit to Australia and New Zealand in 1920–21. During a stopover at Colombo, Doyle was persuaded by a native conjurer to take hold of a cobra, and when he came to describe this incident in his book he recalled his earlier experience with snakes:

I remember that I once had three in my employ when *The Speckled Band* was produced in London, fine, lively rock pythons, and yet in spite of this profusion of realism I had the experience of reading a review which, after duly slating the play, wound up with the scathing sentence, 'The performance ended with the production of a palpably artificial serpent.' Such is the reward of virtue. Afterwards when the necessities of several travelling companies compelled us to use dummy snakes we produced a much more realistic effect. The real article either hung down like a pudgy yellow bell rope, or else when his tail was pinched, endeavoured to squirm back and get level with the stage carpenter, who pinched him, which was not in the plot. The latter individual had no doubts at all as to the dummy being an improvement upon the real.[293]

The critic who had been so disparaging about the snake is given as that of the *Daily Telegraph* in a composite article, 'The Truth about Sherlock Holmes', which appeared in *Collier's* on 29 December 1923 and which used all the relevant paragraphs from Doyle's autobiography. This was, however, a mistake, as Doyle must have realized, for he omitted the reference from the published book. In its original review, the *Daily Telegraph* had spoken of the snake 'waggling horribly', and when the play was revived the following year (then, of course, with a dummy) the critic went out of his way to praise the scene with the snake as one of the most impressive which Doyle's imagination had ever created. The first American production was rather less successful and, if the New York *Bookman* of February 1911 is to be believed, the snake suggested 'nothing more terrible than a large and unwieldy sausage'.[294]

Further reminiscences about the play were given by Arthur Hardy in an interview with the Glasgow *Evening Citizen* of 11 October 1938. He revealed that Doyle had been persuaded against his will to change the title from *The Stonor Case* to *The Speckled Band*, and also that, as he continued to insist on the use of a real snake, he had been invited to compare its performance against that of a dummy. Without telling him, the order was reversed, so that when Doyle chose the first, he chose the dummy, and was therefore forced to agree to its use.

The Speckled Band

An Adventure of Mr Sherlock Holmes, based on the short story, 'The Speckled Band', was first produced under that title at the Adelphi Theatre, London, on 4 June 1910, with the following cast:

Dr Grimesby Rylott	LYN HARDING
Enid Stonor	MISS CHRISTINE SILVER
Mrs Staunton	MISS AGNES THOMAS
Rodgers	A. S. HOMEWOOD
Ali	WILTON ROSS
Mr Scott Wilson	ARTHUR BURNE
Mr Armitage	SPENCER TREVOR
Mr Longbrace	J. J. BARTLETT
Mr Brewer	FRANK RIDLEY
Inspector Downing	GEOFFREY HILL
Coroner's Officer	GEORGE LAUNDY
Mr Holt Loaming	A. G. CRAIG
Mrs Soames	MISS GWENDOLEN FLOYD
Mr James B. Montague	A. CORNEY GRAIN
Mr Milverton	FRANK RIDLEY
Billy	MASTER CECIL F. LOWRIE
Dr Watson	CLAUDE KING
Peters	C. LATER
Mr Sherlock Holmes	H. A. SAINTSBURY

Jurors at the Inquest

The Stonor Case

An Adventure of Mr Sherlock Holmes

DRAMATIS PERSONAE

SHERLOCK HOLMES	The great Detective
DR WATSON	His Friend
BILLY	Page to SHERLOCK HOLMES
DR GRIMESBY RYLOTT	A retired Anglo-Indian surgeon. Owner of Stoke Moran Manor
ENID STONOR	His stepdaughter
ALI	An Indian, valet to DR RYLOTT
RODGERS	Butler to DR RYLOTT
MRS STAUNTON	Housekeeper to DR RYLOTT
MR SCOTT WILSON	Engaged to ENID'S sister
MR LONGBRACE	Coroner
MR BREWER	Foreman of the Jury
MR ARMITAGE	A Juror, the village grocer
MR HOLT LOAMING MR MILVERTON MR JAMES B. MONTAGUE MRS SOAMES	} Clients of SHERLOCK HOLMES
CORONER'S OFFICER	

ACT I

The Hall of Stoke Place, Stoke Moran
(*Two years are supposed to elapse*)

ACT II

Scene 1. A sitting-room in Stoke Place
Scene 2. Mr Sherlock Holmes's Room in Baker Street

ACT III

Scene 1. The Hall of the Stoke Moran Manor House
Scene 2. Enid's Bedroom, Stoke Place

First Act

Scene

Stoke Place at Stoke Moran

A large oak-lined, gloomy hall with everything in disrepair. A staircase leads up at the back. In centre is a door which leads into morning room. To the right, but also facing audience, is another door which leads to the outside hall. There is a long table with chairs round.

(MISS ENID STONOR sits on a couch at one side, her face buried in the cushions, sobbing. RODGERS also discovered, R., the butler, a broken old man. He looks timidly about him and then approaches MISS ENID.)

RODGERS: Don't cry, my dear young lady. You're so good and kind to others that it just goes to my heart to see such trouble come to you. Things will all change for the better now.

ENID: Thank you, Rodgers, you are very kind.

RODGERS: Life can't all be trouble, Miss Enid. There must surely be some sunshine somewhere, though I've waited a weary time for it.

ENID: Poor old Rodgers!

RODGERS: Yes, it used to be 'Poor *young* Rodgers', and now it's 'Poor *old* Rodgers'; and there's the story of my life.

Enter ALI, L., *an Indian servant*

ALI: Mrs Staunton says you are to have beer and sandwiches for the jury, and tiffin for the coroner, sahib.

RODGERS: Very good.

ALI: Go at once.

RODGERS: You mind your own business. You think you are the master.

ALI: I carry the housekeeper's order.

RODGERS: Well, I've got my orders.

ALI: And I see they are done.

RODGERS: You're only the valet, a servant same as me; same as Mrs Staunton for that matter.

ALI: Shall I tell master? Shall I say you will not take the order?

RODGERS: There, there, I'll do it.

Enter DR GRIMESBY RYLOTT

RYLOTT: Well, what's the matter? What are you doing here, Rodgers?

RODGERS: Nothing, sir, nothing.

ALI: I tell him to set out tiffin.

RYLOTT: Go this instant! What do you mean? Ali, stand at the door and show people in. (*To* ENID.) Oh! for God's sake stop your snivelling! Have I not enough to worry me without that? (*Shakes her.*) Stop it, I say! I'll have no more. They'll all be down in a moment.

ENID: Oh, dad! don't be so harsh with me.

RYLOTT: Hark! I think I hear them. What can they be loitering for? They won't learn much by looking at the body. I suppose that consequential ass of a coroner is giving them a lecture. If Professor van Donop and Dr Watson are satisfied, surely that is good enough for him. Ali!

ALI: Yes, sahib.

RYLOTT: How many witnesses have come?

ALI: Seven, sahib.

RYLOTT: All in the morning room?

ALI: Yes, sahib.

RYLOTT: Then put any others in there also. Woman, *will* you dry your eyes and try for once to think of other people besides yourself? Learn to stamp down your private emotions. Look at me. I was as fond of your sister Violet as if she had really been my daughter, and yet I face the situation now like a man. Get up and do your duty.

ENID (*drying her eyes*): What can I do? (*Rises.*)

RYLOTT (*sitting on the settee*): There's a brave girl. I did not mean to be harsh. Thirty years of India sends a man home with a cayenne pepper temper. Did I ever tell you the funny story of the Indian judge and the cabman?

ENID: Oh, how can you?

RYLOTT: Well, well, I'll tell it some other time. Don't look so shocked. I meant well, I was trying to cheer you up. Now look here, Enid! be a sensible girl and pull yourself together – and I say! be careful what you tell them. We may have had our little disagreements, every family has, but don't wash our linen in public. It is a time to forgive and forget. I always loved Violet in my heart.

ENID: Oh! if I could only think so!

RYLOTT: Since your mother died you have both been to me as my own daughters; in every way the same; mind you say so. D'you hear?

ENID: Yes, I hear.

RYLOTT: Don't forget it. (*Turns her face.*) Don't forget it. Curse them! are they never coming, the carrion crows? I'll see what they are after.

Exit

(SCOTT WILSON *enters at the door, and is shown by* ALI *into the morning room. While he is showing him in,* DR WATSON *enters and seeing* ENID STONOR *with her face in the cushions he comes across to her.*)

WATSON: Let me say how sorry I am, Miss Stonor.

ENID (*rises to meet him* C.): I am so glad to see you, Dr Watson. I fear I am a weak, cowardly creature, unfit to meet the shocks of life. It is all like some horrible nightmare.

WATSON: I think you have been splendidly brave. What woman could fail to feel such a shock?

ENID: Your kindness has been the one gleam of light in these dark days. There is such bad feeling between my stepfather and the country doctor that I am sure he would not have come to us. But I remembered the kind letter you wrote when we came home, and I telegraphed on the chance. I could hardly dare hope that you would come from London so promptly.

WATSON: Why, I knew your mother well in India, and I remember you and your poor sister when you were schoolgirls. I was only too glad to be of any use – if indeed I was of any use. Where is your stepfather?

ENID: He has gone upstairs.

WATSON: I trust that he does not visit you with any of that violence of which I hear so much in the village. Excuse me if I take a liberty; it is only that I am interested. You are very lonely and defenceless.

ENID: I am sure you mean well, but indeed I would rather not discuss this matter.

ALI (*advancing*): This way, sir.

WATSON: In a minute.

ALI: Master's orders, sir.

WATSON: In a minute, I say.

ALI: Very sorry, sir. Must go now.

WATSON (*pushing him away*): Stand back, you rascal. I will go in my own time. Don't you dare to interfere with me.

    (ALI *shrugs shoulders and withdraws.*)

Just one last word. It is a true friend who speaks, and you will not resent it. If you should be in any trouble, if anything should come which made you uneasy – which worried you –

ENID: What should come? You frighten me.

WATSON: You have no one in this lonely place to whom you can go. If by chance you should want a friend you will turn to me, will you not?

ENID: How good you are! But you mean more than you say. What is it that you fear?

WATSON: It is a gloomy atmosphere for a young girl. Your stepfather is a strange man. You would come to me, would you not?

ENID: I promise you I will.

WATSON: I can do little enough. But I have a singular friend – a man with strange powers and a masterful personality. We used to live together, and I came to know him well. Holmes is his name – Mr Sherlock Holmes. It is to him I should turn if things looked black for you. If any man in England could help you it is he.

ENID: But I shall need no help. And yet, it is good to think that I am not all alone. Hush! they are coming. Don't delay! Oh! I beg you to go.

WATSON: I take your promise with me.

Exit into the waiting-room

(*The* DOCTOR *comes down the stairs, conversing with the* CORONER. *The* JURY, *in a confused crowd, come behind. There is a* CORONER'S OFFICER.)

CORONER: Very proper sentiments, sir; very proper sentiments. I can entirely understand your feelings.

RYLOTT: At my age it is a great thing to have a soothing female influence around one. Ah! how I shall miss it at every turn. She had the sweet temperament of her dear mother. Enid, my dear, have you been introduced to Mr Longbrace, the Coroner?

CORONER: How do you do, Miss Stonor? You have my sympathy, I am sure. Well, well, we must get to business. Mr Brewer, I understand that you have been elected as foreman. Is that so, gentlemen?

ALL: Yes, yes!

CORONER: Then perhaps you would sit at the further
end. (*Looks at watch.*) Dear me! it is later than I thought.
Now, Dr Rylott, both you and your stepdaughter are
witnesses in this inquiry, so your presence here is irregu-
lar.

RYLOTT: I thought, sir, that under my own roof –

CORONER: Not at all, sir, not at all. The procedure is
entirely unaffected by such a consideration.

RYLOTT: I am quite in your hands.

CORONER: Then you will kindly withdraw.

RYLOTT: Come, Enid.

CORONER: Possibly the young lady would wish to be free, so
we could take her evidence first.

RYLOTT: That would be most considerate. You can understand, sir, that I would wish her spared in this ordeal. I
leave you, dear girl. (*Aside.*) Remember!

Exit

CORONER: Put a chair, officer.

(OFFICER *places chair.*)

That will do. Now, Miss Stonor! Thank you. The officer
will swear you – The truth and nothing but the truth.
Thank you.

(ENID *kisses Book.*)

Exactly. Gentlemen, before I take the evidence, I will
remind you of the general circumstances connected with
the sudden decease of this unhappy young lady. She was
Miss Violet Stonor, the elder of the stepdaughters of Dr
Grimesby Rylott, a retired Anglo-Indian doctor, who has
lived during the last two years at this ancient house of
Stoke Place, in Stoke Moran. She was born and educated
in India, and her health was never robust. There was,
however, no actual physical lesion, nor has any been
discovered by the doctors. You have seen the room on the
ground floor at the end of this passage, and you realize that
the young lady was well guarded, having her sister's
bedroom on one side of her and her stepfather's on the

other. We will now take the evidence of the sister of the deceased as to what actually occurred. Might I ask you to tell us what happened upon the night of April 14th? I understand that your sister was in her ordinary health when you said good-night to her?

ENID: Yes, sir, she seemed as usual. She was never strong.

CORONER: Had she some mental trouble?

ENID (*hesitating*): She was not very happy in her mind.

CORONER: I beg that you will have no reserves. I am sure you appreciate the solemnity of this occasion. Why was your sister unhappy in her mind?

ENID: There were obstacles to her engagement.

CORONER: Proceed.

ENID: I was awakened shortly after midnight by a scream. I ran into the passage. As I reached her door I heard a sound like low music, then the key turn in the lock, and she rushed out in her nightdress. Her face was convulsed with terror. She screamed out a few words and fell into my arms, and then slipped down upon the floor. When I tried to raise her I found that she was dead. Then – then I fainted myself, and I knew no more.

CORONER: When you came to yourself –?

ENID: When I came to myself I had been carried by my stepfather and Rodgers, the butler, back to my bed.

CORONER: You talk of music? What sort of music?

ENID: It was a low, sweet sound.

CORONER: Whence came this music?

ENID: I could not tell. I may say that once or twice I thought that I heard music at night.

CORONER: You say that your sister screamed out some words. What were the words?

ENID: It was incoherent raving. She was wild with terror.

CORONER: But could you distinguish nothing?

ENID: I heard the word 'band'. I also heard the word 'speckled'. I cannot say more. I was myself almost as terrified as she.

CORONER: Dear me! Speckled band! It sounds like delirium. She mentioned no name?

ENID: None.

CORONER: What light was in the passage?

ENID: A lamp against the wall.

CORONER: You could distinctly see your sister?

ENID: Oh, yes.

CORONER: And there was at that time no trace of violence upon her?

ENID: No, no!

CORONER: You are quite clear that she unlocked her door before she appeared?

ENID: Yes, I can swear it.

CORONER: And her window? Did she ever sleep with her window open?

ENID: No, it was always fastened at night.

CORONER: Did you examine it after her death?

ENID: I saw it next morning; it was fastened then.

CORONER: One other point, Miss Stonor. You have no reason to believe that your sister contemplated suicide?

ENID: Certainly not.

CORONER: At the same time when a young lady – admittedly of a nervous, highly strung disposition – is crossed in her love affairs, such a possibility cannot be excluded. You can throw no light upon such a supposition?

ENID: No.

FOREMAN: Don't you think, Mr Coroner, if the young lady had designs upon herself she would have stayed in her room and not rushed out into the passage?

CORONER: Well, that is for your consideration and judgement. You have heard this young lady's evidence. Have any of you any questions to put?

ARMITAGE (*a juryman*): Well, I'm a plain man, a Methodist and the son of a Methodist –

CORONER: What is your name, sir?

ARMITAGE: I'm Mr Armitage, sir. I own the big shop in the village.

CORONER: Well, sir?

ARMITAGE: I'm a Methodist and the son of a Methodist —

CORONER: Your religious opinions are not under discussion, Mr Armitage.

ARMITAGE: But I speaks my mind as man to man. I pays my taxes the same as the rest of them.

CORONER: Have you any question to ask?

ARMITAGE: Yes, sir. I would like to ask this young lady whether her stepfather uses her ill, for there are some queer stories get about in the village.

CORONER: The question would be out of order. It does not bear upon the death of the deceased.

FOREMAN: Well, sir, I will put Mr Armitage's question in another shape. Can you tell us, miss, whether your stepfather ever ill-used the deceased young lady?

ENID: He — he is not always harsh.

ARMITAGE: Does he lay hands on you — that's what I want to know?

CORONER: Really, Mr Armitage!

ARMITAGE: Excuse me, Mr Coroner. I've lived in this village, boy and man, for fifty years, and I can look any man in the face.

CORONER: You have heard the question, Miss Stonor. I don't know that we could insist upon your answering it.

ENID: My stepfather, gentlemen, has spent his life in the tropics. It has affected his health. There are times — there are times when he loses control over his temper. At such times he is liable to be violent. My sister and I thought — hoped — that he was not really responsible for it. He is sorry for it afterwards.

CORONER: Well, Miss Stonor, I am sure I voice the sentiments of the Jury when I express our profound sympathy for the sorrow which has come upon you.

(JURY *all murmur.*)

We need not detain you any longer.

                             ENID *rises and exits,* L.

(*To his* OFFICER.) Call Mr Scott Wilson.

OFFICER (*at door*): Mr Scott Wilson.

Enter SCOTT WILSON — *a commonplace young gentleman*

CORONER: Swear him, officer.

                         (*Mumbling.*)

Exactly. I understand, Mr Scott Wilson, that you were engaged to the deceased.

WILSON: Yes, sir.

CORONER: Since how long?

WILSON: Six weeks, sir.

CORONER: Was there any quarrel between you?

WILSON: None.

CORONER: Were you in a position to marry?

WILSON: Yes.

CORONER: Was there any talk of an immediate marriage?

WILSON: Well, sir, we hoped before the summer was over.

CORONER: We hear of obstacles. What were the obstacles?

WILSON: Dr Rylott, sir. He would not hear of the marriage.

CORONER: Why not?

WILSON: He gave no reason, sir.

CORONER: There was some scandal, was there not?

WILSON: Yes, sir, he assaulted me.

CORONER: What happened?

WILSON: He met me in the village. He was like a raving madman. He struck me several times with his cane, and he set his boar-hound upon me.

CORONER: What did you do?

WILSON: I took refuge in one of the little village shops.

ARMITAGE: I beg your pardon, young gentleman, you took refuge in my shop.

WILSON: Yes, sir, I took refuge in Mr Armitage's shop.

CORONER: And a police charge resulted?

WILSON: I withdrew it, sir, out of consideration for my fiancée.

CORONER: But you continued your engagement?

WILSON: I would not be bullied out of that.

CORONER: Quite so. But this opposition, and her fears as to your safety, caused Miss Stonor great anxiety?

WILSON: Yes.

CORONER: Apart from that, you can say nothing which throws any light on this sad event?

WILSON: No, sir. I had not seen her for a week before her death.

CORONER: She never expressed any particular apprehensions to you?

WILSON: She was always nervous and unhappy.

CORONER: But nothing definite?

WILSON: No.

CORONER: Any questions, gentlemen? (*Pause.*) Very good. You may go. Call Dr Watson.

OFFICER (*at door*): Dr Watson.

Enter DR WATSON

CORONER: You will kindly take the oath. You have had read to you, gentlemen, the evidence of Professor van Donop, the pathologist, who is unable to be present today. Dr Watson's evidence is supplementary to that. You are not in practice, I understand, Dr Watson?

WATSON: No, sir.

CORONER: A retired Army surgeon, I understand?

WATSON: Yes.

CORONER: Dear me! you retired young.

WATSON: I was wounded in the Afghan Campaign.

CORONER: I see, I see. You knew Dr Rylott before this tragedy?

WATSON: No, sir. I knew Mrs Stonor when she was a widow, and I knew her two daughters. That was in India. I heard of her re-marriage and her death. When I heard that the children, with their stepfather, had come to England, I wrote and reminded them that they had at least one friend.

CORONER: Well, what then?

WATSON: I heard no more until I received a wire from Miss Enid Stonor. I at once went out to Stoke Moran.

CORONER: You were the first medical man to see the body?

WATSON: Dr Rylott is himself a medical man.

CORONER: Exactly. You were the first independent medical man?

WATSON: Yes, sir.

CORONER: Without going too far into painful details, I take it that you are in agreement with Professor van Donop's report and analysis?

WATSON: Yes, sir.

CORONER: You found no physical lesion?

WATSON: No, sir.

CORONER: Nothing to account for death?

WATSON: No, sir.

CORONER: No signs of violence?

WATSON: No, sir.

CORONER: Nor of poison?

WATSON: No, sir.

CORONER: Yet there must be a cause?

WATSON: There are many causes of death which leave no sign.

CORONER: For instance –?

WATSON: Well, for instance, the subtler poisons. There are many poisons for which we have no test.

CORONER: No doubt. But you will remember, Dr Watson, that this young lady died some five or six hours after her last meal. So far as the evidence goes it was only then that she could have taken poison, unless she took it of her own free will; in which case we should have expected to find some paper or bottle in her room. But it would indeed be a strange poison which could strike her down so suddenly many hours after it was taken. You perceive the difficulty?

WATSON: Yes, sir.

CORONER: You could name no poison capable of such a belated effect?

WATSON: No, sir.

CORONER: Then what remains?

WATSON: There are other causes. One may die of nervous shock, or one may die of a broken heart, and neither will leave a physical sign.

CORONER: Had you any reason to think that the deceased had undergone nervous shock?

WATSON: Only the narrative of her sister, corroborated by the expression upon the face of the deceased.

CORONER: You have formed no conjecture as to the nature of the shock to which she may have been exposed?

WATSON: No, sir.

CORONER: You spoke of a broken heart. Have you any reason for such an expression in connection with the deceased?

WATSON: Only my general impression that she was not happy.

CORONER: I fear we cannot deal with 'general impressions'. You have no definite reason?

WATSON: None that I can put into words.

CORONER: Has any juror any question to ask?

ARMITAGE: I'm a plain, downright man, and I want to get to the bottom of this thing.

CORONER: We all share your desire, Mr Armitage.

ARMITAGE: Look here, Doctor! you examined this lady. Did you find any signs of violence?

WATSON: I have already said I did not.

ARMITAGE: I mean bruises, or the like? (*Sits.*)

WATSON: No, sir.

CORONER: Any questions?

ARMITAGE: I would like to ask the Doctor whether he wrote to these young ladies because he had any reason to think they were ill-used?

WATSON: No, sir. I wrote because I knew their mother.

ARMITAGE: What did their mother die of?

WATSON: I have no idea.

CORONER: Really, Mr Armitage, you go too far! Anything else?

FOREMAN: May I ask, Dr Watson, whether you examined the window of the room to see if any one from outside could have molested the lady?

WATSON: The window was bolted.

FOREMAN: Yes, but had it been bolted all night?

WATSON: Yes, it had.

CORONER: How do you know?

WATSON: By the dust on the window-latch.

CORONER: Dear me, Doctor, you are very observant!

WATSON: I have a friend, sir, who trained me in such matters.

CORONER: Well, your evidence seems final on that point. We are all obliged to you, and will detain you no longer.

Exit DR WATSON

Call Rodgers, the butler.

OFFICER (*at door*): Mr Rodgers.

Enter RODGERS

CORONER: Swear him!

(*Mumble.*)

Well, Mr Rodgers, how long have you been in the service of Dr Rylott?

RODGERS: Two years, sir.

CORONER: Ever since the family settled here?

RODGERS: Yes, sir. I'm an old man, sir, too old to change. I don't suppose I'd get another place if I lost this one. He tells me it would be the gutter or the workhouse.

CORONER: Who says so?

RODGERS: Him, sir – the master. But I am not saying anything against him, sir. No, no, don't think that – not a word against the master. You won't misunderstand me?

CORONER: You seem nervous?

RODGERS: Well, I'm an old man, sir, and things like this –

CORONER: Quite so, we can understand. Now, Rodgers, you helped to carry Miss Stonor to her bed?

RODGERS: Did I, sir? Who said that?

CORONER: We had it in Miss Stonor's evidence. Was it not so?

RODGERS: Yes, yes, if Miss Enid said it. What Miss Enid says is true. And what the master says is true. It's all true.

CORONER: I suppose you came when you heard the scream?

RODGERS: Yes, yes, the scream in the night; I came to it.

CORONER: And what did you see?

RODGERS: I saw – I saw – (*Puts his hands up as if about to faint.*)

CORONER: Come, come, man, speak out.

RODGERS: I'm – I'm frightened.

CORONER: You have nothing to fear. You are under the protection of the law. Who are you afraid of? Your master?

RODGERS: No, no, gentlemen, don't think that! No, no!

CORONER: Well, then – what did you see?

RODGERS: She was on the ground, sir, and Miss Enid beside her, both in white night clothes. My master was standing over them.

CORONER: Well?

RODGERS: We carried the young lady to her bed. She never spoke, nor moved. I know no more – indeed I know no more.

CORONER: Any questions, gentlemen?

ARMITAGE: You live in the house all the time?

RODGERS: Yes, sir.

ARMITAGE: Does your master ever knock you about?

RODGERS: No, sir, no.

ARMITAGE: Well, Mr Scott Wilson told us what happened to him, and I know he laid the under gardener up for a week and paid ten pound to keep out of court. You know that yourself.

RODGERS: No, no, sir, I know nothing of the kind.

ARMITAGE: Well everyone else in the village knows. What

I want to ask is – was he ever violent to these young ladies?

FOREMAN: Yes, that's it. Was he violent?

RODGERS: No, not to say violent. No, he's a kind man, the master.

(*Pause.*)

CORONER: That will do. Call Mrs Staunton, the house-keeper.

Exit RODGERS

Enter MRS STAUNTON

CORONER: You are housekeeper here?

MRS STAUNTON: Yes, sir.

CORONER: How long have you been here?

MRS STAUNTON: Ever since the family settled here.

CORONER: Can you tell us anything of this matter?

MRS STAUNTON: I knew nothing of it, sir, till after the poor young lady had been laid upon the bed. After that it was I who took charge of things, for Dr Rylott was so dreadfully upset that he could do nothing.

CORONER: Oh! he was very upset, was he?

MRS STAUNTON: I never saw a man in such a state of grief.

CORONER: Living in the house you had numerous opportunities of seeing the relations between Dr Rylott and his two stepdaughters.

MRS STAUNTON: Yes, sir.

CORONER: How would you describe them?

MRS STAUNTON: He was kindness itself to them. No two young ladies could be better treated than they have been.

CORONER: It has been suggested that he was sometimes violent to them.

MRS STAUNTON: Never, sir. He was like a tender father.

ARMITAGE: How about that riding switch? We've heard tales about that.

MRS STAUNTON: Oh, it's you, Mr Armitage? There are good reasons why you should make mischief against the Doctor. He told you what he thought of you and your canting ways.

CORONER: Now then, I cannot have these recriminations. If I had known, Mr Armitage, that there was personal feeling between the Doctor and you –

ARMITAGE: Nothing of the sort, sir. I'm doing my public duty.

CORONER: Well, the evidence of the witness seems very clear in combating your assertion of ill-treatment. Anything more? Very good, Mrs Staunton.

Exit MRS STAUNTON

Call Dr Grimesby Rylott.

OFFICER (*calls at door*): Dr Rylott.

Enter DR RYLOTT

CORONER: Dr Rylott, can you say anything which will throw any light upon this unhappy business?

RYLOTT: You may well say unhappy, sir. It has completely unnerved me.

CORONER: No doubt.

RYLOTT: She was the ray of sunshine in the house. She knew my ways; I am lost without her.

CORONER: No doubt. But we must confine ourselves to the facts. Have you any explanation which will cover the facts of your stepdaughter's death?

RYLOTT: I know just as much of the matter as you do. It is a complete and absolute mystery to me.

CORONER: Speaking as a doctor, you had no misgivings as to her health?

RYLOTT: She was never robust, but I had no reason for uneasiness.

CORONER: It has come out in evidence that her happiness had been affected by your interference with her engagement?

RYLOTT: That is entirely a misunderstanding, sir. As a matter of fact, I interfered in order to protect her from a man who I had every reason to believe was a mere fortune-hunter. She saw it herself in that light and was relieved to see the last of him.

CORONER: Excuse me, sir, but this introduces a new element into the case. Then the young lady had separate means?

RYLOTT: A small annuity under her mother's will.

CORONER: And to whom does it go now?

RYLOTT: I believe that I might have a claim upon it, but I waive it in favour of her sister.

CORONER: Very handsome, I am sure.

ARMITAGE: I expect, sir, so long as she lives under your roof you have the spending of it.

CORONER: Well, well, we can hardly go into that.

ARMITAGE: Has the young lady her own cheque book?

CORONER: Really, Mr Armitage, you get away from the subject.

ARMITAGE: It is the subject.

RYLOTT: I am not here, sir, to submit to impertinence.

CORONER: I must ask you, Mr Armitage. (*Holds up hand.*) Now, Dr Rylott, the medical evidence, as you are aware, gives us no cause of death. You can suggest none?

RYLOTT: No, sir.

CORONER: Your stepdaughter has affirmed that her sister unlocked her door before appearing in the passage. Can you confirm this?

RYLOTT: Yes, I heard her unlock the door.

CORONER: You arrived in the passage simultaneously with the lady?

RYLOTT: Yes, sir.

CORONER: You had been aroused by the scream?

RYLOTT: Yes, sir.

CORONER: And naturally you came at once?

RYLOTT: Quite so. I was just in time to see her rush from her room and fall into her sister's arms. I can only imagine that she had had some nightmare or hideous dream which had been too much for her heart. That is my own theory of her death.

CORONER: We have it on record that she said some incoherent words before she died.

RYLOTT: I heard nothing of the sort.

CORONER: She said nothing so far as you know?

RYLOTT: Nothing.

CORONER: Did you hear any music?

RYLOTT: Music, sir? No, I heard none.

CORONER: Well, what happened next?

RYLOTT: I satisfied myself that the poor girl was dead. Old Rodgers, my butler, had arrived, and together we laid her on her couch. I can really tell you nothing more.

CORONER: You did not at once send for a doctor?

RYLOTT: Well, sir, I was a doctor myself. To satisfy Enid I consented in the morning to telegraph for Dr Watson, who had been the girls' friend in India. I really could do no more.

CORONER: Looking back, you have nothing with which to reproach yourself in your treatment of this lady?

RYLOTT: She was the apple of my eye, I would have given my life for her.

CORONER: Well, gentlemen, any question?

ARMITAGE: Yes, a good many.

(*The other* JURYMEN *show some impatience.*)

Well, I pay my way the same as the rest of you, and I claim my rights. Mr Coroner, I claim my rights.

CORONER: Well, well, Mr Armitage, be as short as you can. (*Looks at his watch.*) It is nearly two.

ARMITAGE: See here, Dr Rylott, what about that great hound of yours? What about that whip you carry? What about the tales we hear down in the village of your bully-raggin' them young ladies?

RYLOTT: Really, Mr Coroner, I must claim your protection! This fellow's insolence is intolerable.

CORONER: You go rather far, Mr Armitage. You must confine yourself to definite questions upon matters of fact.

ARMITAGE: Well then, do you sleep with a light in your room?

RYLOTT: No, I do not.

ARMITAGE: How was you dressed in the passage?

RYLOTT: In my dressing-gown.

ARMITAGE: How did you get it?

RYLOTT: I struck a light, of course, and took it from a hook.

ARMITAGE: Well, if you did all that, how did you come into the passage as quick as the young lady who ran out just as she was?

RYLOTT: I can only tell you it was so.

ARMITAGE: Well, I can only tell *you* I don't believe it.

CORONER: You must withdraw that, Mr Armitage.

ARMITAGE: I says what I mean, Mr Coroner, and I say it again, I don't believe it. I've got common sense if I haven't got education.

RYLOTT: I can afford to disregard his remarks, Mr Coroner.

CORONER: Anything else, Mr Armitage?

ARMITAGE: I've said my say, and I stick to it.

CORONER: Then that will do, Dr Rylott. (*Pause.*)

(DR RYLOTT *is going out* C.)

By the way, can your Indian servant help us at all in the matter?

RYLOTT: Ali sleeps in a garret and knew nothing till next morning. He is my personal valet.

CORONER: Then we need not call him. Very good, Dr Rylott. You can remain if you wish. (*To* JURY.) Well, gentlemen, you have heard the evidence relating to this very painful case. There are several conceivable alternatives. There is death by murder. Of this I need not say there is not a shadow or tittle of evidence. There is death by suicide. Here again, the presumption is absolutely against it. Then there is death by accident. We have nothing to lead us to believe that there had been an accident. Finally, we come to death by natural causes. It must be admitted that these natural causes are obscure, but the processes of nature are often mysterious, and we cannot claim to have such an exact knowledge of them

that we can always define them. We have read the
evidence of Professor van Donop and you have heard that
of Dr Watson. It is for you to form your own conclusions.
(*The* JURY *buzz together for a moment. The* CORONER *rises,*
and goes over to DR RYLOTT.)

(*Looking at watch.*) We are later than I intended.

RYLOTT: These absurd interruptions –!

CORONER: Yes, at these country inquests we generally have
some queer fellows on the jury.

RYLOTT: Lunch must be ready. Won't you join us?

CORONER: Well, well, I shall be delighted.

FOREMAN: All ready, sir.

                    (CORONER *returns to table.*)

CORONER: Well, gentlemen?

FOREMAN: We are for natural causes.

CORONER: Quite so. Unanimous?

ARMITAGE: No, sir, I am for an open verdict. I don't know
it's natural and I won't say it's natural.

CORONER: You are twelve to one – I entirely agree with the
finding. Well, gentlemen, that finishes our labours. I must
thank you all for your attendance.

(*The* JURY *rise.* CORONER *takes* ARMITAGE *by the shoulder*
and leads him out.)

I'm sorry, Mr Armitage, that you are not yet satisfied.

ARMITAGE: No, sir, I am not.

CORONER: You are a little exacting. (*Turns away.*)

RYLOTT (*touching* ARMITAGE *on the shoulder*): I have only
one thing to say to you, sir. Get out of my house. D'you
hear?

ARMITAGE: Yes, Dr Rylott, I hear. And I seem to hear
something else. Something crying from the ground, Dr
Rylott, crying from the ground.

RYLOTT: Impertinent rascal! (*Turns away.*)

Enter WATSON, ENID *and other* WITNESSES *from room behind*
    (*They all file out towards the door.* ENID *has come down*
    stage. DR WATSON *comes back from the door.*)

WATSON: Good-bye, Miss Enid. (*Shakes hands. Then in a lower voice.*) Don't forget that you have a friend.

CURTAIN

(*Two years are supposed to elapse*)

Second Act

Scene One

A sitting-room in Stoke Place

Enter MRS STAUNTON *showing in* MR ARMITAGE

MRS STAUNTON: I can't tell how long the Doctor may be. It's not long since he went out.

ARMITAGE: Well, I'll wait for him, however long it is.

MRS STAUNTON: It's nothing I could do for you, I suppose.

ARMITAGE: No, it is not.

MRS STAUNTON: Well, you need not be so short. Perhaps after you've seen the Doctor you may be sorry.

ARMITAGE: There's the law of England watching over me, Mrs Staunton. I advise you not to forget it – nor your master either. I fear no man so long as I am doing my duty.

Enter ENID

Ah, Miss Stonor, I am very glad to see you.

ENID (*bewildered*): Good-day, Mr Armitage. What brings you up here?

ARMITAGE: I had a little business with the Doctor. But I should be very glad to have a chat with you also.

MRS STAUNTON: I don't think the Doctor would like it, Miss Enid.

ARMITAGE: A pretty state of things. Isn't this young lady able to speak with whoever she likes? Do you call this a prison, or a private asylum, or what? These are fine doings in a free country.

MRS STAUNTON: I am sure the Doctor would not like it.

ARMITAGE: Look here, Mrs Staunton, two is company and

three is none. If I'm not afraid of your master, I'm not
afraid of you. You're a bit beyond your station, you are. Get
to the other side of that door and leave us alone, or else –

MRS STAUNTON: Or what, Mr Armitage?

ARMITAGE: As sure as my father was a Methodist I'll go
down to the J.P. and swear an information that this young
lady is under constraint.

MRS STAUNTON: You need not be so hot about it. It's
nothing to me what you say to Miss Enid. But the Doctor
won't like it.

Exit

ARMITAGE (*looking at the door*): You haven't such a thing as
a hatpin?

ENID: No.

ARMITAGE: If I were to jab it through that keyhole –

ENID: Oh, no, Mr Armitage.

ARMITAGE: You'd hear Sister Jane's top note. But we'll
speak low for I don't mean she shall hear. First of all, Miss
Enid, how are they using you? Are you all right?

ENID: Mr Armitage, I know you mean it all for kindness,
but I cannot discuss my personal affairs with you. I hardly
know you.

ARMITAGE: Only the village grocer, too. I know all about
that. But I've taken an interest in you, Miss Stonor, and
I'm the kind of man that can't leave go his hold. I came
here not to see you, but your stepfather.

ENID: Oh, Mr Armitage, I beg you to go away at once. You
have no idea how violent he is if any one thwarts him.
Please, please go at once.

ARMITAGE (*sitting down*): Well, Miss Stonor, your only
chance of getting me to go is to answer my questions.
When my conscience is clear I'll go, and not before. My
conscience tells me that it is my duty to stay here till I have
some satisfaction.

ENID: But what is it, Mr Armitage?

ARMITAGE: Well, I'll tell you. I make it my business to

know what is going on in this house. It may be that I like you, or it may be that I dislike your stepfather. Or it may be that it's just my nature, but so it is. I've got my own way of finding out, and I do find out.

ENID: What have you found out?

ARMITAGE: Now look here, miss. Cast your mind back to that inquest two years ago.

ENID: Oh!

ARMITAGE: I'm sorry if it hurts you, but I must speak plain. When did your sister meet her death? It was shortly after her engagement, was it not?

ENID: Yes, it was.

ARMITAGE: Well, you're engaged now, are you not?

ENID: Yes, I am.

ARMITAGE: Point number one. Well now, have there not been repairs lately, and are you not forced to sleep in the very room your sister died in?

ENID: Only for a few nights.

ARMITAGE: Point number two. There was talk at the inquest of music heard in the house at night. Have you never heard music of late?

ENID: Good God! only last night I thought I heard it; and then persuaded myself that it was a dream. But how do you know these things, Mr Armitage, and what do they mean?

ARMITAGE: Well, I won't tell you how I know them, and I can't tell you what they mean. But it's devilish, Miss Stonor, devilish! Now I've come up to see your stepfather and to tell him, as man to man, that I've got my eye on him, and that if anything happens to you it will be a bad day's work for him.

ENID: Oh, Mr Armitage, he would beat you within an inch of your life. Mr Armitage, you cannot think what he is like when the fury is on him. He is terrible. For God's sake, Mr Armitage, don't see him. You want to help me, don't you? Well, it would be dreadful to me if anything befell you.

ARMITAGE: The law will look after me.

ENID: It might avenge you, Mr Armitage, but it could not protect you. You would be at his mercy in this lonely house. And besides, Mr Armitage, you are quite mistaken in your fears. There is no possible danger. You know of my engagement to Lieutenant Curtis?

ARMITAGE: I hear he leaves tomorrow.

ENID: That is true. But the next day I am going on a visit to his mother at Fenton. Indeed, there is no danger. I will not deny that there have been times when my stepfather has been very harsh both to my dear sister and myself. But that was long ago. Lately he has been very kind. He made no opposition at all to my engagement. I assure you that I have nothing to fear.

ARMITAGE: Well, I won't deny that I am consoled by what you say and that it puts another colour upon things. It may be that he is just kind in order to deceive you, or it may be as you say. It's not for the pleasure of meeting him that I am here, and if my conscience would let me I would soon be out of it. Now look here, Miss Stonor, there's just one condition on which I would leave it.

ENID: What is that?

ARMITAGE: Well, I remember your friend, Dr Watson, at the inquest – and we've heard of his connection with Mr Sherlock Holmes. If you'll promise me that you'll slip away to London tomorrow, see those two gentlemen and get their advice, I'll wash my hands of it. I should feel that someone stronger than me was looking after you.

ENID: Oh, Mr Armitage, I couldn't.

ARMITAGE (*folding his arms*): Then I stay here.

ENID: It is Lieutenant Curtis's last day in England.

ARMITAGE: When does he leave?

ENID: In the evening.

ARMITAGE: Well, if you go in the morning, you'd be back in time.

ENID: But how can I get away?

ARMITAGE: Who's to stop you? Have you money?

ENID: Yes, I have enough.

ARMITAGE: Then, go.

ENID: It is really impossible.

ARMITAGE: Very good. Then I'll have it out with the Doctor.

ENID: There! there! I'll promise. I'll go. I won't have you hurt. I'll write and arrange it all.

ARMITAGE: Word of honour?

ENID: Yes, yes. Oh! do go. Through here. (*Goes to French window.*) If you keep among the laurels you can get to the high road and no one will meet you.

ARMITAGE: That dog about?

ENID: It is with the Doctor. Oh, do go! and thank you – thank you with all my heart.

ARMITAGE: My wife and I can always take you in. Don't forget it.

Exit

(ENID *stands looking after him. As she does so,* MRS STAUNTON *enters the room.*)

MRS STAUNTON: I saw Mr Armitage going off through the shrubbery.

ENID: Yes, he has gone.

MRS STAUNTON: But why did he not wait to see the Doctor?

ENID: He thought it was not necessary.

MRS STAUNTON: He is the most impertinent busybody in the whole village. Fancy the insolence of him coming up here without a with-your-leave or by-your-leave. What was it he wanted, Miss Enid?

ENID: It is not your place, Mrs Staunton, to ask such questions.

MRS STAUNTON: Oh, indeed! For that matter, Miss Enid, I should not have thought it was your place to have secrets with the village grocer. The Doctor will want to know all about it.

ENID: What my stepfather may do is another matter. I beg,

Mrs Staunton, that you will attend to your own affairs and leave me alone. I wish to have nothing to do with you.

MRS STAUNTON (*putting her arms akimbo*): High and mighty, indeed! I'm to do all the work of the house, but the grocer can come in and turn me out of the room. If you think I am nobody you may find yourself mistaken some of these days.

ENID: You are an odious woman. (*She makes for door.*)

Enter RYLOTT

RYLOTT: Why, Enid, what's the matter? Any one been upsetting you? What's all this, Mrs Staunton?

ENID: This woman has been rude to me.

RYLOTT: Dear, dear! Here's a storm in a teacup. Well now, come and tell me all about it. No one shall bother my little Enid. What would her sailor boy say?

MRS STAUNTON: Mr Armitage from the village has been here.

RYLOTT: Armitage the grocer? What the devil did he want?

MRS STAUNTON: He would speak with Miss Enid alone. I didn't think it right. That is why Miss Enid is offended.

RYLOTT: Where is the fellow?

MRS STAUNTON: He is gone. He went off through the shrubbery.

RYLOTT: Upon my word, he seems to make himself at home. What did he want, Enid?

ENID: He wanted to know how I was. When I assured him that I was quite well, he left.

RYLOTT: This is too funny! You have made a conquest, Enid. You have a rustic admirer.

ENID: I believe he is a true friend who means well to me.

RYLOTT: It was an astounding performance. Perhaps it is as well for him that he did not prolong his visit. But now, my dear girl, go to your room until I send for you. I am very sorry that you have been upset, and I will see that such a thing does not happen again. Tut! tut! my little girl shall not be worried. Leave it to me.

Exit ENID

Well, what is it, then? Why have you upset her?

MRS STAUNTON: Why has she upset me? Why should I be always the last to be considered?

RYLOTT: Why should you be considered at all?

MRS STAUNTON: You dare to say that to me – you that promised me marriage only a year ago. If I was what I should be, then there would be no talk as to who is the mistress of this house. I'll put up with no more of her tantrums, talking to me as if I were the kitchen-maid.

RYLOTT: You forget yourself.

MRS STAUNTON: I forget nothing. I don't forget your promise, and it will be a bad day for you if you don't keep it.

RYLOTT: I'll put you out on the roadside if you dare speak so to me.

MRS STAUNTON: You will, will you? Try it, and see. I saved you once. Maybe I could do the other thing, if I tried.

RYLOTT: Saved me!

MRS STAUNTON: Yes, saved you. If it hadn't been for my evidence at that inquest, that fellow Armitage would have taken the Jury with him. Yes, he would. I've had it from them since.

RYLOTT: Well, you only spoke the truth.

MRS STAUNTON: The truth! Do you think I don't know?

RYLOTT: What do you know?

(*She is silent, and looks hard at him.*)

What do you know?

(*She is still silent.*)

Don't look at me like that, woman. Have you lost your wits? What do you know?

MRS STAUNTON: I know enough.

RYLOTT: Tell me, then! How did she die?

MRS STAUNTON: Only you know that.

RYLOTT: Come, come, you're raving!

MRS STAUNTON: I may not know how she died, but I know very well –

RYLOTT (*interrupting*): There! there! enough said. You were always fanciful, Kate, but I know very well that you have only my own interests at heart. Put it out of your head if I have said anything unkind. Don't quarrel with this little fool, or you may interfere with my plans. Just wait a little longer, and things will come straight with us. You know that I have a hasty temper, but it is soon over.

MRS STAUNTON: You can always talk me round, and you know it. Now, listen to me, for I am the only friend you've got. Don't try it again. You've got clear once. But a second would be too much.

RYLOTT: They would make no more of the second than of the first. No one in the world can tell. It's impossible, I tell you. If she marries, half my income is gone.

MRS STAUNTON: Couldn't she sign it to you?

RYLOTT: She can be strong enough when she likes. She would never sign it to me. I hinted at it once, and she talked of a lawyer. But if anything should happen to her – well, there's an end to all our trouble.

MRS STAUNTON: They must suspect.

RYLOTT: Let them suspect. But they can prove nothing.

MRS STAUNTON: Not yet.

RYLOTT: On Wednesday she goes a-visiting, and who knows when she may return? No, it's tomorrow or never.

MRS STAUNTON: Then let it be never.

RYLOTT: And lose half my income without a struggle? No, Kate, it's all or nothing with me now.

MRS STAUNTON: Well, look out for Armitage.

RYLOTT: What about him?

MRS STAUNTON: He must have known something before he dared to come here.

RYLOTT: What can he know of our affairs?

MRS STAUNTON: But there's Rodgers. You think he's half-witted. So he is. But he may know more and say more than we think. He's a deal down in the village. Maybe Armitage gets hold of him.

RYLOTT (*striking the bell*): We'll soon settle that. I'll twist the old rogue's neck if he has dared to play me false. There's one thing – he can't hold anything in if I want it to come out. Did you ever see a snake and a white mouse?

Enter RODGERS

Come here, Rodgers.

RODGERS: Yes, sir.

RYLOTT: Sit here, where the light falls on your face, Rodgers. I can tell then if you are telling me the truth.

RODGERS: The truth, sir. Surely I would tell that.

RYLOTT (*taking his neck and pressing him into chair*): Sit there! Don't move! Now look at me. That's right. You can't lie to me now. You've been down to see Mr Armitage in the village.

RODGERS: Sir – I hope – there was no harm in that.

RYLOTT: How often?

RODGERS: Two or three times.

RYLOTT: How often?

RODGERS: Two or three –

RYLOTT: How often?

RODGERS: When I go to the village I always see him.

MRS STAUNTON: That's nearly every day.

RODGERS: Yes.

RYLOTT: What have you told him about me?

RODGERS: Oh, sir, nothing.

RYLOTT: What have you told him?

RODGERS: Just the news of the house, sir.

RYLOTT: What news?

RODGERS: Well, about Miss Enid's engagement, sir, and Siva biting the gardener, and the cook giving notice, and the like.

RYLOTT: Nothing more than this?

RODGERS: No, sir.

RYLOTT: Nothing more about Miss Enid?

RODGERS: No, sir.

RYLOTT: You swear it?

RODGERS: No, sir, no. I said nothing more.

RYLOTT (*shaking him*): You doddering old rascal, how came you to say anything at all? I kept you here out of charity, and you dare to gossip about my affairs. I've had enough of you. I'll go to London tomorrow and get a younger man. You pack up your things and go. D'you hear?

RODGERS: Won't you look it over, sir? I'm an old man, sir, and I have no place to go to. Where am I to go?

RYLOTT: You can go to the devil for all I care, or to your friend Armitage, the grocer. There is no place for you here. Get out of the room.

RODGERS: Yes, sir.

RYLOTT: And tell Miss Enid I want her.

RODGERS: Yes, sir.

Exit RODGERS

MRS STAUNTON: You have done wisely. He was not safe.

RYLOTT: The old devil suited me, too, in a way. A younger man may give more trouble.

MRS STAUNTON: You'll soon break him in.

RYLOTT: Yes, I expect I will. Now, make it right with Enid for my sake. You must play the game to the end.

MRS STAUNTON: It is a long game and a hard game, but the day will come when I shall claim the stakes. It is all right, I'm ready for her.

Enter ENID

RYLOTT: My dear, Mrs Staunton is very sorry if she has given you any annoyance. I hope you will accept her apology in the same spirit that it is offered.

MRS STAUNTON: I meant no harm, Miss Enid, and I was only thinking of the master's interests. I hope you'll forgive me.

ENID: Certainly I forgive you, Mrs Staunton.

RYLOTT: There's a good little girl. Now, Mrs Staunton, you had better leave us.

Exit MRS STAUNTON

Now, my dear, you must not be vexed with poor Mrs Staunton, for she is a very hard-working woman and devoted to her duty, though of course her manners are often wanting in polish. Come now, dear, say that it is all right.

ENID: I have said that I forgive her.

RYLOTT: You must tell me anything I can do, dear, to make you happier. Of course you have someone else now, but I would not like you to forget your old stepfather altogether. Until the day when you have to leave me, I wish to do the very best for you.

ENID: You are very kind.

RYLOTT: Can you suggest anything that I can do?

ENID: No, no, there is nothing.

RYLOTT: I was a little too rough last week. I am sorry for that. I am sure that you will often look back to the days which you spent in the dear old house. I should wish your future husband to like me. You will tell him, when you see him, that I have done what I could to make you happy?

ENID: Yes, yes.

RYLOTT: You see him tomorrow?

ENID: Yes.

RYLOTT: And he leaves us tomorrow evening?

ENID: Yes.

RYLOTT: You have all my sympathy, dear, in the sad privation. But he will soon be back again, and then, of course, you will part no more. In his absence you will have this pleasant visit and the time will soon slip by. You will be sorry to hear that old Rodgers has been behaving badly and that I must get rid of him.

ENID: Rodgers! what has he done?

RYLOTT: He grows more foolish and incompetent every day. I propose to go to London myself tomorrow to get a new butler. Would you send a line in my name to the agents to say that I shall call about two o'clock?

ENID: I will do so.

RYLOTT: There's a good little girl. There's nothing on your mind, is there?

ENID: Oh, no.

RYLOTT: Well, then, run away and get your letter written. I dare bet you have another of your own to write. One a day – or two a day? What is his allowance? Well, well, we have all done it at some time.

Enter ALI *with milk, jug, glass, and saucer on tray*

ALI: I beg pardon, sahib, I go.

RYLOTT: Come in! Come in! Put my milk down on the table.

Exit ENID

You fool! why did you not make sure I was alone?

ALI: I thought no one here but sahib.

RYLOTT: Well, as it happens, there's no harm done. (*Goes to door and locks it. Pulls down blind of window.*)

(*While he does so* ALI *opens a cupboard and takes out a peculiar square wicker-work basket.* RYLOTT *pours milk into saucer and puts it before basket. Then he cracks his fingers and whistles while* ALI *plays on an Eastern flute.*)

CURTAIN

Scene Two

Mr Sherlock Holmes's room in Baker Street

Enter PAGE (BILLY), *showing in* DR WATSON

WATSON: I particularly want to see Mr Holmes.

PAGE: Well, sir, I expect he will be back almost immediately.

WATSON: Is he very busy just now?

PAGE: Yes, sir, we are very busy. We don't get much time to ourselves these days.

WATSON: Any particular case?

PAGE: Quite a number of cases, sir. Two German princes

and the Duchess of Ferrers yesterday. The Pope's been bothering us again. Wants us to go to Rome over the cameo robbery. We are very overworked.

WATSON: Well, I'll wait for Mr Holmes.

PAGE: Very good, sir. Here is *The Times*. There's four for him in the waiting-room now.

WATSON: Any lady among them?

PAGE: Not what I would call a lady, sir.

WATSON: All right, I'll wait.

Exit PAGE

(WATSON *lights a cigarette and looks around him.*)

Just the same as ever. There are the old chemicals! Heavens! what have I not endured from those chemicals in the old days? Pistol practice on the wall! Quite so. I wonder if he still keeps tobacco in that Persian slipper? Yes, here it is. And his pipes in the coal-scuttle? Full of them! Black clays, the same as ever. (*Takes one out and smells it.*) Faugh! Bottle of cocaine, dear, dear! and the violin, the same old violin with one string left.

Enter WORKMAN, *with tools*

WORKMAN: You sent for me, Mr Sherlock Holmes.

WATSON: I am not Mr Holmes.

WORKMAN: Beg pardon, sir, it was to mend the gas-bracket.

WATSON: What's wrong with it?

WORKMAN: Leaking, sir, this one near the window.

WATSON: Well, go on with your work.

WORKMAN: Yes, sir. (*Goes to the bracket.*) Hope I won't disturb you, sir?

WATSON (*taking up* The Times): That's all right. Don't mind me.

WORKMAN: Very untidy man, Mr Holmes, sir.

WATSON: What do you mean by that?

WORKMAN: Well, sir, you can't help noticing it. It's all over the room. I've 'eard say he was as tidy as any when he started, but he learned bad 'abits from a cove what lived with him. Watson was his name.

WORKMAN *slips into bedroom*

WATSON: You impertinent fellow! How dare you talk in such a fashion? What do you mean? (*Looks round.*) Why! what the deuce has become of him?

WORKMAN *emerges as* SHERLOCK HOLMES, *in dressing-gown with hands in pockets*

Good Heavens, Holmes! I should never have recognized you.

HOLMES: My dear Watson, when you begin to recognize me it will indeed be the beginning of the end. When your eagle eye penetrates my disguise I shall retire to an eligible poultry farm.

WATSON: But why –?

HOLMES: A case, my dear Watson, a case! One of those small conundrums which a trustful public occasionally confides to my investigation. To the British workman, Watson, all doors are open. His costume is unostentatious, and his habits are sociable. A tool-bag is an excellent passport, and side whiskers will be found to secure the co-operation of the maids. It may interest you to know that my humble double is courting a cook in Battersea.

WATSON: My dear Holmes! is it fair to the girl?

HOLMES: Chivalrous old Watson! It's a game of life and death, and every card must be played. But in this case I have a hated rival, so when I disappear all will readjust itself. We walk out on Saturday evenings. Oh! those walks! But the honour of a Duchess is at stake. A mad world, my masters! (*Lights a cigarette and turns to survey* WATSON.) Well, Watson, what is your news?

WATSON (*smiling*): Well, Holmes, I came here to tell you what I am sure will please you.

HOLMES: Engaged, Watson, engaged! Your coat, your hat, your gloves, your buttonhole, your smile, your blush! The successful suitor shines from you all over. What I had heard of you, or perhaps what I had not heard of you, had already excited my worst suspicions. (*Looks fixedly at* WATSON.) But this is better and better, for I begin to perceive that it is a young lady whom I know and respect.

WATSON: But, Holmes, this is marvellous. The lady is Miss Morstan, whom you have indeed met and admired. But how could you tell –!

HOLMES: By the same observation, my dear Watson, which assures me that you have seen the lady this morning. (*Picks a hair off* WATSON'S *breast, wraps it round his finger, and glances at it with his lens.*) Charming, my dear fellow, charming. There is no mistaking the Titian tint. You lucky fellow! I envy you.

WATSON: Thank you, Holmes. Some of these days I may find myself congratulating you.

HOLMES: No marriage without love, Watson.

WATSON: Then why not love?

HOLMES: Absurd, Watson, absurd! I am not for love, nor love for me. It would disturb my reason, unbalance my faculties. Love is like a flaw in the crystal, sand in the clockwork, iron near the magnet. No, no, I have other work in the world.

WATSON: You have, indeed. Billy says you are very busy just now. (*Comes* L.)

HOLMES: There are one or two small matters.

WATSON: Have you room to consider one other? The case of Miss Enid Stonor.

HOLMES: My dear fellow, if you have any personal interest in it.

WATSON: Yes, I feel keenly about it.

HOLMES (C., *taking out note-book*): Let us see how I stand. There is the Baxter Square murder – I have put the police on the track. The Clerkenwell Jewel Robbery – that is now clearing. The case of the Duchess of Ferrers – I shall settle it on Tuesday week. The Pope's cameos – His Holiness must wait. The Princess who is about to run from

home – let her run. (*Rings bell.*) I must see one or two who
are waiting for me, then I am entirely at your disposal.

Enter PAGE

PAGE: Yes, Mr Holmes.

HOLMES: How many are waiting?

PAGE: Four, sir.

HOLMES: A light morning. Show them in now.

Exit PAGE

WATSON: Well, I'll look in later.

HOLMES: No, no, my dear fellow! Why, good gracious! I
have always looked on you as a partner in the firm.
Holmes, Watson, Billy & Co. That's our brass plate when
we raise one. If you'll sit there I shall soon be free.

Enter PAGE, *with a card on tray.* MR HOLT LOAMING *follows
– a rich, dissipated-looking, middle-aged man in
astrakhan-collared coat.*

(*Reading.*) Mr Holt Loaming. I remember the name. A
racing man, I believe?

LOAMING: Yes, sir.

HOLMES: Pray take a seat.

(LOAMING *draws up near the table.*)

What can I do for you?

LOAMING: Time's money, Mr Holmes, both yours and
mine. I'm pretty quick off the mark and you won't mind
that. I'm not here on the advice gratis line. Don't you
think it. I've got my cheque-book here (*takes it out*) and
there's plenty behind it. I won't grudge you your fees, Mr
Holmes. I promise you that.

HOLMES: Well, Mr Loaming, let us hear the business.

LOAMING: My wife, Mr Holmes – damn her! She's given
me the slip. Got back to her own people and they've hid
her. There's the law, of course, but she'd get out all kinds
of lies about ill-treatment. She's mine, and I'll just take
her when I know where to lay my hands on her.

HOLMES: How would you take her?

LOAMING: I just have to walk up to her and beckon. She's

one of those wincing kind of nervous fillies that kick about in the paddock, but give in when once the bridle's on them and they feel the whip. You show me where she is, and I'll do the rest.

HOLMES: She is with her own people, you say?

LOAMING: Well, there's no man in the case, if that's what you're driving at. Lord! if you knew how straight she is, and how she carries on when I have a fling. She's got a cluster of aunts, and she's lyin' low somewhere among them. It's for you to put her up.

HOLMES: I fancy not, Mr Loaming.

LOAMING: Eh, what's that?

HOLMES: I rather like to think of her among that cluster of aunts.

LOAMING: But, damn it, sir, she's my wife!

HOLMES: That was why.

LOAMING (*getting up*): Well, it's a rum start, this. Look here, you don't know what you're missing. I'd have gone to five hundred. Here's the cheque.

HOLMES: The case does not attract me. (*Rings bell.*)

Enter PAGE

Show Mr Loaming out, Billy.

LOAMING: It's the last you'll see of me, Mr Holmes.

HOLMES: Life is full of little consolations.

LOAMING: Damn!

Exit LOAMING *and* PAGE

HOLMES: I'm afraid I shall never be a rich man, Watson.

Re-enter PAGE

Well?

PAGE: Mrs Soames, sir.

Enter MRS SOAMES — *needy, gentlewoman type*

HOLMES: Ah yes, Mrs Soames, I remember you very well. Husband left you penniless with two children on your hands upon the ninth of last September. Supposed to have gone to America.

MRS SOAMES: Yes, sir. He *did* go to America.

HOLMES: Indeed?

MRS SOAMES: And he's dead.

HOLMES: How do you know?

MRS SOAMES: This cutting, sir. (*Hands envelope to* HOLMES.)

HOLMES: Chicago post-mark; red wax seal, pressed down by an obliging gentleman with a scar on his thumb. Dear me! how very interesting. What's this? *Chicago Democrat,* 'Mr Josiah Soames of London, England, run over by a street car.' Look at it, Watson. I regard it as conclusive.

WATSON: That the man is dead?

HOLMES: That the man has married again.

WATSON: My dear Holmes!

HOLMES: Four misprints in six lines, Watson! An absurd advertisement at the back. No real paper ever published such stuff. The sub-editor would be shot out of the office. It's a forgery. And why should he take the trouble if he had not a strong reason for stalling off his first wife? Of course he is going to take a second. (*To* MRS SOAMES.) Go straight out to Chicago, Mrs Soames, and he'll be at your mercy. The police will help you to find him. At least he will have to make you an allowance.

MRS SOAMES: Oh, Mr Holmes! how can I reach Chicago?

HOLMES: Tut, tut! Take this card to my friend Marbrook of the Transatlantic office. He'll see to it. (*Rings.*)

MRS SOAMES: Oh, Mr Holmes –

Enter PAGE

HOLMES: There, there! that will do! Quite so, goodbye.

Exit MRS SOAMES *and* PAGE

Heroic little woman! Selfish brute of a man.

Re-enter PAGE

Well, Billy?

PAGE: Mr James B. Montague, sir.

Enter MR MONTAGUE

Exit PAGE

HOLMES: Good-morning, Mr Montague. Pray take a chair. What can I do?

MONTAGUE (*a furtive-looking man with slimy ways*): Anything fresh about the death of my brother, sir? The police said it was murder, and you said it was murder; but we don't get any further do we?

HOLMES: I have not lost sight of it.

MONTAGUE: That man Henderson was a bad man, Mr Holmes, an evil liver and a corruption. Yes, sir, a corruption and a danger. Who knows what passed between them? I've my suspicions – I've always had my suspicions.

HOLMES: So you said.

MONTAGUE: Have you worked any further on that line, sir? Because, if you tell me from time to time how it is shaping, I may be able to give you a word in season.

HOLMES: I have my eye on him – a very cunning rascal, as you say. We have not enough to arrest him on, but we work away in the hope.

MONTAGUE: Good, Mr Holmes, good! You are on the line. Watch him; you'll get him, as safe as judgement.

HOLMES: I'll let you know if anything comes of it. (*Rings.*)

MONTAGUE (*rising*): That's right, sir. I'm his brother, sir. It's me that should know. It's never out of my mind.

Enter PAGE

HOLMES: Very good, Mr Montague. Good morning.

Exit MR MONTAGUE *and* PAGE

Curious little murder, Watson; done for most inadequate motive. That was the murderer.

WATSON: Good Heavens!

HOLMES: My case is almost complete. Meanwhile I amuse him and myself by the pretended pursuit of the wrong man – a very ancient device, Watson.

Re-enter PAGE

Well, any more?

PAGE: Mr Milverton is here, Mr Holmes.

HOLMES: Show him in when I ring.

Exit PAGE

I am sorry to delay the business upon which you wished to

consult me; but this, I hope, will be the last. You remember Milverton?

WATSON: No.

HOLMES: Ah, it was after your time. The most crawling reptile in London – the king of the blackmailers – a cunning, ruthless devil. I have traced seventeen suicides to that man's influence. It is he who is after the Duchess of Ferrers.

WATSON: The beautiful Duchess, whose re-marriage is announced?

HOLMES: Exactly. He has a letter which he thinks would break off the wedding. (*Rings.*) I am endeavouring to regain it.

Enter MILVERTON

Well, Mr Milverton. Pray take a seat.

MILVERTON: Who is this?

HOLMES: My friend, Dr Watson. Do you mind?

MILVERTON: Oh! I have no object in secrecy. It is your client's reputation, not mine, which is at stake.

HOLMES: Your reputation! Good Heavens!

MILVERTON: Not much to lose there, is there, Mr Holmes? I can't hurt. But she can. Hardly a fair fight, is it?

HOLMES: What are the terms now?

MILVERTON: Steady at seven thousand. No money, no marriage.

HOLMES: My advice to her is to tell the whole story to the Marquis. Then your letter is not worth sixpence. He would condone all.

MILVERTON: Would he, though?

HOLMES: Come, now, what harm is in the letter?

MILVERTON: Sprightly – very sprightly. However, it is purely a matter of business. If you think it is in the best interests of your client that the Marquis should see the letter – why, you would be very foolish to pay a large sum to regain it.

HOLMES: The lady has no great resources.

MILVERTON: But her marriage is a most suitable time for her friends and relations to make some little effort. I can assure you that this envelope would give more joy than all the tiaras and bracelets in Regent Street.

HOLMES: No, it is impossible.

MILVERTON: Dear me! dear me! how unfortunate. Look here! (*Takes out a pocket book.*)

(HOLMES *takes a quick step forward.*)

No, no, Mr Holmes, you can't seriously think I would carry the letter into your rooms. But there are others. Look at this! This belongs to – well – I withhold the name till tomorrow morning. At that time it will be in the hands of the lady's husband. And all because she will not find a beggarly sum which she could get in an hour by turning her jewels into paste. It *is* such a pity. What are her advisers about? And here I find you – a man of sense – boggling about terms when a Duchess' honour is at stake. You surprise me, Mr Holmes.

HOLMES: The money cannot be found, I tell you. Would it not be better to ask some reasonable sum? It can profit you in no way to push matters to an end.

MILVERTON: There you mistake. I have eight or ten other cases maturing. If it were known that I had been severe on the Duchess the others would be more open to reason.

HOLMES: Well, well, you give us to the 14th? (*Rings.*)

MILVERTON: But not an hour longer.

Enter PAGE

HOLMES: Very good. Show Mr Milverton out, Billy.

Exit PAGE and MILVERTON

A fumigator would be useful, Watson. Pah!

WATSON: What can you do?

HOLMES: My remedy will be heroic. It is this gentleman's cook who has honoured me. In the intervals of philandering I have made an acquaintance with the lock of his safe. I should not be surprised if there were a burglary upon the 13th, at the Firs, Battersea, and some valuable papers missing. (*Rings.*)

WATSON: Holmes, you are splendid!

Enter PAGE

HOLMES: Tut, tut! (*To* PAGE.) Well, any more?

PAGE: One lady, sir – just come – Miss Enid Stonor, of Stoke Moran.

WATSON: Ah! this is the case.

HOLMES: I'll ring, Billy.

Exit PAGE

Now, Watson! Stonor! Stonor! Surely I associate the name with something?

WATSON: I told you of the case at the time. Sudden mysterious death of a girl at an old house in Stoke Moran, some two years ago.

HOLMES: My dear fellow! it all comes back to me. An inquest, was it not, with a string of most stupid and ineffectual witnesses?

WATSON: I was one of them.

HOLMES: Of course, so you were, so you were. I docketed the evidence. It introduced to my notice a gentleman of singular and most interesting personality. I have a few notes. (*Takes down a scrapbook from a row.*) Let's see – it's R is it not? Ranter – Romanez – Rylott! That's our man. Fifty-five years of age, killed his khitmutgar in India; once in a madhouse; married money – wife died; distinguished surgeon. Well, Watson, what has the distinguished surgeon been up to now?

WATSON: Devilry, I fear.

HOLMES: I have the case very clear in my mind.

WATSON: Then you may remember that the death of the lady followed close upon her engagement?

HOLMES: Exactly.

WATSON: Miss Enid Stonor in turn became engaged, about a month ago, to a neighbour, Lieutenant Curtis.

HOLMES: Ah!

WATSON: Unhappily, the young man leaves for the Mediterranean today. She will henceforward be alone at Stoke Place.

HOLMES: I see.

WATSON: And some circumstances have excited her alarm.

HOLMES: I gather that the amiable stepfather stands to lose in case of marriage.

WATSON: That is so. Of course, supposing that Rylott did the other girl to death, it seems unlikely, on the face of it, that he would try it on again, as two sudden deaths in the house could hardly pass the coroner –!

HOLMES: No, no, Watson! You are making the mistake of putting your normal brain into Rylott's abnormal being. The born criminal is often a monstrous egotist. His mind is unhinged from the beginning. What he wants he must have. Because he thinks a thing, it is right. Because *he* does a thing, it will escape detection. You can't say *a priori* that he will take this view or that one. Perhaps we had best have the young lady in. (*Rings bell.*) My dear fellow, you'll get into trouble if you go about righting the wrongs of distressed damsels. It won't do, Watson, it really won't.

Enter ENID

WATSON: How do you do, Miss Enid? This is my friend, Mr Holmes, of whom I spoke.

(HOLMES *shakes hands with* ENID.)

HOLMES: How do you do, Miss Stonor. Dear me! You must find a dog-cart a cold conveyance in this weather.

ENID: A dog-cart, Mr Holmes?

HOLMES: One can hardly fail to observe the tell-tale splashes on the left sleeve. A white horse and a clay soil are indicated. But what is this? You are trembling. Watson, a chair!

ENID (*looking round*): Tell me, Mr Holmes, my stepfather has not been here?

HOLMES: No.

ENID: He saw me in the street. I dashed past him in a cab. But he saw me; our eyes met, and he waved me to stop.

HOLMES: Why is your stepfather in London?

ENID: He came up on business.

HOLMES: It would be interesting to know what the business was.

ENID: It was to get a new butler. Poor old Rodgers, who has been with us for years, is quite broken up. He is to leave us and a new butler is to come at once. I doubt if any servant would come to such a place.

HOLMES: He may certainly find some difficulty. He would, no doubt, apply to an agent.

ENID: At two o'clock, to Patterson & Green, of Cavendish Street.

HOLMES: Exactly. I know them. But this is a digression, is it not? We get back to the fact that he saw you in the street?

ENID: It was in Pall Mall. I fancy he followed me.

HOLMES: Would he imagine you would come here?

ENID: No, he would think I was going to Dr Watson's. He knows that Dr Watson is my only friend in London.

HOLMES: But I had been given to understand that Dr Rylott has treated you more kindly of late?

ENID: Yes, he has. Because he knows I have some one to protect me. But even so, there have been moments –

(HOLMES *raises her sleeve.*)

HOLMES: Good Heavens!

ENID: He does not realize his own strength. When he is angry he is like a fierce wild beast. Only last week he thrashed the village blacksmith.

HOLMES: He is welcome to the blacksmith, but not to my clients. This shall not occur again. Does your fiancé know of this?

ENID: I would not dare to tell him. Besides, as I say, my stepfather has, on the whole, been kinder. But there is a look in his eyes, when I turn on him suddenly, that chills me to the bone. This kindness is from the head, not from the heart. I feel as if he were waiting – waiting –

HOLMES: Waiting for what?

ENID: Waiting for Lieutenant Curtis to leave. Waiting till

he has me at his mercy. That room freezes my blood. Often I cannot sleep for horror.

WATSON: What? he has changed your room?

ENID: The change was necessary. It is a tumbledown old house and much of it is really uninhabitable. My old room is under repair. I go on a visit tomorrow and when I return my room will be ready.

WATSON: You sleep, then, in the room where your sister died?

ENID: In the same room. And other things have happened. The music has come again.

HOLMES: What is that? The music?

ENID: It came before my sister's death. She spoke of it, and then I heard it myself the night she died. But it has come again. Oh, Mr Holmes, I am terrified.

HOLMES (*going over and laying his hand on her shoulder*): There, there! you've had enough to break any one's nerve. This – music – does it seem to be *inside* the house or *outside*?

ENID: Indeed, I could not say.

HOLMES: What is it like?

ENID: A sort of soft, droning sound.

HOLMES: You sleep with your door and window fastened?

ENID: Yes, but so did poor Violet. It did not save *her*, and it may not save *me*.

HOLMES: Could there be anything in the nature of secret doors or panels?

ENID: I have searched again and again. No, there is nothing.

HOLMES: And nothing peculiar in the room?

ENID: No, I cannot say there is.

HOLMES: I must really drop in and have a look at this most interesting apartment. Suggestive – very suggestive. When did you hear this music last?

ENID: Last night.

HOLMES: And your fiancé leaves today?

ENID: He leaves today. What shall I do?

HOLMES: Well, Miss Stonor, I take up your case. It presents features which commend it to me. You must put yourself into my hands.

ENID: I do, most unreservedly.

(HOLMES *rings bell*.)

Enter PAGE

HOLMES: Billy, a gentleman will probably call presently. Keep him in the waiting room and let me know at once.

Exit PAGE

(*To* WATSON.) It is a question whether we are justified in letting her return at all to Stoke Moran.

ENID: I must return. At five o'clock Charles leaves, and I shall not see him again for months.

HOLMES: Ah! that is a complication. Where is the A.B.C. Stonehouse – Stowell – Stoke –

ENID: I know my train, Mr Holmes.

HOLMES: I was looking for mine.

ENID: You are coming down?

HOLMES: I shall not be content until I have seen this room of yours. Yes, that will do. I could get up to you between eleven and twelve. Would you have the goodness to leave your shutter open? The room is, I understand, upon the ground floor? Perhaps you would wait up for my coming?

ENID: Oh! it is not safe, Mr Holmes. You cannot think of the danger.

HOLMES: I have taken up your case, Miss Stonor, and this is part of it. Have you any friends in the village?

ENID: Mr Armitage, the grocer, and his wife.

HOLMES: That is most fortunate. Now, listen to me, Miss Stonor. When you have returned home certain circumstances may arise which will ensure your safety. In that case you will stay at Stoke Place until I come in the evening. On the other hand, things may miscarry, and you may not be safe. In that case I will so manage that a warning will reach you. You will then break away from home and take refuge with the Armitages. Is that clear?

ENID: Who will bring me the warning?

HOLMES: I cannot say. But you have my assurance that it will come.

ENID: Then, until it does, I will stay at Stoke Place.

HOLMES: And should any new development occur you could always send me a telegram, could you not?

ENID: Yes, I could do that.

HOLMES: Then it is not goodbye, but au revoir.

Enter PAGE

PAGE: Please, Mr Holmes, a gentleman to see you, at once.

HOLMES: Who is he?

PAGE: A very impatient gentleman, sir. It was all I could do to get him to stay in the waiting-room. I had to turn the key on him.

ENID: Is he tall, broad, dark, with a black beard, and a long white scar in his cheek?

PAGE: That's him, miss.

ENID: It is my stepfather. Oh, Mr Holmes, what shall I do? He has surely followed me.

WATSON: If he went to my rooms, my landlady had instructions to send any one on.

HOLMES: Exactly.

ENID: Oh! I dare not meet him, I dare not.

PAGE: All safe, miss; he can't get out.

ENID: Then I can slip away.

HOLMES: I see no reason why you should stay. Show the lady out, Billy.

PAGE: Yes, Mr Holmes. Don't be alarmed, miss, I'll see you through.

Exit PAGE *and* ENID

WATSON: This fellow is dangerous, Holmes. You may need a weapon.

HOLMES: There's something of the kind in that drawer at your right.

Enter PAGE

PAGE: Shall I stay when I show him in, Mr Holmes?

HOLMES: Why so?

PAGE: An ugly customer, Mr Holmes.

HOLMES: Tut, tut! Show him up.

Exit PAGE

Well, Watson, I must thank you for a most interesting morning. You are certainly the stormy petrel of crime.

Enter DR RYLOTT

RYLOTT: So, sir, this is pretty treatment. Does this young rascal act on your instructions? Is it your habit to lock up all your visitors?

HOLMES: Not all.

RYLOTT: Not all? Not all? What do you mean, sir?

HOLMES: Only those who seem inclined to be troublesome.

RYLOTT: Insolence! My name, sir, is Dr Grimesby Rylott, of Stoke Moran.

HOLMES: A very pretty place, sir, and obviously good for the lungs.

RYLOTT: I have come here to ask whether you have seen my stepdaughter here, Miss Enid Stonor.

HOLMES: The first law in my profession, Doctor, is never to answer questions.

RYLOTT: Sir, you *shall* answer me.

HOLMES: We could do with warmer weather.

RYLOTT: I insist upon an answer.

HOLMES: But I hear the crocuses are coming on.

RYLOTT: Curse your crocuses! I've heard of you, you meddling busybody. Look here, Dr Watson, I expected to find you here. What do you mean by interfering with my lawful affairs?

WATSON: So long as they are lawful, Dr Rylott, no one is likely to interfere with them.

RYLOTT: Now look here, Mr Holmes, perhaps I may seem to you a little hot-headed –

HOLMES: Dear me, Dr Rylott, what put that idea into your head?

RYLOTT: I apologize if I have seemed rude –

HOLMES: Robust – a little robust – nothing more.

RYLOTT (*sitting down*): I wish to put the matter to you as man to man. You know what girls are, how sudden and unreasonable their prejudices may be. Imagine how painful my position must be, to be distrusted by one whom I have loved.

HOLMES: You have my deep sympathy, Dr Rylott.

RYLOTT (*pleased*): Ah!

HOLMES: You are a most unfortunate man. There was that sad tragedy two years ago –

RYLOTT: Yes, indeed!

HOLMES: I think I could help you in that matter.

RYLOTT: How so?

HOLMES: As a friend, and without a fee.

RYLOTT: You are very good.

HOLMES: I am very busy, but your case seems so hard that I will put everything aside to assist you.

RYLOTT: In what way, sir?

HOLMES: I will come down at once, examine the room in which the tragedy occurred, and see if such small faculties as I possess can throw any light upon the matter.

RYLOTT: Sir, this is an intolerable liberty.

HOLMES: What! you don't want help?

RYLOTT: It is intolerable, I say. What I ask you to do – what I order you to do is to leave my affairs alone. Alone, sir – do you hear me?

HOLMES: You are perfectly audible.

RYLOTT: I'll have no interference – none! Don't dare to meddle with me. D'you hear, the pair of you? You, Holmes – I'm warning you.

HOLMES (*looking at his watch*): I fear I must end this interview. Time flies when one is chatting. Life has its duties as well as its pleasures, Doctor.

RYLOTT: Insolent rascal! I'll – I'll – (*Turns to the grate and picks up the poker.*)

HOLMES: No, Watson, no! It does need poking, but perhaps you would put on a few coals first?

RYLOTT: You laugh at me? You don't know the man you are dealing with. Perhaps you think that my strength fails because my hair is turned. I was the strongest man in India once. See that! (*Bends the poker and throws it down at HOLMES'S feet.*) I am not a safe man to play with, Mr Holmes.

HOLMES: Nor am I a safe man to play with, Dr Rylott. See that! (*Bends the poker straight again.*) I think we have taken too many liberties with Mrs Hudson's fire-irons. Let me see – what were we talking about before the Sandow performance?

RYLOTT: You shall not overcrow me with your insolence! I tell you now, and you too, Dr Watson, that you interfere with my affairs to your own danger. No one has ever crossed my path without being the worse for it. You have your warning.

HOLMES: I'll make a note of it.

RYLOTT: And you refuse to tell me if Miss Stonor has been here?

HOLMES: Don't we seem to be travelling just a little in a circle?

RYLOTT: Well, you can't prevent me from finding out from her.

HOLMES: Ah! there I must talk a little seriously to you, Dr Grimesby Rylott. You have mentioned this young lady, and I know something of her circumstances. If anything should befall her I hold you responsible. My eye is on you, sir, and the Lord help you, the Lord help you if I catch you tripping. Now leave this room, and take my warning with you.

RYLOTT: You cursèd fool! I may teach you both not to meddle with what does not concern you. Keep clear of

Stoke Moran, or you'll get a charge of shot into your hide.

Exit RYLOTT, *slamming door*

HOLMES: I had a presentiment he would slam the door. Stoke Moran must be less dull than many country villages. Quite a breezy old gentleman, Watson. Well, I must thank you for a very pretty problem. What the exact danger may be which destroyed one sister and now threatens the other, may be suspected, but cannot yet be defined. That is why I must visit the room.

WATSON: I will come with you, Holmes.

HOLMES: My dear fellow, you are no longer an unattached knight-errant. Dangerous quests are forbidden. What would Miss Morstan say?

WATSON: She would say that the man who could desert his friend would never make a good husband.

HOLMES: Well, my dear Watson, it may be our last adventure together, so I welcome your co-operation. I am rather busy now, so I bid you goodbye. You will leave Victoria tonight at eleven fifteen for Stoke Moran. Perhaps you will see me at the station. Perhaps you won't. In any case, eleven fifteen for Stoke Moran. (*Shakes hands.*)

CURTAIN

Third Act

Scene One

The Hall of the Stoke Moran Manor House

(MRS STAUNTON *discovered with a telegram in her hand,
reading it.*)

Enter ALI *from the outside door. He is wrapped up in a dark
overcoat, which he discards. Looks about him anxiously.*

ALI: Has she come back?

MRS STAUNTON: Yes, quarter of an hour ago; she has gone to her room.

ALI: I lost her at the Pendale Wood, but I thought she was coming home.

MRS STAUNTON: Well, what happened?

ALI: I did all that the master telegraphed. I went to the station and waited. She came alone by the third train. She walked from the station to Fenton. I followed far behind. She met Lieutenant Curtis. For an hour I waited in the hedge; then she left him, but I dared not stir, for it would have gone ill with me had he seen me; so I lost her.

MRS STAUNTON: It will go ill with you if you do not do what the Doctor tells you. But she came. The first thing she asked was whether there was a note or a message for her. Now, who can she be expecting a message from? What friend has she?

ALI: There is that Dr Watson of London.

MRS STAUNTON: Yes, that's true.

ALI: Or there is the man, Armitage, in the village.

MRS STAUNTON: That low busybody!

ALI: He speaks to her when he can. Does master return?

MRS STAUNTON: I have a telegram from him. He comes and brings the butler, and a young girl, too, the butler's daughter. We shall see the last of Mr Rodgers, the doddering old fool! He has lost his wits completely these last days. What has become of him? (*Goes to back and calls.*) Mr Rodgers! Mr Rodgers!

Enter RODGERS

RODGERS: Well, Mrs Staunton?

MRS STAUNTON: So! you've got your marching orders, Mr Rodgers?

RODGERS: I don't think the master meant it, Mrs Staunton. He was in one of his tempers when he said it.

MRS STAUNTON: Don't make any mistake about that, Mr Rodgers. There's a new man – Mr Peters, by name – and you'll have to hand over tonight.

RODGERS: Tonight! It's all so sudden, Mrs Staunton. Where can I go, and what can I do? I've no home, no friends, and little money. I'm not strong enough now to go out into the world.

MRS STAUNTON: Well, I suspect the Doctor thinks you are not strong enough to stay here. Look out! here is Miss Enid coming. (*Motions to* ALI *and* RODGERS *to go.*)

They exit

ENID *enters* R.

Can I get you a cup of tea, miss?

ENID (*sitting down*): No, thank you.

MRS STAUNTON: Is there nothing I can do?

ENID: Has any message come for me?

MRS STAUNTON: No, miss.

ENID: Very good, you can go.

MRS STAUNTON: I beg your pardon, miss, but I would be glad to know what I have done to offend you?

ENID: I have no wish to discuss it.

MRS STAUNTON: For two years and more, Miss Enid, you have behaved to me like this. I'd like to know the reason.

ENID: The reason is that you are my enemy. The reason is that you have been my sister's enemy. Do you think I do not know – that we both did not know – of your spying and mischief-making? You have been the only woman with us under this dreadful roof. You might have been our comfort and our help. Your own conscience will tell you what you have been.

MRS STAUNTON: I'm surprised at you, miss. What have I ever been except a good servant to my master?

ENID: That will do. I have said more than I intended. (*Rises.*)

MRS STAUNTON: I beg pardon, miss, but what are you going to do?

ENID: I am going down to the village.

MRS STAUNTON: What for?

ENID: How dare you ask me such a question? What do you mean by it?

MRS STAUNTON: I thought it was something we could do for you.

ENID: It is not.

MRS STAUNTON: Then I am sorry, miss, but it can't be done. The Doctor's orders were that you should not go out again.

ENID: You insolent woman! I am going out now.

MRS STAUNTON: Ali! Ali!

ALI runs in

Get to the door, Ali! It's no use, miss, we must obey our orders. You don't budge from here.

ENID: What is the meaning of it?

MRS STAUNTON: It is not for the likes of us to ask the meaning. The Doctor is a good master and he pays good money; but his servants have to obey him.

ENID: I will go out. (*Tries to rush past.*)

(*MRS STAUNTON seizes her and so does ALI. They push her into the settee.*)

Help! Help!

MRS STAUNTON: If you don't like it, you can tell him so. He'll be here very soon. Till he comes we have to hold you.

ENID: Well, leave me alone!

MRS STAUNTON: Will you promise not to make a bolt of it?

ENID: I'll promise nothing.

MRS STAUNTON: Lock the door, Ali.

(*ALI crosses and locks the door.*)

The other doors are locked as well. You needn't try the windows, for Siva is loose and Ali will be with him in the park. All right, Ali, you can go!

Exit ALI

Now, miss, don't kick against the pricks. That's my advice to you.

Exit

(ENID *waits until she has gone; then she rushes across to the writing-table and scribbles a telegram.*)

(RODGERS *passes at back.*)

ENID: Rodgers!

RODGERS: Yes, miss.

ENID: Come here, Rodgers!

(RODGERS *comes down.*)

I want to speak to you. I hear that you are leaving us. I wanted to say how sorry I am.

RODGERS: God bless you, Miss Enid. My heart is sore to part with you. All the kindness I've ever had in this house has been from poor Miss Violet and you.

ENID: Rodgers, if ever I have done anything for you, you can repay it now a hundredfold.

RODGERS: Nothing against the master, Miss Enid! Don't ask me to do anything against the master.

ENID: How can you love him!

RODGERS: Love him! No, no, I don't love him, Miss Enid. But I fear him – Oh! I fear him. One glance of his eyes seems to cut me – to pierce me like a sword. I wouldn't even listen to anything against him, for I feel it would come round to him, and then – then –!

ENID: Be a man, Rodgers. What can he do to you?

RODGERS: Oh, I couldn't, Miss Enid – don't ask me. What a man! what a man! Has he a child in his room, Miss Enid?

ENID: A child?

RODGERS: What is it he plays music to?

ENID: Ah! you have heard it.

RODGERS: Yes, yes, the music. And who drinks the milk? He drinks no milk.

ENID: What milk?

RODGERS: A jug of milk, Miss Enid. Every morning I take up the jug of milk. Surely it is a child.

ENID: Nonsense, Rodgers, you are raving.

RODGERS: Yes, poor old Rodgers is soft-headed. They all

tell me. Mrs Staunton told me; Ali told me. You wouldn't
let them put me in an asylum, Miss Enid, would you, now?
No, no, you wouldn't let them. That's what master said
would happen if ever I crossed him.

ENID: No, no, Rodgers. You are in no danger. It is I – I who
am in danger.

RODGERS: You, Miss Enid?

ENID: And you can save me.

RODGERS: Oh, Miss Enid, I couldn't – I couldn't! I have no
nerve. I couldn't.

ENID: All I want you to do is to take a telegram.

RODGERS: A telegram, Miss Enid?

ENID: They won't let me out, and yet I must send it.

RODGERS: Perhaps they won't let me out.

ENID: You could wait a little and then slip away to the
village.

RODGERS: What is the telegram, Miss Enid? Say it slowly.
My poor old head is not as clear as it used to be.

ENID: Give it to the clerk.

RODGERS: No, no, I must be sure it is nothing against the
master.

ENID: It is my business – only mine. Your master's name is
not even mentioned. See – it is to Mr Sherlock Holmes –
he is a friend of mine – Baker Street, London. 'Come
to me as soon as you can. Hurry.' That is all. Dear Rodgers, it means so much to me, please – please take it for
me.

RODGERS: So long as it isn't against the master. I can't
understand things like I used.

ENID: Oh! do take it, Rodgers! You said yourself that I had
always been kind to you. You *will* take it, won't you?
(*Holds out telegram to* RODGERS.)

RODGERS: Yes, yes, I will take it, Miss Enid. (*Takes telegram and puts it in his pocket.*)

ENID: Oh! you don't know what a service you are doing. It
may save me – it may save my going all the way to town.

RODGERS: Well, well, of course I will take it. What's that?
(*Wheels heard outside.*)

Enter MRS STAUNTON *and* ALI

MRS STAUNTON: Quick, Ali! Get the door unlocked. He won't like to be kept waiting.

ENID (*to* RODGERS): Don't forget! as soon as you can. (*Rises.*)

MRS STAUNTON: Rodgers, be ready to receive your master. (*Follows* ENID.)

ENID: I did not ask you to come, Mrs Staunton.

MRS STAUNTON: I have my duty, Miss Enid.

ENID *exits, followed by* MRS STAUNTON

ALI *throws open door and salaams. Enter* DR RYLOTT, *followed by* PETERS, *the new butler, who is followed by a young girl, with a big hat-box.*

RYLOTT (*taking off things and handing to* ALI): Where is Miss Enid? Did she return?

ALI: Yes, sir, she is in her room.

RYLOTT: Ah! (*To* RODGERS.) What! still here?

RODGERS: I had some hopes, sir –

RYLOTT: Get away! Lay the supper! I'll deal with you presently.

Exit RODGERS

You can go also, Ali. Show this young girl to the kitchen. (*To* PETERS.) What is her name?

PETERS: Amelia – the same as her mother's.

RYLOTT: Go to the kitchen, child, and make yourself useful.

Exit ALI, *followed by* AMELIA

(*To* PETERS.) Now, my man, we may as well understand each other first as last. I'm a man who stands no nonsense in my own house. I give good pay, but I exact good service. Do you understand?

PETERS: Yes, sir.

RYLOTT: I've had a man for the last two years, but he is old and useless. I want a younger man to keep the place in order. Rodgers will show you the cellar and the other things you should know. You take over from tomorrow morning.

PETERS: Very good, sir. I'm sure, sir, it was very good of you to take me with such an encumbrance as my poor little orphaned Amelia.

RYLOTT: I've taken you not only with a useless encumbrance, but without references and without a character. Why have I done that? Because I expect I shall get better service out of you. Where are you to find a place if you lose this one? Don't you forget it.

PETERS: I won't forget it, sir. I'll do all I can. If I can speak to your late butler, sir, I have no doubt he will soon show me my duties.

RYLOTT: Very good. (*Rings bell.*)

Enter MRS STAUNTON *up* R.

Where is Miss Enid now?

MRS STAUNTON: She is in her room, sir.

RYLOTT: Where is Siva?

MRS STAUNTON: Loose in the park, sir.

RYLOTT: By the way, I had best warn you, Peters, not to go out till my dog comes to know you. He's not safe with strangers – not very safe with anyone but myself.

PETERS: I'll remember, sir.

RYLOTT: Warn that girl of yours.

PETERS: Yes, I will.

RYLOTT (*to* MRS STAUNTON): What have you on the tray?

MRS STAUNTON: Tea for Miss Enid.

RYLOTT: Let her take her tea here. Set it down and tell her. But first of all, tell Rodgers I want him.

MRS STAUNTON (*sets tea down*): Yes, sir.

Exit

(DR RYLOTT *turns towards the fire, lost in thought.* PETERS *gets near the tea-tray.* DR RYLOTT *turns round.*)

PETERS: Shall I carry in this tray, sir?

RYLOTT: Leave it alone.

PETERS: Very good, sir.

Enter RODGERS

RYLOTT: Rodgers, you will hand your keys over to Peters. When you have done so, come to me in the study.

RODGERS: Yes, sir.

Exit DR RYLOTT

PETERS (*after looking round*): Well, I'm not so sure that I think much of this place. Maybe you are the lucky one after all. I hope I am not doing you out of your job. I'd chuck it for two pins.

RODGERS: If it wasn't you it would be someone else. Old Rodgers is finished – used up. But he said he wanted to see me in the study. What do you think he wants with me in the study?

PETERS: Maybe to thank you for your service; maybe to make you a parting present.

RODGERS: His eyes were hard as steel. What can he want with me? I get nervous these days, Mr Peters. What was it he told me to do?

PETERS: To hand over the keys.

RODGERS: Yes, yes, the keys. They are here, Mr Peters. That's the cellar key, Mr Peters. Be careful about the cellar. That was the first time he struck me – when I mistook the claret for the burgundy. He's often hasty, but he always kept his hands off till then.

PETERS: Well, beggars can't be choosers, but the more I see of this place the less I fancy it. I'd be off tonight, but it's not so easy these days to get a place if your papers ain't in order. See here, Mr Rodgers, I'd like to know a little more about my duties. The study is there, is it not?

RODGERS: Yes, he is there now waiting – waiting for me.

PETERS: Where is his room?

RODGERS: You see the passage yonder. Well, the first room you come to is the master's room; the next is Miss Enid's; the next is the spare room, but the builders have been at it.

PETERS: I see. Well, now, could you take me along to the master's room and show me any duties I have there?

RODGERS: The master's room? no one ever goes into the master's room. All the time I've been here I've never put my head inside the door.

PETERS (*surprised*): What! no one at all?

RODGERS: Ali goes. Ali is the Indian valet. But no one else.

PETERS: I wonder you never mistook the door and just walked in.

RODGERS: You could not do that, for the door is locked.

PETERS: Oh! he locks his door, does he? Dear me! None of the keys here any use, I suppose?

RODGERS: Don't think of such a thing! What are you saying? Why should you wish to enter the master's room?

PETERS: I don't want to enter it. The fewer rooms the less work. Why do you suppose he locks the door?

RODGERS: It is not for me, nor for you, to ask why the master does things. He chooses to do so. That is enough for us.

PETERS: Well, Mr Rodgers, if you'll excuse my saying so, this old 'ouse 'as taken some of the spirit out of you. I'm sure I don't wonder. I don't see myself staying here very long. Wasn't there someone died here not so long ago?

RODGERS: I'd rather not talk of that, Mr Peters.

PETERS: A woman died in the room next the doctor's. The cabman was telling me as we drove up.

RODGERS: Don't listen to them, Mr Peters. The master would not like it. Here is Miss Enid, and the Doctor wants me.

Enter ENID

ENID: Rodgers, can I have a word with you?

RODGERS: Very sorry, Miss Enid, the master wants me.

RODGERS *exits into study*

ENID (*to* PETERS): Who are you?

PETERS: I am Peters, miss, the new butler.

(ENID *sits down beside the tea.* PETERS *stands still with his eyes upon her.*)

ENID: Why do you stand there? Are you a spy set to watch me? Am I to have no one but enemies around me? What have they told you, or what have they paid you, to turn against me? Am I never to have one moment of privacy?

PETERS: I beg pardon, miss, I am sorry if you are in trouble.

ENID: Excuse me if I have spoken bitterly. I have had enough to make me bitter.

PETERS: I'm very sorry, miss. I'm new to the place and don't quite know where I am yet. May I ask, miss, if your name is Enid Stonor?

ENID: Yes, why do you ask?

PETERS: There was a lad at the station with a message for you.

ENID: A message for me! Oh! it is what I want of all things on earth! Why did you not take it?

PETERS: I did take it, miss, it is here. (*Hands her a note.*)

ENID (*tears it open, reads*): 'Fear nothing, and stay where you are. All will be right. Holmes.' Oh! It is a ray of sunshine in the darkness – such darkness. Tell me, Peters, who was this boy?

PETERS: I don't know, miss, just a very ordinary nipper. The Doctor had gone on to the cab. He touched my sleeve and asked me to give you this note in your own hand.

ENID: You said nothing to the Doctor?

PETERS: Well, miss, it seemed to be your business, not his. I just took it, and there it is.

ENID: God bless you for it. (*She conceals the note in her bosom.*)

PETERS: I'm only a servant, miss, but if I can be of any help to you, you must let me know.

Exit PETERS

(ENID *takes the note out of her bosom, reads it again, then hurriedly replaces it as* DR RYLOTT *and* RODGERS *enter.*)

RYLOTT: Very good. You can go and pack your box.

RODGERS (*cringing*): Yes, sir. You won't –!

RYLOTT: That's enough! Get away!

Exit RODGERS

(ENID *sits at tea-table.*)

(*Comes over to* ENID.) There you are! I must have a word or two with you. What the devil did you mean by slipping off to London the moment my back was turned? And what did you do when you got there?

ENID: I went there on my own business.

RYLOTT: Oh! your own business, was it? Perhaps what you call your own business may prove to be my business also. Who did you see? Come, woman, tell me?

ENID: It was my own business. I am of age and I have my own rights. You have no claim to control me.

RYLOTT: I know exactly where you went. Deny it if you can. You went to the rooms of Mr Sherlock Holmes, where you met Dr Watson, who advised you to go there. Was it not so?

ENID: I will answer no questions. If I did as you say I was within my rights.

RYLOTT: What did you go to consult Mr Holmes about?

(ENID *remains silent.*)

D'you hear? What did you go about? By God, I'll find a way to make you speak! (*Seizes her by the arm.*) Come!

Enter PETERS

PETERS: Yes, sir.

RYLOTT: I did not ring for you.

PETERS: I thought you called.

RYLOTT: Get out of this! What do you mean?

PETERS: I beg your pardon, sir.

Exit

RYLOTT: Look here, Enid, let us be sensible. I was too hot just now. But you must realize the situation. It will be best for both of us if you do. Your wisest and safest course is complete submission. If you do what I tell you there need be no friction between us.

ENID: What do you wish me to do?

RYLOTT: Your marriage will complicate the arrangement which was come to at your mother's death. I want you, of your own free will, to bind yourself to respect it. Come, Enid, you would not wish that your happiness should cause loss and even penury to me. I am an elderly man, and accustomed to certain little luxuries. I have had losses, too, which make it the more necessary that I should preserve what is left. If you will sign a little deed it will be best for both of us.

ENID: I have promised to sign nothing until a lawyer has seen it.

RYLOTT: Promised? Promised whom?

ENID: I promised Charles.

RYLOTT: Oh! you did, did you. I always felt that he was plotting against me. But why should lawyers come between you and me, Enid? I beg you – I urge you to do what I ask.

ENID: No, no, I cannot.

RYLOTT: Very good! on your own head be it. Tell me, Enid, what are your suspicions of me?

ENID: I have no suspicions.

RYLOTT: Did I not receive your fiancé with civility?

ENID: Yes, you did.

RYLOTT: Have I not, on the whole, been kind to you all this winter?

ENID: Yes, you have.

RYLOTT: Then tell me, child, why do you suspect me?

ENID: I don't suspect you.

RYLOTT: Why do you send out messages to get help against me?

ENID: I don't understand you.

RYLOTT: Don't you send out for help? Tell me the truth, child.

ENID: No.

RYLOTT (*with a yell*): You damned little liar! (*Bangs the telegram down before her.*) What was this telegram that you gave to Rodgers?

(ENID *sinks back, half fainting.*)

Ah! you infernal hypocrite. Shall I read it to you? 'Come to me as soon as you can. Hurry.' What did you mean by that? What did you mean, I say? What is it you suspect? None of your lies – Out with it.

ENID: Keep your hands off me, you coward! You know that my protector is gone, or you would not dare to treat me so.

RYLOTT: Answer me, then!

ENID: I will answer you! I believe that you murdered my mother by your neglect. I believe that in some way you drove my sister to her grave. Now I am certain that you mean to do the same to me. You're a murderer! a murderer! We were left to your care – helpless girls. You have ill-used us. You have tortured us. Now you have murdered one of us, and you would do the same to me. But if I am on the brink of the grave I will tell you that you are a coward, a monster, a man fit only for the gallows!

RYLOTT: You'll pay for this, you little devil! Get to your room.

ENID: I will – and I will lock myself in until someone comes to my help. I'm not without friends, as you may find.

RYLOTT: You've got some plot against me. What have you been arranging in London? What is it? (*Clutches her.*)

ENID: Let me go!

RYLOTT: What did you tell them? Answer me, damn you, or I'll screw the arm off you! By God, I'll twist your head off your shoulders if you dare to cross me! (*Seizes her by the neck.*)

ENID: Help! Help!

Enter PETERS

PETERS: Keep your hands off, Dr Rylott.

RYLOTT: You infernal scoundrel! (*Releases* ENID.)

PETERS: You had best go to your room, young lady. I'll see

that you are not molested. Never fear for me. Go right away!

RYLOTT: I'll soon settle you. (*Runs to a rack at the side.*)

ENID: He'll murder you.

RYLOTT: Go at once, I tell you, go! (*Pushes her.*)

                                        Exit ENID

(DR RYLOTT *gets a whip, opens the hall door, stands near it with his whip.*)

RYLOTT: Now then, out you go!

PETERS: I am going. I'd made up my mind it was no place for me. I wonder at a gentleman like you. I won't stand by and see a lady ill-used.

RYLOTT: Come on! (*Cracking whip.*) Out with you!

PETERS: With your permission, sir, I'll call my little Amelia and put on my hat and coat. Amelia, dear! (*Calling.*) The box I'll send for in the morning.

    Enter AMELIA, *who hands* PETERS *his coat and hat,
                    which he takes*

RYLOTT: Come on!

PETERS: Yes, sir. I'm not in service any more, so I'll take the liberty of lighting this cigarette. I'll borrow a match.

            (AMELIA *lights one for him.*)

Thank you, Amelia. Now I think we are ready.

RYLOTT: I think I am ready, too. By George! you'll remember Stoke Moran.

PETERS: Excuse me, sir, but is that a whip?

RYLOTT: You'll soon see what it is.

PETERS: I am afraid I must ask you to put it down.

RYLOTT: Oh, indeed! must you?

PETERS (*taking out a revolver*): Yes, sir! You'll please put down that whip.

RYLOTT (*falling back*): You villain!

PETERS: Stand right back, sir. I have no wish to do you a mischief. But I'll take no risks with a man like you. Right back, I say! Thank you, sir.

(*Approaches door.*) Hurry up, Billy, shift that key! Quick!

Business of key, revolver, and exit PETERS *and* AMELIA
(HOLMES *and* BILLY)

ALI *comes rushing in.* DR RYLOTT *runs to door.*

RYLOTT: The infernal villain! I'll be level with you.

ALI: No, no, sahib. He is gone. What can you do? besides
people come – police come.

RYLOTT: You're right. (*Puts whip down.*) We have another
game to play; Ali, you will watch outside Miss Enid's
window.

ALI: Yes, sahib, shall I watch all night?

RYLOTT: All night? No, not all night! You will learn when
you may cease your watch.

CURTAIN

Scene Two

Enid's Bedroom, Stoke Place

Bed on left. Door facing audience, on right.
Window on left of bed.

(ENID *discovered seated near lamp at small table near win-*
dow. Knock heard at door.)

ENID: Who is there?

RYLOTT (*speaking off*): It is I.

ENID: What do you want?

RYLOTT: Why is your light still burning?

ENID: I have been reading.

RYLOTT: You are not in bed, then?

ENID: Not yet.

RYLOTT: Then I desire to come in.

ENID: But it is so late.

RYLOTT (*rattles door*): Come, come, let me in this instant.

ENID: No, no, I cannot!

RYLOTT: Must I break the door in?

ENID: I will open it, I will open it. (*Opens door.*) Why do
you persecute me so?

RYLOTT *enters, in his dressing-gown*

RYLOTT: Why are you so childish and so suspicious? Your mind has brooded upon your poor sister's death until you have built up these fantastic suspicions against me. Tell me now, Enid – I'm not such a bad sort, you know, if you only deal frankly with me. Tell me, have you any idea of your own about how your sister died? Was that what you went to Mr Holmes about this morning? Couldn't you take me into your confidence as well as him? Is it not natural that I should feel hurt when I see you turn to a stranger for advice?

ENID: How my poor sister met her death only your own wicked heart can know. I am as sure that it came to her through you as if I had seen you strike her down. You may kill me, if you like, but I *will* tell you what I think.

RYLOTT: My dear child, you are overwrought and hysterical. What can have put such wild ideas into your head? After all, I may have a hasty temper – I have often deplored it to you – but what excuse have I ever given you for such monstrous suspicions?

ENID: You think that by a few smooth words you can make me forget all your past looks, your acts. You cannot deceive me. I know the danger, and I face it.

RYLOTT: What, then, is the danger?

ENID: It is near me tonight, whatever it is.

RYLOTT: Why do you think so?

ENID: Why is that Indian watching in the darkness? I opened my window just now, and there he was. Why is he there?

RYLOTT: To prevent your making a public fool of yourself. You are capable of getting loose and making a scandal.

ENID: He is there to keep me in my room, as the sheep is kept in the pen, until it is time for the slaughter.

RYLOTT: Upon my word, I think your brain is unhinged! Now, look here, Enid, be reasonable for a moment. Listen to me. If there is friction between us – and I don't for a moment deny that there is – why is it? You think I mean to hurt you. I could only have one possible motive for hurting you. Why not remove that motive? Then you could no longer work yourself into these terrors. Here is that little legal paper I spoke of. Mrs Staunton could witness it. All I want is your signature. It would be best for you and best for me.

ENID: No, never.

RYLOTT: Never!

ENID: Unless my lawyer advises it.

RYLOTT: Is that final?

ENID: Yes, it is. I will never sign it.

RYLOTT: You little fool! I have done my best for you. It was your last chance.

ENID: Ah! then you do mean murder.

RYLOTT: The last chance of regaining my favour. Get to your bed, and may you wake in a more rational mood tomorrow. You will not be permitted to make a scandal. Ali will be at his post outside, and I shall sit in the hall; so you may reconcile yourself to being quiet. Nothing more to say to me? Very good!

Exit

(*When he has gone* ENID *listens to his departing footsteps. Then she locks the door once again, and looks round her.*)

ENID: What is that tapping? Surely I heard tapping! Perhaps it is the pulse within my own brain? Yes! there it is again. Where was it? Is it the signal of death? (*Looks wildly round the walls.*) Ah! it grows louder. It is the window. (*Goes towards window.*) A man! a man crouching in the darkness. Still tapping. It's not Ali! The face was white. Ah!

The window opens and HOLMES *enters*

HOLMES: My dear young lady, I trust that I don't intrude. Old-fashioned window-catches are most inefficient.

ENID: Oh, Mr Holmes! I'm so glad to see you! Save me! Mr Holmes, they mean to murder me.

HOLMES: Tut, tut! we mean that they shall do nothing of the sort.

ENID: I had given up all hope of your coming. How did you pass the Indian and the dog?

HOLMES: Well, as to the Indian, we chloroformed him. Watson is busy tying him up in the arbour at the present moment. The dog I was compelled to shoot at an earlier stage of the proceedings.

ENID: You shot Siva!

HOLMES: I might have been forced to shoot his master also. It was after I sent you to your room. He threatened me with a whip.

ENID: You were – you were Peters, the butler.

HOLMES: A rough disguise, but it served. I wanted to be near you. So this is the famous room, is it? Dear me! Very much as I had pictured it. You will excuse me for not discovering myself to you, but any cry or agitation upon your part would have betrayed me.

ENID: But your daughter Amelia?

HOLMES: Ah yes, I always take Billy when I can.

ENID: Then you intended to watch over me till night?

HOLMES: Exactly. But the man's brutality caused me to show my hand too soon. However, I have never been far from your window. I gather the matter is pressing.

ENID: He means to murder me.

HOLMES: I was watching him. He is certainly in an ugly humour. He is not in his room at present.

ENID: No, he is in the hall.

HOLMES: So we can talk with safety. What has become of the excellent Watson? (*Approaches window.*) Come in, Watson, come in!

Enter WATSON *from window*

How is our Indian fellow-subject?

WATSON: He is coming out of the chloroform; but he can neither move nor speak. Good evening, Miss Stonor, what a night it is.

HOLMES: The wind is good. Its howling will cover all sounds. Just sit in the window, Watson, and see that our rear is safe. With your leave, I will inspect the room a little more closely. Now, my dear young lady, I can see that you are frightened to death, and no wonder. Your courage has been admirable. Sit over here by the fire and all will be well.

ENID: If he should come –!

HOLMES: In that case answer him. Say that you have gone to bed. (*Holds up the lamp.*) A most interesting old room – very quaint indeed! Old-fashioned comfort without modern luxury. The passage is, as I understand, immediately outside?

ENID: Yes.

HOLMES: Mr Peters made two attempts to explore the ground, but without avail. By the way, I gather that you tried to send me a message, and that old Rodgers gave it to your stepfather.

ENID: Yes, he did.

HOLMES: He is not to be blamed. His master controls him. He *had* to betray you.

ENID: It was my fault for trusting him.

HOLMES: Well, well, it was an indiscretion, but it didn't matter. Let me see now, on this side is the room under repair. On this other side the genial old gentleman sleeps when he is so innocently employed. Hush! what's that?

ENID: It's his step in the passage.

(HOLMES *holds his hat over the light. Knock at door.*)

RYLOTT (*heard outside door*): Enid!

ENID: What is it?

RYLOTT: Are you in bed?

ENID: Yes.

RYLOTT: Are you still of the same mind?

ENID: Yes, I am.

RYLOTT: Very good, then it's finished.

(*Pause. They all listen.*)

HOLMES (*whispering*): Has he gone into his room?

ENID: No, he went down the passage to the hall.

HOLMES: Then we must make the most of the time. Might I trouble you, Watson, for the gimlet and the yard-measure? Thank you. The lantern also, thank you! You can screen the lamp, but don't put it out. I am interested in this partition wall. No little surprise, I suppose? No trap-doors and sliding panels? Funny folk, our ancestors, with a quaint taste in practical joking. (*Gets on bed and fingers the wall.*) No, it seems solid enough. Dear me! and yet you say your sister fastened both door and window. Remarkable! My lens, Watson. A perfectly respectable wall – in fact a commonplace wall. Trap-door in the floor? No, nothing suspicious in that direction. Ancient carpeting – oak wainscot – nothing more. Hullo! hullo! hullo! hullo!

WATSON: What is it?

HOLMES: Why is your bed clamped to the floor?

ENID: I really don't know.

HOLMES: Was the bed in your other room clamped?

ENID: No, I think not.

HOLMES: Very interesting. Most interesting and instructive. And this bell-pull – where does it communicate with?

ENID: It does not work.

HOLMES: But if you want to ring?

ENID: There is another over here.

HOLMES: Then why this one?

ENID: I don't know. There were some changes after we came here.

HOLMES: Quite a burst of activity apparently. It took some strange shapes. (*Standing on bed.*) You may be interested to know that the bell-rope ends in a brass hook. No wire attachment; it is a dummy. Dear me! how very singular. I see a small screen above it, which covers a ventilator, I suppose?

ENID: Yes, Mr Holmes, there is a ventilator.

HOLMES: Curious fad to ventilate one room into another when one could as well get the open air. Most original man, the architect. Very singular indeed! There is no means of opening the flap from here; it must open on the other side.

WATSON: What do you make of it, Holmes?

HOLMES: Suggestive, my dear Watson, very suggestive. Bear in mind that this opening, concealed by a flap of wood, leads into the room of our cheery Anglo-Indian neighbour. I repeat the adjective, Watson – Anglo-Indian.

WATSON: Well, Holmes?

HOLMES (*steps off the bed*): The bed is clamped so that it cannot be shifted. He has a dummy bell-pull which leads to the bed. He has a hole above it which opens on his room. He is an Anglo-Indian doctor. Do you make nothing of all this? The music, too? The music, too. What is the music?

WATSON: A signal, Holmes.

HOLMES: A signal! A signal to whom?

WATSON: An accomplice.

HOLMES: Yes, an accomplice who could enter a room with locked doors – an accomplice who could give a death which leaves no trace.

ENID: Hush! he is gone to his room.

(*Door heard to close outside.*)

Listen! the door is shut.

HOLMES: Turn out that lamp, Watson. Keep your dark lantern handy. We must wait in the dark. I fancy we will not have long to wait.

ENID: I am so frightened.

HOLMES: I wish we could send you away. It is too much for you.

WATSON: Can I do nothing, Holmes?

HOLMES: You can hand me my cane. Hush! What's that?

My stick, Watson – quick, be quick! (*The music comes again.*) Now take the lantern! Have you got it? When I cry, 'Now!' turn it full blaze upon the top of the bell-rope. Do you understand?

WATSON: Rely on me!

HOLMES: Down that bell-rope comes the messenger of death. It can only reach the pillow. Hush! the flap!

(*The flap opens, disclosing a small square of light. This light is obscured.*)

(*Cries sharply.*) Now!

(WATSON *turns lantern full on to bell-rope. A snake is seen half through the hole.* HOLMES *lashes at it with a stick. It disappears backwards.*)

WATSON: It has gone.

HOLMES: Yes, it has gone, but we know the truth.

(*A loud cry is heard.*)

WATSON: What is that?

HOLMES: I believe the devil has turned on its master.

(*Another cry.*)

It is in the passage. (*Throws open the door.*)

(*In the doorway is seen the* DOCTOR, *in shirt and trousers, the snake round his head and neck.*)

RYLOTT: Save me! save me!

RYLOTT *rushes in and falls on floor*

(WATSON *and* HOLMES *strike at the snake as it writhes across the room.*)

WATSON (*looking at snake*): The brute is dead.

HOLMES (*looking at* DR RYLOTT): So is the other.

(*They both run to support the fainting lady.*)

Miss Stonor, there is no more danger for you under this roof.

CURTAIN

THE CROWN DIAMOND

Whether *The Crown Diamond* preceded 'The Adventure of the Mazarin Stone' or was a dramatization of that story is not known, though the play is popularly believed to have come first. The autograph manuscript runs to twenty-five pages, but it is not dated and does not give the place at which it was written. A comparison between the play and the story shows many points of similarity and, although a few names are changed – Colonel Sebastian Moran becomes Count Negretto Sylvius and Van Seddor appears as Van Seddar (though this may be a misreading of the text) – the lines in the play are in many cases direct or shortened transcripts of the words spoken in the story, the manuscript of which offers little help even though it was first called 'The Adventure of the Mazarin Diamond'. The main argument in favour of the play preceding the story is that Dr Watson is not the narrator and the action is confined to one room. This, however, is less conclusive than may appear. The story was the first in a new series, some of which were to be told by Holmes himself, and it followed shortly after *The Valley of Fear* which, in its preliminary stages, was also a third person narrative.

An agreement for the play was signed on 18 April 1921 between Doyle's literary agent, A. P. Watt, and the Daniel Mayer Company, and there was a fee of twelve guineas for the week's production given at the Bristol

Hippodrome where Dennis Neilson-Terry's company opened on 2 May. It was Neilson-Terry's first appearance on the variety stage, and the 'playlet', as the theatrical papers called it, was performed twice nightly along with other acts and turns. On 16 May it reached the London Coliseum, where it played for one week in a variety programme which included Bournonville's *La Sylphide* given by the Danish dancers of the Royal Theatre in Copenhagen, and performances by popular revue artists like Muriel George and Ernest Butcher, Walter Williams and Gertrude Lawrence. It may be that the manager of the Coliseum, Arthur Croxton, or the producer, 'Colonel' Stanley Bell, had commissioned the piece for that theatre which had for many years included one-act plays by famous writers in its programmes; or it may be that Sir Oswald Stoll, who had just purchased the film rights for most of the Sherlock Holmes stories for his film company and who was the owner of the Coliseum, had approached Doyle for the play; or, possibly, Doyle had been so struck by what he saw of Eille Norwood, the actor who was playing Holmes in the new films, that he wrote the play or script without any prompting. A final possibility is that Dennis Neilson-Terry was the person who first approached Conan Doyle. There is no known evidence either to support or contradict these theories.

After playing at the London Coliseum, *The Crown Diamond* toured the major provincial theatres for three months, visiting, among others, the Liverpool Olympia, the Birmingham Grand, and the Hippodrome in Manchester, Huddersfield, and Sheffield. Back in London for further performances from 30 August, it then resumed its tour starting at the Brighton Hippodrome.

Charles Farrell, the actor who made his début on the London stage in the rôle of Sam Merton in *The Crown Diamond*, recalls that the tour lasted nearly fourteen months, with only a fortnight's break before Christmas and a week at Christmas; he did not leave the company until August or September 1922 when he accepted a part in *Bulldog Drummond*. He remembers that the play did the full circuit of the Stoll, Moss, and Gulliver theatres, as well as a number of independent dates, and adds that it topped the bill in the provincial theatres, being both a popular and a financial success. The only mishap was the loss of Rex Vernon Taylour, who played Watson; he was taken away by the police in July 1921 or thereabouts for stealing a watch and compromising a local barmaid. The part was then taken by Paul Ashwell.

Mr Farrell has also, in the course of a letter to the *Stage* on the subject of voice projection, given the following reminiscence of how he was chosen for the part:

> As a very young actor in April 1921, my manager, Lee Ephraim, arranged that I should read a part for Sir Arthur Conan Doyle in his sketch *The Crown Diamond*.
>
> I arrived one very cold morning, shivering with fright, and was pushed on to the enormous London Coliseum stage with Conan Doyle, Lee Ephraim and the director, Stanley Bell, standing at the back of the gallery.
>
> No sooner had I uttered the first two lines when the booming voice of Conan Doyle was heard, 'Stop shouting, my boy – speak naturally!'
>
> Thereupon I came down to about half volume and after the next few lines the great man said, 'All right, my boy, he will do Mr Ephraim.'[295]

'The Adventure of the Mazarin Stone' was first published in the *Strand Magazine* of October 1921, having been advertised as forthcoming the previous month. The manuscript of the play, written in a school exercise book, was one of a number discovered in a bank vault at Crowborough, Sussex, in July 1947; these were in a hat-box deposited by Conan Doyle in 1922. There are a number of discrepancies between the original and the version presented at the Coliseum. The latter is the one which is given here.

An edition of the play, purporting to be limited to 59 copies (though some were oddly numbered, '58a' or whatever, and others were out of sequence), was published in July 1958 by the Baskerrette Press of New York.

The Crown Diamond

Or, An Evening with Sherlock Holmes, was first produced at the Bristol Hippodrome on 2 May 1921 and at the London Coliseum on 16 May 1921, with the following cast:

Sherlock Holmes	DENNIS NEILSON-TERRY
Dr Watson	R. V. TAYLOUR
Billy	RONALD HAMMOND
Colonel Sebastian Moran	NORMAN LEYLAND
Sam Merton	CHARLES FARRELL

Produced by STANLEY BELL

The Crown Diamond

An Evening with Sherlock Holmes

CHARACTERS

MR SHERLOCK HOLMES	The famous Detective
DR WATSON	His Friend
BILLY	Page to MR SHERLOCK HOLMES

COLONEL SEBASTIAN
   MORAN   An intellectual Criminal

SAM MERTON   A Boxer

   Scene: Sherlock Holmes's Room in Baker Street

Scene

Mr Holmes's room at Baker Street

It presents the usual features, but there is a deep bow window to it, and across there is drawn a curtain running upon a brass rod fastened across eight feet above the ground, and enclosing recess of the window.

Enter WATSON *and* BILLY

WATSON: Well, Billy, when will he be back?

BILLY: I'm sure I couldn't say, sir.

WATSON: When did you see him last?

BILLY: I really couldn't tell you.

WATSON: What, you couldn't tell me?

BILLY: No, sir. There was a clergyman looked in yesterday, and there was an old bookmaker, and there was a workman.

WATSON: Well?

BILLY: But I'm not sure they weren't all Mr Holmes. You see, he's very hot on a chase just now.

WATSON: Oh!

BILLY: He neither eats nor sleeps. Well, you've lived with him same as me. You know what he's like when he's after someone.

WATSON: Yes, I know.

BILLY: He's a responsibility, sir, that he is. It's a real worry to me sometimes. When I asked him if he would order dinner, he said, 'Yes, I'll have chops and mashed potatoes at seven-thirty the day after tomorrow.' 'Won't you eat before then, sir?' I asked. 'I haven't time, Billy, I'm busy,' said he. He gets thinner and paler, and his eyes get brighter. It's awful to see him.

WATSON: Tut, tut, this will never do. I must certainly stop and see him.

BILLY: Yes, sir, it will ease my mind.

WATSON: But what is he after?

BILLY: It's this case of the Crown diamond.

WATSON: What, the hundred-thousand-pound burglary?

BILLY: Yes, sir. They must get it back, sir. Why, we had the Prime Minister and the Home Secretary both sitting on that very sofa. Mr Holmes promised he'd do his very best for them. Quite nice to them he was. Put them at their ease in a moment.

WATSON: Dear me! I've read about it in the paper. But I say, Billy, what have you been doing to the room? What's this curtain?

BILLY: I don't know, sir. Mr Holmes had it put there three days ago. But we've got something funny behind it.

WATSON: Something funny?

BILLY (*laughing*): Yes, sir. He had it made.

(BILLY *goes to the curtain and draws it across, disclosing a wax image of* HOLMES *seated in a chair, back to the audience.*)

WATSON: Good heavens, Billy!

BILLY: Yes, sir. It's like him, sir. (*Picks the head off and exhibits it.*)

WATSON: It's wonderful! But what's it for, Billy?

BILLY: You see, sir, he's anxious that those who watch him should think he's at home sometimes when he isn't. There's the bell, sir. (*Replaces head, draws curtain.*) I must go.

BILLY *exits*

(WATSON *sits down, lights a cigarette, and opens a paper.*)

Enter a tall, bent OLD WOMAN *in black with veil and side-curls*

WATSON (*rising*): Good day, ma'm.

WOMAN: You're not Mr Holmes?

WATSON: No, ma'm. I'm his friend, Dr Watson.

WOMAN: I knew you couldn't be Mr Holmes. I'd always heard *he* was a handsome man.

WATSON (*aside*): Upon my word!

WOMAN: But I must see him at once.

WATSON: I assure you he is not in.

WOMAN: I don't believe you.

WATSON: What!

WOMAN: You have a sly, deceitful face – oh, yes, a wicked, scheming face. Come, young man, where is he?

WATSON: Really, madam!

WOMAN: Very well, I'll find him for myself. He's in there, I believe. (*Walks towards bedroom door and gets behind settee.*)

WATSON (*rising and crossing*): That is his bedroom. Really, madam, this is outrageous!

WOMAN: I wonder what he keeps in this safe.

(*She approaches it and, as she does so, the lights go out, and the room is in darkness save for* 'DON'T TOUCH' *in red fire over the safe. Four red lights spring up, and between them the inscription* 'DON'T TOUCH.' *After a few seconds, the lights go on again and* HOLMES *is standing beside* WATSON.)

WATSON: Good heavens, Holmes!

HOLMES: Neat little alarm, is it not, Watson? My own invention. You tread on a loose plank and so connect the circuit, or I can turn it on myself. It prevents inquisitive people becoming too inquisitive. When I come back I know if anyone has been fooling with my things. It switches off again automatically, as you saw.

WATSON: But, my dear fellow, why this disguise?

HOLMES: A little comic relief, Watson. When I saw you sitting there looking so solemn, I really couldn't help it. But I assure you, there is nothing comic in the business I am engaged upon. Good heavens! (*Rushes across room, and draws curtain which has been left partly open.*)

WATSON: Why, what is it?

HOLMES: Danger, Watson. Airguns, Watson. I'm expecting something this evening.

WATSON: Expecting what, Holmes?

HOLMES (*lighting pipe*): Expecting to be murdered, Watson.

WATSON: No, no, you are joking, Holmes!

HOLMES: Even my limited sense of humour could evolve a better joke than that, Watson. No, it is a fact. And in case it should come off – it's about a two to one chance – it would perhaps be as well that you should burden your memory with the name and address of the murderer.

WATSON: Holmes!!

HOLMES: You can give it to Scotland Yard, with my love and a parting blessing. Moran is the name, Colonel Sebastian Moran. Write it down, Watson, write it down! 136, Moorside Gardens, N.W. Got it?

WATSON: But surely something can be done, Holmes. Couldn't you have this fellow arrested?

HOLMES: Yes, Watson, I could. That's what's worrying him so.

WATSON: But why don't you?

HOLMES: Because I don't know where the diamond is.

WATSON: What diamond?

HOLMES: Yes, yes, the great yellow Crown diamond, seventy-seven carats, lad, and without flaw. I have two fish in the net. But I haven't got the stone there. And what's the use of taking *them*? It's the stone I'm after.

WATSON: Is this Colonel Moran one of the fish in the net?

HOLMES: Yes, and he's a shark. He bites. The other is Sam Merton, the boxer. Not a bad fellow, Sam, but the Colonel has used him. Sam's not a shark. He's a great big silly gudgeon. But he's flopping about in my net all the same.

WATSON: Where is this Colonel Moran?

HOLMES: I've been at his elbow all morning. Once he picked up my parasol. 'By your leave, ma'm,' he said. Life is full of whimsical happenings. I followed him to old

Straubenzee's workshop in the Minories. Straubenzee made the airgun – fine bit of work, I understand.

WATSON: An airgun?

HOLMES: The idea was to shoot me through the window. I had to put up that curtain. By the way, have you seen the dummy? (*Draws curtain.*)

(WATSON *nods.*)

Ah! Billy has been showing you the sights. It may get a bullet through its beautiful wax head at any moment.

Enter BILLY

Well, Billy?

BILLY: Colonel Sebastian Moran, sir.

HOLMES: Ah! the man himself. I rather expected it. Grasp the nettle, Watson! A man of nerve. He felt my toe on his heels. (*Looks out of window.*) And there is Sam Merton in the street – the faithful but fatuous Sam. Where is the Colonel, Billy?

BILLY: Waiting-room, sir.

HOLMES: Show him up when I ring.

BILLY: Yes, sir.

HOLMES: Oh, by the way, Billy, if I am not in the room, show him in just the same.

BILLY: Very good, sir.

Exit BILLY

WATSON: I'll stay with you, Holmes.

HOLMES: No, my dear fellow, you would be horribly in the way. (*Goes to table and scribbles note.*)

WATSON: He may murder you.

HOLMES: I shouldn't be surprised.

WATSON: I can't possibly leave you.

HOLMES: Yes, you can, my dear Watson, for you've always played the game, and I am very sure that you will play it to the end. Take this note to Scotland Yard. Come back with the police. The fellow's arrest will follow.

WATSON: I'll do that with joy.

HOLMES: And before you return I have just time to find out

where the diamond is. (*Rings bell.*) This way, Watson. We'll go together. I rather want to see my shark without his seeing me.

Exit WATSON *and* HOLMES *into bedroom*
Enter BILLY *and* COLONEL MORAN, *who is a fierce, big man, flashily dressed; he carries a heavy cudgel*

BILLY: Colonel Sebastian Moran.

Exit BILLY

(COLONEL MORAN *looks round, advances slowly into the room, and starts as he sees the dummy figure sitting in the window. He stares at it, then crouches, grips his stick, and advances on tip-toe. When close to the figure he raises his stick.*)

HOLMES *comes quickly out of the bedroom door*

HOLMES: Don't break it, Colonel! Don't break it!

COLONEL (*staggering back*): Good Lord!

HOLMES: It's such a pretty little thing. Tavernier, the French modeller, made it. He is as good at waxwork as Straubenzee is at airguns. (*Shuts curtains.*)

COLONEL: Airguns, sir. Airguns! What do you mean?

HOLMES: Put your hat and stick on the side table. Thank you. Pray take a seat. Would you care to put your revolver out also? Oh, very good, if you prefer to sit upon it.

(COLONEL *sits down.*)

I wanted to have five minutes' chat with you.

COLONEL: I wanted to have five minutes' chat with you.

(HOLMES *sits down near him and crosses his legs.*)

I won't deny that I intended to assault you just now.

HOLMES: It struck me that some idea of that sort had crossed your mind.

COLONEL: And with reason, sir, with reason.

HOLMES: But why this attention?

COLONEL: Because you have gone out of your way to annoy me. Because you have put your creatures on my track.

HOLMES: My creatures?

COLONEL: I have had them followed. I know that they come to report to you here.

HOLMES: No, I assure you.

COLONEL: Tut, sir! Other people can observe as well as you. Yesterday there was an old sporting man; today it was an elderly lady. They held me in view all day.

HOLMES: Really, sir, you compliment me! Old Baron Dowson, before he was hanged at Newgate, was good enough to say that in my case what the law had gained the stage had lost. And now you come along with your kindly words. In the name of the elderly lady and of the sporting gentleman I thank you. There was also an out-of-work plumber who was an artistic dream – you seem to have overlooked him.

COLONEL: It was you – you!

HOLMES: Your humble servant! If you doubt it, you can see the parasol upon the settee which you so politely handed to me this morning down in the Minories.

COLONEL: If I had known, you might have never –

HOLMES: Never have seen this humble home again. I was well aware of it. But it happens you didn't know, and here we are, quite chatty and comfortable.

COLONEL: What you say only makes matters worse. It was not your agents, but you yourself, who have dogged me. Why have you done this?

HOLMES: You used to shoot tigers?

COLONEL: Yes, sir.

HOLMES: But why?

COLONEL: Pshaw! Why does any man shoot a tiger – the excitement – the danger!

HOLMES: And, no doubt, the satisfaction of freeing the country from a pest which devastates it and lives on the population?

COLONEL: Exactly!

HOLMES: My reasons in a nutshell!

COLONEL (*springing to his feet*): Insolent!

HOLMES: Sit down, sir, sit down! There was another, more practical reason.

COLONEL: Well?

HOLMES: I want that yellow Crown diamond.

COLONEL: Upon my word! Well, go on.

HOLMES: You knew that I was after you for that. The real reason why you are here tonight is to find out how much I know about the matter. Well, you can take it that I know *all* about it, save one thing, which you are about to tell me.

COLONEL (*sneering*): And, pray, what is that?

HOLMES: Where the diamond is.

COLONEL: Oh, you want to know that, do you? How the devil should I know where it is?

HOLMES: You not only know, but you are about to tell me.

COLONEL: Oh, indeed!

HOLMES: You can't bluff me, Colonel. You're absolute plate-glass. I see to the very back of your mind.

COLONEL: Then, of course, you see where the diamond is!

HOLMES: Ah, then you do know. You have admitted it!

COLONEL: I admit nothing.

HOLMES: Now, Colonel, if you will be reasonable, we can do business together. If not, you may get hurt.

COLONEL: And *you* talk about bluff!

HOLMES (*raising a book from the table*): Do you know what I keep inside this book?

COLONEL: No, sir, I do not.

HOLMES: You!

COLONEL: Me?

HOLMES: Yes, sir, *you*! You're all here, every action of your vile and dangerous life.

COLONEL: Damn you, Holmes! Don't go too far!

HOLMES: Some interesting details, Colonel. The real facts as to the death of Miss Minnie Warrender of Laburnum Grove. All here, Colonel.

COLONEL: You – you devil!!

HOLMES: And the story of young Arbuthnot, who was found drowned in the Regent's Canal just before his intended exposure of you for cheating at cards.

COLONEL: I – I never hurt the boy.

HOLMES: But he died at a very seasonable time. Do you want some more, Colonel? Plenty of it here. How about the robbery in the train-de-luxe to the Riviera, February 13th, 1892? How about the forged cheque on the Crédit Lyonnais the same year?

COLONEL: No; you're wrong there.

HOLMES: Then I'm right on the others! Now, Colonel, you are a card-player. When the other fellow holds all the trumps, it saves time to throw in your hand.

COLONEL: If there was a word of truth in all this, would I have been a free man all these years?

HOLMES: I was not consulted. There were missing links in the police case; but I have a way of finding missing links. You may take it from me that I could do so.

COLONEL: Bluff, Mr Holmes, bluff!

HOLMES: Oh, you wish me to prove my words! Well, if I touch this bell it means the police, and from that instant the matter is out of my hands. Shall I?

COLONEL: What has all this to do with the jewel you speak of?

HOLMES: Gently, Colonel! Restrain that eager mind! Let me get to the point in my own humdrum way. I have all this against you; and I also have a clear case against both you and your fighting bully in this case of the Crown diamond.

COLONEL: Indeed!

HOLMES: I have the cabman who took you to Whitehall and the cabman who brought you away. I have the commissionaire who saw you beside the case. I have Ikey Cohen who refused to cut it up for you. Ikey has peached, and the game is up.

COLONEL: Hell!

HOLMES: That's the hand I play from. But there's one card missing. I don't know where this King of Diamonds is.

COLONEL: You never shall know.

HOLMES: Tut, tut! don't turn nasty. Now, consider. You're going to be locked up for twenty years. So is Sam Merton. What good are you going to get out of your diamond? None in the world. But if you let me know where it is – well, I'll compound a felony. We don't want you or Sam. We want the stone. Give that up, and so far as I am concerned you can go free so long as you behave yourself in the future. If you make another slip – then, God help you. But this time my commission is to get the stone, not you. (*Rings bell.*)

COLONEL: But if I refuse?

HOLMES: Then – alas – it must be you, not the stone.

Enter BILLY

BILLY: Yes, sir.

HOLMES (*to* COLONEL): I think we had better have your friend Sam at this conference. Billy, you will see a large and very ugly gentleman outside the front door. Ask him to come up, will you?

BILLY: Yes, sir. Suppose he won't come, sir?

HOLMES: No force, Billy! Don't be rough with him. If you tell him Colonel Moran wants him he will come.

BILLY: Yes, sir.

Exit BILLY

COLONEL: What's the meaning of this, then?

HOLMES: My friend Watson was with me just now. I told him that I had a shark and a gudgeon in my net; now I'm drawing the net and up they come together.

COLONEL (*leaning forward*): You won't die in your bed, Holmes!

HOLMES: D'you know, I have often had the same idea. For that matter, your own finish is more likely to be perpendicular than horizontal. But these anticipations are morbid. Let us give ourselves up to the unrestrained enjoyment of the present. No good fingering your revolver, my friend, for you know perfectly well that you dare not use it. Nasty, noisy things revolvers. Better stick to airguns,

Colonel Moran. Ah! I think I hear the fairy footstep of your estimable partner.

Enter BILLY

BILLY: Mr Sam Merton.

Enter SAM MERTON, *in check suit and loud necktie,*
yellow covert coat

HOLMES: Good day, Mr Merton. Rather damp in the street, is it not?

Exit BILLY

MERTON (*to* COLONEL): What's the game? What's up?

HOLMES: If I may put it in a nutshell, Mr Merton, I should say it is *all* up.

MERTON (*to* COLONEL): Is this cove tryin' to be funny, or what? I'm not in the funny mood myself.

HOLMES: You'll feel even less humorous as the evening advances, I think I can promise you that. Now, look here, Colonel, I'm a busy man and I can't waste time. I'm going into the bedroom. Pray make yourselves entirely at home in my absence. You can explain to your friend how the matter lies. I shall try over the Barcarolle upon my violin. In (*looks at his watch*) five minutes I shall return for your final answer. You quite grasp the alternative, don't you? Shall we take you, or shall we have the stone?

Exit HOLMES, *taking his violin with him*

MERTON: What's that? He knows about the stone?

COLONEL: Yes, he knows a dashed sight too much about it. I'm not sure that he doesn't know *all* about it.

MERTON: Good Lord!

COLONEL: Ikey Cohen has split.

MERTON: He has, has he? I'll do him down a thick 'un for that.

COLONEL: But that won't help us. We've got to make up our minds what to do.

MERTON: Half a mo'. He's not listening, is he? (*Approaches bedroom door.*) No, it's shut. Looks to me as if it was locked.

(*Music begins.*)

Ah! there he is, safe enough. (*Goes to curtain.*) Here, I say! (*Draws it back, disclosing the figure.*) Here's that cove again, blast him!

COLONEL: Tut! it's a dummy. Never mind it.

MERTON: A fake is it? (*Examines it, and turns the head.*) By gosh, I wish I could twist his own as easy! Well, strike me! Madame Tussaud ain't in it.

(*As* MERTON *returns towards the* COLONEL, *the lights suddenly go out, and the red* 'DON'T TOUCH' *signal goes up. Figures must transpose at that moment. After a few seconds the lights readjust themselves.*)

MERTON: Well, dash my buttons! Look 'ere, guv'nor, this is gettin' on my nerves. Is it unsweetened gin, or what?

COLONEL: Tut! it is some childish hanky-panky of this fellow Holmes, a spring or an alarm or something. Look here, there's no time to lose. He can lag us for the diamond.

MERTON: The hell he can!

COLONEL: But he'll let us slip if we only tell him where the stone is.

MERTON: What, give up the swag! Give up a hundred thousand?

COLONEL: It's one or the other.

MERTON: No way out? You've got the brains, guv'nor, surely you can think a way out of it.

COLONEL: Wait a bit! I've fooled better men than he. Here's the stone in my secret pocket. It can be out of England tonight, and cut into four pieces in Amsterdam before Saturday. He knows nothing of Van Seddor.

MERTON: I thought Van Seddor was to wait till next week.

COLONEL: Yes, he *was*. But now he must get the next boat. One or other of us must slip round with the stone to the *Excelsior*, and tell him.

MERTON: But the false bottom ain't in the hat-box yet!

COLONEL: Well, he must take it as it is and chance it. There's not a moment to lose. As to Holmes, we can fool him easily enough. You see, he won't arrest us if he thinks he can get the stone. We'll put him on the wrong track about it, and before he finds it *is* the wrong track, the stone will be in Amsterdam and we out of the country.

MERTON: That's prime.

COLONEL: You go off now and tell Van Seddor to get a move on him. I'll see this sucker and fill him up with a bogus confession. The stone's in Liverpool – that's what I'll tell him. By the time he finds it isn't, there won't be much of it left, and we'll be on the blue water. (*He looks carefully round him, then draws a small leather box from his pocket and holds it out.*) Here is the Crown diamond.

HOLMES (*taking it, as he rises from chair*): I thank you!

COLONEL (*staggering back*): Curse you, Holmes! (*Puts hand in pocket.*)

MERTON: To hell with him!

HOLMES: No violence, gentlemen – no violence, I beg of you! It must be very clear to you that your position is an impossible one. The police are waiting below.

COLONEL: You – you devil! How did you get there?

HOLMES: The device is obvious but effective; lights off for a moment and the rest is common sense. It gave me a chance of listening to your racy conversation, which would have been painfully constrained by a knowledge of my presence. No, Colonel, no! I am covering you with a .450 Derringer through the pocket of my dressing-gown. (*Rings bell.*)

Enter BILLY

Send them up, Billy.

Exit BILLY

COLONEL: Well, you've got us, damn you!

MERTON: A fair cop! But, I say, what about that bloomin' fiddle?

HOLMES: Ah, yes, these modern gramophones – wonderful invention, wonderful!

CURTAIN

PREFACES

Although the first edition of A *Study in Scarlet* had a preface, the second did not. Doyle told his mother on 14 October 1891: 'Ward, Lock & Co. wrote to ask me to write a preface for A *Study in Scarlet.* I refused. Then they wrote for leave to use a subtitle with the name of Sherlock Holmes. I refused again.'[296] He had by then realized what a mistake he had made in selling the copyright for a mere £25, and his anger was directed against the publisher rather than against Sherlock Holmes. When the Warwick House Library edition of A *Study in Scarlet* was issued at the end of 1891, despite the publisher's assurances, there was no preface. The book was reprinted a number of times during the following year and still no preface was forthcoming, then, with Harry How's article about Conan Doyle in the August 1892 *Strand* and Joseph Bell's review of *The Adventures of Sherlock Holmes* in the December 1892 *Bookman*, the situation was saved. Sherlock Holmes made his way on to the title page and the book had an excellent and highly appropriate preface.

Neither *The Adventures* nor *The Memoirs of Sherlock Holmes* had a preface, nor did *The Sign of Four*, though when this was reissued on 10 March 1896 in Newnes's Penny Library of Famous Books it did have an editorial note by C.S.C. (Charles Smith Cheltnam) who gave details of Doyle's background and of his literary achievements, saying of Sherlock Holmes: 'The creation of the character of the great amateur detective was a literary revelation, and was instantly accepted by the public with something like an enthusiastic expression of favour.'[297]

It was the twelve volume Author's Edition which was to reveal Doyle's true feelings towards Sherlock Holmes and to give the lie to those who had suggested that he did not rate the stories at all highly. All the Sherlock Holmes stories were included and, as the edition coincided with the writing of *The Hound of the Baskervilles*, plans were also in hand to include the new story in the edition, the publication of which, the author said, had given him the opportunity of 'casting off what my more mature judgement told me to be unworthy and of retaining what my conscience approved'. Of his 'police romances' he did approve, though he admitted that they were 'on a different and humbler plane'[298] than his historical novels.

The Author's Edition was a joint publishing venture between Smith, Elder and D. Appleton of New York who were each to produce limited editions of one thousand copies. The English publisher had a decided advantage, as Doyle agreed to sign the first volumes and as there were two illustrations per volume rather than the single illustration in the American edition. 'In the case of each book,' Doyle explained in his general preface, 'I have added in this edition some small explanation as to the scope and object of the work. A preface had always seemed to me an unnecessary impertinence, until I found by experience how easily one may be misunderstood.'[299] There was, however, only one preface to the Sherlock Holmes stories in *The Adventures of Sherlock Holmes*, while the volume containing *A Study in Scarlet* and *The Sign of Four* had the publisher's note and the article by Joseph Bell which had been used in the 1893 Ward, Lock edition, and *The Memoirs of Sherlock Holmes* had no

introductory matter. The three volumes were published
in England on 15 October 1903.

Watson said in 'The Adventure of the Second Stain'
that he could not communicate more of the exploits of his
friend as Holmes had 'definitely retired from London and
betaken himself to study and bee-farming on the Sussex
Downs'[300] and notoriety had become hateful to him.
Watson, or his creator, may have felt that *The Return of
Sherlock Holmes* required no preface – certainly it had
none, nor did *The Valley of Fear* but it was John H.
Watson himself who supplied the preface for *His Last Bow*
which was published on 22 October 1917; and it also
served as the blurb on the dust-jacket. The preface gives
details of Sherlock Holmes's farm and of how he had been
employing the time between his retirement and his
involvement in the Von Bork affair. What may be a
misprint did, however, occur in both the English and the
American editions. Holmes is described as dividing his
time between 'philosophy and agriculture', whereas Watson is more likely to have written 'apiculture', for Holmes's *magnum opus*, the 'fruit of pensive nights and
laborious days',[301] was *The Practical Handbook of Bee
Culture* and this had occupied all his time. The blurb on
the dust-jacket, in its turn, referred to 'music and philosophy' as the pursuits which had engaged Holmes's attention, and, as it was put into the third person, also
mentioned that the details of the other cases had been
lying in 'Mr Watson's portfolio'. Watson, no doubt, like
Doyle before him preferred this form of address having
given up his medical practice so as to devote himself to
literature. The preface to *His Last Bow* shows Doyle's
sense of humour and that he was prepared to play the
game in which many people in all walks of life were
engaged, the so-called 'higher criticism'.

The Casebook of Sherlock Holmes, which was published
in 1927, has the longest preface. It was the article which

introduced the Sherlock Holmes Competition in the *Strand Magazine* and as such will be found elsewhere in this volume (pp. 317 ff.).

The two omnibus volumes published by John Murray containing the short and the long stories each had a new preface. *The Complete Sherlock Holmes Short Stories* was published on 15 October 1928; its preface contains two apparent inaccuracies. Doyle says that 'A Scandal in Bohemia' 'came out in 1892', whereas it was, in fact, published in the *Strand Magazine* in July 1891, though *The Adventures of Sherlock Holmes* did appear in 1892; he also says that Holmes made his final exit in 'The Adventure of Shoscombe Abbey' in 1925. This is the title used on the manuscript which was changed, when it appeared in *Liberty* on 5 March 1927 and in the *Strand Magazine* of April 1927, to 'The Adventure of Shoscombe Old Place', but Doyle did not complete the series until the end of 1926. The 'witty critic' whose judgement on the Sherlock Holmes stories is referred to is mentioned in 'Some Personalia about Mr Sherlock Homes' as having been a Cornish boatman. The famous remark was probably made early in 1909 when Doyle was in Cornwall with his wife convalescing after an operation.

The Complete Sherlock Holmes Long Stories was published on 26 June 1929, and its preface contains an interesting account of how the novels came to be written. The 'ambassador' sent over by Lippincott was Joseph Marshall Stoddart; Bertram Fletcher Robinson, whose remark led to *The Hound of the Baskervilles* and whose premature death is mentioned, had died at the age of 35 on 21 January 1907; and the 'graphic account' of the Molly Maguires was *The Molly Maguires and the Detectives* by Allan Pinkerton.

Doyle's last preface was to the twenty-four volume Crowborough Edition published in 1930 by Doubleday, Doran and Company. This had been intended to be definitive; but failing health prevented Doyle from making the corrections and alterations which he had planned, so the edition is unremarkable except for the presence of the new preface which does little more than summarize and classify his achievement as an author. He again says that most of the Sherlock Holmes books have a preface of their own, but none were new.

Author's Edition
(1903)

Preface to the Sherlock Holmes Stories

So elementary a form of fiction as the detective story hardly deserves the dignity of a preface. The purpose of such narrative is obvious and the means transparent. There are, however, a few things which might be said upon this theme, and in saying them I include in my remarks all that I have ever written of this nature – namely, the three short books, A Study in Scarlet, The Sign of Four, and The Hound of the Baskervilles, with the two collections of tales which are called The Adventures, and The Memoirs of Sherlock Holmes. All are equally concerned with the experiences and exploits of that mythical person.

I can well imagine that some of my critics may express surprise that, in an edition of my works from which I have rigorously excluded all that my literary conscience rejects, I should retain stories which are cast in this primitive and conventional form. My own feeling upon the subject is that all forms of literature, however humble, are legitimate if the writer is satisfied that he has done them to the highest of his power. To take an analogy from a kindred art, the composer may range from the oratorio to the comic song and be ashamed of neither, so long as his work in each is as honest as he can make it. It is insincere work, scamped work, work which is consciously imitative, which a man should voluntarily suppress before time saves him the trouble. As to work which is unconsciously imitative, it is not to be expected that a man's style and mode of treatment should spring fully formed from his own brain. The most that he can hope is that as he advances the outside influences should decrease and his own point of view become clearer and more distinctive.

Edgar Allan Poe, who, in his carelessly prodigal fashion, threw out the seeds from which so many of our present forms of literature have sprung, was the father of the detective tale, and covered its limits so completely that I fail to see how his followers can find any fresh ground which they can confidently call their own. For the secret of the thinness and also of the intensity of the detective story is, that the writer is left with only one quality, that of intellectual acuteness, with which to endow his hero. Everything else is outside the picture and weakens the effect. The problem and its solution must form the theme, and the character-drawing be limited and subordinate. On this narrow path the writer must walk, and he sees the footmarks of Poe always in front of him. He is happy if he ever finds the means of breaking away and striking out on some little side-track of his own.

It was my own good fortune to have found the qualities of my hero in actual life, although it was towards the detection of disease rather than of crime that his remarkable talents were directed. Yet, as in my young student days, I saw and heard the ease with which my teacher reasoned from points which were hardly visible to me, and arrived at just conclusions from the most trivial details, there grew upon me the conviction that the resources of the human brain in this direction had never been appreciated, and that a scientific system might give results more remarkable than any of the arbitrary and inexplicable triumphs which so often fall to the lot of the detective in fiction. Monsieur Dupin had, of course, already demonstrated this, and I can only claim the very limited credit of doing it from a fresh model and from a new point of view.

Some few words upon the chronology of these stories may not be out of place. The first of them, *A Study in Scarlet*, published in '87, was the very first separate booklet of mine which ever appeared. *The Sign of Four* followed two years later. Then, in '91, *The Adventures of Sherlock Holmes* began to appear in the *Strand Magazine*. The public having shown them some favour I was persuaded to continue them into another series, *The Memoirs of Sherlock Holmes*, which came to an end in 1893. That it was an end, and that I had no intention of abusing the patience of the public, was shown by the last story in which, wisely or unwisely, I brought my hero as well as my stories to an end. The subject had begun to weary me, and it seemed to me that, while there was no reason to be ashamed of doing detective stories, it was unjustifiable that I should allow myself to be tempted into doing nothing else. *The Hound of the Baskervilles* represents the inevitable relapse after repentance.

One strong objection to the detective story has always been that it must deal with crime, and that the idea of crime is not a wholesome one for the young. It must be admitted that there is some force in this contention. If no crime were ever committed in these stories the reader might feel that he was the victim of a practical joke, but it is a fact (never observed, as far as I remember, by any critic), that in a considerable number of these stories the effect is produced by the anticipation of what might have been, not of what is, and that there has actually been no grave legal crime whatever.

A. CONAN DOYLE

UNDERSHAW, HINDHEAD, 1901

His Last Bow:
Some Reminiscences of
Sherlock Holmes
(1917)

Preface

The friends of Mr Sherlock Holmes will be glad to learn that he is still alive and well, though somewhat crippled by occasional attacks of rheumatism. He has, for many years, lived in a small farm upon the Downs five miles from Eastbourne, where his time is divided between philosophy and agriculture. During this period of rest he has refused the most princely offers to take up various cases, having determined that his retirement was a permanent one. The approach of the German war caused him, however, to lay his remarkable combination of intellectual and practical activity at the disposal of the Government, with the historical results which are recounted in 'His Last Bow'. Several previous experiences which have lain long in my portfolio, have been added to 'His Last Bow' so as to complete the volume.

JOHN H. WATSON, M.D.

Sherlock Holmes
The Complete Short Stories
══════ (1928) ══════

Preface

This book contains the whole series of stories concerning Sherlock Holmes apart from the four novels, *A Study in Scarlet, The Sign of Four, The Hound of the Baskervilles, The Valley of Fear.*

It begins with his first appearance in this form in 'A Scandal in Bohemia' which came out in 1892, until he made his final exit in the 'Adventure of Shoscombe Abbey' in 1925. As his methods and character became familiar to the public there was naturally less element of surprise, and the later stories suffered by comparison. As a witty critic remarked, 'He may not have been killed when he fell over the cliff, but he was never quite the same man afterwards.' I hope, however, that the reader who can now take them in any order will not find that the end shows any conspicuous falling off from the modest merits of the beginning.

ARTHUR CONAN DOYLE

CROWBOROUGH, 1928

Sherlock Holmes
The Complete Long Stories
═══════ (1929) ═══════

Preface

The following stories paint Mr Sherlock Holmes and his activities upon a somewhat broader canvas where there is room for expansion. This expansion must express itself in action, for there is no room for character development in the conception of a detective. Whatever you add to the one central quality of astuteness must in my opinion detract from the general effect. Other writers may however succeed where I fail.

The *Study in Scarlet* was the first completed long story which I ever wrote, though I had served an apprenticeship of nearly ten years of short stories, most of which were anonymous. It represented a reaction against the too facile way in which the detective of the old school, so far as he was depicted in literature, gained his results. Having endured a severe course of training in medical diagnosis, I felt that if the same austere methods of observation and reasoning were applied to the problems of crime some more scientific system could be constructed. On the whole, taking the series of books, my view has been justified, as I understand that in several countries some change has been made in police procedure on account of these stories. It is all very well to sneer at the paper detective, but a principle is a principle, whether in fiction or in fact. Many of the great lessons of life are to be learned in the pages of the novelist.

There was no American copyright in 1887 when the *Study in Scarlet* was written, so that the book had a circulation in the United States, and attracted some attention. As a consequence Mr Lippincott sent an ambassador over to treat for a successor. He had commissions for several British authors, and invited Oscar Wilde and myself to dinner to discuss the matter. The result was *The Picture of Dorian Gray* and *The Sign of Four*.

Then came *The Hound of the Baskervilles*. It arose from a remark by that fine fellow, whose premature death was a loss to the world, Fletcher Robinson, that there was a spectral dog near his home on Dartmoor. That remark was the inception of the book, but I should add that the plot and every word of the actual narrative was my own.

Finally, there is *The Valley of Fear*, which had its origin through my reading a graphic account of the Molly McQuire outrages in the coalfields of Pennsylvania, when a young detective drawn from Pinkerton's Agency acted exactly as the hero is represented as doing. Holmes plays a subsidiary part in this story.

I trust that the younger public may find these romances of interest, and that here and there one of the older generation may recapture an ancient thrill.

ARTHUR CONAN DOYLE

June, 1929

Crowborough Edition
(1930)

Extract from the

Preface

My first long story was *The Firm of Girdlestone*, which stands for that crude and imitative stage through which an undeveloped writer may pass. It is a book which I could eliminate from my list without compunction. And yet I find that it appeals strongly to a certain type of reader who tunes in to my own mind at that point. It was mostly written before many of the '*Polestar*' stories, though published much later.

I then, in 1887, wrote *A Study in Scarlet*, in which I first evolved the character of Sherlock Holmes with his faithful chronicler Watson. Having met with approbation, I two years later wrote another little book, *The Sign of Four*, about Holmes. Shortly afterwards, having started as an eye surgeon in London, I found much time upon my hands, and in my deserted consulting room I began that series of short stories about Holmes which ran eventually to such an unconscionable length, my only excuse being that the demand was always greater than the supply. This covers *The Adventures, The Memoirs, The Return*, and *The Case Book of Sherlock Holmes*, together with *The Hound of the Baskervilles, His Last Bow*, and *The Valley of Fear*. As most of these books have a preface of their own I need not enlarge. I might remark, however, that it had long struck me that a serial story in a magazine was a mistake, since if a single number was missed, the interest was gone. A series in which each was complete in itself seemed to me to be the ideal, and as far as I know I was a pioneer in this direction.

ARTHUR CONAN DOYLE

Windlesham, Crowborough, Sussex
December, 1929

SOME PERSONALIA
ABOUT
MR SHERLOCK HOLMES

'Some Personalia about Mr Sherlock Holmes' was written at the bidding of the Editor of the *Strand Magazine*, Herbert Greenhough Smith, who persuaded Doyle to round off the series of stories, which ended in September 1917 with the publication of 'His Last Bow' in the *Strand Magazine*, by describing the effect they had had on the reading public and by giving examples of his own attempts to emulate his famous character. The article, which ran to ten pages of manuscript, was completed on 9 September 1917 and was published in the Christmas number of the magazine; it also appeared in America in the *Detective Story Magazine* on 15 January 1918 under the title, 'An Intimate Study of Sherlock Holmes'.

This was Doyle's first article about Sherlock Holmes, though he had referred to the subject in earlier interviews and speeches. Most of the letters to Sherlock Holmes (about which further information is given in the main introduction, p. 104) dated from those years when Holmes's reputation was at a peak abroad; a number had already been published by St John Adcock in an article about Conan Doyle in the *Bookman* of November 1912 which also mentioned the char-à-banc of French schoolboys who had wanted to see Baker Street – a story which greatly pleased Conan Doyle and one which he recalled on many later occasions. The credulity of French schoolboys and the reputation of Sherlock Holmes in France were both great. Lady Eleanor Smith, the daughter of Lord Birkenhead, in her column for the *Weekly Dispatch* of 16 December 1928 described a similar incident. She had been asked to show a French boy round the sights of London:

> But he had one ambition, touristically, and one only. That was to visit the house of Mr Sherlock Holmes in Baker Street; and, if it would not be carrying presumption too far, to catch a glimpse of the great man on his way to unravel some national problem.

The two took a taxi to Baker Street and Lady Eleanor asked the driver to stop outside a 'gloomy narrow house'. The boy gazed in rapture and showed no inclination to move:

> 'I will stay here,' said the ardent Sherlock-fan, 'on the chance of seeing either Monsieur Holmes or even *le docteur* Watson. I would never forgive myself, nor would my family forgive me, if I left without seeing them.'
>
> My teeth were chattering with the cold. 'I am sorry,' I said, 'but Mr Holmes retired three months ago and is now running a bee farm in Sussex. The taxi driver here has just told me so, and he seems a most reliable man.'
>
> My young friend was desolated and proceeded to look ten years older. He sighed repeatedly and resignedly.[302]

The French interest in Sherlock Holmes had been increased by Maurice Leblanc's Arsène Lupin, though he could hardly have been responsible for the message contained in the piece of chalk (p. 291, below) – other, that is, than indirectly. Doyle, who was coached by John Mannock, had been fond of billiards since his days in Southsea where his friend, Major-General Drayson, was an expert. The occasion to which he refers appears to have been the 1913 Billiard Association Amateur Championship which he entered more with a view to encouraging the competition than with any idea of winning. He had a bye in the first round and won the second, his best break being forty-two off the red, and, although he was defeated, he could take some comfort from the fact that his opponent reached the finals. Doyle had a full-sized billiard table at his house in Crowborough and was, by all accounts, a good player. Greenhough Smith described in 1919 how, after scoring a few points himself, Doyle had proceeded to beat him with a break of a hundred. In 1926 Doyle entered for the Wright Cup but was defeated by J. B. Evans at the Stadium Club.

Doyle's example of how he used the reasoning of Sherlock Holmes in the case of a young man who had disappeared from his hotel was often held up as proof that he was as able as his detective. His wife described it as the case of a young officer: 'He told me,' she said of her husband in an interview with the *Sunday Express*, 'that the vanished man would reappear either in Glasgow or in Edinburgh in three days' time. He was so certain that he wrote it to the boy's family. On the third day a telegram told my husband that he had turned up, precisely as had been deduced.'[303] Cases of disappearances were the ones which most frequently came Doyle's way. That of the young foreigner, who is mentioned in the article, occurred in the summer of 1909. A nurse had become engaged to a Danish merchant seaman who then vanished. She wrote to Doyle from the North-Western Hospital in Hampstead begging help. He contacted the sailor's cousin in Copenhagen and learnt that she was well rid of the man. On 7 August 1909 she told him: 'I don't know how to thank you sufficiently for all your kindness, please accept my most grateful thanks for all you have done for me. As you say, I have had an extraordinary escape, and I dread to think what might have happened . . .'[304] The invitation to visit Warsaw and investigate an aristocratic murder case had come from Felix de Halpert who wrote on 19 October 1913; Doyle was particularly amused by the suggestion that he might name his own terms.

The treasure chart which Doyle reproduces is of particular interest. It relates to the East Indiaman, the *Grosvenor*, which was wrecked off the Pondoland coast of South Africa on 4 August 1782 (W. Clark Russell may have borrowed the name for his novel, *The Wreck of the Grosvenor*, but his book is otherwise unconnected). An attempt to find the remains of the ship was made in 1880 by Sidney Turner of Durban and Lieutenant Beddoes; it was reported in *The Times* on 29 June 1880, where reference was made to 'an idea in the minds of the local Caffres that a box of treasure is buried near the spot where the *Grosvenor* came ashore, but although a stone is said to have been marked to show where it is, there is as yet little clue to the whereabouts of the hidden prize'.[305] Turner appears to have had a copy of the chart, but it was Robert Raleigh, who arrived in Natal in 1880, who was the first to take it seriously. He persuaded a mesmerist called William Whittaker to use his powers with a young medium called 'Andy'. In a trance, the boy interpreted the symbols 'NBG' and 'SWK' as 'nine bags of gold' and, read backwards, 'kegs with silver'; the first he believed were buried in one spot, and the silver, which he said was contained in thirteen kegs, was buried in another. He also gave an unconvincing explanation of the remainder of the chart. At another seance he located the exact position of the treasure. The search party reached the scene on 11 August 1883, but a single gun was all that was discovered.

Alexander Lindsay was the next to explore the site of the wreck. He started in 1896 and in August 1905 registered the Grosvenor Recovery Syndicate. A few months earlier Doyle (and not Sherlock Holmes) received the chart from R. G. Pearson of Durban who thought that it would interest the author of 'The Adventure of the Dancing Men'. In his letter, dated 10 March 1905, Pearson explained that the ship had been carrying the Crown jewels and other bullion from the sack of Delhi. The crew had come ashore bearing a chest which they had buried at a short distance from the wreck; they had then attempted to make their way overland to Cape Town, and, with the exception of four sailors, had all died or been killed on the way. 'On the chart arriving at London,' he added, 'the Admiralty – together with the only key to the cipher – was burned down. It appears that in those days each Indiaman had her own private code of semaphore signals, as, being at war with France, it was considered better that they should not be acquainted with all the signals by capturing one vessel. Three armed semaphore were then used.' He hoped that the ciphers from other ships might still be available in London which would enable the chart to be deciphered. 'The X,' he continued, 'evidently represents the spot of burial and the semi-circle may represent a line of quartz or rock inland or possibly a line of bush-edge.'[306]

In his article, Doyle repeated what Pearson had told him and he was later criticized for doing so as the semaphore, though invented in 1767, had not been adopted for maritime use until 1816 and then only with two arms. Whether he took any further interest in the pre-war syndicate is not known. It became a company in 1907 and was wound up in 1911. After the war he did become more closely involved. At the beginning of March 1921 a new company, the Grosvenor Bullion Syndicate, was registered and a prospectus was issued in the early summer giving details of the treasure thought to be on board. One went to Conan Doyle and he expressed interest in it:

'I have written to the syndicate asking certain questions with regard to the method by which they hope to salve the treasure,' he told a representative of the *Daily Express* on 24 August 1921. 'If the answers are satisfactory – and I am an old sea-going man myself, having been a ship's surgeon, with knowledge of such matters – I may take up one thousand shares. I certainly believe the treasure is worth a million.'[307]

His interest provoked some ribald correspondence. Stuart C. Cumberland asked whether Doyle could not use his 'mystic powers' to locate the wreck and suggested that the spirits might show their gratitude by actually raising the treasure. Doyle replied to the 'good-natured banter' in a letter published on 30 August:

There is no mystery at all about the *Grosvenor*, and her position is known to an inch. Her deck has already been explored. The problem lies in the skill needed by submarine workers in such uneasy waters. These human and mechanical difficulties are for our own wits to solve, otherwise the human race would lose all initiative and become mere automata upon the earth.[308]

Doyle took a thousand shares and it is possible that he eventually held twice that number. When a new prospectus was issued in March 1922 it included a facsimile of a letter from Conan Doyle, whose connection with the scheme was used to give added respectability. His name was also occasionally taken in vain, as at the Annual General Meeting of 1923, when one shareholder told the chairman: 'As Sir Conan Doyle has got a lot of shares in this concern I suggest that he be asked to call up the spirit of the wreck and prove to us that this is the wreck of the *Grosvenor*.'[309]

When Doyle wrote his autobiography in 1923 he included some sections of the article in the chapter about

Sherlock Holmes. He made no reference to his own involvement in the Grosvenor Syndicate but he did add, after saying that he expected someone to set to work to solve the mystery, 'indeed at the present moment (1923) there is a small company working to that end'.[310] He may still have hoped that the treasure would be discovered, but it was not. The Syndicate was dissolved in 1929 and, like the Spanish galleon in the bay of Tobermory in which he had also invested, the *Grosvenor* 'took treasure rather than gave it'.[311]

One unexplained mystery mentioned in 'Some Personalia about Mr Sherlock Holmes' was later used in 'The Problem of Thor Bridge': Watson there refers to a number of unfinished cases, among them 'that of Mr James Phillimore, who, stepping back into his own house to get his umbrella, was never more seen in this world'.

At the request of the Editor I have spent some days in looking over an old letter-box in which from time to time I have placed letters referring directly or indirectly to the notorious Mr Holmes. I wish now that I had been more careful in preserving the references to this gentleman and his little problems. A great many have been lost or mislaid. His biographer has been fortunate enough to find readers in many lands, and the reading has elicited the same sort of response, though in many cases that response has been in a tongue difficult to comprehend. Very often my distant correspondent could neither spell my own name nor that of my imaginary hero, as in a recent instance which I here append. Many such letters have been from Russians. Where the Russian letters have been in the vernacular I have been compelled, I am afraid, to take them as read, but when they have been in English they have been among the most curious in my collection.

There was one young lady who began all her epistles with

the words 'Good Lord'. Another had a large amount of guile underlying her simplicity. Writing from Warsaw she stated that she had been bedridden for two years, and that my novels had been her only, etc., etc. So touched was I by this flattering statement that I at once prepared an autographed parcel of them to complete the fair invalid's collection. By good luck, however, I met a brother author upon the same day to whom I recounted the touching incident. With a cynical smile he drew an identical letter out of his pocket. His novels also had been for two years her only, etc., etc. I do not know how many more the lady had written to, but if, as I imagine, her correspondence had extended to several countries, she must have amassed a rather interesting library.

The young Russian's habit of addressing me as 'Good Lord' had an even stranger parallel at home, which links it up with the subject of this article. Shortly after I received a knighthood I had a bill from a tradesman which was quite correct and businesslike in every detail save that it was made out to Sir Sherlock Holmes. I hope that I can stand a joke as well as my neighbours, but this particular piece of humour seemed rather misapplied, and I wrote sharply upon the subject. In response to my letter there arrived at my hotel a very repentant clerk, who expressed his sorrow at the incident, but kept on repeating the phrase, 'I assure you, sir, that it was *bonâ fide.*'

'What do you mean by *bonâ fide?*' I asked.

'Well, sir, my mates in the shop told me that you had been knighted, and that when a man was knighted he changed his name, and that you had taken that one.'

I need not say that my annoyance vanished, and that I laughed as heartily as his pals were probably doing round the corner.

There are certain problems which are continually recurring in these Sherlock Holmes letters. One of them has exercised men's minds in the most out-of-the-way places, from Labrador to Tibet; indeed, if a matter needs thought it is just the men in these outlying stations who have the time and solitude for it. I dare say I have had twenty letters upon the one point alone. It arises in 'The Adventure of the Priory School', where Holmes, glancing at the track of a bicycle, says, 'It is evidently going from us, not towards us.' He did not give his reasoning, which my correspondents resent, and all assert that the deduction is impossible. As a matter of fact it is simple enough upon soft undulating ground such as the moor in question. The weight of the rider falls most upon the hind wheel, and in soft soil it makes a perceptibly deeper track. Where the machine goes up a slope this hind mark would be very much deeper; where it goes down a slope rapidly it would be hardly deeper at all. Thus the depth of the mark of the hind wheel would show which way the bike was travelling.

I never realized what an actual living personality Mr Holmes was to many people until I heard the very pleasing story of the char-à-banc of French schoolboys on a tour to London, who, when asked what they wanted to see first, replied unanimously that they wanted to see Mr Holmes's lodgings in Baker Street. Rather less pleasing, though flattering in their way, were the letters of abuse which showered upon me when it was thought that I had killed him. 'You brute!' was the promising opening on one lady's epistle. The most trenchant criticism of the stories as a series came from a Cornish boatman, who remarked to me: 'When Mr Holmes had that fall he may not have been killed, but he was certainly injured, for he was never the same man afterwards.' I hope the allegation is not true – and, indeed, those who have read the stories backward, from the latest to the first, assure me that it is not so – but it was a shrewd thrust none the less.

One of the quaintest proofs of his reality to many people is that I have frequently received autograph books by post, asking me to procure his signature. When it was announced that he was retiring from practice and intended to keep bees on the South Downs I had several letters offering to help him in his project. One says: 'Will Mr Sherlock Holmes require a housekeeper for his country cottage at Christmas? I know someone who loves a quiet country life, and bees especially – an old-fashioned, quiet woman.' The other, which is addressed to Holmes himself, says: 'I see by some of the morning papers that you are about to retire and take up bee-keeping. If correct I shall be pleased to render you service by giving any advice you may require. I trust you will read this letter in the same spirit in which it is written, for I make this offer in return for many pleasant hours.' Many other letters have reached me in which I have been implored to put my correspondents in touch with Mr Holmes, in order that he might elucidate some point in their private affairs.

Occasionally I have been so far confused with my own character that I have been asked to take up professional work upon these lines. I had, I remember, one offer, in the case of an aristocratic murder trial in Poland some years ago, to go across and look into the matter upon my own terms. I need not say that I would not do such a thing for money, since I am diffident as to how far my own services would be of any value; but I have several times as an amateur been happy to have been of some assistance to people in distress. I can say, though I touch wood as I say it, that I have never entirely failed in any attempt which I have made to reduce Holmes's methods to practical use, save in one instance to which I allude later.

For the case of Mr Edalji I can claim little credit, for it did not take any elaborate deduction to come to the conclusion that a man who is practically blind did not make a journey at night which involved crossing a main line of railway, and would have tested a trained athlete had he been called upon to do it in the time. The man was obviously innocent, and it is a disgrace to this country that he has never received a penny of compensation for the three years which he spent in jail.

A more complex case is that of Oscar Slater, who is still working out his sentence as a convict. I have examined the evidence carefully, including the supplementary evidence given at the very limited and unsatisfactory commission appointed to inquire into the matter, and I have not the faintest doubt that the man is innocent. When the judge asked him at the trial whether he had anything to say why the sentence of death for the murder of Miss Gilchrist should not be pronounced upon him, he cried aloud, 'My Lord, I did not know there was such a woman in the world.' I am convinced that this was the literal truth. However, it is proverbially impossible to prove a negative, so there the matter must stand until the people of Scotland insist upon a real investigation into all the circumstances which surround this deplorable case.

A few of the problems which have come my way have been very similar to some which I had invented for the exhibition of the reasoning of Mr Holmes. I might perhaps quote one in which that gentleman's method of thought was copied with complete success. The case was as follows. A gentleman had disappeared. He had drawn a bank balance for forty pounds, which was known to be on him. It was feared that he had been murdered for the sake of the money. He had last been heard of stopping at a large hotel in London, having come from the country that day. In the evening he went to a music-hall performance, came out of it about ten o'clock, returned to his hotel, changed his evening clothes, which were found in his room next day, and disappeared utterly. No one saw him leave the hotel, but a man occupying a neighbouring room declared that he had heard him moving during the night. A week had elapsed at the time that I was consulted, but the police had discovered nothing. Where was the man?

These were the whole of the facts as communicated to me by his relatives in the country. Endeavouring to see the matter through the eyes of Mr Holmes, I answered by return of post that he was evidently either in Glasgow or in Edinburgh. It proved later that he had as a fact gone to Edinburgh, though in the week that had passed he had moved to another part of Scotland.

There I should leave the matter, for, as Dr Watson has often shown, a solution explained is a mystery spoiled. However, at this stage the reader can lay down the magazine and show how simple it all is by working out the problem for himself. He has all the data which were ever given to me. For the sake of those, however, who have no turn for such conundrums I will try to indicate the links which make the chain. The one advantage which I possessed was that I was familiar with the routine of London hotels – though, I fancy, it differs little from that of hotels elsewhere.

The first thing was to look at the facts and separate what was certain from what was conjecture. It was *all* certain except the statement of the person who heard the missing man in the night. How could he tell such a sound from any other sound in a large hotel? That point could be disregarded if it traversed the general conclusions. The first clear deduction was that the man had meant to disappear. Why else should he draw all his money? He had got out of the hotel during the night. But there is a night-porter in all hotels, and it is impossible to get out without his knowledge when the door is once shut. The door is shut after the theatre-goers return – say at twelve o'clock. Therefore the man left the hotel before twelve o'clock. He had come from the music-hall at ten, had changed his clothes, and had departed with his bag. No one had seen him do so. The inference is that he had done it at the moment when the hall was full of the returning guests, which is from eleven to eleven-thirty. After that hour, even if the door were still open, there are few people coming and going; so that he with his bag would certainly have been seen.

Having got so far upon firm ground we now ask ourselves why a man who desires to hide himself should go out at such an hour. If he intended to conceal himself in London he need never have gone to the hotel at all. Clearly, then, he was going to catch a train which would carry him away. But a man who is deposited by a train in any provincial station during the night is likely to be noticed, and he might be sure that when the alarm was raised and his description given some guard or porter would remember him. Therefore his destination would be some large town, which he would reach in daylight hours, as a terminus, where all his fellow-passengers would disembark and where he would lose himself in the crowd. When one turns up the time-table and sees that the great Scotch expresses bound for Edinburgh and Glasgow start about midnight, the goal is reached. As for his dress-suit, the fact that he abandoned it proved that he intended to adopt a line of life where there were no social amenities. This deduction also proved to be correct.

I quote such a case in order to show that the general lines of reasoning advocated by Holmes have a real practical application to life. In another case where a girl had become engaged to a young foreigner who suddenly disappeared I was able by a similar process of deduction to show her very clearly both whither he had gone and how unworthy he was of her affections. On the other hand, these semi-scientific methods are occasionally laboured and slow as compared with the results of the rough-and-ready practical man. Lest I should seem to have been throwing bouquets either to myself or to Mr Holmes, let me state that on the occasion of a burglary of the village inn, within a stone-throw of my house, the village constable, with no theories at all, had seized the culprit, while I had got no farther than that he was a left-handed man with nails in his boots.

The unusual or dramatic effects which lead to the invocation of Mr Holmes in fiction are, of course, great aids to him in reaching a conclusion. It is the case where there is nothing to get hold of which is the deadly one. I heard of such a one in America which would certainly have presented a formidable problem. A gentleman of blameless life, starting off for a Sunday evening walk with his family, suddenly observed that he had forgotten his stick. He went back into the house, the door of which was still open, and he left his people waiting for him outside. He never reappeared, and from that day to this there has been no clue as to what befell him. This was certainly one of the strangest cases of which I ever heard in real life.

Another singular case came within my own observation. It was sent to me by an eminent London publisher. This gentleman had in his employment a head of department whose name we shall take as Musgrave. He was a hard-working person with no special feature in his character. Mr Musgrave died, and several years after his death a letter was received addressed to him, care of his employers. It bore the postmark of a tourist resort in the West of Canada, and had the note 'Confl films' upon the outside of the envelope, with the word 'Report Sy' in one corner. The publishers naturally opened the envelope, as they had no note of the dead man's relatives. Inside were two blank sheets of paper. The letter, I may add, was registered. The publisher, being unable to make anything of this, sent it on to me, and I submitted the blank sheets to every possible chemical and heat test, with no result whatever. Beyond the fact that the writing appeared to be that of a woman, there is nothing to add to this account. The matter was, and remains, an insoluble mystery. How the correspondent could have something so secret to say to Mr Musgrave and yet not be aware that this person had been dead for several years is very hard to understand – or why blank sheets should be so carefully registered through the post. I may add that I did not trust the sheets to my own chemical tests, but had the best expert advice, without getting any result. Considered as a case it was a failure – and a very tantalizing one.

Mr Sherlock Holmes has always been a fair mark for practical jokers, and I have had numerous bogus cases of various degrees of ingenuity, marked cards, mysterious warnings, cipher messages, and other curious communications. It is astonishing the amount of trouble which some people will take with no object in view save a mystification. Upon one occasion, as I was entering the hall to take part in an amateur billiard competition, I was handed by the attendant a small packet which had been left for me. Upon opening it I found a piece of ordinary green chalk such as is used in billiards. I was amused by the incident, and I put the chalk in my waistcoat pocket and used it during the game. Afterwards I continued to use it until one day, some months later, as I rubbed the tip of my cue, the face of the chalk crumbled in, and I found it was hollow. From the recess thus exposed I drew out a small slip of paper with the words, 'From Arsène Lupin to Sherlock Holmes'. Imagine the state of mind of the joker who took such trouble to accomplish such a result!

One of the mysteries submitted to Mr Holmes was rather upon the psychic plane, and therefore beyond his powers. The facts as alleged are most remarkable, though I have no proof of their truth save that the lady wrote earnestly and gave both her name and address. The person, whom we will call Mrs Seagrave, had been given a curious second-hand ring, snake-shaped, and of dull gold. This she took from her finger at night. One night she slept in it, and had a fearsome dream in which she seemed to be pushing off some furious creature which fastened its teeth into her arm. On awakening the pain in the arm continued, and the next day the imprint of a double set of teeth appeared upon the arm, with one tooth of the lower jaw missing. The marks were in the shape of blue-black bruises which had not broken the skin. 'I do not know,' says my correspondent, 'what made me think the ring had anything to do with the matter, but I took a dislike to the thing and did not wear it for some months, when, being on a visit, I took to wearing it again.' To make a long story short, the same thing happened, and the lady settled the matter for ever by dropping her ring into the hottest corner of the kitchen-range. This curious story, which I believe to be genuine, may not be as supernatural as it seems. It is well known that in some subjects a strong mental impression does produce a physical effect. Thus a very vivid nightmare-dream with the impression of a bite might conceivably produce the mark of a bite. Such cases are well attested in medical annals. The second incident would, of course, arise by unconscious suggestion from the first. None the less, it is a very interesting little problem, whether psychic or material.

Buried treasures are naturally among the problems which have come to Mr Holmes. One genuine case was accompanied by the diagram here reproduced. It refers to an Indiaman which was wrecked upon the South African coast in the year 1782. If I were a younger man I should be seriously inclined to go personally and look into that matter. The ship contained a remarkable treasure, including, I believe, the old crown regalia of Delhi. It is surmised that they buried these near the coast and that this chart is a note of the spot. Each Indiaman in those days had its own semaphore code, and it is conjectured that the three marks upon the left are signals from a three-armed semaphore. Some record of their meaning might perhaps even now be found in the old papers of the India Office. The circle upon the right gives the compass bearings. The larger semicircle may be the curved edge of a reef or of a rock. The figures above are the indications how to reach the X which marks the treasure. Possibly they may give the bearings as 186 feet from the 4 upon the semicircle. The scene of the wreck is a lonely part of the country, but I shall be surprised if sooner or later someone does not seriously set to work to solve the mystery.

One last word before I close these jottings about my imaginary character. It is not given to every man to see the child of his brain endowed with life through the genius of a great sympathetic artist, but that was my good fortune when Mr Gillette turned his mind and his great talents to putting Holmes upon the stage. I cannot end my remarks more fittingly than by my thanks to the man who changed a creature of thin air into an absolutely convincing human being.

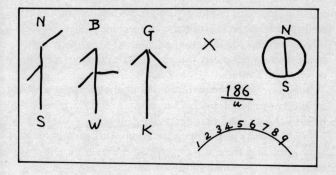

SHERLOCK HOLMES
ON THE SCREEN

'I think these photographs of Sherlock Holmes quite wonderful',[312] Conan Doyle was quoted as saying at the beginning of Fenn Sherie's interview with Eille Norwood, 'Sherlock Holmes on the Film', which appeared in the *Strand Magazine* in July 1921. He was speaking of the disguises used by Norwood in the Stoll films which had been in production since November 1920, and of the sets at the Cricklewood studios which included, Sherie said, 'a perfect replica of Holmes's famous residence at 144, Baker Street'![313] Eille Norwood, in his turn, was delighted to learn that his disguises, which were so good that they often fooled the producer Maurice Elvey, had won Doyle's approval. It was therefore very fitting that the creator and the impersonator of Sherlock Holmes should come together at the Stoll Convention Dinner.

'I dine with Stoll's picture people at the Trocadero (7.30 Tuesday next). I believe I am expected to speak about Sherlock,' Doyle informed Greenhough Smith a few days before, and added: 'I wish you were there – if I am his father you were the "Accoucheur".'[314] His wish was granted. The dinner, held in the Balmoral ballroom of the Trocadero on 28 September 1921 with the Managing Director of Stoll Films, Jeffrey Bernerd, in the chair, was attended by 130 guests among whom were two from the

Strand Magazine, the proprietor, Frank Newnes, and the editor.

The first toast was to the film of *The Fruitful Vine*, based on the novel by Robert Hichens, which had had its trade show the previous day. The producer, Maurice Elvey, replied. Next came a toast to 'The Stoll Film Company, Limited, its work, and its workers' by Ernest W. Peall of the Cinematograph Exhibitors' Association. He paid tribute to Sir Oswald Stoll for making British films and to Conan Doyle for entrusting the Sherlock Holmes films to a British company. A letter from the Managing Director of the Associated Cinematograph Theatres was then read out, after which the special guest, Sir Arthur Conan Doyle, was introduced by the chairman, who was able to inform the guests that the new Sherlock Holmes films had just been sold in the United States for what he 'estimated was one of the largest prices ever paid for pictures in America'.[315] After the speech by Conan Doyle and the reply by Eille Norwood, both of which were well-received, A. E. Newbould, MP, proposed a further toast expressing the film industry's debt to Conan Doyle. He was followed by the chairman, who proposed a toast to the guests. He said that Doyle had done the company an honour by being present and that the guests would appreciate how great that honour was when he told them that Doyle had not attended any public dinner since August 1914. He then read out a message from Lord Riddell, a personal friend of Lloyd George, which said:

Among the first to read Sir A. Conan Doyle's new Sherlock Holmes story just published in the October issue of the *Strand Magazine* has been the Prime Minister, who considers it to be one of the best Sherlock Holmes stories that he has read. Mr Lloyd George is not only a great admirer of Sherlock Holmes, but also of the

stories of Brigadier Gerard, the other great hero of Sir
A. Conan Doyle.[316]

This was greeted with applause (though the story, 'The
Adventure of the Mazarin Stone', is far from being the
best – indeed many consider that it is the worst – of the
Sherlock Holmes stories). The chairman ended by assuring the assembled guests that Stoll films were being seen
throughout the world, and that Sherlock Holmes had
gone as far as Japan, Australia, and the whole of the Far
East, and that he would be shown throughout the world.
There were replies by A. E. W. Mason and Edgar Wal-
lace, and a number of final toasts, after which the evening
drew to its close.

Doyle had sold the Sherlock Holmes film rights to a
French film company, Eclair, who made one film in
France in 1911 and eight in Great Britain during 1912.
These were released in America at the end of 1912 and
the beginning of 1913, and in England during 1913 and
1914. A number of other films were also made in Britain,
the most notable being those of the Samuelson film
company. Doyle eventually bought back the rights and
these were taken by Stoll Film Productions, who had
made and released sixteen by the time of the Stoll
Convention Dinner. The most recent, which Doyle had
seen, *The Hound of the Baskervilles*, had received its
premiere on 8 August. A further sixteen films were made
in 1922, and a final sixteen in 1923.

Doyle's speech was reprinted in *Stoll's Editorial News* on
6 October 1921. It is one of the few occasions on which he
refers to a cricketer as having inspired the name 'Sherlock' (which is more fully discussed in the main introduction), and the reference to the messages which he had
sent to the Magdeburg Military Prison is also of interest. It
was in 1915 that he established his secret correspondence, and the book he used appears to have been *The*

Valley of Fear, which was published on 3 June 1915. The friend in the camp was Willie Loder-Symonds, the brother of Jean Conan Doyle's closest friend, Lily Loder-Symonds. She made her home at Windlesham during the war, while her brother eventually escaped with J. L. Hardy, though he was killed in a flying accident shortly afterwards. The officer who showed the 'extraordinary sagacity' was Rupert Oswald Derek Keppel of the Cold-stream Guards, the third son of the Earl of Albemarle, who had been wounded and taken prisoner on 25 August 1914. In his autobiography Doyle explained in greater detail how and why the correspondence had come about:

A dear friend of my wife, Miss Lily Loder-Symonds, had a brother, Captain Willie Loder-Symonds, of the Wiltshires, who had been wounded and taken in the stand before Le Cateau. He was an ingenious fellow and had written home a letter which passed the German censor, because it seemed to consist in the description of a farm, but when read carefully it was clear that it was the conditions of himself and his comrade which he was discussing. It seemed to me that if a man used such an artifice he would be prepared for a similar one in a letter from home. I took one of my books, therefore, and beginning with the third chapter – I guessed the censor would examine the first – I put little needle-pricks under the various printed letters until I had spelled out all the news. I then sent the book and also a letter. In the letter I said that the book was, I feared, rather slow in the opening, but that from Chapter III onwards he might find it more interesting. That was as plain as I dared to make it. Loder-Symonds missed the allusion altogether, but by good luck he showed the letter to Captain the Hon. Rupert Keppel, of the Guards, who had been taken at Landrecies. He smelled a rat, borrowed the book, and found my cipher. A message came back to his father, Lord Albemarle, to the effect that he hoped Conan Doyle would send more books. This was sent on to me, and of course showed me that it was all right. From that time onwards every month or two I pricked off my bulletin, and a long job it was. Finally, I learned that the British papers were allowed for the prisoners, so that my budget was superfluous. [317]

Conan Doyle's Speech at the Stoll Convention Dinner

'He was, I take it, the most perfect reasoning and observing machine that the world has seen' – 'A Scandal in Bohemia'.

I must begin by apologizing for the somewhat vainglorious quotation which I find printed here on the toast list. You must remember that these are the words of a certain gentleman named Watson whose opinions were not generally very weighty ones.

If my little creation of Sherlock Holmes has survived longer perhaps than it deserved, I consider that it is very largely due to those gentlemen who have, apart from myself, associated themselves with him. In the early days it was Sidney Paget who illustrated those stories so well that he made a type which the whole English-reading race came to recognize, and I may say here that in his premature death English art lost a very great asset. Afterwards there came along William Gillette, with his wonderful impersonation in the play written entirely by himself – so entirely that I remember his sending me a cable from America in which he said: 'May I marry Sherlock Holmes?' I had such confidence in him that I cabled back: 'You may marry him, murder him, or do anything you like with him.' Then there came Mr Saintsbury with his excellent personation in *The Speckled Band*, and now, finally, but not least important, there comes Mr Eille Norwood, who has carried his extraordinarily clever personation of Sherlock Holmes, not only all over Great Britain, but, as I learn with very great pleasure, over the United States of America as well.

I suffer sometimes from some little confusion between the author and the character. I am afraid that in my own personality I rather represent that gentleman already quoted – Dr Watson. But the psychologists tell us that we really are very multiplex people; that we are like a bundle of faggots, or rather a rope with many strands, and that sometimes in the most commonplace rope there may be one single strand which, if you only isolate it, produces unexpected effects. There may be represented in my being some strand of Sherlock. If so all the villains I have created may be also represented by strands in my personality, and there is only one man who, having made more villains, is in a worse case than myself, and that is my friend Mr Phillips Oppenheim.

I can remember someone attacking me by attributing to me those vices of self-conceit and self-complacency which existed in Sherlock Holmes, and he did it in some clever doggerel published in a magazine. I took the liberty of answering him also in doggerel, which I remember ran thus:

> Pray master this, my esteemed commentator,
> That the created is not the creator.
> Just grasp this fact with your cerebral tentacle,
> That the doll and its maker are never identical.

But I suffer from that confusion between author and character. I remember when lecturing in New York I avoided the newspapers all I could, but I remember one caught my eye and I read: 'As the author advanced to deliver his lecture a thrill of disappointment ran through the assembly.' I was naturally rather disappointed myself at reading that, but I learned afterwards that they all expected to see in me a cadaverous looking person with marks of cocaine injections all over him.

My creation of Holmes did, after all, a small bit of war

work. It is hardly worth mentioning, but I had a friend who was shut up in the Magdeburg Military Prison in Germany. As he and his brother officers were getting no news from England, I took a volume of Sherlock Holmes and in it I pricked out all the news letter by letter, beginning with the third chapter – pricking under each letter of the message with a needle. I sent the book to him with a note saying: 'This may relieve your prison captivity and afterwards be placed in the prison library. It is slow but perhaps you might find the third chapter to be a little more interesting.' I thought that would be good enough for him, but as a matter of fact he missed it. There was, however, another officer, Capt. The Hon. Keppel, of the Guards who, with extraordinary sagacity, 'got on' to it. The result was that the British officers in captivity got the whole of the news of England at that time. I then got another letter saying: 'Please send us another Sherlock Holmes story.' I continued to send them with all the news pricked out in them to those officers until I learned that they were actually being allowed to have English newspapers, and then I desisted.

As to the birth of Sherlock Holmes, I have several times been asked how he began and how he got his name. That is rather curious. The name Holmes is simple. In those old days – pretty early in the nineties – there was a reaction against what I look upon as the one blot in Charles Dickens, and I give way to no one in my admiration for that great man. But I think that if he had dropped all the Turveydrops and the Tittletits and the other extraordinary names he gave to people, he would have made his work more realistic. If you call a detective Inspector Sharp or Inspector Ferret, you knock the bottom out of him at once. It is much better to call him by an ordinary name. I don't know how we got the name of Holmes, but I think you can trace the Sherlock. If you will read the old *Lillywhites* and the old cricketing news, I think that is the most productive line to follow. I remember playing in a match and my old friend, Colonel English, who is present, played in it too, between the United Services and the MCC. The MCC brought down against us two fine bowlers in Attewell and Sherlock. I had the good fortune to scrape up twenty or thirty runs against them, and I think the name of Sherlock impressed itself on my mind. Through that small incident, when you remember his brother's name was Mycroft, I think you will see where the cricketing line runs. I am afraid even my villains have a taint of cricket, and when I think of Dr Grimesby Rylott I feel I owe an apology to that excellent bowler.

My first two little books were A *Study in Scarlet* and *The Sign of Four*, both dealing with Holmes, but they made no hit at all, and it was not until my friend, Mr Smith here, piloted the early fortunes of the *Strand Magazine*, and was kind enough to take aboard that promising ship my Sherlock as passenger that I was able to 'get home' with the public. Since then I have had considerable correspondence from all parts of the world about this imaginary character. It is extraordinary how realistic some people take it to be. I remember a Russian lady who used to write to me in English about it, and who always began her letters with 'Good Lord'. I don't know whether she alluded to me or whether it was the effect the stories produced on her.

I have suffered also from my mystifications. People tried to pull my leg, I hope with not undue success. But the most remarkable thing occurred at a billiard match. Just as I was going in somebody handed me a bit of chalk saying 'Use it for luck', and I did. I took it home with me and used it for some time until one day I was marking my cue and the cue broke through the chalk. I then found that inside was a paper bearing these words: 'From Arsène Lupin to Sherlock Holmes'.

I think of all the little incidents that have pleased me in connection with Holmes, the most pleasing was when a party of schoolboys from the Paris lycées were brought to London, crammed into charabancs, asked what they would

like to see first, and, when everybody thought they would say
Westminster Abbey, all replied 'Baker Street'.

I couple the toast with the name of Mr Eille Norwood,
whose wonderful personation of Holmes has amazed me. On
seeing him in the *The Hound of the Baskervilles* I thought I had
never seen anything more masterly.

Sherlock Holmes Replies
(in the person of Eille Norwood)

Ladies and Gentlemen and Dr Watson, ever since I knew
that I was to respond to this toast I have been on the rack – I
mean to say on the toast rack. For it is not easy for anyone to
follow in the wake of so gifted an author and so fluent a
speaker as Sir Arthur Conan Doyle without running the risk
of being capsized in the back wash of his eloquence. I do not
think there is any writer living who has achieved such
popularity as Sir A. Conan Doyle, and no character in
modern fiction has gained such world-wide popularity as
Sherlock Holmes.

I know that Sherlock Holmes as a character is very
difficult for an actor to undertake to portray. I do not think,
in my opinion, there is any actor who could adequately
portray it, but there is no actor who would not jump at the
chance of attempting it. If I could feel that I deserved
one-half of the generous tribute so handsomely paid by Sir
A. Conan Doyle to my attempt I should feel that I was not
worthy to undo the latchet of my own shoes. I want to
express my profound sense of gratitude to Sir A. Conan
Doyle for the kind things he has said of me. If my enthusiasm
has enabled me to cover up my many deficiencies and to give
but a faint suggestion of his brilliant creation, I feel I have
achieved as much as I dared hope to achieve when before me
lies the task of appearing in another fifteen of his adventures.
With that prospect in the future I envy no man.

I suppose every actor has a pet ambition. It is on record that Wilson Barrett once saw the play of *Hamlet* from the gallery of the old Princess's Theatre, and that on leaving he made a vow that he would play Hamlet twenty-five years later in that very theatre. On indisputable authority we are assured that he did so. It is not given to all of us to have our ambitions so completely realized, but had I such an ambition, it was not to play Hamlet at the Princess's Theatre; it was to play Sherlock Holmes. But my hope never soared beyond the narrow environment of the theatre. I never dreamt in my wildest moments of the vastly wider publicity of the screen. In the theatre an actor has one audience; on the screen he has his hundreds. Thus for the actor arises the paradox that the shadow is of greater value than the substance.

From all parts of the United Kingdom and from our Overseas possessions I have received hundreds of letters from book-lovers of the famous detective who have extended their affection to his celluloid successor. Cinema stars must be a source of considerable revenue to the Post Office. As their success increases so does their correspondence. It seems to me that Mr Kellaway* must be well pleased to have their success so well stamped. From the success of the Stoll Film Company in filming his excellent stories Sir A. Conan Doyle can rest assured that if he gives more Sherlock Holmes his multitudinous public will love and thank him for it, and I think I can say for Mr Jeffrey Bernerd the more films will they want. In association with the memory of this wonderful character when I make my last adieu let my epitaph be:

> Lies Sherlock Holmes beneath the soil,
> His still remains disarmed, destroyed,
> But thanks to Stoll and Conan Doyle,
> He still remains in celluloid.

* Frederick George Kellaway, the Postmaster-General in 1921.

SIDELIGHTS ON
SHERLOCK HOLMES

This article, the title of which was probably based on his earlier lecture 'Sidelights on History', was written in 1923 as a part of Conan Doyle's autobiography, *Memories and Adventures*, and may be read in conjunction with 'The Background to Sherlock Holmes' (p. 327 ff.) which is from the same source. 'I may as well interrupt my narrative here in order to say what may interest my readers about my most notorious character,'[318] Doyle writes at the beginning of the chapter entitled 'Sidelights on Sherlock Holmes', though the three final paragraphs of the previous chapter had already touched on the subject. The article appeared in the *Strand Magazine* in January 1924 and parts of it were published in *Collier's Weekly* on 29 December 1923. The sections taken from 'Some Personalia about Mr Sherlock Holmes' and the parody by J. M. Barrie with Doyle's comments about it, which appeared in the same chapter of the book, will be found elsewhere (pp. 277 ff., 366 ff.).

There are certain differences between the serial publication in the magazines and the book. The American magazine (following a typescript of the original manuscript) gives the names of the Paget brothers as Arthur and Harold, while the *Strand* has Sidney and Harold; only the autobiography is correct, with Sidney and Walter Paget (Harold, or H. M. Paget was Sidney's brother, but he was not the model for Sherlock Holmes). The American magazine also gives the critic who spoke so disparagingly about the real snake used in *The Speckled Band* as that of the *Daily Telegraph*, which is not given elsewhere; and where Doyle explains how he decided to play a 'bold and energetic game' following the failure of his boxing play, both magazines have 'and certainly I never played a bolder', while the book has 'for an empty theatre spells ruin'. *Collier's* and the book both refer to 'Sherlockholmitos', while the *Strand* gives the South American word as 'Sherlockolmitos'. *Collier's* also has a few extra lines, which are included here, about the plot of 'The Adventure of the Sussex Vampire'; this was not given either in the *Strand* (though the story appeared in the same issue) or in the book.

The poem, 'The Inner Room', was first collected in Doyle's *Songs of Action* in 1898. In that volume and in the collected edition of his poetry the final line appears as 'Through', rather than 'In', the gloom.

The article mentions a number of unrecorded cases of Sherlock Holmes, 'Rigoletto and his abominable wife', 'The Adventure of the Tired Captain', and 'The Curious Experience of the Patterson Family in the Island of Uffa'. The first is mentioned in 'The Adventure of the Musgrave Ritual' as the case of 'Ricoletti of the club foot and his abominable wife'; the second comes from 'The Adventure of the Naval Treaty'; and the third appears in 'The Adventure of the Five Orange Pips' as 'the singular adventures of the Grice Patersons in the island of Uffa'.

The editor who was concerned about the lack of a second line of rails was, of course, Greenhough Smith of the *Strand Magazine*. He later admitted that Doyle was 'no pedant as to accuracy of details so long as he obtained the effect at which he aimed'.[319] The problem arose in 'The Man with the Watches' ('IV' referring to 'The Lost

Special'). When it was brought to his attention, Doyle replied:

> About the trains in the text that is all right. You see it is not an integral part of the story but merely a theoretical explanation put forward by a theorist. If the facts are wrong he is wrong but that does not matter to us. Though for that matter I should not in my own person hesitate at laying down a fresh line of rails – or a fresh railway line as I did in Story IV – if by so doing I could get my effect. One must be masterful in telling a story.[320]

He did, however, feel that criticism of another story in the series, 'The Black Doctor', was justified as he had in the opening sentence inadvertently located a village 10 miles in a 'south-westerly' direction from Liverpool!

Some criticism did strike home. The article about 'Silver Blaze', for example, was to prevent him from placing the story among his favourites, but a legal critique by A. C. Fox-Davies was to have a more beneficial outcome. As a barrister, Fox-Davies was intrigued by the Sherlock Holmes stories. He wrote a sequel to one of them in which he showed that the criminal could easily be acquitted on the evidence given by Holmes. He sent this to Conan Doyle, who was impressed by it and who encouraged him to turn to fiction, which in due course he did.

Various versions of the story about the cabman who correctly deduced Doyle's identity are given in the main introduction, but one which is contemporary with the composition of the article (though in this version it had been current for over a decade) may be given here. It appeared in *Cassell's Weekly* on 5 September 1923:

> The other day Sir Arthur went from Lyons to Paris, and at the station took a taxicab from the station to his

hotel, the cabby, receiving his fare with a *douceur* added, saluted and said:

'Merci, M. Conan Doyle.'

'Why, how do you know my name?' questioned Sir Arthur.

'Well, sir, I noticed in the paper that you were coming to Paris from the South of France, your general appearance is English, and I could see that your hair had lately been cut by a barber in the South of France.'

'That is remarkable,' said Sir Arthur. 'Had you no other evidence to go on?'

'Well,' said the man, 'there was also the fact that your name was on your luggage.'[321]

'You will be amused to hear that I am at work upon a Sherlock Holmes story,' Doyle once informed Greenhough Smith, adding: 'So the old dog returns to his vomit.'[322] This, the editor felt, was 'pretty strong', and he may have thought the same about the two apocryphal tales – the one about a goat and the one about Sherlock Holmes in Heaven – as neither was included in the *Strand Magazine*. The first was taken from the *Daily Sketch* of 21 November 1910; the point of the second was that Adam did not have a navel. This type of joke was popular and many were far worse, as the following, which is taken from *To-Day* of 10 February 1894, will show:

YOUNG SHERLOCK (*in churchyard*): Look, mamma! A man has been buried there.

MRS HOLMES: Why, child – it may just as likely have been a woman.

YOUNG SHERLOCK: But, mamma, don't you see that cigar end lying there?[323]

Doyle mentions the stage début of Eille Norwood as Holmes. This was in *The Return of Sherlock Holmes* by J. E. Harold Terry and Arthur Rose which was first performed in London at the Princes Theatre on 9 October

1923. He was himself present on the opening night and such was the 'approbation of the London public' that he was called upon to make a short curtain speech. As far as the play was concerned, he said, he was only the grandfather of Sherlock Holmes.

Perhaps Doyle's most unjust assertion – one which he had previously mentioned in a letter to Ronald Knox – is that Watson never shows a single gleam of humour; however the reference to the conversation between Goldsmith and Dr Johnson is very apt. When Dr Johnson said that the little fishes in a proposed fable should talk like little fishes, Goldsmith, according to the *Life of Johnson* (27 April 1773), replied: 'Why, Dr Johnson, this is not so easy as you seem to think; for if you were to make little fishes talk, they would talk like whales.' At a very early stage, Watson acquired and thereafter retained his reputation as a slow thinker and as one inclined to opt for the least likely alternatives.

That Sherlock Holmes was anything but mythical to many is shown by the fact that I have had many letters addressed to him with requests that I forward them. Watson has also had a number of letters in which he has been asked for the address or for the autograph of his more brilliant *confrère*. A press-cutting agency wrote to Watson asking whether Holmes would not wish to subscribe. When Holmes retired several elderly ladies were ready to keep house for him and one sought to ingratiate herself by assuring me that she knew all about bee-keeping and could 'segregate the queen'. I had considerable offers also for Holmes if he would examine and solve various family mysteries. Once the offer – from Poland – was that I should myself go, and my reward was practically left to my own judgement. I had judgement enough, however, to avoid it altogether.

I have often been asked whether I had myself the qualities which I depicted, or whether I was merely the Watson that I look. Of course I am well aware that it is one thing to grapple with a practical problem and quite another thing when you are allowed to solve it under your own conditions. I have no delusions about that. At the same time a man cannot spin a character out of his own inner consciousness and make it really life-like unless he has some possibilities of that character within him – which is a dangerous admission for one who has drawn so many villains as I. In my poem 'The Inner Room', describing our multiplex personality, I say:

> There are others who are sitting,
>   Grim as doom,
> In the dim ill-boding shadow
>   Of my room.
> Darkling figures, stern or quaint,
> Now a savage, now a saint,
> Showing fitfully and faint
>   In the gloom.

Among those figures there may perhaps be an astute detective also, but I find that in real life in order to find him I have to inhibit all the others and get into a mood when there is no one in the room but me. Then I get results and have several times solved problems by Holmes's methods after the police have been baffled. Yet I must admit that in ordinary life I am by no means observant and that I have to throw myself into an artificial frame of mind before I can weigh evidence and anticipate the sequence of events.

The impression that Holmes was a real person of flesh and blood may have been intensified by his frequent appearance upon the stage. After the withdrawal of my dramatization of *Rodney Stone* from a theatre upon which I held a six months' lease, I determined to play a bold and energetic game, for an empty theatre spells ruin. When I saw the course that things were taking I shut myself up and devoted my whole mind to making a sensational Sherlock Holmes drama. I wrote it in a week and called it *The Speckled Band* after the short story of that name. I do not think that I exaggerate if I say that within a fortnight of the one play shutting down I had a company working upon rehearsals of a second one, which had been written in the interval. It was a considerable success. Lyn Harding, as the half epileptic and wholly formidable Doctor Grimesby Rylott, was most masterful, while Saintsbury as Sherlock Holmes was also very good. Before the end of the run I had cleared off all that I had lost upon the other play, and I had created a permanent property of some value. It became a stock piece and is even now touring the country. We had a fine rock boa to play the title-rôle, a snake which was the pride of my heart, so one can imagine my disgust when I saw that one critic ended his disparaging review by the words: 'The crisis of the play was produced by the appearance of a palpably artificial serpent.' I was inclined to offer him a goodly sum if he would undertake to go to bed with it. We had several snakes at different times, but they were none of them born actors and they were all inclined either to hang down from the hole in the wall like inanimate bell-pulls, or else to turn back through the hole and get even with the stage carpenter who pinched their tails in order to make them more lively. Finally we used artificial snakes, and every one, including the stage carpenter, agreed that it was more satisfactory.

This was the second Sherlock Holmes play. I should have spoken about the first, which was produced very much earlier, in fact at the time of the African war. It was written and most wonderfully acted by William Gillette, the famous American. Since he used my characters and to some extent my plots, he naturally gave me a share in the undertaking, which proved to be very successful. 'May I marry Holmes?' was one cable which I received from him when in the throes of composition. 'You may marry or murder or do what you like with him,' was my heartless reply. I was charmed both with the play, the acting and the pecuniary result. I think that every man with a drop of artistic blood in his veins would agree that the latter consideration, though very welcome when it does arrive, is still the last of which he thinks.

Before I leave the subject of the many impersonations of Holmes I may say that all of them, and all the drawings, are very unlike my own original idea of the man. I saw him as very tall – 'over 6 feet, but so excessively lean that he seemed considerably taller', said *A Study in Scarlet*. He had, as I imagined him, a thin razor-like face, with a great hawks-bill of a nose, and two small eyes, set close together on either side of it. Such was my conception. It chanced, however, that poor Sidney Paget who, before his premature death, drew all the original pictures, had a younger brother whose name, I think, was Walter, who served him as a model. The handsome Walter took the place of the more powerful but uglier Sherlock, and perhaps from the point of view of my lady readers it was as well. The stage has followed the type set up by the pictures.

Films of course were unknown when the stories appeared, and when these rights were finally discussed and a small sum offered for them by a French company it seemed treasure trove and I was very glad to accept. Afterwards I had to buy them back again at exactly ten times what I had received, so the deal was a disastrous one. But now they have been done by the Stoll Company with Eille Norwood as Holmes, and it was worth all the expense to get so fine a production. Norwood has since played the part on the stage and won the approbation of the London public. He has that rare quality which can only be described as glamour, which compels you to watch an actor eagerly even when he is doing nothing. He has the brooding eye which excites expectation and he has also a quite unrivalled power of disguise. My only criticism of the films is that they introduce telephones, motor cars and other luxuries of which the Victorian Holmes never dreamed.

People have often asked me whether I knew the end of a

Holmes story before I started it. Of course I do. One could not possibly steer a course if one did not know one's destination. The first thing is to get your idea. We will suppose that this idea is that a woman is suspected of biting a wound in her child, when she was really sucking that wound for fear of poison injected by some one else. Having got that key idea one's next task is to conceal it and lay emphasis upon everything which can make for a different explanation. Holmes, however, can see all the fallacies of the alternatives, and arrives more or less dramatically at the true solution by steps which he can describe and justify. He shows his powers by what the South Americans now call 'Sherlock-holmitos', which means clever little deductions, which often have nothing to do with the matter in hand, but impress the reader with a general sense of power. The same effect is gained by his offhand allusion to other cases. Heaven knows how many titles I have thrown about in a casual way, and how many readers have begged me to satisfy their curiosity as to 'Rigoletto and his abominable wife', 'The Adventure of the Tired Captain', or 'The Curious Experience of the Patterson Family in the Island of Uffa'. Once or twice, as in 'The Adventure of the Second Stain', which in my judgement is one of the neatest of the stories, I did actually use the title years before I wrote a story to correspond.

There are some questions concerned with particular stories which turn up periodically from every quarter of the globe. In 'The Adventure of the Priory School' Holmes remarks in his offhand way that by looking at a bicycle track on a damp moor one can say which way it was heading. I had so many remonstrances upon this point, varying from pity to anger, that I took out my bicycle and tried. I had imagined that the observations of the way in which the track of the hind wheel overlaid the track of the front one when the machine was not running dead straight would show the direction. I found that my correspondents were right and I was wrong, for this would be the same whichever way the cycle was moving. On the other hand the real solution was much simpler, for on an undulating moor the wheels make a much deeper impression uphill and a more shallow one downhill; so Holmes was justified of his wisdom after all.

Sometimes I have got upon dangerous ground where I have taken risks through my own want of knowledge of the correct atmosphere. I have, for example, never been a racing man, and yet I ventured to write 'Silver Blaze', in which the mystery depends upon the laws of training and racing. The story is all right, and Holmes may have been at the top of his form, but my ignorance cries aloud to heaven. I read an excellent and very damaging criticism of my story in some sporting paper, written clearly by a man who *did* know, in which he explained the exact penalties which would have come upon every one concerned if they had acted as I described. Half would have been in jail and the other half warned off the turf for ever. However, I have never been nervous about details, and one must be masterful sometimes. When an alarmed editor wrote to me once: 'There is no second line of rails at that point,' I answered: 'I make one.' On the other hand, there are cases where accuracy is essential.

I do not wish to be ungrateful to Holmes, who has been a good friend to me in many ways. If I have sometimes been inclined to weary of him, it is because his character admits of no light or shade. He is a calculating machine, and anything you add to that simply weakens the effect. Thus the variety of the stories must depend upon the romance and compact handling of the plots. I would say a word for Watson also, who in the course of seven volumes never shows one gleam of humour or makes one single joke. To make a real character one must sacrifice everything to consistency and remember Goldsmith's criticism of Johnson that 'he would make the little fishes talk like whales'.

I do not think that I ever realized what a living actual

personality Holmes had become to the more guileless readers, until I heard of the very pleasing story of the char-à-banc
of French schoolboys who, when asked what they wanted to
see first in London, replied unanimously that they wanted to
see Mr Holmes's lodgings in Baker Street. Many have asked
me which house it is, but that is a point which for excellent
reasons I will not decide.

There are certain Sherlock Holmes stories, apocryphal I
need not say, which go round and round the press and turn
up at fixed intervals with the regularity of a comet. One is the
story of the cabman who is supposed to have taken me to an
hotel in Paris. 'Dr Doyle,' he cried, gazing at me fixedly, 'I
perceive from your appearance that you have been recently
at Constantinople. I have reason to think also that you have
been at Buda, and I perceive some indication that you were
not far from Milan.' 'Wonderful. Five francs for the secret of
how you did it?' 'I looked at the labels pasted on your trunk,'
said the astute cabby. Another perennial is of the woman
who is said to have consulted Sherlock. 'I am greatly puzzled,
sir. In one week I have lost a motor horn, a brush, a box of
golf balls, a dictionary and a bootjack. Can you explain it?'
'Nothing simpler, madame,' said Sherlock. 'It is clear that
your neighbour keeps a goat.' There was a third about how
Sherlock entered heaven, and by virtue of his power of
observation at once greeted Adam, but the point is perhaps
too anatomical for further discussion.

A SHERLOCK HOLMES COMPETITION

'Which are the best Sherlock Holmes stories?' was the question on the cover of the *Strand Magazine* for March 1927 which contained 'A Novel Competition set by A. Conan Doyle'. He had selected the twelve short stories which he considered the best of the forty-four already published in book form, and had given the list in a sealed envelope to the editor. A prize of £100 and a signed copy of his autobiography, *Memories and Adventures*, was offered to the person who sent a list which coincided most closely with his own, and there were to be a hundred signed copies of his autobiography for the runners-up.

An illustration from each story was given on the competition pages and on the half title of the magazine; these were numbered in the order in which they had appeared, so that 'The Adventure of the Cardboard Box', for example, was number 14. The readers were asked to make their choice by placing the numbers on a coupon which was printed at the end of the advertisement section and to return it by 26 March 1927.

The article inaugurating the competition was written in January 1927 and was originally called, 'Mr Sherlock Holmes to his Friends'; where Conan Doyle had put, 'now contains no fewer than fifty-six stories', the editor added, 'including "The Adventure of Shoscombe Old Place", to appear in next month's *Strand Magazine*'; and the page was given on which the details of the competition were set out: 'It is as a little test of the opinion of the public that I inaugurate the small competition announced on page 281.' The article was subsequently used, with two of the final paragraphs omitted, as the preface to *The Case-Book of Sherlock Holmes* which was published by John Murray on 16 June 1927.

The Sherlock Holmes Competition was by no means the first. One of the earliest, a 'Sherlock Holmes Examination Paper', had appeared in *Tit-bits* on 21 October 1893. It consisted of twelve questions about the detective's methods and there were three prizes. The examination proved very successful and there were a great many correct entries. The winner, Adam R. Thomson, was named on 16 December 1893, his entry having been chosen on account of the answer he had given to the one question which depended on personal ingenuity. As well as the prizes already announced, the editor was able to offer additional ones. He explained: 'Mr Conan Doyle, who has taken an interest in the competition, has been kind enough to send autographed copies of *The Memoirs of Sherlock Holmes* to a number of the senders of the next best competitions.'[324]

On 6 January 1894, after the presumed death of Sherlock Holmes, *Tit-bits* announced another competition; the readers were asked to state which Sherlock Holmes story was their favourite. The one which had most supporters would be judged the most popular, and the person who gave the best reasons for his choice would receive the 'Sherlock Holmes Memorial Prize'. As with the later competition, 'The Speckled Band' proved to be the most popular, with 'Silver Blaze' and 'The Final Problem' close behind.

Shortly after Doyle had finished 'The Problem of Thor Bridge' in September 1921, using an idea suggested by Greenhough Smith, he was contemplating a new longer story and a further series of six short stories about Sherlock Holmes. He explained to the editor that it was the need for good plots which made the stories so hard to do:

> I can write them if I have good initial ideas, but have rather exhausted my own stock. No wonder! I wonder if a competition for the best mystery idea would be possible – probably you would get no fish worth taking out of the net.[325]

This competition was never held, as the editor felt that Doyle's prediction of the result would have been 'assuredly borne out'. But a competition to select the twelve best stories was one which would work well. It would settle the long argument over whether the later stories were inferior to the early ones and would show whether the author's own feelings were at variance with those of his readers. Doyle had often been surprised when people told him that they considered a certain story was the best, often choosing one of which he was not particularly fond or one which he thought among the weakest.

The winner of the 1927 competition was R. T. Norman, who named ten of the twelve selected by Conan Doyle. Seven competitors chose nine, and a great number were correct with eight. It was not surprising that nobody had managed the full twelve, as Doyle's choice was idiosyncratic, which makes his explanation, which is given in 'How I made my list', the more interesting. 'I think I was wrong not to include *both* "The Naval Treaty" and "The Second Stain",' he admitted afterwards. 'Otherwise I think my choice is reasonable.'[326] The results were published in the June 1927 issue of the *Strand Magazine* and, at the same time, it was announced that the *Grand Magazine* would reprint the first six stories on the author's list. These began the following month, and, in fact, all twelve were printed between then and June 1928. The remaining six, which Doyle had mentioned as among the best, were also reprinted in the *Grand Magazine* between May and October 1930, in the following order: 'The Naval Treaty', 'The Resident Patient', 'The Man with a Twisted Lip', 'The Greek Interpreter', 'The Bruce-Partington Plans', and 'The Crooked Man'.

Mr Sherlock Holmes to His Readers

I fear that Mr Sherlock Holmes may become like one of those popular tenors who, having outlived their time, are still tempted to make repeated farewell bows to their indulgent audiences. This must cease and he must go the way of all flesh, material or imaginary. One likes to think that there is some fantastic limbo for the children of imagination, some strange, impossible place where the beaux of Fielding may still make love to the belles of Richardson, where Scott's heroes still may strut, Dickens's delightful Cockneys still raise a laugh, and Thackeray's worldlings continue to carry on their reprehensible careers. Perhaps in some humble corner of such a Valhalla, Sherlock and his Watson may for a time find a place, while some more astute sleuth with some even less astute comrade may fill the stage which they have vacated.

His career has been a long one – though it is possible to exaggerate it; decrepit gentlemen who approach me and declare that his adventures formed the reading of their boyhood do not meet the response from me which they seem to expect. One is not anxious to have one's personal dates handled so unkindly. As a matter of cold fact, Holmes made his *début* in *A Study in Scarlet* and in *The Sign of Four*, two small booklets which appeared between 1887 and 1889. It was in 1891 that 'A Scandal in Bohemia', the first of the long series of short stories, appeared in the *Strand Magazine*. The public seemed appreciative and desirous of more, so that from that date, thirty-six years ago, they have been produced in a broken series which now contains no fewer than fifty-six stories. These have been re-published in *The Adventures*, *The Memoirs*, *The Return*, and *His Last Bow*, and there remain twelve published during the last few years which Sir John Murray is about to produce under the title of *The Case-Book of Sherlock Holmes*. He began his adventures in the very heart of the later Victorian era, carried it through the all-too-short reign of Edward, and has managed to hold his own little niche even in these feverish days. Thus it would be true to say that those who first read of him as young men have lived to see their own grown-up children following the same adventures in the same magazine. It is a striking example of the patience and loyalty of the British public.

I had fully determined at the conclusion of *The Memoirs* to bring Holmes to an end, as I felt that my literary energies should not be directed too much into one channel. That pale, clear-cut face and loose-limbed figure were taking up an undue share of my imagination. I did the deed, but, fortunately, no coroner had pronounced upon the remains, and so, after a long interval, it was not difficult for me to respond to the flattering demand and to explain my rash act away. I have never regretted it, for I have not in actual practice found that these lighter sketches have prevented me from exploring and finding my limitations in such varied branches of literature as history, poetry, historical novels, psychic research, and the drama. Had Holmes never existed I could not have done more, though he may perhaps have stood a little in the way of the recognition of my more serious literary work.

There has been some debate as to whether the adventures of Holmes, or the narrative powers of Watson, declined with the passage of the years. When the same string is still harped upon, however cunningly one may vary the melody, there is still the danger of monotony. The mind of the reader is less fresh and responsive, which may unjustly prejudice him against the writer. To compare great things to small, Scott in his autobiographical notes has remarked that each of Voltaire's later pamphlets was declared to be a declension from the last one, and yet when the collected works were assembled they were found to be among the most brilliant. Scott also was depreciated by critics for some of his most solid work. Therefore, with such illustrious examples before one, let me preserve the hope that he who in days to come may read my series backwards will not find that his impressions are very different from those of his neighbour who reads them forwards.

It is as a little test of the opinion of the public that I inaugurate this small competition. I have drawn up a list of the twelve short stories contained in the four published volumes which I consider to be the best, and I should like to know to what extent my choice agrees with that of *Strand* readers. I have left my list in a sealed envelope with the Editor of the *Strand Magazine*.

And so, reader, farewell to Sherlock Holmes! I thank you for your constancy, and can but hope that some return has been made in the shape of that distraction from the worries of life and stimulating change of thought which can only be found in the fairy kingdom of romance.

How I Made My List

When this competition was first mooted I went into it in a most light-hearted way, thinking that it would be the easiest thing in the world to pick out the twelve best of the Holmes stories. In practice I found that I had engaged myself in a serious task. In the first place I had to read the stories myself with some care. 'Steep, steep, weary work,' as the Scottish landlady remarked.

I began by eliminating altogether the last twelve stories, which are scattered through the *Strand* for the last five or six years. They are about to come out in volume form under the title *The Case-Book of Sherlock Holmes*, but the public could not easily get at them. Had they been available I should have put two of them in my team – namely, 'The Lion's Mane' and 'The Illustrious Client'. The first of these is hampered by being told by Holmes himself, a method which I employed only twice, as it certainly cramps the narrative. On the other hand, the actual plot is among the very best of the whole series, and for that it deserves its place. 'The Illustrious Client', on the other hand, is not remarkable for plot, but it has a certain dramatic quality and moves adequately in lofty circles, so I should also have found a place for it.

However, these being ruled out, I am now faced with some forty odd candidates to be weighed against each other. There are certainly some few an echo of which has come to me from all parts of the world, and I think this is the final proof of merit of some sort. There is the grim snake story, 'The Speckled Band'. That I am sure will be on every list. Next to that in popular favour and in my own esteem I would place 'The Red-Headed League' and 'The Dancing Men', on account in each case of the originality of the plot. Then we could hardly leave out the story which deals with the only foe who ever really extended Holmes, and which deceived the public (and Watson) into the erroneous inference of his death. Also, I think the first story of all should go in, as it opened the path for the others, and as it has more female interest than is usual. Finally, I think the story which essays the difficult task of explaining away the alleged death of Holmes, and which also introduces such a villain as Colonel Sebastian Moran, should have a place. This puts 'The Final Problem', 'A Scandal in Bohemia', and 'The Empty House' upon our list, and we have got our first half-dozen.

But now comes the crux. There are a number of stories which really are a little hard to separate. On the whole I think I should find a place for 'The Five Orange Pips', for though it is short it has a certain dramatic quality of its own. So now only five places are left. There are two stories which deal with high diplomacy and intrigue. They are both among the very best of the series. The one is 'The Naval Treaty' and the other 'The Second Stain'. There is no room for both of them in the team, and on the whole I regard the latter as the better story. Therefore we will put it down for the eighth place.

And now which? 'The Devil's Foot' has points. It is grim and new. We will give it the ninth place. I think also that 'The Priory School' is worth a place if only for the dramatic moment when Holmes points his finger at the Duke. I have only two places left. I hesitate between 'Silver Blaze', 'The Bruce-Partington Plans', 'The Crooked Man', 'The Man with the Twisted Lip', 'The "Gloria Scott"', 'The Greek Interpreter', 'The Reigate Squires', 'The Musgrave Ritual', and 'The Resident Patient'. On what principle am I to choose two out of those? The racing detail in 'Silver Blaze' is very faulty, so we must disqualify him. There is little to choose between the others. A small thing would turn the scale. 'The Musgrave Ritual' has a historical touch which gives it a little added distinction. It is also a memory from Holmes's early life. So now we come to the very last. I might as well draw the name out of a bag, for I see no reason to put one before the other. Whatever their merit – and I make no claim for that – they are all as good as I could make them. On the whole Holmes himself shows perhaps most ingenuity in 'The Reigate Squires', and therefore this shall be twelfth man in my team.

It is proverbially a mistake for a judge to give his reasons, but I have analysed mine if only to show any competitors that I really have taken some trouble in the matter.

The List is therefore as follows:
The Speckled Band
The Red-Headed League
The Dancing Men
The Final Problem
A Scandal in Bohemia
The Empty House
The Five Orange Pips
The Second Stain
The Devil's Foot
The Priory School
The Musgrave Ritual
The Reigate Squires

THE BACKGROUND TO
SHERLOCK HOLMES

'The Background to Sherlock Holmes' is a composite article derived from Conan Doyle's autobiography, *Memories and Adventures*, which was published on 18 September 1924. Some details of his life and of his life style have been included as well as all the material which has a direct bearing on the background and composition of the Sherlock Holmes stories. It does not attempt to do full justice to Sir Arthur Conan Doyle's rich and varied career; one which he summarized thus:

I have had a life which, for variety and romance, could, I think, hardly be exceeded. I have known what it was to be a poor man and I have known what it was to be fairly affluent. I have sampled every kind of human experience. I have known many of the most remarkable men of my time. I have had a long literary career after a medical training which gave me the M.D. of Edinburgh. I have tried my hand at very many sports, including boxing, cricket, billiards, motoring, football, aeronautics and ski-ing, having been the first to introduce the latter for long journeys into Switzerland. I have travelled as Doctor to a whaler for seven months in the Arctic and afterwards in the West Coast of Africa. I have seen something of three wars, the Soudanese, the South African and the German. My life has been dotted with adventures of all kinds.[327]

And in the preface to the Crowborough Edition he admitted that he had, in Savage Landor's phrase, thoroughly 'warmed both hands before the fire of life':

> Few men living have, I should think, had so varied an experience or seen life from so many angles. Perhaps some reflection of this may be found in my books, which, in spite of the predominance of the detective story in the public eye, really open up many different channels of imaginative thought.[328]

The excuse for this article is that a similar one appeared in *Collier's Weekly* on 29 December 1923 under the title, 'The Truth About Sherlock Holmes'. 'In this article,' the blurb stated, 'Sir Arthur answers all our questions about Holmes – how he was born and developed and why it became necessary to kill him.'[329] It was one of three which used material from the autobiography, the others dealt with his career in politics and with his spiritual beliefs. It is unlikely that Doyle was responsible for the choice of material, for it jumps from section to section with poorly concealed joins. It may have been done by his secretary, but it is more likely that someone connected with the magazine created the article using a typed copy of the manuscript. As Doyle wished to complete his autobiography before he sailed to America in 1923, the later years were dealt with in less detail. On his return he rewrote the last chapter and rearranged some of the material before its appearance in book form.

In the serial publication, both in England and America, there was one major error or ambiguity which, though omitted from the book, did resurface on many occasions. When Doyle describes how he had determined to kill Sherlock Holmes, he originally put: 'The idea was in my mind when I went with my wife for a short holiday in Switzerland, in the course of which we walked down the Lauterbrunnen Valley. I saw there the wonderful falls of Reichenbach, a terrible place, and that, I thought, would make a worthy tomb for poor Sherlock, even if I buried my banking account along with him.' As many people were quick to point out the Reichenbach Falls are not in, or near, the Lauterbrunnen Valley. Doyle therefore crossed out that line so that it read, rather clumsily, 'a short holiday in Switzerland, in the course of which we saw there the wonderful falls of Reichenbach'.

In the new edition of *Memories and Adventures* published shortly after his death in July 1930, Doyle had made very few changes, though he did add some lines about his impersonation of Professor Challenger and, in passing, about the value of the early editions of the Sherlock Holmes stories. 'It seems strange to me to hear that the original edition of *Sherlock Holmes* is now selling at about twenty pounds. I wish I had laid in a few of them.'[330] He would have been even more surprised had he known what they were to fetch half a century later.

I was born on May 22, 1859, at Picardy Place, Edinburgh. Of my boyhood I need say little, save that it was Spartan at home and more Spartan at the Edinburgh school where a tawse-brandishing schoolmaster of the old type made our young lives miserable. I was in my tenth year when I was sent to Hodder, which is the preparatory school for Stonyhurst, the big Roman Catholic public school in Lancashire. From Hodder I passed on to Stonyhurst. The general curriculum, like the building, was medieval but sound. There were seven classes – elements, figures, rudiments, grammar, syntax, poetry and rhetoric – and you were allotted a year for each, or seven in all – a course with which I faithfully complied, two having already been completed at Hodder. In the last year I edited the College magazine and wrote a good deal of indifferent verse. I also went up for the Matriculation examination of London University, a good all-round test which winds up the Stonyhurst curriculum, and I surprised every one by taking honours, so after all I emerged from Stonyhurst at the age of sixteen with more credit than seemed probable from my rather questionable record. I had yet another year with the Jesuits, for it was determined that I was still too young to begin any professional studies, and that I should go to Germany and learn German.

When I returned to Edinburgh, with little to show, either mental or spiritual, for my pleasant school year in Germany, I found that the family affairs were as straitened as ever. It had been determined that I should be a doctor, chiefly, I think, because Edinburgh was so famous a centre for medical learning. I entered as a student in October 1876, and I emerged as a Bachelor of Medicine in August 1881. Between these two points lies one long weary grind at botany, chemistry, anatomy, physiology, and a whole list of compulsory subjects, many of which have a very indirect bearing upon the art of curing.

The most notable of the characters whom I met was one Joseph Bell, a surgeon at the Edinburgh Infirmary. Bell was a very remarkable man in body and mind. He was thin, wiry, dark, with a high-nosed acute face, penetrating grey eyes, angular shoulders, and a jerky way of walking. His voice was high and discordant. He was a very skilful surgeon, but his strong point was diagnosis, not only of disease, but of occupation and character. For some reason which I have never understood he singled me out from the drove of students who frequented his wards and made me his out-patient clerk, which meant that I had to array his out-patients, make simple notes of their cases, and then show them in, one by one, to the large room in which Bell sat in state surrounded by his dressers and students. Then I had ample chance of studying his methods and of noticing that he often learned more of his patient by a few quick glances than I had done by my questions. Occasionally the results were very dramatic, though there were times when he blundered. In one of his best cases he said to a civilian patient:

'Well, my man, you've served in the army.'

'Aye, sir.'

'Not long discharged?'

'No, sir.'

'A Highland regiment?'

'Aye, sir.'

'Stationed at Barbados?'

'Aye, sir.'

'You see, gentlemen,' he would explain, 'the man was a respectful man but did not remove his hat. They do not in the army, but he would have learned civilian ways had he been long discharged. He has an air of authority and he is obviously Scottish. As to Barbados, his complaint is elephantiasis, which is West Indian and not British.' To his audience of Watsons it all seemed very miraculous until it was explained, and then it became simple enough. It is no wonder that after the study of such a character I used and amplified his methods when in later life I tried to build up a scientific detective who solved cases on his own merits and not through the folly of the crimjnal. Bell took a keen interest in these detective tales and even made suggestions which were not, I am bound to say, very practical. I kept in touch with him for many years and he used to come upon my platform to support me when I contested Edinburgh in 1900.

When I took over his out-patient work he warned me that a knowledge of Scottish idioms was necessary, and I, with the confidence of youth, declared that I had got it. The sequel was amusing. On one of the first days an old man came who, in response to my question, declared that he had a 'bealin' in his oxter'. This fairly beat me, much to Bell's amusement. It seems that the words really mean an abscess in the armpit.

I endeavoured almost from the first to compress the classes for a year into half a year, and so to have some months in which to earn a little money as a medical assistant, who would dispense and do odd jobs for a doctor. My first venture, in the early summer of '78, was with a Dr Richardson, running a low-class practice in the poorer quarters of Sheffield. I did my best, and I dare say he was patient, but at the end of three weeks we parted by mutual consent. I went on to London, where I renewed my advertisements in the medical papers, and found a refuge for some weeks with my Doyle relatives, then living at Clifton Gardens, Maida Vale. I fear that I was too Bohemian for them and they too conventional for me. However, they were kind to me, and I roamed about London for some time with pockets so empty that there was little chance of idleness breeding its usual mischief.

Soon, however, there came an answer to my advertisement: 'Third year's student, desiring experience rather than remuneration, offers his services, &c., &c.' It was from a Dr Elliot living in a townlet in Shropshire which rejoiced in the extraordinary name of 'Ruyton-of-the-eleven-towns'. It was not big enough to make one town, far less eleven. There for four months I helped in a country practice. It was a very quiet existence and I had a good deal of time to myself under very pleasant circumstances, so that I really trace some little mental progress to that period, for I read and thought without interruption.

After a winter's work at the University my next assistantship was a real money-making proposition to the extent of some two pounds a month. This was with Dr Hoare, a well-known Birmingham doctor, who had a five-horse City practice, and every working doctor, before the days of motors, would realize that this meant going from morning to night. I had long lists of prescriptions to make up every day, for we dispensed our own medicine, and one hundred bottles of an evening were not unknown. I had my own visiting list, also, the poorest or the most convalescent, and I saw a great deal, for better or worse, of very low life. Twice I returned to this Birmingham practice and always my relations with the family became closer.

It was at this time that I first learned that shillings might be earned in other ways than by filling phials. Some friend remarked to me that my letters were very vivid and surely I could write some things to sell. I may say that the general aspiration towards literature was tremendously strong upon me, and that my mind was reaching out in what seemed an aimless way in all sorts of directions. I used to be allowed twopence for my lunch, that being the price of a mutton pie, but near the pie shop was a second-hand book shop with a barrel full of old books and the legend 'Your choice for 2*d*.' stuck above it. Often the price of my luncheon used to be spent on some sample out of this barrel, and I have within reach of my arm as I write these lines, copies of Gordon's *Tacitus*, Temple's works, Pope's *Homer*, Addison's *Spectator* and Swift's works, which all came out of the twopenny box. Any one observing my actions and tastes would have said that so strong a spring would certainly overflow, but for my own part I never dreamed I could myself produce decent prose, and the remark of my friend, who was by no means given to flattery, took me greatly by surprise. I sat down, however, and wrote a little adventure story which I called 'The Mystery of Sasassa Valley'. To my great joy and surprise it was accepted by *Chambers's Journal*, and I received three guineas. It mattered not that other attempts failed. I had done it once and I cheered myself by the thought that I could do it again.

It was in the *Hope*, under the command of the well-known whaler, John Gray, that I paid a seven months' visit to the Arctic Seas in the year 1880. I went in the capacity of surgeon, but as I was only twenty years of age when I started, and as my knowledge of medicine was that of an average third year's student, I have often thought that it was as well that there was no very serious call upon my services. I went on board the whaler a big, straggling youth, I came off it a powerful, well-grown man. Now I had a straight run in to my final examination, which I passed with fair but not notable distinction at the end of the winter session of 1881. I was now a Bachelor of Medicine and a Master of Surgery, fairly launched upon my professional career.

It had always been my intention to take a voyage as ship's surgeon when I had taken my degree, as I could in this way see something of the world, and at the same time earn a little of the money which I so badly needed if I were ever to start in practice for myself. I had no reason to think that I would find a billet upon a passenger ship and had nearly forgotten that I had my name down, when I suddenly received a telegram telling me to come to Liverpool and to take medical charge of the African Steam Navigation Company's *Mayumba*, bound for the West Coast. In a week I was there, and on October 22, 1881, we started on our voyage. On January 14 we were in Liverpool once more, and West Africa was but one more of the cinema reels of memory.

I have now reached the time when, under very curious circumstances, I endeavoured to establish myself in medical practice. In a book written some years afterwards called *The Stark Munro Letters*, I drew in very close detail the events of the next few years, and there the curious reader will find them more clearly and fully set out than would be to scale in these pages. There are some few incidents there which are imaginary, otherwise the whole history of my association with the man whom I called Cullingworth, his extraordinary character, our parting and the way in which I was left to what seemed certain ruin, were all as depicted.

My mother had greatly resented my association with Cullingworth. Her family pride had been aroused, and justly as I can now see, though my wanderings had left me rather too Bohemian and careless upon points of etiquette. She wrote me several letters of remonstrance which certainly dealt rather faithfully with his character as it appeared to her. I was careless of my papers and these letters were read both by Cullingworth and his wife. One day he came to me and told me that he thought my presence complicated his practice and that we had better part. He then strongly advised me to go into practice myself. I replied that I had no capital. He answered that he would see to that, that he would allow me a pound a week until I got my feet under me, and that I could repay it at leisure. I thanked him warmly, and after looking at Tavistock I finally decided that Portsmouth would be a good place, the only reason being that I knew the conditions at Plymouth, and Portsmouth seemed analogous.

I spent a week in marking down the unoccupied houses, and finally settled at £40 a year into Bush Villa. I fixed up the plate which I had brought from Plymouth, bought a red lamp on tick, and fairly settled down in receipt of custom. As the weeks passed and I had no one with whom to talk I began to think wistfully of the home circle at Edinburgh, and to wonder why, with my eight-roomed house, one or more of them should not come to keep me company. My sisters were already governessing or preparing to do so, but there was my little brother Innes. It would relieve my mother and yet help me if he could join me. So it was arranged, and one happy evening the little knicker-bockered fellow, just ten years old, joined me as my comrade.

For some time Innes and I lived entirely alone, doing the household tasks between us, and going on long walks in the evening to keep ourselves fit. Then I had a brain-wave and I put an advertisement in the evening paper that a groundfloor was to let in exchange for services. From then onwards our meals were cooked for us, and we became in all ways normal.

In the year 1885 my brother left me to go to a public school in Yorkshire. Shortly afterwards I was married. In many ways my marriage marked a turning-point in my life. A bachelor, especially one who had been a wanderer like myself, drifts easily into Bohemian habits, and I was no exception. Up to now the main interest in my life lay in my medical career.

But with the more regular life and the greater sense of responsibility, coupled with the natural development of brain-power, the literary side of me began slowly to spread until it was destined to push the other entirely aside.

During the years before my marriage I had from time to time written short stories which were good enough to be marketable at very small prices – £4 on an average – but not good enough to reproduce. I can hardly have earned more than £10 or £15 a year from this source, so that the idea of making a living by it never occurred to me. But though I was not putting out I was taking in. It was about a year after my marriage that I realized that I could go on doing short stories for ever and never make any headway. What is necessary is that your name should be on the back of a volume. Only so do you assert your individuality, and get the full credit or discredit of your achievement. I had for some time from 1884 onwards been engaged upon a sensational book of adventure which I had called *The Firm of Girdlestone*, which represented my first attempt at a connected narrative.

I felt now that I was capable of something fresher and crisper and more workmanlike. Gaboriau had rather attracted me by the neat dovetailing of his plots, and Poe's masterful detective, M. Dupin, had from boyhood been one of my heroes. But could I bring an addition of my own? I thought of my old teacher Joe Bell, of his eagle face, of his curious ways, of his eerie trick of spotting details. If he were a detective he would surely reduce this fascinating but unorganized business to something nearer to an exact science. I would try if I could get this effect. It was surely possible in real life, so why should I not make it plausible in fiction? It is all very well to say that a man is clever, but the reader wants to see examples of it – such examples as Bell gave us every day in the wards. The idea amused me. What should I call the fellow? I still possess the leaf of a notebook with various alternative names. One rebelled against the elementary art which gives some inkling of character in the name, and creates Mr Sharps or Mr Ferrets. First it was Sherringford Holmes; then it was Sherlock Holmes. He could not tell his own exploits, so he must have a commonplace comrade as a foil – an educated man of action who could both join in the exploits and narrate them. A drab, quiet name for this unostentatious man. Watson would do. And so I had my puppets and wrote my *Study in Scarlet*.

I knew that the book was as good as I could make it, and I had high hopes. When *Girdlestone* used to come circling back with the precision of a homing pigeon, I was grieved but not surprised, for I acquiesced in the decision. But when my little Holmes book began also to do the circular tour I was hurt, for I knew that it deserved a better fate. James Payn applauded but found it both too short and too long, which was true enough. Arrowsmith received it in May 1886, and returned it unread in July. Two or three others sniffed and turned away. Finally, as Ward, Lock & Co. made a speciality of cheap and often sensational literature, I sent it to them. They said:

> Dear Sir, – We have read your story and are pleased with it. We could not publish it this year as the market is flooded at present with cheap fiction, but if you do not object to its being held over till next year, we will give you £25 for the copyright.
>
> Yours faithfully, WARD, LOCK & Co.
> Oct. 30, 1886

It was not a very tempting offer, and even I, poor as I was, hesitated to accept it. It was not merely the small sum offered, but it was the long delay, for this book might open a road for me. I was heart-sick, however, at repeated disappointments, and I felt that perhaps it was true wisdom to make sure of publicity, however late. Therefore I accepted, and the book became *Beeton's Christmas Annual* of 1887. I never at any time received another penny for it.

Having a long wait in front of me before this book could

appear, and feeling large thoughts rise within me, I now determined to test my powers to the full, and I chose a historical novel for this end, which I called *Micah Clarke*. But, alas! although my Holmes booklet was out, and had attracted some little favourable comment, the door still seemed to be barred. James Payn had first peep, and he began his letter of rejection with the sentence 'How can you, can you, waste your time and your wits writing historical novels!' I was on the point of putting the worn manuscript into hospital with its mangled brother *Girdlestone* when as a last resource I sent it to Longmans, whose reader, Andrew Lang, liked it and advised its acceptance. It was to 'Andrew of the brindled hair', as Stevenson called him, that I owe my first real opening, and I have never forgotten it. The book duly appeared in February 1889, and though it was not a boom book it had extraordinarily good reviews.

British literature had a considerable vogue in the United States at this time for the simple reason that there was no copyright and they had not to pay for it. It was hard on British authors, but far harder on American ones, since they were exposed to this devastating competition. One good result, however, from my point of view was that a British author, if he had anything in him, soon won recognition over there, and afterwards, when the Copyright Act was passed, he had his audience all ready for him. My Holmes book had met with some American success and presently I learned that an agent of Lippincott's was in London and that he wished to see me, to arrange for a book. Needless to say that I gave my patients a rest for a day and eagerly kept the appointment. Stoddart, the American, proved to be an excellent fellow, and had two others to dinner. They were Gill, a very entertaining Irish M.P., and Oscar Wilde, who was already famous as the champion of aestheticism. It was indeed a golden evening for me. Wilde to my surprise had read *Micah Clarke* and was enthusiastic about it, so that I did not feel a complete outsider. The result of the evening was that both Wilde and I promised to write books for *Lippincott's Magazine* – Wilde's contribution was *The Picture of Dorian Gray*, a book which is surely upon a high moral plane, while I wrote *The Sign of Four*, in which Holmes made his second appearance.

Encouraged by the kind reception which *Micah Clarke* had received from the critics, I now determined upon an even bolder and more ambitious flight. Hence came my two books *The White Company*, written in 1889, and *Sir Nigel*, written fourteen years later. Of the two I consider the latter the better book, but I have no hesitation in saying that the two of them taken together did thoroughly achieve my purpose, that they made an accurate picture of that great age, and that as a single piece of work they form the most complete, satisfying and ambitious thing that I have ever done. All things find their level, but I believe that if I had never touched Holmes, who has tended to obscure my higher work, my position in literature would at the present moment be a more commanding one. The work needed much research and I have still got my notebooks full of all sorts of lore. I cultivate a simple style and avoid long words so far as possible, and it may be that this surface of ease has sometimes caused the reader to underrate the amount of real research which lies in all my historical novels.

My life had been a pleasant one with my steadily-increasing literary success, my practice, which was enough to keep me pleasantly occupied, and my sport. Suddenly, however, there came a development which shook me out of my rut, and caused an absolute change in my life and plans. It arose when in 1890 Koch announced that he had discovered a sure cure for consumption and that he would demonstrate it upon a certain date in Berlin. A great urge came upon me suddenly that I should go to Berlin and see him do so. I came back a changed man. I had spread my wings and had felt something of the powers within me. Especially I had been influenced by a long talk with Malcolm

Morris, in which he assured me that I was wasting my life in the provinces and had too small a field for my activities. He insisted that I should leave general practice and go to London. I answered that I was by no means sure of my literary success as yet, and that I could not so easily abandon the medical career which had cost my mother such sacrifices and myself so many years of study. He asked me if there was any special branch of the profession on which I could concentrate so as to get away from general practice. I said that of late years I had been interested in eye work and had amused myself by correcting refractions and ordering glasses in the Portsmouth Eye Hospital under Mr Vernon Ford. 'Well,' said Morris, 'why not specialize upon the eye? Go to Vienna, put in six months' work, come back and start in London. Thus you will have a nice clean life with plenty of leisure for your literature.' I came home with this great suggestion buzzing in my head and as my wife was quite willing and Mary, my little girl, was old enough now to be left with her grandmother, there seemed to be no obstacle in the way. There were no difficulties about disposing of the practice, for it was so small and so purely personal that it could not be sold to another and simply had to dissolve. We set forth upon a bitter winter day at the close of 1890.

With the spring my work at Vienna had finished, if it can be said to have begun, and we returned viâ Paris, putting in a few days there with Landholt, who was the most famous French oculist of his time. We took rooms in Montague Place, and I went forth to search for some place where I could put up my plate as an oculist. I searched the doctors' quarters and at last found suitable accommodation at 2 Devonshire Place, which is at the top of Wimpole Street and close to the classical Harley Street. There for £120 a year I got the use of a front room with part use of a waiting-room. I was soon to find that they were both waiting-rooms, and now I know that it was better so.

A number of monthly magazines were coming out at that

time, notable among which was the *Strand*, under the very able editorship of Greenhough Smith. Considering these various journals with their disconnected stories it had struck me that a single character running through a series, if it only engaged the attention of the reader, would bind that reader to that particular magazine. On the other hand, it had long seemed to me that the ordinary serial might be an impediment rather than a help to a magazine, since, sooner or later, one missed one number and afterwards it had lost all interest. Clearly the ideal compromise was a character which carried through, and yet instalments which were each complete in themselves, so that the purchaser was always sure that he could relish the whole contents of the magazine. I believe that I was the first to realize this and the *Strand Magazine* the first to put it into practice.

Looking round for my central character I felt that Sherlock Holmes, whom I had already handled in two little books, would easily lend himself to a succession of short stories. These I began in the long hours of waiting in my consulting-room. Greenhough Smith liked them from the first, and encouraged me to go ahead with them.

I was now once more at a crossroads of my life, and Providence, which I recognize at every step, made me realize it in a very energetic and unpleasant way. I was starting off for my usual trudge one morning from our lodgings when icy shivers passed over me, and I only got back in time to avoid a total collapse. It was a virulent attack of influenza, at a time when influenza was in its deadly prime. It was then, as I surveyed my own life, that I saw how foolish I was to waste my literary earnings in keeping up an oculist's room in Wimpole Street, and I determined with a wild rush of joy to cut the painter and to trust for ever to my power of writing. I haunted house-agents, got lists of suburban villas, and spent some weeks, as my strength returned, in searching for a new home. Finally I found a suitable house, modest but comfortable, isolated and yet one of a row. It was 12 Tennison Road,

South Norwood. There I settled down with a stout heart to do some literary work worthy of the name.

The difficulty of the Holmes work was that every story really needed as clear-cut and original a plot as a longish book would do. One cannot without effort spin plots at such a rate. They are apt to become thin or to break. I was determined, now that I had no longer the excuse of absolute pecuniary pressure, never again to write anything which was not as good as I could possibly make it, and therefore I would not write a Holmes story without a worthy plot and without a problem which interested my own mind, for that is the first requisite before you can interest any one else. If I have been able to sustain this character for a long time and if the public find, as they will find, that the last story is as good as the first, it is entirely due to the fact that I never, or hardly ever, forced a story. Some have thought there was a falling off in the stories, and the criticism was neatly expressed by a Cornish boatman who said to me, 'I think, sir, when Holmes fell over that cliff, he may not have killed himself, but all the same he was never quite the same man afterwards.' I think, however, that if the reader began the series backwards, so that he brought a fresh mind to the last stories, he would agree with me that, though the general average may not be conspicuously high, still the last one is as good as the first.

I was weary, however, of inventing plots and I set myself now to do some work which would certainly be less remunerative but would be more ambitious from a literary point of view. I had long been attracted by the epoch of Louis XIV and by those Huguenots who were the French equivalent of our Puritans. I had a good knowledge of the memoirs of that date, and many notes already prepared, so that it did not take me long to write *The Refugees*. During this Norwood interval, I was certainly working hard, for besides *The Refugees* I wrote *The Great Shadow*, a booklet which I should put near the front of my work for merit, and two other little books on a very inferior plane – *The Parasite* and *Beyond the City*. All these books had some decent success, though none of it was remarkable.

It was still the Sherlock Holmes stories for which the public clamoured, and these from time to time I endeavoured to supply. At last, after I had done two series of them I saw that I was in danger of having my hand forced, and of being entirely identified with what I regarded as a lower stratum of literary achievement. Therefore as a sign of my resolution I determined to end the life of my hero. The idea was in my mind when I went with my wife for a short holiday in Switzerland, in the course of which we saw the wonderful falls of Reichenbach, a terrible place, and one that I thought would make a worthy tomb for poor Sherlock, even if I buried my banking account along with him. So there I laid him, fully determined that he should stay there – as indeed for some years he did. I was amazed at the concern expressed by the public. They say that a man is never properly appreciated until he is dead, and the general protest against my summary execution of Holmes taught me how many and how numerous were his friends. 'You Brute' was the beginning of the letter of remonstrance which one lady sent me, and I expect she spoke for others besides herself. I heard of many who wept. I fear I was utterly callous myself, and only glad to have a chance of opening out into new fields of imagination, for the temptation of high prices made it difficult to get one's thoughts away from Holmes.

THE TRUE STORY OF SHERLOCK HOLMES

'Conan Doyle Tells the True Story of Sherlock Holmes' was published in a special double number of *Tit-bits* on 15 December 1900. Extracts from it were also published in the *Westminster Gazette* on 13 December 1900, under the title: 'Birth and Burial of "Sherlock Holmes". An Agreeable Prospect.'

To interview Dr Conan Doyle, the creator of Sherlock Holmes, is not an easy matter. Dr Doyle has a strong objection to the interview, even though he has no personal antipathy to the interviewer. Considerations, however, of the peculiar interest attached to the thousandth number of *Tit-bits*, coupled with the recollection of his long and friendly relationship with the firm of George Newnes, Ltd, in the pages of whose popular and universally read *Strand Magazine* Sherlock Holmes lived, and moved, and had his being, overcame Dr Doyle's reluctance to be interviewed, and he consented to give the following particulars, which will be read with interest by his admirers all over the world.

'Before I tell you of Sherlock Holmes's death and how it came about,' said Dr Conan Doyle, 'it will probably be interesting to recall the circumstances of his birth. He originally made his appearance, you will remember, in a book which I wrote called *A Study in Scarlet*. The idea of the detective was suggested by a professor under whom I had worked in Edinburgh, and in part by Edgar Allan Poe's detective, which, after all, ran on the lines of all other detectives who have appeared in literature.

'In work which consists in the drawing of detectives there are only one or two qualities which one can use, and an author is forced to hark back upon them constantly, so that every detective must really resemble every other detective to a greater or lesser extent. There is no great originality required in devising or constructing such a man, and the only possible originality which one can get into a story about a detective is in giving him original plots and problems to solve, as in his equipment there must be of necessity an alert acuteness of mind to grasp facts and the relation which each of them bears to the other.

'At the time I first thought of a detective – it was about 1886 – I had been reading some detective stories, and it struck me what nonsense they were, to put it mildly, because for getting the solution of the mystery the authors always depended on some coincidence. This struck me as not a fair way of playing the game, because the detective ought really to depend for his success on something in his own mind and not on merely adventitious circumstances, which do not, by any means, always occur in real life. I was seedy at the time, and, not working much, had leisure to read, so I read half-a-dozen or so detective stories, both in French and English, and they one and all filled me with dissatisfaction and a sort of feeling how much more interesting they might be made if one could show that the man deserved his victory over the criminal or the mystery he was called upon to solve.

'Then I began to think, suppose my old professor at Edinburgh were in the place of one of these lucky detectives, he would have worked out the process of effect from cause just as logically as he would have diagnosed a disease, instead of having something given to him by mere luck, which, as I said just now, does not happen in real life.

'For fun, therefore, I started constructing a story and

giving my detective a scientific system, so as to make him reason everything out. Intellectually that had been done before by Edgar Allan Poe with M. Dupin, but where Holmes differed from Dupin was that he had an immense fund of exact knowledge to draw upon in consequence of his previous scientific education. I mean by this, that by looking at a man's hand he knew what the man's trade was, as by looking at his trousers leg he could deduce the character of the man. He was practical and he was systematic, and his success in the detection of crime was to be the fruit, not of luck, but of his qualities.

'With this idea I wrote a small book on the lines I have indicated, and produced *A Study in Scarlet*, which was made *Beeton's Christmas Annual* in 1887. That was the first appearance of Sherlock; but he did not arrest much attention, and nobody recognized him as being anything in particular. About three years later, however, I was asked to do a small shilling book for *Lippincott's Magazine*, which publishes, as you know, a special story in each number. I didn't know what to write about, and the thought occurred to me, "Why not try to rig up the same chap again?" I did it, and the result was *The Sign of Four*. Although the criticisms were favourable, I don't think even then Sherlock attracted much attention to his individuality.

'About this time I began thinking about short stories for magazines. It occurred to me that a serial story in a magazine was a mistake, for those who had not begun the story at the beginning would naturally be debarred from buying a periodical in which a large number of pages were, of necessity, taken up with a story in which they had no particular interest.

'It occurred to me, then, that if one could write a serial without appearing to do so – a serial, I mean, in which each instalment was capable of being read as a single story, while each retained a connecting link with the one before and the one that was to come by means of its leading characters – one would get a cumulative interest which the serial pure and simple could not obtain. In this respect I was a revolutionist, and I think I may fairly lay claim to the credit of being the inaugurator of a system which has since been worked by others with no little success.

'It was about this time that the *Strand Magazine* was started, and I asked myself, "Why not put my idea in execution and write a series of stories with Sherlock Holmes?" whose mental processes were familiar to me. I was then in practice in Wimpole Street as a specialist, and, while waiting for patients to come, I began writing to fill up my waiting hours. In this way I wrote three stories, which were afterwards published as part of *The Adventures of Sherlock Holmes*. I sent them to the *Strand Magazine*. The editor liked them, seemed keen on them, and asked for more. The more he asked for the more I turned out, until I had done a dozen. That dozen constituted the volume which was afterwards published as *The Adventures of Sherlock Holmes.*

'That dozen stories being finished, I determined they should be the end of all Sherlock's doings. I was, however, approached to do some more. My instincts were against this, as I believe it is always better to give the public less than it wants rather than more, and I do not believe in boring it with this sort of stuff. Besides, I had other subjects in my mind. The popularity of Sherlock Holmes, however, and the success of the new stories with the common thread running through them brought a good deal of pressure on me, and at last, under that pressure, I consented to continue with Sherlock, and did twelve more stories, which I called *The Memoirs of Sherlock Holmes.*

'By the time I had finished those I was absolutely determined it would be bad policy to do any more Holmes stories. I was still a young man and a young novelist, and I have always noticed that the ruin of every novelist who has come up has been effected by driving him into a groove. The public gets what it likes, and, insisting on getting it, makes him go on until he loses his freshness. Then the public turns round and says: "He has only one idea, and can only write one sort of story." The result is that the man is ruined, for, by that time, he has probably himself lost the power of adapting himself to fresh conditions of work. Now, why should a man be driven into a groove and not write about what interests him? When I was interested in Holmes I wrote about Holmes, and it amused me making him get involved in new conundrums; but when I had written twenty-six stories, each involving the making of a fresh plot, I felt that it was becoming irksome this searching for plots – and if it were getting irksome to me, most certainly, I argued, it must be losing its freshness for others.

'I knew I had done better work in other fields of literature, and in my opinion *The White Company*, for example, was worth a hundred Sherlock Holmes stories. Yet, just because the Sherlock Holmes stories were, for the moment, more popular, I was becoming more and more known as the author of Sherlock Holmes instead of as the author of *The White Company*. My lower work was obscuring my higher.

'I therefore determined to stop my Holmes stories, and as my mind was fully made up I couldn't see any better way than by bringing Holmes to an end as well as the stories.

'I was in Switzerland for the purpose of giving a lecture at the time when I was thinking out the details of the final story. I was taking a walking tour through the country, and I came to a waterfall. I thought if a man wanted to meet a gaudy kind of death that was a fine romantic place for the purpose. That started the train of ideas by which Holmes just reached that spot and met his death there.

'That is really how I came to kill Holmes. But when I did it I was surprised at the amount of interest people took in his fate. I never thought they would take it so to heart. I got letters from all over the world reproaching me on the subject. One, I remember, from a lady whom I did not know, began "you beast".

'From that day to this I have never for an instant regretted the course I took in killing Sherlock. That does not say, however, that because he is dead I should not write about him again if I wanted to, for there is no limit to the number of papers he left behind or the reminiscences in the brain of his biographer.

'My objection to detective stories is that they only call for the use of a certain portion of one's imaginative faculty, the invention of a plot, without giving any scope for character drawing.

'The best literary work is that which leaves the reader better for having read it. Now, nobody can possibly be the better – in the high sense in which I mean it – for reading Sherlock Holmes, although he may have passed a pleasant hour in doing so. It was not to my mind high work, and no detective work ever can be, apart from the fact that all work dealing with criminal matters is a cheap way of rousing the interest of the reader.

'For this reason, at the outset of my career it would have been bad to devote too much attention to Sherlock Holmes. If I had continued with him I should by this time have worn him out, and also the patience of the public, and I should not have written *Rodney Stone*, *Brigadier Gerard*, *The Stark Munro Letters*, *The Refugees*, and all the other books which treat of life from many different standpoints, some of which represent my own views, which Sherlock Holmes never did.

'There is one fact in connection with Holmes which will probably interest those who have followed his career from the beginning, and to which, so far as I am aware, attention has never been drawn. In dealing with criminal subjects one's natural endeavour is to keep crime in the background. In nearly half the number of the Sherlock Holmes stories, however, in a strictly legal sense no crime was actually committed at all. One heard a good deal about crime and the criminal, but the reader was completely bluffed. Of course, I could not bluff him always, so sometimes I had to give him a crime, and occasionally I had to make it a downright bad one.

'My own view of Sherlock Holmes – I mean the man as I saw him in my imagination – was quite different from that which Mr Paget pictured in the *Strand Magazine*. I, however, am eminently pleased with his work, and quite understand the aspect which he gave to the character, and am even prepared to accept him now as Mr Paget drew him. In my own mind, however, he was a more beaky-nosed, hawk-faced man, approaching more to the Red Indian type, than the artist represented him, but, as I have said, Mr Paget's pictures please me very much.'

THE LAST OF
SHERLOCK HOLMES

This interview with Conan Doyle, which may have been written by Sidney Dark*, appeared in the 'Daily Mail on 8 October 1904. It was responsible for a number of letters addressed to Sherlock Holmes from people offering their services during his retirement.

* Sidney Dark joined the staff of the *Daily Mail* in 1899. He says in his autobiography that he was sent to interview Conan Doyle, who was then living in Hindhead: 'He was delightfully kind and helpful, and, thanks much more to him than to myself, the result was an article that received editorial commendation' (*Mainly About Other People*, London, 1925, p. 233).

GREAT DETECTIVE TO RETIRE AT CHRISTMAS.
FROM CRIME TO BEE-KEEPING

The world will learn with very great regret that December next will mark the final retirement from public life of the eminent detective, Sherlock Holmes.

Despite his iron constitution and nerves of steel, Mr Holmes is at last feeling the strain of his great achievements. He will take a little place in the country, and with his magnificent record behind him will settle down to enjoy the remainder of his days in the simple pleasures of the idyllic life.

The bald announcement of his retirement is chronicled in the *Bookman* as follows:

We hear that Sir Arthur Conan Doyle has written for the Christmas number of the *Strand Magazine* the last adventure of the famous Sherlock Holmes which he will ever chronicle. It is said to be 'The Adventure of the Second Stain'.

Yesterday a representative of the *Daily Mail* journeyed to the lovely Hindhead home of Sir Arthur Conan Doyle to ascertain, if possible, the reasons and circumstances of the famous detective's retirement.

SIMPLE COUNTRY LIFE

'A man must retire some time,' he said, 'he can't go on for ever. Yes, his retirement is now absolute and final. So far as I know there is not the slightest intention of his ever again entering on the work of the detection of crime. His last adventure will be a strenuous one, and will, I think, be on a level with some of his higher achievements. After it, he retires for good.

'For a long time he has nursed the idea of a country life with its simple delights. He will take a little place and will go in for bee-keeping.'

'Is it not a probability that a period of rest and country solitude may result in a reaction and throw him once more into the consideration of complex and dangerous problems?'

'From what I know,' replied Sir Arthur emphatically, 'Sherlock Holmes's retirement will be final. He will not again emerge.'

It was pointed out to Sir Arthur that some years ago, after the memorable occasion of his encounter with Moriarty on the mountain-side, the detective was lost to view for a considerable time; was, indeed, believed to be dead.

'Yes,' said the author thoughtfully, 'and I, for one, firmly believed that he was dead. It was merely by accident that I didn't chronicle the finding of his body. This time, however, his exit will be final.'

MAY WRITE A BOOK

'No, he won't marry. You will remember he has always wanted time to write a work on the scientific side of his experience. It is possible that in his retirement he will put his mind on that.'

Speaking of incidents in the life of Sherlock Holmes, Sir Arthur recalled Mr Gillette's preparation for the presentation of the famous detective on the stage. 'Mr Gillette,' he said, 'wired to me from America asking if he might marry Sherlock Holmes in the play. I replied at once, "Marry him, kill him, or do what you like with him!"'

'Yes,' added Sir Arthur, 'I am rather tired of Sherlock Holmes. I expect the public is too. My first idea of him sprang from Dr Bell, of Edinburgh University, whom I knew when I was a medical student there. He had the clear-cut mind of Sherlock Holmes. He would tell the trade of a patient by little signs about him, and would often state what a person was suffering from before a word passed. Thinking of a detective story I decided that reasoning rather than coincidence should form its basis. Then my experience of Dr Bell suggested Sherlock Holmes to me.

'A *Study in Scarlet* was the first book I published. It made no particular stir. Sherlock Holmes caught on when I began to write the short stories which appeared month by month. I had taken rooms in Wimpole Street with the idea of becoming a consultant on eye-troubles. I used to wait there three or four hours every day for the patients who didn't turn up. I utilized my time in writing the first of the Sherlock Holmes short stories.'

From that casual beginning sprang the prominent public life of the renowned detective, who makes his farewell bow at Christmas.

PLOT FOR SHERLOCK
HOLMES STORY

This 'scenario for an uncompleted tale' was discovered by Hesketh Pearson, who included it in his biography of Conan Doyle. Although attributed to Doyle there is no evidence to show that it is by him and strong internal evidence to suggest that it is not.

A girl calls on Sherlock Holmes in great distress. A murder has been committed in her village – her uncle has been found shot in his bedroom, apparently through the open window. Her lover has been arrested. He is suspected on several grounds:

1. He had had a violent quarrel with the old man, who has threatened to alter his will, which is in the girl's favour, if she ever speaks to her lover again.
2. A revolver has been found in his house, with his initials scratched on the butt, and one chamber discharged. The bullet found in the dead man's body fits this revolver.
3. He possesses a light ladder, the only one in the village, and there are the marks of the foot of such a ladder on the soil below the bedroom window, while similar soil (fresh) has been found on the feet of the ladder.

His only reply is that he never possessed a revolver, and that it had been discovered in a drawer of the hatstand in his hall, where it would be easy for anyone to place it. As for the mould on the ladder (which he has not used for a month) he has no explanation whatever.

Notwithstanding these damning proofs, however, the girl persists in believing her lover to be perfectly innocent, while she suspects another man, who has also been making love to her, though she has no evidence whatever against him, except that she feels by instinct that he is a villain who would stick at nothing.

Sherlock and Watson go down to the village and inspect the spot, together with the detective in charge of the case. The marks of the ladder attract Holmes's special attention. He ponders – looks about him – inquires if there is any place where anything bulky could be concealed. There is – a disused well, which has not been searched because apparently nothing is missing. Sherlock, however, insists on the well being explored. A village boy consents to be lowered into it, with a candle. Before he goes down Holmes whispers something in his ear – he appears surprised. The boy is lowered and, on his signal, pulled up again. He brings to the surface *a pair of stilts!*

'Good Lord!' cries the detective, 'who on earth could have expected this?'

'I did,' replies Holmes.

'But why?'

'Because the marks on the garden soil * were made by two perpendicular poles – the feet of a ladder, which is on the slope, would have made depressions slanting towards the wall.'

This discovery lessened the weight of the evidence of the ladder, though the other evidence remained.

The next step was to trace the user of the stilts, if possible. But he had been too wary, and after two days nothing had

* The soil was a strip beside a gravel path on which the stilts left no impression.

been discovered. At the inquest the young man was found guilty of murder. But Holmes is convinced of his innocence. In these circumstances, and as a last hope, he resolves on a sensational stratagem.

He goes up to London, and, returning on the evening of the day when the old man is buried, he and Watson and the detective go to the cottage of the man whom the girl suspects, taking with them a man whom Holmes has brought from London, who has a disguise which makes him the living image of the murdered man, wizened body, grey shrivelled face, skull-cap, and all. They have also with them the pair of stilts. On reaching the cottage, the disguised man mounts the stilts and stalks up the path towards the man's open bedroom window, at the same time crying out his name in a ghastly sepulchral voice. The man, who is already half mad with guilty terrors, rushes to the window and beholds in the moonlight the terrific spectacle of his victim stalking towards him. He reels back with a scream as the apparition, advancing to the window, calls in the same unearthly voice – 'As you came for me, I have come for you!' When the party rush upstairs into his room he darts to them, clinging to them, gasping, and, pointing to the window, where the dead man's face is glaring in, shrieks out, 'Save me! My God! He has come for me as I came for him.'

Collapsing after this dramatic scene, he makes a full confession. He has marked the revolver, and concealed it where it was found – he has also smeared the ladder-foot with soil from the old man's garden. His object was to put his rival out of the way, in the hope of gaining possession of the girl and her money.

THE ADVENTURES OF SHERLOCK HOLMES:

A REVIEW BY JOSEPH BELL

This review, first published in the *Bookman* in December 1892, was reprinted the following year as the introduction to *A Study in Scarlet*. This, however, is the first time that it has been reprinted in its entirety.

It is not entirely a bad sign of this weary, worn-out century that in this, its last decade, even the petty street-bred people are beginning, as the nurses say, to take notice. An insatiable and generally prurient curiosity as to the doings of the class immediately above is pandered to by the society journals, and encouraged even by the daily newspapers. Such information is valueless intellectually, and tends to moral degradation; it exercises none of the senses, and pauperizes the imagination. Celebrities at home, illustrated interviews, society scandal on all levels merely titillate the itching ear of the gossip. Memoirs, recollections, anecdotes of the Bar or of the Academy, are much more interesting, and may be valuable as throwing sidelights on history, but still only amuse and help to kill the time of which we forget the value. But in the last few years there has been a distinct demand for books which, to a certain poor extent, encourage thought and stimulate observation. The whole *Gamekeeper at Home* series and its imitations opened the eyes of town dwellers, who had forgotten or never known White of Selborne, to the delightful sights and sounds that were the harvest of the open eye and ear.

Something of the same interest is given to the 'crowded city's horrible street' by the suggestion of crime and romance, of curiosity and its gratification, we find written with more or less cleverness in the enormous mass of so-called detective literature under which the Press groans. Every bookstall has its shilling shocker, and every magazine which aims at a circulation must have its mystery of robbery or murder. Most of these are poor enough stuff; complicated plots, which can be discounted in the first chapter, extraordinary coincidences, preternaturally gifted detectives, who make discoveries more or less useless by flashes of insight which no one else can understand, become wearisome in their sameness, and the interest, such as it is, centres only in the results and not in the methods. We may admire Lecoq, but we do not see ourselves in his shoes.

Dr Conan Doyle has made a well-deserved success for his detective stories, and made the name of his hero beloved by the boys of this country by the marvellous cleverness of his method. He shows how easy it is, if only you can observe, to find out a great deal as to the works and ways of your innocent and unconscious friends, and by an extension of the same method to baffle the criminal and lay bare the manner of his crime. There is nothing new under the sun. Voltaire taught us the method of Zadig, and every good teacher of medicine or surgery exemplifies every day in his teaching and practice the method and its results. The precise and intelligent recognition and appreciation of minor differences is the real essential factor in all successful medical diagnosis. Carried into ordinary life, granted the presence of an insatiable curiosity and fairly acute sense, you have Sherlock Holmes as he astonishes his somewhat dense friend Watson; carried out in a specialized training, you have Sherlock Holmes the skilled detective.

Dr Conan Doyle's education as a student of medicine

taught him how to observe, and his practice, both as a general practitioner and a specialist, has been a splendid training for a man such as he is, gifted with eyes, memory, and imagination. Eyes and ears which can see and hear, memory to record at once and to recall at pleasure the impressions of the senses, and an imagination capable of weaving a theory or piecing together a broken chain or unravelling a tangled clue, such are implements of his trade to a successful diagnostician. If in addition the doctor is also a born story-teller, then it is a mere matter of choice whether he writes detective stories or keeps his strength for a great historical romance as is *The White Company*.

Syme, one of the greatest teachers of surgical diagnosis that ever lived, had a favourite illustration which, as a tradition of his school, has made a mark on Dr Conan Doyle's method, 'Try to learn the features of a disease or injury as precisely as you know the features, the gait, the tricks of manner of your most intimate friend.' Him, even in a crowd, you can recognize at once; it may be a crowd of men dressed alike, and each having his complement of eyes, nose, hair, and limbs; in every essential they resemble each other, only in trifles do they differ; and yet, by knowing these trifles well, you make your diagnosis or recognition with ease. So it is with disease of mind or body or morals. Racial peculiarities, hereditary tricks of manner, accent, occupation or the want of it, education, environment of all kinds, by their little trivial impressions gradually mould or carve the individual, and leave finger marks or chisel scores which the expert can recognize.

The great broad characteristics which at a glance can be recognized as indicative of heart disease or consumption, chronic drunkenness or long-continued loss of blood, are the common property of the veriest tyro in medicine, while to masters of their art there are myriads of signs eloquent and instructive, but which need the educated eye to detect. A fair-sized and valuable book has lately been written on the one symptom, the pulse; to any one but a trained physician it seems as much an absurdity as is Sherlock Holmes's immortal treatise on the one hundred and fourteen varieties of tobacco ash. The greatest stride that has been made of late years in preventive and diagnostic medicine consists in the recognition and differentiation by bacteriological research of those minute organisms which disseminate cholera and fever, tubercle and anthrax. The importance of the infinitely little is incalculable. Poison a well at Mecca with the cholera bacillus, and the holy water which the pilgrims carry off in their bottles will infect a continent, and the rags of the victims of the plague will terrify every seaport in Christendom.

Trained as he has been to notice and appreciate minute detail, Dr Doyle saw how he could interest his intelligent readers by taking them into his confidence, and showing his mode of working. He created a shrewd, quick-sighted, inquisitive man, half doctor, half virtuoso, with plenty of spare time, a retentive memory, and perhaps with the best gift of all – the power of unloading the mind of all the burden of trying to remember unnecessary details. Holmes tells Watson: 'A man should keep his little brain-attic stocked with all the furniture that he is likely to use, as the rest he can put away in the lumber-room of his library, where he can get it if he wants it.' But to him the petty results of environment, the sign-manuals of labour, the stains of trade, the incidents of travel, have living interest, as they tend to satisfy an insatiable, almost inhuman, because impersonal curiosity. He puts the man in the position of an amateur, and therefore irresponsible, detective, who is consulted in all sorts of cases, and then he lets us see how he works. He makes him explain to the good Watson the trivial, or apparently trivial, links in his chain of evidence. These are at once so obvious, when explained, and so easy, once you know them, that the ingenious reader at once feels, and says to himself, I also could do this; life is not so dull after all; I will keep my eyes open, and find out things. The gold watch, with its scratched keyhole and pawnbroker's marks, told such an easy tale about Watson's brother. The dusty old billycock hat revealed that its master had taken to drinking some years ago, and had got his hair cut yesterday. The tiny thorn-prick and fearsome footmark of the thing that was neither a child nor a monkey enabled Holmes to identify and capture the Andaman Islander. Yet, after all you say, there is nothing wonderful; we could all do the same.

The experienced physician and the trained surgeon every day, in their examinations of the humblest patient, have to go through a similar process of reasoning, quick or slow according to the personal equations of each, almost automatic in the experienced man, laboured and often erratic in the tyro, yet requiring just the same simple requisites, senses to notice facts, and education and intelligence to apply them. Mere acuteness of the senses is not enough. Your Indian tracker will tell you that the footprint on the leaves was not a redskin's, but a paleface's, because it marked a shoe-print, but it needs an expert in shoe-leather to tell where that shoe was made. A sharp-eyed detective may notice the thumb-mark of a grimy or bloody hand on the velvet or the mirror, but it needs all the scientific knowledge of a Galton to render the ridges and furrows visible and permanent, and then to identify by their sign-manual the suspected thief or murderer.

Sherlock Holmes has acute senses, and the special education and information that makes these valuable; and he can afford to let us into the secrets of his method. But in addition to the creation of his hero, Dr Conan Doyle in this remarkable series of stories has proved himself a born story-teller. He has had the wit to devise excellent plots, interesting complications; he tells them in honest Saxon-English with directness and pith; and, above all his other merits, his stories are absolutely free from padding. He knows how delicious brevity is, how everything tends to be too long, and he has given us stories that we can read at a sitting between dinner and coffee, and we have not a chance to forget the beginning before we reach the end. The ordinary detective story, from Gaboriau or Boisgobey down to the latest shocker, really needs an effort of memory quite misplaced to keep the circumstances of the crimes and all the wrong scents of the various meddlers before the wearied reader. Dr Doyle never gives you a chance to forget an incident or miss a point.

No wonder the stories have been successful. Of the twelve, some are much better than others. One man will enjoy the 'Red-Headed League'; another the 'Blue Carbuncle'; for the average reader the 'Speckled Band' has special charms. The story of the 'Five Orange Pips' will probably come home to the American, and the 'Noble Bachelor' will interest Mayfair. In the 'Engineer's Thumb' Mr Holmes has less to do, but what he does is done with his usual directness of action, guided by simplicity of method. Not one of the twelve is a failure, and the handsome volume in which they have been collected will be a prize for all those young and old who are not ashamed to read good stories. Had the handsome volume been divided into two, it would not have been so heavy to hold.

SHERLOCK HOLMES PARODIES

BY J. M. BARRIE

'The Adventure of the Two Collaborators', written on the fly-leaves of *A Window in Thrums*, was first published in Conan Doyle's autobiography; the second parody, 'The Late Sherlock Holmes', first appeared in the *St James's Gazette* on 29 December 1893.

The following introductory note by Conan Doyle is taken from his autobiography and from its serial publication in *Collier's Weekly* (where there is an additional paragraph).

James Barrie is one of my oldest literary friends, and I knew him within a year or two of the time when we both came to London. He had just written his *Window in Thrums*, and I, like all the world, acclaimed it. When I was lecturing in Scotland in 1893 he invited me to Kirriemuir, when I stayed some days with his family – splendid types of the folk who have made Scotland great. His father was a fine fellow, but his mother was wonderful with a head and a heart – rare combinations – which made me class her with my own mother.

Great as are Barrie's plays – and some of them I think are very great – I wish he had never written a line for the theatre. The glamour of it and the – to him – easy success have diverted from literature the man with the purest style of his age. Plays are always ephemeral, however good, and are limited to a few, but Barrie's unborn books might have been an eternal and a universal asset of British literature.

Barrie and I had one unfortunate venture together, in which I may say that the misfortune was chiefly mine, since I had really nothing to do with the matter, and yet shared all the trouble. However, I should have shared the honour and profit in case of success, so that I have no right to grumble. The facts were that Barrie had promised Mr D'Oyly Carte that he would provide the libretto of a light opera for the Savoy. This was in the Gilbert days, when such a libretto was judged by a very high standard. It was an extraordinary commission for him to accept, and I have never yet been able to understand why he did so, unless, like Alexander, he wanted fresh worlds to conquer.

I was brought into the matter because Barrie's health failed on account of some family bereavement. I had an urgent telegram from him at Aldeburgh, and going there I found him very worried because he had bound himself by this contract, and he felt in his present state unable to go forward with it. There were to be two acts, and he had written the first one, and had the rough scenario of the second, with the complete sequence of events – if one may call it a sequence. Would I come in with him and help him to complete it as part author? Of course I was very happy to serve him in any way. My heart sank, however, when, after giving the promise, I examined the work. The only literary gift which Barrie has not got is the sense of poetic rhythm, and the instinct for what is permissible in verse. Ideas and wit were there in abundance. But the plot itself was not strong, though the dialogue and the situations also were occasionally excellent. I did my best and wrote the lyrics for the second act, and much of the dialogue, but it had to take the predestined shape. The result was not good, and on the first night I felt inclined, like Charles Lamb, to hiss it from my box. The opera, *Jane Annie*, was one of the few failures in Barrie's brilliant career. However, the actual comradeship of production was very amusing and interesting, and our failure was mainly painful to us because it let down the producer and the cast. We were well abused by the critics, but Barrie took it all in the bravest spirit, and I still retain the comic verses of consolation which I received from him next morning.

There followed a parody on Holmes, a gay gesture of resignation over the failure which we had encountered, written on the fly leaves of one of his books.

This parody, the best of all the numerous parodies, may be taken as an example not only of the author's wit but of his debonnaire courage, for it was written immediately after our joint failure which at the moment was a bitter thought for both of us. There is indeed nothing more miserable than a theatrical failure, for you feel how many others who have backed you have been affected by it. It was, I am glad to say, my only experience of it, and I have no doubt that Barrie could say the same.

It ran thus:

To A. Conan Doyle, from his friend J. M. Barrie

The Adventure of the Two Collaborators

In bringing to a close the adventures of my friend Sherlock Holmes I am perforce reminded that he never, save on the occasion which, as you will now hear, brought his singular career to an end, consented to act in any mystery which was concerned with persons who made a livelihood by their pen. 'I am not particular about the people I mix among for business purposes,' he would say, 'but at literary characters I draw the line.'

We were in our rooms in Baker Street one evening. I was (I remember) by the centre table writing out 'The Adventure of the Man without a Cork Leg' (which had so puzzled the Royal Society and all the other scientific bodies of Europe), and Holmes was amusing himself with a little revolver practice. It was his custom of a summer evening to fire round my head, just shaving my face, until he had made a photograph of me on the opposite wall, and it is a slight proof of his skill that many of these portraits in pistol shots are considered admirable likenesses.

I happened to look out of the window, and perceiving two gentlemen advancing rapidly along Baker Street asked him who they were. He immediately lit his pipe, and, twisting himself on a chair into the figure 8, replied:

'They are two collaborators in comic opera, and their play has not been a triumph.'

I sprang from my chair to the ceiling in amazement, and he then explained:

'My dear Watson, they are obviously men who follow some low calling. That much even you should be able to read in their faces. Those little pieces of blue paper which they fling angrily from them are Durrant's Press Notices. Of these they have obviously hundreds about their person (see how their pockets bulge). They would not dance on them if they were pleasant reading.'

I again sprang to the ceiling (which is much dented), and shouted: 'Amazing! but they may be mere authors.'

'No,' said Holmes, 'for mere authors only get one press notice a week. Only criminals, dramatists and actors get them by the hundred.'

'Then they may be actors.'

'No, actors would come in a carriage.'

'Can you tell me anything else about them?'

'A great deal. From the mud on the boots of the tall one I perceive that he comes from South Norwood. The other is as obviously a Scotch author.'

'How can you tell that?'

'He is carrying in his pocket a book called (I clearly see)

"Auld Licht Something". Would any one but the author be likely to carry about a book with such a title?'

I had to confess that this was improbable.

It was now evident that the two men (if such they can be called) were seeking our lodgings. I have said (often) that my friend Holmes seldom gave way to emotion of any kind, but he now turned livid with passion. Presently this gave place to a strange look of triumph.

'Watson,' he said, 'that big fellow has for years taken the credit for my most remarkable doings, but at last I have him – at last!'

Up I went to the ceiling, and when I returned the strangers were in the room.

'I perceive, gentlemen,' said Mr Sherlock Holmes, 'that you are at present afflicted by an extraordinary novelty.'

The handsomer of our visitors asked in amazement how he knew this, but the big one only scowled.

'You forget that you wear a ring on your fourth finger,' replied Mr Holmes calmly.

I was about to jump to the ceiling when the big brute interposed.

'That Tommy-rot is all very well for the public, Holmes,' said he, 'but you can drop it before me. And, Watson, if you go up to the ceiling again I shall make you stay there.'

Here I observed a curious phenomenon. My friend Sherlock Holmes *shrank*. He became small before my eyes. I looked longingly at the ceiling, but dared not.

'Let us cut the first four pages,' said the big man, 'and proceed to business. I want to know why —'

'Allow me,' said Mr Holmes, with some of his old courage. 'You want to know why the public does not go to your opera.'

'Exactly,' said the other ironically, 'as you perceive by my shirt stud.' He added more gravely, 'And as you can only find out in one way I must insist on your witnessing an entire performance of the piece.'

It was an anxious moment for me. I shuddered, for I knew

that if Holmes went I should have to go with him. But my friend had a heart of gold. 'Never,' he cried fiercely, 'I will do anything for you save that.'

'Your continued existence depends on it,' said the big man menacingly.

'I would rather melt into air,' replied Holmes, proudly taking another chair. 'But I can tell you why the public don't go to your piece without sitting the thing out myself.'

'Why?'

'Because,' replied Holmes calmly, 'they prefer to stay away.'

A dead silence followed that extraordinary remark. For a moment the two intruders gazed with awe upon the man who had unravelled their mystery so wonderfully. Then drawing their knives —

Holmes grew less and less, until nothing was left save a ring of smoke which slowly circled to the ceiling.

The last words of great men are often noteworthy. These were the last words of Sherlock Holmes: 'Fool, fool! I have kept you in luxury for years. By my help you have ridden extensively in cabs, where no author was ever seen before. *Henceforth you will ride in buses!*'

The brute sunk into a chair aghast.

The other author did not turn a hair.

The Late Sherlock Holmes

SENSATIONAL ARREST
WATSON ACCUSED OF THE CRIME

(By Our Own Extra-Special Reporters)

12.30 p.m. – Early this morning Mr W. W. Watson, MD (Edin.), was arrested at his residence, 12a, Tennison-road, St John's-wood, on a charge of being implicated in the death of Mr Sherlock Holmes, late of Baker-street. The arrest was quietly effected. The prisoner, we understand, was found by the police at breakfast with his wife. Being informed of the cause of their visit he expressed no surprise, and only asked to see the warrant. This having been shown him, he quietly put himself at the disposal of the police. The latter, it appears, had instructions to tell him that before accompanying them to Bow-street he was at liberty to make arrangements for the carrying on during his absence of his medical practice. Prisoner smiled at this, and said that no such arrangements were necessary, as his patient had left the country. Being warned that whatever he said would be used as evidence against him, he declined to make any further statement. He was then expeditiously removed to Bow-street. Prisoner's wife witnessed his removal with much fortitude.

THE SHERLOCK HOLMES MYSTERY

The disappearance of Mr Holmes was an event of such recent occurrence and gave rise to so much talk that a very brief *résumé* of the affair is all that is needed here. Mr Holmes was a man of middle age and resided in Baker-street, where he carried on the business of a private detective. He was extremely successful in his vocation, and some of his more notable triumphs must still be fresh in the minds of the public – particularly that known as 'The Adventure of the Three Crowned Heads', and the still more curious 'Adventure of the Man without a Wooden Leg', which had puzzled all the scientific bodies of Europe. Dr Watson, as will be proved out of his own mouth, was a great friend of Mr Holmes (itself a suspicious circumstance) and was in the habit of accompanying him in his professional peregrinations. It will be alleged by the prosecution, we understand, that he did so to serve certain ends of his own, which were of a monetary character. About a fortnight ago news reached London of the sudden death of the unfortunate Holmes, in circumstances that strongly pointed to foul play. Mr Holmes and a friend had gone for a short trip to Switzerland, and it was telegraphed that Holmes had been lost in the terrible Falls of Reichenbach. He had fallen over or been precipitated. The Falls are nearly a thousand feet high; but Mr Holmes in the course of his career had survived so many dangers, and the public had such faith in his turning-up as alert as ever next month, that no one believed him dead. The general confidence was strengthened when it became known that his companion in this expedition was his friend Watson.

WATSON'S STATEMENT

Unfortunately for himself (though possibly under the compulsion of the police of Switzerland), Watson felt called upon to make a statement. It amounted in brief to this: that the real cause of the Swiss tour was a criminal of the name of Moriarty, from whom Holmes was flying. The deceased gentleman, according to Watson, had ruined the criminal business of Moriarty, who had sworn revenge. This shattered the nerves of Holmes, who fled to the Continent, taking Watson with him. All went well until the two travellers reached the Falls of Reichenbach. Hither they were followed by a Swiss boy with a letter to Watson. It purported to come from the innkeeper of Meiringen, a neighbouring village, and implored the Doctor to hasten to the inn and give his professional attendance to a lady who had fallen ill there. Leaving Holmes at the Falls, Watson hurried to the inn, only to discover that the landlord had sent no such letter. Remembering Moriarty, Watson ran back to the Falls, but arrived too late. All he found there was signs of a desperate struggle and a slip of writing from Holmes explaining that he and Moriarty had murdered each other and then flung themselves over the Falls.

POPULAR TALK

The arrest of Watson this morning will surprise no one. It was the general opinion that some such step must follow in the interests of public justice. Special indignation was expressed at Watson's statement that Holmes was running away from Moriarty. It is notorious that Holmes was a man of immense courage, who revelled in facing danger. To represent him as anything else is acknowledged on all hands to be equivalent to saying that the People's Detective (as he was called) had

IMPOSED UPON THE PUBLIC.

We understand that printed matter by Watson himself will be produced at the trial in proof of the public contention. It may also be observed that Watson's story carried doubt on the face of it. The deadly struggle took place on a narrow path along which it is absolutely certain that the deceased must have seen Moriarty coming. Yet the two men only wrestled on the cliff. What the Crown will ask is,

WHERE WERE HOLMES'S PISTOLS?

Watson, again, is the authority for stating that the deceased never crossed his threshold without several loaded pistols in his pockets. If this were so in London, is it not quite incredible that Holmes should have been unarmed in the comparatively wild Swiss mountains, where, moreover, he is represented as living in deadly fear of Moriarty's arrival? And from Watson's sketch of the ground, nothing can be clearer than that Holmes had ample time to shoot Moriarty after the latter hove in sight. But even allowing that Holmes was unarmed, why did not Moriarty shoot him? Had he no pistols either? This is the acme of absurdity.

WHAT WATSON SAW

Watson says that as he was leaving the neighbourhood of the Falls he saw in the distance the figure of a tall man. He suggests that this was Moriarty, who (he holds) also sent the bogus letter. In support of this theory it must be allowed that Peter Steiler, the innkeeper, admits that some such stranger did stop at the inn for a few minutes and write a letter. This clue is being actively followed up, and doubtless with the identification of this mysterious person, which is understood to be a matter of a few hours' time, we shall be nearer the unravelling of the knot. It may be added, from the information supplied us from a safe source, that the police do not expect to find that this stranger was Moriarty, but rather

AN ACCOMPLICE OF WATSON'S,

who has for long collaborated with him in his writings, and has been a good deal mentioned in connection with the deceased. In short, the most sensational arrest of the century is on the *tapis*.

The murdered man's

ROOMS IN BAKER-STREET

are in possession of the police. Our representative called there in the course of the morning and spent some time in examining the room with which the public has become so familiar through Watson's descriptions. The room is precisely as when deceased inhabited it. Here, for instance, is his favourite chair in which he used to twist himself into knots when thinking out a difficult problem. A tin canister of tobacco stands on the mantelpiece (shag), and above it hangs the long-lost Gainsborough 'Duchess', which Holmes discovered some time ago, without, it seems, being able to find the legal owner. It will be remembered that Watson, when Holmes said surprising things, was in the habit of 'leaping to the ceiling' in astonishment. Our representative examined the ceiling and found it

MUCH DENTED.

The public cannot, too, have forgotten that Holmes used to amuse himself in this room with pistol practice. He was such a scientific shot that one evening while Watson was writing he fired all round the latter's head, shaving him by an infinitesimal part of an inch. The result is a portrait on the wall, in pistol-shots, of Watson, which is considered an excellent likeness. It is understood that, following the example set in the Ardlamont case, this picture will be produced in court. It is also in contemplation to bring over the Falls of Reichenbach for the same purpose.

THE MOTIVE

The evidence in the case being circumstantial, it is obvious that motive must have a prominent part in the case for the Crown. Wild rumours are abroad on this subject, and at this stage of the case they must be received with caution. According to one, Watson and Holmes had had a difference about money matters, the latter holding that the former was making a gold-mine out of him and sharing nothing. Others allege that the difference between the two men was owing to Watson's change of manner; Holmes, it is stated, having complained bitterly that Watson did not jump to the ceiling in amazement so frequently as in the early days of their intimacy. The blame in this case, however, seems to attach less to Watson than to the lodgers on the second floor, who complained to the landlady. We understand that the legal fraternity look to

THE DARK HORSE

in the case for the motive which led to the murder of Mr Holmes. This dark horse, of course, is the mysterious figure already referred to as having been seen in the vicinity of the Falls of Reichenbach on the fatal day. He, they say, had strong reasons for doing away with Mr Holmes. For a long time they were on excellent terms. Holmes would admit frankly in the early part of his career that he owed everything to this gentleman; who, again, allowed that Holmes was a large source of income to him. Latterly, however, they have not been on friendly terms, Holmes having complained frequently that whatever he did the other took the credit for.

On the other hand, the suspected accomplice has been heard to say 'that Holmes has been getting too uppish for anything', that he 'could do very well without Holmes now', that he 'has had quite enough of Holmes', that he 'is sick of the braggart's name', and even that 'if the public kept shouting for more Holmes he would kill him in self-defence'. Witnesses will be brought to prove these statements, and it is believed that the mysterious man of the Falls and this gentleman will be found to be one and the same person. Watson himself allows that he owes his very existence to this dark horse, which supplies the important evidence that the stranger of the Falls is also a doctor. The theory of the Crown, of course, is that these two medical men were accomplices. It is known that he whom we have called the dark horse is still in the neighbourhood of the Falls.

DR CONAN DOYLE

Dr Conan Doyle is at present in Switzerland.

AN EXTRAORDINARY RUMOUR

reaches us as we go to press, to the effect that Mr Sherlock Holmes, at the entreaty of the whole British public, has returned to Baker-street, and is at present (in the form of the figure 8) solving the problem of The Adventure of the Novelist and His Old Man of the Sea.

SIR ARTHUR CONAN DOYLE
OR,
AN UNGRATEFUL FATHER
BY BEVERLEY NICHOLS

'Sir Arthur Conan Doyle or, An Ungrateful Father' by Beverley Nichols was first published in the *Sketch* on 10 November 1926 as one of a series of 'Celebrities in Undress', and was collected the following year in *Are They the Same at Home?* The meeting and the discussion about Sherlock Holmes is believed to have taken place over lunch at the St James's Club at 106 Piccadilly.

We were sitting in front of a blazing fire, talking about Sherlock Holmes. It was just the sort of day on which one should talk about Holmes, for there was a thick mist in the streets outside, and it was Sunday – the day on which, one imagines, all the best criminals feel most creative.

Now, when Conan Doyle talks about Sherlock Holmes, he is obviously talking about a real person. So obviously, in fact, that I had an almost uncomfortable feeling, as though at any moment a voice would be heard in the corridors outside, shouting 'Watson!', or a thin hand be laid on my shoulder, and the rustle of a familiar dressing-gown echo behind my chair. Even now, I am convinced that Sherlock Holmes *was* somewhere near, and I was a little anxious lest he should overhear some of the not entirely laudatory things which Sir Arthur had to say about him.

'Of course, I'm grateful to Holmes,' said Sir Arthur, much

as he would say that he was grateful to a bright stockbroker or a competent physician – but certainly not as though he were speaking of a creature of his own. 'I'm grateful to him,' he repeated. 'He's been a very good friend to me, in a pecuniary way. But, quite frankly, I get very tired of him.' (I wished he would speak more softly, because the door was open, and I could have sworn that I heard the rattling of a hypodermic syringe.)

'I fancy it may be that I know him too well,' he went on. 'I know exactly how he would behave in any circumstance, in any emergency, and that's always a bad thing to know about any of one's friends, isn't it?' (You notice the word 'friends'.) 'I've always felt,' he said, 'that he's hardly human. He's got so few angles from which one can approach him. At first, he used to interest me much more. But I soon realized that he was really nothing more than a calculating machine. I feel he, and all his doings, probably appeal to a lower level of intelligence than the things which absorb me now.' (Meaning, of course, the study of spiritualism.)

Now, I thought, if Holmes is outside the door, the fat is in the fire. To be told that one is nothing more nor less than a calculating machine, and that one is really apt to be a little tiresome, and that one's activities appeal to a comparatively low level of intelligence – to be told all this in the face of the fact that one has brought fame and glory to one's accuser, and has invariably provided him with an exclusive account of one's most sensational activities – surely that is a little hard? If I were Holmes, I should treat Sir Arthur very coldly the next time I met him.

'Don't you think,' I said, by way of apologizing for this maligned creature, 'that you might try to find out a little more about his human side? His, er' – I wanted to say 'love affairs', but it was a little difficult with that ghostly presence so near – 'his affections?'

But Sir Arthur was relentless. 'You can't bring love affairs into detective stories,' he said. 'As soon as you begin to make your detective too human, the story flops. It falls to the ground. You have to be ruthlessly analytical about the whole thing. If I had made Holmes human . . .'

I could not bear it any longer. I therefore decided to draw a red herring across the trail. I had seen in an American newspaper an extraordinary theory that Conan Doyle composed his detective stories simply 'by imagining any sort of muddle and then clearing it up'. For instance, he would describe a room in appalling confusion, with a dead man on the carpet. He would fill the room with baffling clues, and then sit down to work the whole thing out, inventing the story to fit the clues, which, when he first laid them, were as meaningless to him as to anybody else. I asked him if there was any truth in this theory, and, not greatly to my surprise, he answered, 'None.'

'This is how I write a detective story,' he said. 'First of all, I get my central idea. When I say I "get" it, I mean that it comes of its own accord. I can no more sit down and command ideas than I can sit down and command rain. Take "The Speckled Band" as an example. The first stage of that story was when suddenly, and for no particular reason, the idea came to me of a man killing somebody with a snake. I thought the idea a good one, and thinking of it made it gradually grow. The man, I decided, should be an Anglo-Indian, and the person he should kill would be, naturally, somebody whose death would be to his advantage – preferably a woman. To heighten the gruesome effect of the story, I decided that it should be laid in remote surroundings, which would make the pathos of the victim the more acute.

'Already, therefore, we had arrived, after a very little thought, at the conception of an unscrupulous man who has lived in India planning to murder his stepdaughter by means of a snake, in order that he may reap the benefits of a will which should rightly be hers. Well – there's the basis of your story. The rest consists in two tasks – the concoction of false scents to put the reader off the track and to keep him guessing until the last minute, and the provision of clues, as ingenious as one can make them, for the detective to follow up. Obviously, in the basis of "The Speckled Band", there are dozens of clues which one can lay in front of the detective. The Anglo-Indian might have books on snakes in his library, he might – oh, really, there are so many ways in which he might give himself away that the difficulty is not in imagining them but in selecting them.'

'I see,' I said, not seeing in the least.

'In fact, it is really too easy,' said Sir Arthur. 'The other day I wrote a whole Sherlock Holmes story, and finished it, and played two rounds of golf on the same day. You see – Holmes isn't *big* enough. Now, if you take Professor Challenger, that's a different story.'

I knew that he would say that. Spiritualism has given him, in these later years of his life, so absorbing and so passionate an interest that one can well understand his aversion from such comparatively childish pursuits as the writing of detective stories. One can see the ardour in his pale, distant eyes, hear it in the very tone of his soft and even voice. I need not here concern myself with that belief. But I cannot forget one thing which he told me. 'There are now between five and six hundred little Spiritualist churches in the kingdom,' he said. 'Most of them are very humble places, with tin roofs and wooden benches. Many of the preachers in these churches are uneducated men, with no gift of speech, with nothing in them but the truth as they see it. You may not think much of the movement in this stage. *But don't forget that it was in exactly this way that Christianity began to sweep the world.*'

I think that the man, whatever his convictions, who scoffs at a spirit like that is something worse than a fool.

Notes

Introduction

1 *Memories and Adventures*, Sir Arthur Conan Doyle, London: Hodder and Stoughton Limited, 1924, p. 108. See p. 314.

2 See p. 321.

3 *Moments of Memory*. Recollections and Impressions, Herbert Asquith, London: Hutchinson & Co. (Publishers) Ltd, 1937, p. 107.

4 J. Bliss Austin Collection, Pittsburg, Mass. DOYLE. A.MS.S. *Memories and Adventures*.

5 DOYLE. A. L. S. to Charlotte Thwaites Drummond, n.d. (*c.* Autumn 1883).

6 DOYLE. A. L. S. to Charlotte Thwaites Drummond, n.d. (*c.* 1882).

7 'Arthur Conan Doyle. Some Early Recollections', the Rev. E. Elliot, *Heywood Advertiser*, 11 July 1930.

8 *Op. cit.* (1), p. 17. See p. 332.

9 DOYLE. A. L. S. to Charlotte Thwaites Drummond, n.d. (*c.* January 1883).

10 'Sir Arthur Conan Doyle. Old Friend and Message Report', George Sanderson, *Belfast Telegraph*, 17 July 1930.

11 *Life has been Good*. Memoirs of The Marqués de Villavieja. With a Foreword by The Duke of Berwick & Alba, London: Chatto & Windus, 1938, p. 46.

12 *Uncollected Stories*. The Unknown Conan Doyle, London: Secker & Warburg, 1982, 'The Recollections of Captain Wilkie', p. 342.

13 *Leaves from the Life of a Country Doctor* (Clement Bryce Gunn, M. D., J. P.), edited by Rutherford Crockett. With a Foreword by John Buchan, Edinburgh & London: The Moray Press, 1935, p. 35.

14 *Op. cit.* (12), pp. 345–6.

15 'A Talk with Dr Conan Doyle', Raymond Blathwayt, *Bookman*, May 1892, II, p. 50.

16 Brigadier J. N. Stisted Family Papers, Edinburgh. DOYLE. A. L. S. to Joseph Bell, 4 May 1892.

17 *Ibid.*, DOYLE. A. L. S. to Joseph Bell, 7 May 1892.

18 'A Day with Dr Conan Doyle', Harry How, *Strand Magazine*, August 1892, IV, p. 186.

19 *Loc. cit.* (16). DOYLE. A. L. S. to Joseph Bell, n.d. (June 1892).

20 *Op. cit.* (18), p. 188.

21 *Loc. cit.* (16). DOYLE. A. L. S. to Joseph Bell, 16 July 1892.

22 *The Letters of Robert Louis Stevenson* to his Family and Friends, selected and edited with notes and introductions by Sidney Colvin, London: Methuen and Co., 1899, Vol. II, p. 286. Vailima, Apia, Samoa, 5 April 1893.

23 *Loc. cit.* (16). DOYLE. A. L. S. to Joseph Bell, 7 July 1892.

24 *Some Piquant People*, Lincoln Springfield, London: T. Fisher Unwin Ltd, 1924, p. 104.

25 *Op. cit.* (13), p. 37.

26 'The Original of "Sherlock Holmes". An Interview with Dr Joseph Bell', (Lincoln Springfield), *Pall Mall Gazette*, 28 December 1893, LVII, pp. 1–2.

27 'Holmes's Early Mistake', *Evening Standard*, 8 July 1930.

28 *Alloquia*. Experiences & some Reflections of a Medical Practitioner, D. Marinus. With Preface by Sir Arthur Conan Doyle, London: The C. W. Daniel Company, 1928, p. 36.

29 *Op. cit.* (26), p. 1.

30 *Joseph Bell, M.D., F.R.C.S., J.P., D.L., Etc.* An Appreciation by an old Friend, (Jessie M.E. Saxby), Edinburgh and London: Oliphant, Anderson & Ferrier, 1913, p. 18.

31 'The Real Sherlock Holmes', Handasyde (Emily Handasyde Buchanan), *Good Words*, March 1902, XLIII, p. 159.

32 'The Election Campaign', *Evening Dispatch*, Edinburgh, 2 October 1900.

33 'Detective of the Surgery', *Daily Express*, 5 October 1911.

34 'Sir Arthur Conan Doyle in Reminiscent Mood', *East African Standard*, Nairobi, 9 March 1929.

35 'The Original of Sherlock Holmes', Dr Harold Emery Jones, *Collier's Weekly*, New York, 9 January 1904, XXXII, p. 14.

36 'Conan Doyle as he appears here', *New York Times*, 3 October 1894.

37 *Sir Arthur Conan Doyle.* Centenary 1859–1959, London: John Murray, 1959, p. 104. The notes for A Study in Scarlet were reproduced on the dust-jacket of the first American edition of *Memories and Adventures* (Boston: Little, Brown, and Company, 1924).

38 *The Penguin Complete Sherlock Holmes*, Sir Arthur Conan

Doyle, London: Penguin Books, 1981, *A Study in Scarlet*, p. 24.

39 *The Complete Tales and Poems of Edgar Allan Poe*, London: Penguin Books, 1982, 'The Purloined Letter', p. 208.

40 *Op. cit.* (38), 'The Adventure of the Cardboard Box', p. 888 (see also p. 423).

41 *Through the Magic Door*, Arthur Conan Doyle, London: Smith, Elder & Co., 1907, p. 121.

42 *Op. cit.* (12), 'The Fate of the Evangeline', p. 203.

43 *Op. cit.* (39), 'The Murders in the Rue Morgue', p. 157.

44 *Op. cit.* (38), *The Sign of Four*, p. 111.

45 *Round the Fire Stories*, Arthur Conan Doyle, London: Smith, Elder & Co., 1908, 'The Lost Special', p. 187.

46 See p. 162.

47 *Op. cit.* (41), pp. 114–16.

48 'The Poe Centenary', *The Times*, 2 March 1909.

49 *Our American Adventure*, Arthur Conan Doyle, London: Hodder and Stoughton Ltd, 1923, pp. 168–9.

50 *The Life of Sir Arthur Conan Doyle*, John Dickson Carr, London: John Murray, 1949, p. 60.

51 *Op. cit.* (15), p. 50.

52 'Mr Stevenson's Methods in Fiction', A. Conan Doyle, *National Review*, January 1890, XIV, p. 648.

53 *Op. cit.* (50), 'Extract from Southsea notebook No. 1, the first ideas for *A Study in Scarlet*, 1885', p. 63.

54 'Sir Arthur Conan Doyle Tells of His Career and Work, His Sentiments Towards America, and His Approaching Marriage', Bram Stoker, *World*, New York, 28 July 1907; reprinted in a shortened form, *Daily Chronicle*, 14 February 1908.

55 *Op. cit.* (1), p. 75. See p. 336.

56 *Essays on Photography*. The Unknown Conan Doyle, London. Secker & Warburg, 1982, 'After Cormorants with a Camera', p. 2. This article was first published in the *British Journal of Photography*, 14, 21 October 1881; reprinted, *Anthony's Photographic Bulletin*, New York, November 1881.

57 *Op. cit.* (49), p. 66.

58 *Op. cit.* (41), p. 255.

59 'The Making of Sherlock Holmes', A.M. (Arthur Mee), *Young Man*, October 1900, XIV, p. 335.

60 *Belfast Telegraph, Portsmouth Evening News, Yorkshire Telegraph & Star*, 7 July 1930.

61 'Enter Mr Sherlock Holmes', Vincent Starrett, *Atlantic Monthly*, Concord, New Hampshire, July 1932, CL, p. 84; *The Private Life of Sherlock Holmes*, Vincent Starrett, New York: The Macmillan Company, 1933, p. 8; London: Ivor Nicholson & Watson, Limited, 1934, p. 8.

In answer to a query from Howard Haycraft, Starrett admitted in *American Notes & Queries* (June 1941, I, p. 42) that he knew of no direct evidence to suggest that Conan Doyle surnamed his detective after Oliver Wendell Holmes; his own 'categorical statement to that effect' was 'a bold assumption – or deduction' based on Doyle's tribute to the American author in *Through the Magic Door*.

62 See pp. 301–2.

63 Obituary. 'Doyle, Sir Arthur Conan, M.D. (Edin.)', *John Wisden's Cricketers' Almanack* for 1931, p. 255.

This would appear to be the source for the 'Useless Information. Facts and Figures about Cricket contributed by Ian Peebles' in the *Strand Magazine*, August 1949, which states: 'Sherlock Holmes was christened after Conan Doyle had played a successful innings against F. Shacklock of Nottingham.'

64 *The Wanderings of a Spiritualist*, Sir Arthur Conan Doyle, London: Hodder and Stoughton Limited, 1921, p. 23.

65 'Window on East Anglia. Blueprint for Dr Watson', Clement Court, *Eastern Daily Press*, Norwich, 15 November 1969.

66 *Op. cit.* (50), p. 68.

67 Sir Arthur Conan Doyle Foundation, Lausanne, Scrapbook 1, 'L. and A. Conan Doyle, August 6th, 1885'.

68 *Mr J. W. Arrowsmith's Business Jubilee, 1862–1912*. Proceedings at Dinner, December 30th, 1911, Printed for private circulation (Bristol: J. W. Arrowsmith Ltd. Publishers), 1912, p. 36.

69 *Op. cit.* (50), p. 68.

70 *Loc. cit.* (67).

71 'Personal Memories of Sherlock Holmes', Coulson Kernahan, *London Quarterly and Holborn Review*, October 1934, CLIX, p. 449.

72 'The Younger Writers of To-Day', F. G. Bettany, *Young Man*, February 1900, XIV, p. 52.

73 *Op. cit.* (71), p. 450.

74 *A Study in Scarlet*, A. Conan Doyle, London: Ward, Lock & Co., 1888, Publishers' Preface, p. (v).

75 'At the Sign of the Ship', A. Lang, *Longman's Magazine*, January 1889, XIII, pp. 335–6.

76 *Our Second American Adventure*, Arthur Conan Doyle, London: Hodder and Stoughton Limited, 1924, pp. 86–7.

77 'Literature. Present and Past. Some Reminiscences', Sir Arthur Conan Doyle, *Daily Telegraph*, Sydney, 17 November 1920.

78 Redmond A. Burke Collection, Oshkosh, Wisconsin. DOYLE. A. L. S. to Joseph Marshall Stoddart, 3 September 1889. Letter No. 1.

79 *Ibid.*, DOYLE. A. L. S. to Joseph Marshall Stoddart, 1 October 1889. Letter No. 2.

80 *Ibid.*, DOYLE. A. L. S. to Joseph Marshall Stoddart, 6 March 1890. Letter No. 3.

81 *Ibid.*, DOYLE. A. L. S. to Joseph Marshall Stoddart, 17 March 1890. Letter No. 4.

82 *The Last Bookman*, A Journey into the Life & Times of Vincent Starrett, edited by Peter Ruber, New York: The Candlelight Press, 1968, 'Sherlock, Tobacco, and a Gold-Headed Cane', David A. Randall, p. 78.

83 'Novels of the Week', *Athenaeum*, 6 December 1890, p. 773.

84 'Authors I Have Known. Thumbnail Sketches', H. Greenhough Smith, *John O'London's Weekly*, 19 April 1919, I, p. 36.

85 'The Man Who Made "The Strand"', *World's Press News*, 18 December 1930, IV, p. 3.

86 *Loc. cit.* (4).

87 Arthur Conan Doyle Collection, Metropolitan Toronto Central Library. DOYLE. A. L. S. to Herbert Greenhough Smith, 24 September (1921). Letter No. 48.

88 Humanities Research Center, University of Texas, Austin. DOYLE. A. MS. S. 'The Adventure of the Golden Pince-Nez'.

89 Bernard Halliday, Leicester, Catalogue No. 194 (1935), p. 19. DOYLE. A. L. S. to Herbert Greenhough Smith, 9 July 1891.

90 'The Truth About Sherlock Holmes', Sir Arthur Conan Doyle, *Collier's Weekly*, New York, 29 December 1923, LXXII, p. 28.

91 'He Made Holmes Real', Winifred Paget, *John O'London's Weekly*, 17 February 1954, LXIII, p. 177.
   Some uncertainty existed over the identity of the original model for Dr Watson; Winifred Paget believed it was Alfred Morris Butler (as did Butler's daughter), but her brother, the Rev. Gordon Paget, thought it was based on his uncle, Stephen Martin (*vide, Sunday Times*, 5 February 1950).

92 'Artists of "The Strand Magazine". Mr Sidney Edward Paget', *Strand Magazine*, December 1895, X, p. 786.

93 *Op. cit.* (91).

94 Formerly in the Rev. J.R. Paget Collection, Sussex. HOUNS-FIELD (MRS). A. L. S. to her daughter, Edith Paget, 2 June 1893.

95 *Loc. cit.* (67), Château de Lucens, DOYLE. A. L. S. to his mother, 14 October 1891.

96 *Ibid.*, DOYLE. A. L. S. to his mother, 11 November 1891.

97 *Ibid.*, DOYLE. A. L. S. to his mother, 6 January 1892.

98 'Portraits of Celebrities at Different Times of their Lives. A. Conan Doyle', *Strand Magazine*, December 1891, II, p. 606.

99 *Loc. cit.* (67), Château de Lucens, DOYLE. A. L. S. to his mother, 4 February 1892.

100 *Op. cit.* (18), pp. 187–8.

101 'A London Woman's Diary. Memories', *News Chronicle*, 9 July 1930.

102 'Author and Sportsman', *Argus*, Melbourne, 2 October 1920.

103 *The Greenwood Hat*. Being a Memoir of James Anon, 1885–1887, (J. M. Barrie), Fifty Copies Privately Printed, 1930, p. 202; London: Peter Davis Limited, 1937, p. 183.

104 *Peaceful Personalities and Warriors Bold*, Frederic Villiers, London and New York: Harper & Brothers, 1907, pp. 114–15.

105 *Loc. cit.* (67), Château de Lucens, DOYLE. A. L. S. to his mother, 6 April 1893.

106 *Loc. cit.* (88), Ellery Queen Collection, DOYLE. A. L. S. to his publisher, 28 August 1893.

107 Berg Collection, New York Public Library, DOYLE. A. L. S. to A. P. Watt, 5 November 1893.

108 'Conan Doyle's Error. Memoirs of Sherlock Holmes', Henry S. Lunn, *Sunday Times*, 28 September 1930.

109 'Men and Women of To-Day. XXXVIII – Dr Lunn', *Tit-bits*, 8 August 1896, XXX, p. 329.

110 'Glorious Grindelwald', W. J. Dawson, *Young Man*, April 1894, VIII, p. 118.

111 'A Holiday with Conan Doyle', Silas K. Hocking, *New Age*, 24 January 1895, I, p. 273.

112 *Memoirs of a Clubman*, G. B. Burgin, London: Hutchinson & Co., 1921, p. 110.

113 *My Book of Memory*. A String of Reminiscences and Reflections, Silas K. Hocking, London: Cassell and Company, Ltd, 1923, p. 153.

114 *Op. cit.* (38), 'His Last Bow', p. 980.

115 'Sherlock Holmes', J. H. Marlow, *The Times*, 7 March 1941.

116 *The Sherlock Holmes Exhibition*. Catalogue, Adrian M. Conan Doyle, New York, 1952, p. 6, No. 28. Norwood Notebook, No. 1. 'In a brief diary at the end of this notebook Conan Doyle made the following entry: 1893 December: – Killed Holmes.'

117 'Answers to Correspondents', *Tit-bits*, 6 January 1894, XXV, p. 247.

118 *The Strand Magazine 1891–1950*, Reginald Pound, London: Heinemann, 1966, p. 45.

119 *Op. cit.* (117).

120 'Small Talk', *Sketch*, 20 December 1893, IV, p. 406.

121 'The Adventures of Picklock Holes. No. VII – The Stolen March (cont.)', Cunnin Toil (R. C. Lehmann), Note, *Punch*, 30 December 1893, CV, p. 301.

122 'This Busy World', E. S. Martin, *Harper's Weekly*, New York, 16 December 1893, XXXVII, p. 1191.

123 'Dr Conan Doyle: A Character Sketch', W. J. Dawson, *Young Man*, July 1894, VIII, p. 222.

124 *Op. cit.* (15).

125 'A Chat with Dr Conan Doyle', *Cassell's Saturday Journal*, 15 February 1893, XI, p. 422.

126 'The Conan Doyle Banquet at the Authors' Club', *Queen*, 4 July 1896, C, p. 19.

127 See p. 349.

128 *Op. cit.* (1), p. 99. See p. 343.

129 *Op. cit.* (126).

130 *Op. cit.* (117).

131 'The Bookmarker. In Memoriam – Sherlock Holmes', *To-Day*, 30 December 1893, I, p. 10.

132 *Recollections*, David Christie Murray, London: John Long,

1908, p. 296, 'Copy of Letter to David Christie Murray, 8th May 1896'.

133 'Real Conversations. V. A Dialogue between Conan Doyle and Robert Barr', Robert Barr, *McClure's Magazine*, New York, November 1894, III, p. 511.

134 'Dr Doyle and Sherlock Holmes', *New York Daily Tribune*, 13 November 1894.

135 *Op. cit.* (1), p. 109. See p. 315.

136 *Eccentricities of Genius*. Memories of Famous Men and Women of the Platform and Stage, Major J. B. Pond, New York: G. W. Dillingham Company, Publishers, 1900, pp. 507–8. English issue, London: Chatto & Windus, 1901.

137 '"Cab, Sir?" True Tales told by a Taxicabman for 20 Years', *Sunday Express*, 6 July 1930.

138 *The Wheels of Chance*. A Holiday Adventure, H. G. Wells, London: J. M. Dent and Co., 1896, p. 9.

139 'Dr Conan Doyle and his Stories. II. An Appreciation of Dr Doyle's Work', Hugh S. Maclauchlan, *Windsor Magazine*, October 1896, IV, pp. 369–70.

140 'The Reader. Arthur Conan Doyle', J. E. Hodder Williams, *Bookman*, April 1902, XXII, p. 10; *Bookman*, New York, August 1903, XVII, p. 651.

141 *Loc. cit.* (87), DOYLE. A. L. S. to Herbert Greenhough Smith, n.d. (*c*. April 1898). Letter No. 9.

142 *Op. cit.* (45), 'The Man with the Watches', p. 49.

143 *Ibid.*, 'The Lost Special', p. 187.

144 *The Pursuit of the House-Boat*, John Kendrick Bangs, New York and London: Harper & Brothers Publishers, 1897, p. (iii).

145 *Loc. cit.* (107), DOYLE. A. L. S to John Kendrick Bangs, 27 June 1897.

146 *The Amateur Cracksman*, E. W. Hornung, London: Methuen & Co., 1899, p. (v).

147 *Op. cit.* (1), p. 259.

148 *Old Offenders and a Few Old Scores*, E. W. Hornung, With Preface by Sir A. Conan Doyle, London: John Murray, 1923, p. vi.

149 'Chronicle and Comment. Sherlock and Raffles', *Bookman*, New York, January 1903, XVI, p. 449.

150 'An Editorial Adventure Story', Trumbull White, *Bookman*, New York, July 1922, LV, p. 457.

151 *Whatever Goes Up* – The Hazardous Fortunes of a Natural Born

Gambler, George C. Tyler (in collaboration with J. C. Furnas), Indianapolis: The Bobbs-Merrill Company, 1934, p. 187.

152 *Op. cit.* (1), p. 259.
153 *Links in the Chain of Life*, Baroness Orczy, London: Hutchinson & Co. (Publishers) Ltd, 1946, p. 86.
154 *The A. E. W. Mason Omnibus.* Inspector Hanaud's Investigations, London: Hodder and Stoughton Ltd, 1931, p. 10.
155 *Those Days*, E. C. Bentley, London: Constable & Co. Ltd, 1940, pp. 252, 254.
156 *An Autobiography*, Agatha Christie, London: Collins, 1977, p. 254.
157 'Green Room Gossip', *Daily Mail*, 15 December 1897.
158 *Op. cit.* (116), p. 7, No. 32.
159 'The Theatres', *Candid Friend*, 9 November 1901, p. 74.
160 'Mr William Gillette as Sherlock Holmes', Harold J. Shepstone, *Strand Magazine*, December 1901, XXII, p. 615.
161 'San Francisco Hotel Fire. Charles Frohman's Loss Heavy', *New York Times*, 24 November 1898.
162 The Stowe-Day Library, Hartford, Conn., Gillette Family Collection, GILLETTE. TS. *Sherlock Holmes*, 26 October 1901, Act II, scene 2, p. 23; also TS, 30 November 1931, p. 23.
163 *Charles Frohman: Manager and Man*, Isaac F. Marcosson and Daniel Frohman, London: John Lane, The Bodley Head, 1916, p. 197.
164 *Op. cit.* (159).
165 DOYLE. A. L. S. to William Gillette, n.d. (*c.* December 1901).
166 *Sir Arthur Conan Doyle Archives* (Lew David Feldman), n.d., p. 4.
167 *Op. cit.* (160).
168 *Sherlock Holmes. Farewell Appearances of William Gillette. 1929–1930*, New York, 1929, 'Sherlock Holmes. A Little History of the World's Most Famous Fictional Character', Frederic Dorr Steele, p. 5, reprinted in a revised form in *Sherlock Holmes. A Play*, William Gillette, New York: Doubleday, Doran & Company, Inc., 1935, 'Reminiscent Notes', Frederic Dorr Steele, p. xxvii.
169 'Sherlock Holmes in Pictures', Frederic Dorr Steele, *New Yorker*, 22 May 1937, XIII, p. 37.

170 'The Fun Behind the Veil', Sir A. Conan Doyle, *Sunday Express*, 8 April 1928.

171 'A Londoner's Diary. "I am Sherlock"', *Evening Standard*, 10 November 1943.

172 *Loc. cit.* (162), DOYLE. A. L. S. to William Gillette, 25 October 1929. *Op. cit.* (168), 'The Return of William Gillette', p. 15; *Letters of Salutation and Felicitation received by William Gillette* on the occasion of His Farewell to the Stage in 'Sherlock Holmes', (compiled by Clayton Hamilton, 1929), p. 20.

173 DOYLE (DENIS P. S. CONAN). T. L. S. to James F. Reilly (of Charles Frohman, Inc.), 4 October 1934.

174 *My Autobiography*, Charles Chaplin, London: The Bodley Head, 1964, p. 81. Also, *My Early Years*, 1979.

175 *Ibid.*, p. 91.

176 '"Brother Savages". University of Bohemia', *Daily Telegraph*, 7 December 1925.

177 *Op. cit.* (76), p. 143.

178 'Conan Doyle at the Front. A Detective at Fault', A Painter's Youngest Daughter (Dorothy Menpes), *M.A.P.*, 14 July 1900, V, p. 34.

179 *Op. cit.* (1), p. 188.

180 *Loc. cit.* (67), Château de Lucens, DOYLE. A. L. S. to his mother, n.d. (March 1901).

181 *Op. cit.* (140), p. 13.

182 *Loc. cit.* (67), Château de Lucens, DOYLE. A. L. S. to his mother, 2 April 1901.

183 *The Hound of the Baskervilles*, Conan Doyle, *Strand Magazine*, August 1901, XXII, p. 123 (footnote).

184 *The Hound of the Baskervilles*, A. Conan Doyle, London: George Newnes, 1902, p. (v).

185 *The Hound of the Baskervilles*, A. Conan Doyle, New York: McClure, Phillips, & Co., 1902, p. (vii).

186 'Chronicle and Comment. The New Sherlock Holmes Story', *Bookman*, New York, October 1901, XIV, p. 110.

187 *Out and About*. Random Reminiscences, Archibald Marshall, London: John Murray, 1933, pp. 4–5.

188 *A Book of the West*, Being an Introduction to Devon and Cornwall, S. Baring-Gould, Vol. I, Devon, London: Methuen & Co., 1899, p. 183.

189 *Ladies and Gentlemen*, A Parcel of Reconsiderations, Branch

Cabell, New York: Robert M. McBride & Company, 1934, p. 215.

190 See p. 275.

191 'The man's name is Baskerville and what he says today brings a big argument over the Sherlock Holmes Legend', Peter Evans, *Daily Express*, 16 March 1959; *New York World-Telegram and Sun*, 28 March 1959.

192 'Baskerville anger over holiday home offer', *The Times*, 9 November 1981.

193 'Some Letters of Conan Doyle. With Notes and Comments', H. Greenhough Smith, *Strand Magazine*, October 1930, LXXX, p. 391.

194 *Ibid.*

195 *Op. cit.* (89), DOYLE. A. L. S. to Herbert Greenhough Smith, n.d.

196 *Op. cit.* (187), p. 5.

197 *Op. cit.* (140), p. 13.

198 'Sherlock Holmes among the Illustrators', Edmund Pearson, *Bookman*, New York, August 1932, LXXV, pp. 356–7.

199 'Chronicle and Comment. More Sherlock Holmes Theories', *Bookman*, New York, May 1902, XV, pp. 215, 217.

200 *Op. cit.* (50), p. 200.

201 *Op. cit.* (116), p. 9, No. 41; *op. cit.* (50), p. 200. DOYLE. A. L. S. to his mother, (Spring 1903).

202 *Loc. cit.* (87), DOYLE. A. L. S. to Herbert Greenhough Smith, 14 May 1903. Letter No. 23.

203 *Ibid.*, DOYLE. A. L. S to Herbert Greenhough Smith, n.d. (May 1903). Letter No. 24.

204 *Ibid.*, DOYLE. A. L. S. to Herbert Greenhough Smith, n.d. (May 1903). Letter No. 26.

205 *Op. cit.* (50), p. 202.

206 'A Case of Coincidence Relating to Sir A. Conan Doyle', Lyndon Orr, *Bookman*, New York, April 1910, XXXI, p. 179.

207 *Op. cit.* (38), 'The Greek Interpreter', p. 444.

208 *Loc. cit.* (87), DOYLE. A. L. S. to Herbert Greenhough Smith, n.d. (1904). Letter No. 29.

209 'Dr Conan Doyle on Cycling', *Hub*, 22 August 1896, I, p. 101.

210 'An Eminent Novelist as a Motor Cyclist', *Motor Cycle*, 27 February 1905, III, p. 189.

211 '"Sherlock Holmes'" Future', *Evening News*, 8 June 1903.

212 *Op. cit.* (37), p. 73.

213 *Ibid.*, p. 107.

214 *Ibid.*

215 'The Reader. Sir Arthur Conan Doyle', A. St John Adcock, *Bookman*, November 1912, XLIII, p. 104; *Strand Magazine*, New York, April 1913, XLV, pp. 304–13.

216 *Op. cit.* (64), p. 247.

217 *Loc. cit.* (67), Lausanne.

218 *Op. cit.* (116), p. 19, No. 75, AN ADMIRER. A. L. S. to Sherlock Holmes, 10 June 1910.

219 *Arsène Lupin contre Herlock Sholmès*, Maurice Leblanc, Paris: Pierre Lafitte & Cie, 1908. The first English edition, as *Arsène Lupin versus Holmlock Shears*, was translated by Alexander Teixeira de Mattos and was published in 1909 by Grant Richards, being issued in America by Doubleday, Page, & Company: 'And then, of course, he is Holmlock Shears, that is to say, a sort of miracle of intuition, of insight, of perspicacity, of shrewdness. It is as though nature had amused herself by taking the two most extraordinary types of detective that fiction had invented, Poe's Dupin and Gaboriau's Lecoq, in order to build up one in her own fashion, more extraordinary yet and more unreal. And, upon my word, any one hearing of the adventures which have made the name of Holmlock Shears famous all over the world must feel inclined to ask if he is not a legendary person, a hero who has stepped straight from the brain of some great novel-writer, of a Conan Doyle, for instance.' The indigenous American translations by George Morehead and Olive Harper (Mrs Helen D'Apery) retained the original name.

220 'Arsène Lupin at Home', Charles Henry Meltzer, *Cosmopolitan*, New York, May 1913, LIV, p. 772.

221 '"England Articulate". Sir A. Conan Doyle's Tribute to Mr Kipling', *The Times*, 7 December 1925.

222 'Sherlock Holmes and His Creator', Arthur Bartlett Maurice, *Collier's Weekly*, New York, 15 August 1908, XLI, 'Concerning Mr Sherlock Holmes. (7) Sherlock Holmes on the Stage – At Home and abroad', p. 14.

223 *Sherlock Holmes, Raffles und ihre Vorbilder*. Ein Beitrag zur Entwicklungsgesichte und Technik der Kriminalerzählung, Friedrich Depken, Heidelberg: Carl Winter's Universitäts-buchhandlung, 1914, p. 88: 'It is certain that Europe is just now suffering from a complaint which one may call Sherlock-

ismus – a literary disease comparable to the Werthermania or to Romantic Byronismus.'

224 'After Thirty-five Years', *The Times*, 10 December 1926.

225 'Chronicle and Comment. Señor Sherlock Holmes', *Bookman*, New York, April 1915, XLI, p. 118.

226 'Mistaken for Holmes!' Reverend Gerald Herring. This letter is reprinted in *The Sherlock Holmes Scrapbook*, London: New English Library, 1973, p. 57, as having come from the *Church Times* of May 1910.

227 *Op. cit.* (225), p. 121.

228 'Misunderstood', *The Times*, 4 October 1946.

229 *Op. cit.* (1), p. 228.

230 *Golden Horn*, Francis Yeats-Brown, London: Victor Gollancz Ltd, 1932, p. 56.

231 'Sherlock Holmes', Frederick Hamer, *The Times*, 10 July 1930.

232 *Op. cit.* (1), pp. 260–1. Stevenson told Doyle in a letter dated 23 August 1893 that he had re-narrated 'The Engineer's Thumb' to his native overseer Simelè: 'It was necessary, I need hardly say, to go somewhat further afield than you have done. To explain (for instance) what a railway is, what a steam hammer, what a coach and horse, what coining, what a criminal, and what the police. I pass over other and no less necessary explanations. But I did actually succeed; and if you could have seen the drawn, anxious features and the bright, feverish eyes of Simelè, you would have (for the moment at least) tasted glory. You might perhaps think that, were you to come to Samoa, you might be introduced as the Author of "The Engineer's Thumb". Disabuse yourself. They do not know what it is to make up a story. "The Engineer's Thumb" (God forgive me) was narrated as a piece of actual and factual history.'

233 'The odd things that happen. Elementary', *Sunday Express*, 20 March 1949.

234 'A Swiss Ban on "Sherlock Holmes"', *The Times*, 14 February 1910.

235 'Conan Doyle as a Detective', *Pictorial Magazine* (Penny Pictorial), 8 July 1905, p. 243.

236 *Op. cit.* (222), 'Concerning Conan Doyle. (2) Conan Doyle as Sherlock Holmes', p. 26.

237 *Op. cit.* (159), pp. 73–4.

238 '"Jack the Ripper". How "Sherlock Holmes" would have tracked him', *Evening News*, Portsmouth, 4 July 1894.

239 *Life and Memoirs of John Churton Collins*, L. C. Collins, London: John Lane The Bodley Head, 1912, p. 200.

240 'The Real Sherlock Holmes', *Tit-bits*, 21 October 1911, LXI, p. 127.

241 *Op. cit.* (239), p. 246.

242 *Ibid.*, p. 204.

243 '*G. H. Darby*' *Captain of the Wyrley Gang*, G. A. Atkinson, With Prefaces by Sir Arthur Conan Doyle and Capt. the Hon. G. A. Anson, Walsall: T. Kirby & Sons Ltd, 1914, p. (11).

244 'Case of George Edalji. The "Martin Molton" Letters – No. 3', Sir A. Conan Doyle, *Daily Telegraph*, 27 May 1907.

245 *Op. cit.* (1), p. 220.

246 '"Peculiarities" in the Writing. George Edalji concludes his story', G. E. T. Edalji, *Pearson's Weekly*, 6 June 1907, p. 845.

247 *Sixty Years Ago and After*, Max Pemberton, London: Hutchinson & Co. (Publishers) Ltd, 1936, pp. 243–4.

248 'The Late Sir Conan Doyle. A Reminiscence', Dr Lindsay Johnson, *Natal Mercury*, Durban, 16 July 1930.

249 *The Case of Oscar Slater*, Arthur Conan Doyle, London: Hodder and Stoughton, 1912, p. 5.

250 '"The Case of Oscar Slater"', A. Conan Doyle, *Daily Mail*, 2 September 1912.

251 *The Case of Oscar Slater*, Arthur Conan Doyle, London: Hodder and Stoughton, Third Edition, 1914, p. (4).

252 'Oscar Slater. My Last Words on the Case', Sir A. Conan Doyle, *Sunday Times*, 29 July 1928.

253 *Memories and Adventures*, Arthur Conan Doyle, London: John Murray, Revised Edition, 1930, p. 445.

254 'Oscar Slater's Fight to Clear his Name', Sir Arthur Conan Doyle, *Sunday Pictorial*, 15 July 1928.

255 'Western Wanderings', Sir Arthur Conan Doyle, *Cornhill Magazine*, January 1915, XXXVIII, p. 5.

256 'Sir A. Conan Doyle and the Thorne Case', *Morning Post*, 21 April 1925. See also *Daily Sketch*, 21 April 1925.

257 DOYLE. A. L. S. to Arthur Whitaker, 7 March 1911.

258 *The Knox Brothers*, Penelope Fitzgerald, London: Macmillan, 1977, p. 106, DOYLE. A. L. S. to Ronald Knox, 5 July 1912.

259 *Op. cit.* (1), p. 108. See p. 315.

260 Philip S. Hench Collection, University of Minnesota, Min-

neapolis, BRIGGS (GRAY CHANDLER). A. L. S. to Frederic Dorr Steele, 30 October 1921.

261 Loc. cit. (87). DOYLE. A. L. S. to Herbert Greenhough Smith, 17 April 1908. Letter No. 35.

262 Loc. cit. (87).

263 Loc. cit. (88), Ellery Queen Collection. DOYLE. A. L. S. to Herbert Greenhough Smith, 6 February 1914.

264 Ibid., DOYLE. A. L. S. to Herbert Greenhough Smith, n.d. (February 1914).

265 Ibid., DOYLE. A. L. S. to Herbert Greenhough Smith, n.d. (1914).

266 Op. cit. (225), p. 121.

267 The Pinkertons. The Detective Dynasty That Made History, James D. Horan, London: Robert Hale & Company, 1970, p. 499. An interview with the late Ralph Dudley, general manager, and the author, 1948.

268 See pp. 136–7.

269 'Sherlock Holmes. A magazine dies – and a fifty year secret comes out', Daily Express, 14 December 1949.

270 'Chronicle and Comment. Secret Service', Bookman, New York, December 1914, XL, p. 368.

271 'Warfare in a Forest. With the French Army in the Argonne', the Editor of the Daily Chronicle (Robert Donald), War Budget, 13 July 1916, VIII, p. 269.

272 A Visit to Three Fronts, Arthur Conan Doyle, London: Hodder and Stoughton, 1916, p. 72; op. cit. (1), pp. 376–7.

273 Op. cit. (222), 'Concerning Mr Sherlock Holmes. (4) The Suppressed and Unwritten Sherlock Holmes Stories', p. 12.

274 The Private Life of Sherlock Holmes, Vincent Starrett, Chicago: The University of Chicago Press, Revised and Enlarged, 1960, p. 24, DOYLE. A. L. S. (facsimile) to Vincent Starrett, n.d. (1918). English issue, London: George Allen & Unwin Ltd, 1961.

275 'Clairvoyants as Detectives', Arthur Conan Doyle, Daily Express, 21 October 1921.

276 'Murder Mysteries Mediums Did Solve', Sir A. Conan Doyle, Sunday News, 1 September 1929.

277 'Mediums No Use to Police. Cold Reception for Novelist's Idea', Evening Chronicle, Manchester, 20 December 1926.

278 'A London Newsletter', The Old Stager (John Gore), Sphere, 12 November 1932, CXXXI, pp. 242–3.

279 *Op. cit.* (224).

280 *Op. cit.* (89).

281 *Ibid.* For the competition, see pp. 317 ff., above.

282 'Conan Doyle Speaking (First Record)', Sir Arthur Conan Doyle, His Master's Voice (The Gramophone Co. Ltd), 1930. Plum Label, Cat. No. C1983 (32–1453); 'Sherlock Holmes explained by his creator Sir Arthur Conan Doyle and presented in action by William Gillette', The National Vocarium, New York, 1939, TNV-109, CS 045829. *Loc. cit.* (88), DOYLE. TS.A.emend. as 'A Chat with Conan Doyle'.

283 'Sir Arthur Conan Doyle', Movietone (Fox Film Corporation, U.S.A., 1927).

The Field Bazaar

284 'A. Conan Doyle, M.D.', *Student*, Edinburgh, 10 February 1892, VI (NS), pp. 233–4.

How Watson Learned the Trick

285 *Loc. cit.* (67), Lausanne, PRINCESS MARIE LOUISE. T. L. S. to Sir Arthur Conan Doyle, 29 August 1922.

286 Royal Archives. Add. A18 Box 9. WOOD (ALFRED HERBERT). A. L. S. to Princess Marie Louise, 28 May 1923. With the gracious permission of Her Majesty The Queen.

The Stonor Case

287 *Op. cit.* (1), p. 232.

288 'Sir Arthur Conan Doyle on Play Writing and Play Producing', *Referee*, 18 September 1910, p. 4.

289 *Op. cit.* (1), p. 233.

290 *Loc. cit.* (107), DOYLE. A. L. S. to Lyn Harding, 18 February 1914.

291 'Adelphi Theatre. "The Speckled Band"', *Daily Telegraph*, 6 June 1910.

292 *Op. cit.* (116), p. 10, No. 46. DOYLE. A. L. S. to his mother, 5 June 1910.

293 *Op. cit.* (64), p. 50.

294 'Chronicle and Comment. Sherlock Holmes', *Bookman*, New York, February 1911, XXXII, p. 563.

The Crown Diamond

295 'Projection', Charles Farrell, *Stage*, 17 January 1974.

Prefaces

296 *Conan Doyle*, Pierre Nordon, London: John Murray, 1966, p. 281, DOYLE. A. L. S. to his mother, 14 October 1891.
297 *The Sign of Four*, A. Conan Doyle, London: George Newnes Limited, 1896, Penny Library of Famous Books, No. 9, Editorial Note, C.S.C. (Charles Smith Cheltnam), p. (2).
298 Author's Edition, *The White Company*, A. Conan Doyle, London: Smith, Elder & Co., 1903, Preface to the Author's Edition, pp. v–vi.
299 *Ibid.*, p. vi.
300 *Op. cit.* (38), 'The Adventure of the Second Stain', p. 650.
301 *Ibid.*, 'His Last Bow', p. 978.

Some Personalia about Mr Sherlock Holmes

302 'From My Window in Vanity Fair', Lady Eleanor Smith, *Sunday Dispatch*, 16 December 1928.
303 'The Trials of Marriage do not exist', Lady Conan Doyle, *Sunday Express*, 20 October 1929.
304 *Op. cit.* (116), p. 17, No. 70. A. L. S. to Sir Arthur Conan Doyle, 7 August 1909.
305 'Relics of a Wreck', *The Times*, 29 June 1880.
306 *Loc. cit.* (88). PEARSON (R. G.). A. L. S. to Sir Conan Doyle, 10 March 1905.
307 'Sunken Gold. Romantic Quest interests Sir A. Conan Doyle', *Daily Express*, 25 August 1921.
308 'Too much for the Spirits', Arthur Conan Doyle, *Daily Express*, 30 August 1921.
309 'Treasure Hunting. Affairs of the Grosvenor Syndicate', *Rand Daily Mail*, Johannesburg, 16 February 1923.
310 *Op. cit.* (1), p. 116.
311 *Ibid.*, p. 240.

Sherlock Holmes on the Screen

312 'Sherlock Holmes on the Film', Fenn Sherie, *Strand Magazine*, July 1921, LXII, p. 72.
313 *Ibid.*
314 *Op. cit.* (87).
315 'Sherlock Holmes consults the Author of his being at the Stoll Convention Dinner', *Stoll's Editorial News*, 6 October 1921, V, p. 11.
316 *Ibid.*, p. 15.
317 *Op. cit.* (1), p. 338.

Sidelights on Sherlock Holmes

318 *Op. cit.* (1), p. 101.
319 *Op. cit.* (193), p. 392.
320 *Loc. cit.* (87). DOYLE. A. L. S. to Herbert Greenhough Smith, n.d. (1904). Letter No. 29.
321 'A Sherlock Holmes Story', *Cassell's Weekly*, 5 September 1923, p. 778.
322 *Op. cit.* (193), p. 393.
323 *To-Day*, 10 February 1894, II, p. 24.

A Sherlock Holmes Competition

324 'Answers to Correspondents', *Tit-bits*, 16 December 1893, XXV, p. 193.
325 *Op. cit.* (87).
326 *Loc. cit.* (87). DOYLE. A. L. S. to Herbert Greenhough Smith, n.d. (1927). Letter No. 56.

The Background to Sherlock Holmes

327 *Op. cit.* (1), Preface, p. 1.
328 The Crowborough Edition, 1, *Rodney Stone*, A. Conan Doyle, New York: Doubleday, Doran & Company, Inc., 1930, Preface to the Crowborough Edition, p. v.
329 *Op. cit.* (90), p. 9.
330 *Op. cit.* (253), p. 136.